International Accounting and Multinational Enterprises

Jeffrey S. Arpan (D.B.A., Indiana University) is professor of international business and director of the Asian/Pacific programs of the College of Business Administration at the University of South Carolina. He was formerly a member of the accounting faculty and of the Institute of International Business at Georgia State University.

Dr. Arpan also serves as special editor for international accounting of the *Journal of International Business Studies,* and is a member and former vice-president of the Academy of International Business and a member of the International Section of the American Accounting Association. His doctoral dissertation was selected as the most outstanding one of the year by the Academy of International Business.

Along with Lee Radebaugh, Dr. Arpan conducts semiannual seminars in international accounting at the IBM education facility in New York, and recently codirected a project sponsored by the Touche Ross Foundation to develop a model for an internationalized accounting curriculum.

Lee H. Radebaugh (D.B.A., Indiana University) is associate professor of accounting at Brigham Young University. He has also been a visiting professor at the Escuela de Administracion de Negocios para Graduados (ESAN) in Lima, Peru.

Dr. Radebaugh has served as chairman of the International Section of the American Accounting Association, and is currently a member of its advisory board. He is also a member of the European Accounting Association and served as chairman of the Multinational Accounting session at its Third Annual Congress in Amsterdam in 1980.

Dr. Radebaugh has published widely in the area of international accounting and business, and with Jeff Arpan is a member of the National Academic Advisory Council of the International Affairs Committee of the AACSB.

International Accounting and Multinational Enterprises

Jeffrey S. Arpan
University of South Carolina

Lee H. Radebaugh
Brigham Young University

JOHN WILEY & SONS

New York • Chichester • Brisbane • Toronto • Singapore

To Kathy and Tanya

Library of Congress Cataloging in Publication Data

Arpan, Jeffrey S.
    International accounting and multinational
enterprises.

    Bibliography: p.
    Includes index.
    1. International business enterprises–Accounting.
2. Accounting. I. Radebaugh, Lee H., joint author.
II. Title.
HF5686.I56A76   657'.A95   80-26070
ISBN 0-471-87746-8

Contents

Preface

A truly phenomenal growth in international business activity has occurred in the past two decades. Because international business events now affect almost everyone's life either directly or indirectly, there has been a commensurate increase in interest in the subject by practitioners, academics, and governments.

Although the formal recognition of the importance of international business was somewhat slower in the United States than in several other countries, it markedly accelerated during the 1970s. In 1974, the American Assembly of Collegiate Schools of Business changed its accreditation standards to include a requirement that the international dimension of business be added to the curricula. In 1978, the American Accounting Association specifically recommended the internationalization of the accounting curricula. The federal government, through many of its departments and agencies, has promoted programs to enhance the international competence of American industry.

Despite the attention being paid today to international business, there are still many questions to be answered and many problems to be solved. In reality, in many areas of international business people are still trying to identify which questions need to be answered and what are the major issues to be addressed. And of all the subareas of the general field of international business, accounting has remained the least developed. In fact, only in 1980 was the first systematic effort made to identify and rank the major international problems and to assess the appropriate research methodologies for resolving them.* Comparatively

---

*Eighty Eight International Accounting Problems in Rank Order of Importance—A Delphi Evaluation was conducted for the American Accounting Association by George Scott with Pontus Troberg of the University of Oklahoma. All the major categories of problems identified in Scott's monograph are addressed in this book.

speaking, there remain fewer courses, books, articles, and instruction materials concerning the international aspects of accounting than in the other major areas of business such as management, finance, and marketing. While *International Accounting and Multinational Enterprises* will not fill the void by any means, it should certainly help close the gap. We also hope it will encourage others to do additional work in the area, for it is truly one of great importance and need.

This book is intended to benefit graduate and upper-division students of accounting, as well as accountants working for public accounting firms, corporations, and other enterprises engaged in international business, and governmental institutions and international organizations. One needs to have a fundamental grasp of accounting principles in order to appreciate and be challenged by the principles contained in the book. We have attempted to cover a broad range of issues in order to convey a fundamental understanding of the problems faced by multinational enterprises, as well as an appreciation for the ways different countries perceive certain accounting problems and the rationale for how they deal with those problems. In most chapters, one or more cases are provided to illustrate the kinds of problems that are encountered in a day-to-day business operation. In addition, all the chapters provide study questions.

The authors of any book are always indebted to numerous other scholars whose work helped form the foundation of knowledge on which their book is based. We are no exception. The pioneering efforts of Paul Garner, Emeritus Dean of the University of Alabama, Gerhard G. Mueller of the University of Washington, and Vernon K. Zimmerman of the University of Illinois are especially notable in that they provided the impetus and inspiration for the field of international accounting in its infancy period in the United States, and we have striven to emulate the standards of excellence set by the cadre of international accounting researchers whose contributions are woven throughout this book.

We would also like to acknowledge the constructive comments of the reviewers of the manuscript for this book: Vinod Bavishi of the University of Connecticut, Thomas G. Evans of the University of South Carolina, and Helen Morsicato of the University of Oregon. Special thanks are also due to the typists who struggled tirelessly and with only minor complaints to type, retype, and type again the countless drafts of the manuscript: Renetta Aldrich, Janice Clower, Elly Rogers, and Susan Akbulut at Georgia State University; Dee Williams at the University of South Carolina; and LuAnn Jaworski, Elaine Martins, and Crystal Stover of The Pennsylvania State University.

We also owe a great deal of thanks to our publisher, Warren, Gorham & Lamont, for their perseverence and the high degree of professionalism given to every aspect of the book. Particularly, we would like to thank Eugene Simonoff who convinced us we could and should write the book, and Cynthia Hausdorff, the text editor, who steadfastly badgered us into improving the format of the book and thus its readability and substance!

And finally, unmeasurable gratitude is due to our wives and children who suffered through late nights and weekend absences as we put all the pieces together.

Despite all this help, there will undoubtedly remain some errors and omissions in our book. Such is the imperfect nature of man. As authors, we assume full responsibility for errors in judgment and communication and all unintended omissions. At some point, however, the book has to go to press. . . . We welcome the opportunity to receive comments from anyone who has occasion to use this book, and to learn from them how it can be improved further.

Jeffrey S. Arpan
Lee H. Radebaugh

November 1980

1

An Overview of International Accounting

Despite rumors to the contrary, the field of accounting has had a notable international history and promises to have an even better future. Like the other functional areas of business, accounting has changed as the environments it serves have changed, moving sequentially from the more rudimentary to the more complex and sophisticated. This chapter (1) traces the international development of accounting, (2) highlights some of the critical factors which determine national differences in accounting systems, and provides an initial perspective on these differences and their importance for accountants in the modern world, and (3) discusses the evolution of world trade and investment patterns, together with some of the accounting implications of these developments.

THE INTERNATIONAL DEVELOPMENT
OF THE ACCOUNTING DISCIPLINE

Record keeping, the foundation of accounting, has been traced back as far as 3600 B.C. Concepts such as depreciation were evident during the early Greek and Roman civilizations, where, for example, walls were depreciated at 1/80th per year. Yet most accounting historians agree that modern accounting dates from the fourteenth century, when the double entry system began.

The first record of a complete system was found in Genoa, in what is now Italy, in 1340. The Genoan system assumed the concept of a business entity, and because it recorded items in money terms, it was the first to imply that unlike items could be compared in terms of a

1

common monetary unit; in other words, that economic events were quantifiable. The Genoan system also implied some understanding of the distinction between capital and income, as it included both expenses and equity accounts.

The Italian domination of accounting was further cemented in 1494 with the publication of the first formal treatise on accounting, *Summa de Arithmetica, Geometria Proportioni et Proportionalita*, by Luca Pacioli, a Franciscan friar residing in Venice. His treatise was unique also because it was one of the earliest printed books (printed in fact on Gutenberg's printing press).

Although one might argue that accounting made little progress from 3600 B.C. to A.D. 1494, one must recognize that several important antecedents had to take place—including the art of writing, the development of arithmetic, the widespread use of money, the development of business organizations such as partnerships, the concept of private property, the development of credit, and a significant accumulation of private capital.

Pacioli's accounting system represented a landmark in accounting development. Its major objective was to provide information for the owner, reporting on stewardship and serving as a basis for granting credit. However, little distinction was made between the entity and the owner, as Pacioli's system reported together all the personal and business affairs of the owner. In addition, there was no concept of an accounting period or the continuing nature of a business; profit was calculated only at the termination of a venture, with no accruals or deferrals.

The concept of an accounting period did not emerge until the seventeenth and eighteenth centuries, when end-of-the-year reconciliations became prominent. During this period the center of commerce shifted sequentially from Italy to Spain, to Portugal, to Northern Europe. With this commercial shift was an accompanying shift in accounting development. In 1673, France adopted the first official accounting code, which required, among other things, that balance sheets be drawn up every two years. This period also saw the first *personification* of accounts (the practice of treating accounts as independent, living entities) and the standardization of debits on the left, credits on the right.

While accounting took a long time to get rolling, it really surged in the nineteenth and early twentieth centuries. The major force in this development was the Industrial Revolution. As the scale of enterprises increased following technological breakthroughs such as mass production, and as fixed assets grew in importance, accounting had to accommodate for depreciation, allocating overhead, and inventory. In addition, the basic form of business organization shifted from proprietorships and partnerships to limited liability and stock companies and ultimately to full-blown corporations. Accounting had to accommodate to these new needs. Massive railroad and canal construction during this period once and for all forced the distinction between income and capital. Increased government regulation of business made new demands and generated new accounting systems which were harbingers of bigger moves to come. Most notable was the increased taxation of businesses and individuals, which brought with it new tax accounting systems and procedures.

Since the early years of this century the rapidity of change and the increasing complexity of the world's industrial economies has necessitated still more changes in accounting. Mergers, acquisitions, and the growth of giant multinational corporations fostered new internal reporting and control systems. With widespread ownership of modern corporations came new audit and reporting procedures, and new agencies became involved in promulgating accounting standards: stock exchanges, securities regulating commissions, internal revenue agencies, and so on.

And finally, with the dramatic increase in foreign investments and world trade and the formation of regional economic groups such as the European Economic Community, problems arose concerning the international activities of business. This phenomenon remains particularly complex, for it involves reconciling the accounting practices of different nations in which each multinational operates, as well as dealing with accounting problems unique to international business.

NATIONAL DIFFERENCES
IN ACCOUNTING SYSTEMS

One might infer that these developments had a uniform effect on accounting systems throughout the world, yet nothing could be further from the truth. There are at least as many accounting systems as there are countries, and no two systems are exactly alike. The underlying reasons for these differences are essentially environmental; accounting systems evolve from and reflect the environments they serve. The reality of the world is that environments have not evolved uniformly or simultaneously. Countries today are at stages of economic development ranging from subsistence, barter economies to highly complex industrial societies.

In some countries there is no private ownership; in others there is virtually no manufacturing. In some countries there have been inflation rates of 200 to 300 percent per year; in others there has been no significant economic growth in years. Given these differences in economic conditions, differences in accounting practices should not be surprising. Just as the accounting needs of a small proprietorship are different from those of a multinational giant, so are the accounting needs of an underdeveloped agrarian country different from those of a highly developed industrial country.

Economic factors are not the only influences. Educational systems, legal systems, political systems, and sociocultural characteristics also influence the need for accounting and the direction and speed of its development. For example, in countries where religious doctrine does not permit the charging of interest, there is unlikely to be elaborate accounting procedures related to interest.

The ways in which environmental factors affect the evolution and development of accounting practices are covered in greater detail in Chapter 2. For the moment, it is sufficient to acknowledge their role and the fact that in each country their unique combination results in a unique system of accounting.

Pragmatic Implications of National Differences in Accounting

There is some benefit in understanding how different nations do things. After all, there is always something to be learned from the experiences of others. As a case in point, consider inflation. Suppose a country has never experienced any significant inflation and has therefore never developed accounting procedures related to inflation. What would happen the first time the country experienced substantial and persistent inflation?

It could independently try to devise appropriate accounting procedures. It could also benefit from the experiences of other countries, which, having experienced significant inflation for some time, have developed inflation accounting procedures that work and make sense. However, one has to acknowledge that another country's solution may not be appropriate or feasible for our hypothetical country. The nature of the inflation may be different, its effects may be different, and the other country's practices for dealing with inflation may be incompatible or inconsistent with our country's accounting system.

On the other hand, if the practices are suitable and feasible, they could significantly shorten the time it would take our country to adapt its system so as to account properly for the effects of inflation. In this sense, accounting is a form of technology which can be borrowed or shared, depending on its suitability.

At the present time the most important reason for understanding different national accounting systems lies in the increasingly internationalized world of business, in which people buy and sell, invest and disinvest from one country to another. If an enterprise is considering granting credit to or acquiring a company in another country, it must be able to assess the financial position of that company. This is easier said than done.

When the foreign company offers a balance sheet and income statement for analysis, several things become immediately evident. First, the language and the currency are different. Second, the terminology is different: certain terms (accounts) have no counterparts in the other language or accounting system, or they mean different things. Third, the types and amount of information disclosed are likely to be different. In addition, there are a host of less obvious but perhaps more important differences. For example, the procedures which were followed to arrive at the final figures are likely to be different, and less likely to be explained. Differences in procedures, such as rules of valuation, recognition, or realization, render the financial statements meaningless unless the analyst is familiar with the foreign country's accounting system.

Significance of the Activity

If the amount of international business activity were insignificant, the differences in accounting practices among nations would not be terribly important except for a few firms, or from the academic/philosophical viewpoint. But such is not the case, nor is it likely to be the case again. Between 1963 and 1970, total world trade jumped to more than double its 1966 level. In terms of manufactured goods, trade increased even faster (165 percent). From 1970 to 1976, world trade nearly tripled in value.

Yet trade is only one aspect of the increase in international business activity. The other phenomenon is international investment. From 1966 to 1970, the value of total foreign investment also increased significantly. By and large these international investments represent the establishment of foreign subsidiaries in countries different from that of the parent company. From 1970 to 1976, the value of international investment continued to surge, more than doubling the 1970 amount. With Americans investing in France, Frenchmen investing in Germany, Germans in Japan, and Japanese in the United States, and vice versa, the managers of these multinational enterprises had to understand not only each foreign market's legal, economic, and political systems but also each country's accounting system. At the same time, each country had to design a system of taxation and regulation for both its own multinational companies and the domestic subsidiaries of other countries' multinationals.

Combine the increased internationalization of business and economies and the emergence of multinational enterprise with the differences in national accounting systems, and you have international accounting problems. The rest of this book considers the most significant of these problems, offers alternative approaches to solving or circumventing them, and analyzes the costs and benefits of the various approaches.

EVOLUTION OF INTERNATIONAL BUSINESS

International business can be traced back to 300 B.C., give or take a few hundred years. And as far as anyone can tell, the reasons and motives were the same then as they are today: people wanted something they did not have in their own country, and they found someone in another country able to provide them with what they wanted—for a fee, of course. Yet this early trade was really a fetal stage, for trade on a major and planned scale did not really begin until the Greeks started exporting inexpensive mass-produced goods around the fifth century B.C. By the end of the Greek period there was sufficient trade to have permitted not only full-time professional traders but even some traders who specialized by area of the world or by commodities.

During the Roman period, traders roamed freely through the empire, and with better transportation, political stability, and no tariffs and trade restrictions, trade flourished. In fact, the Roman Empire established the feasibility and desirability of what is now known as the European Economic Community.

During the Middle Ages, international business flourished in some areas of the world, sputtered in others, died and was resurrected in still others. It flourished in Byzantium (present-day Constantinople) until the Crusades, facilitated by the development of banking and insurance and by the first large-scale international trade fairs. International trade did not fare as well in Europe until much later. Wars, plagues, and a generally anticommercial religious doctrine hindered commerce both domestically and internationally. Not until the twelfth century did commercial activity and trade break out of their comotose state. Yet with their resurgence came laws and regulations regarding commerce and trade. Initially developed by guilds, then by city states, then much later by nation states, international commercial regulations have continued to proliferate to the present day.

The Pre-industrial Period

As Europe emerged from the Dark Ages, merchants sought ways to increase international business. By this time, however, the right to trade had become a privilege granted by the states, a phenomenon that has persisted to modern times. The privilege was based on what was to be known as *mercantilism*, a concept by which each state sought to become more pervasive and powerful militarily, economically, and politically than its rivals. During this period of mercantilism, the state was the driving and controlling force behind domestic and international economic activity, a phenomenon which like several others seems to have come back into vogue during recent decades.

The sixteenth and seventeenth centuries saw the first major foreign investments, under the rubric of colonialism. Governments invested directly in colonies, or gave individuals the right to do so, with the express purpose of obtaining raw materials, then products, in a near monopoly control of trade. Finally, during this period of mercantilism the center of commercial and financial activity shifted steadily westward, from Byzantium to Italy, to Holland and Belgium, and ultimately to London. This dominating influence of Western Europe was to last until the twentieth century.

U.S. Expansion Overseas

The second half of the nineteenth century saw the beginning of a continuing phenomenon: U.S. investment abroad. Pioneered by such well-known companies as Standard Oil and Singer, an ever-increasing number of U.S. companies established foreign operations and expanded international trade as well. The process would last without much disruption, except for World War I, until the Great Depression of the 1930s.

While there was relatively little U.S. government interference or involvement with international trade or investment during this period, there was growing foreign government involvement, particularly in trade. This prompted many U.S. and foreign firms to begin displacing exports with direct investments in the more protectionist countries in order to keep their established markets. And despite the continued increase in both trade and investments, a trend was established: investments were becoming more influential than trade.

The Post-World War II Period

The Great Depression and World War II stunted the growth of international business. The reasons are fairly obvious: drastic reductions in income, the bankruptcy of individuals, companies, and governments, then war, the destruction of property, and an end to the stability of money. Throughout this period, trade protectionism and the regulation of capital flows were on the rise. And these, when combined with the other factors just mentioned, put a damper on international business activity.

When World War II ended, there was a tremendous demand for products and services. With some semblance of order restored in international politics and the international monetary system, both trade and investment increased sharply.

The remnants of the protectionism of the 1930s and early 1940s conspired to emphasize investment. The formation of the European

Economic Community (EEC), with its surging demand and the elimination of its internal trade restrictions, resulted in an unparalleled growth of U.S. manufacturing investment abroad. By the 1970s this had abated considerably, but it was followed by an equally significant surge of foreign investments by foreign-based companies into the United States and other countries.

The Multinational Era

The proliferation of multinational enterprises and their activities has constituted perhaps the most significant development in international business—not only in the past three decades, but possibly in the entire span of international business history. Their wealth and influence are gargantuan, as suggested by the fact that by 1971, of the fifty largest economic entities in the world (companies, countries, states) approximately 20 percent were multinational companies, and of the top hundred, nearly 40 percent were multinationals. Yet the impressive role that they now play is far from the whole story of the tremendous increase in international business. For virtually all the world's economies, trade has increased in importance as a percentage of all their economic activity. From 1965 to 1977, total trade expressed as a percentage of gross national product (GNP) rose from 7 to 14 percent for the United States, from 20 to 35 percent for France, from 30 to 42 percent for Germany, from 28 to 49 percent for the United Kingdom, from 23 to 46 percent for Italy, from 70 to 83 percent for the Netherlands, and from 74 to 94 percent for Belgium. In addition, exports from the top 15 noncommunist exporting countries rose from under $15 billion in 1960 to nearly $1,023 billion in 1977.

Even these statistics do not show the whole picture, because they say nothing about international investment flows. In 1974 the total value of *foreign direct investment* (FDI) in the noncommunist world was estimated at $248 billion, compared to $108 billion in 1967. The United States remains the largest foreign investor, with nearly 48 percent of the total, followed by the United Kingdom (14 percent), Switzerland (7 percent), West Germany (6 percent), Japan, France, and The Netherlands (approximately 5 percent each). Data limitations and deficiencies and the fact that most fixed assets values are understated (particularly due to inflation) make a realistic estimate difficult, but total foreign direct investment today may be $400 billion to $500 billion.

Foreign direct investments by foreign-based companies have grown at higher rates than those for U.S.-based companies. In addition, foreign direct investments have changed their emphasis from mining and petroleum to manufacturing. As of 1976, manufacturing accounted for approximately 60 percent of foreign production, while mining and petroleum totaled about 30 percent.

The Importance of International Business to the United States

Before considering the accounting implications of international business activities, a few words are in order about the relative importance to the United States of international business. The United States has become increasingly involved in and dependent on international business activities of *all* varieties. As was mentioned previously, the portion of U.S. GNP involved in international trade grew from 7 percent in 1965 to 14 percent in 1976 and has continued to grow. Foreign direct investments by U.S. companies increased from under $52 billion in 1966 to more than $168 billion in 1978, while direct investments in the United States by *foreign*-based companies increased from $9 billion in 1966 to nearly $41 billion in 1978. In addition, these direct investment figures represent just a fraction of the value of all the foreign assets owned by U.S. firms ($450 billion in 1978) and all the U.S. assets owned by foreigners ($373 billion in 1978). And finally, the United States has become increasingly dependent on the importation of oil, virtually every mineral, and most other natural resources.

Together, these points lead to the conclusion that U.S. involvement in and dependence on international business will continue to grow. Thus anyone contemplating a career in business should prepare for the international aspects in addition to the domestic aspects. This prognostication applies not only to those in marketing, purchasing, finance, production, and management, but also to those in accounting.

ACCOUNTING ASPECTS OF INTERNATIONAL BUSINESS

A firm's first exposure to international accounting usually occurs as a result of an import- or export-related opportunity. In the case of *exports*, a domestic company may receive an unsolicited inquiry or purchase order from a foreign buyer. Assuming the domestic company desires to make the sale, it needs to investigate the foreign buyer, particularly when the buyer asks for the extension of credit. This procedure is not often as easy as it appears.

First of all, the buyer may not be listed in any of the international credit rating directories, such as Standard & Poor's. If this is the case, the seller may need to ask its bank to have its foreign affiliates check on the buyer's creditworthiness. Alternatively, it may ask the buyer to supply financial information. The buyer may be willing to supply financial statements, but these statements will probably be difficult for the domestic company to interpret. The statements may be in a foreign language and are undoubtedly based on accounting assumptions and procedures unfamiliar to the company's accountants. Most companies new to international business must then get help, either from a bank or from an accounting firm with international expertise. Even if the foreign buyer is willing to pay *before* receiving the shipment, if it wants to pay in its own currency, the selling company must become familiar with the gains and losses from changes in the exchange rate which may occur between the time when the order is confirmed and the time when the payment is received.

Then the selling company must deal with a host of other international details—special international shipping and insurance documents, customs declaration forms, international legal documents, and so on. Once again, the services of lawyers, shippers, bankers, and accountants with international expertise are needed.

In the case of a potential *import,* the international accounting aspects are not as involved because most of the details are the responsibility of the foreign seller. However, if the foreign seller requires payment in his nation's currency, the domestic buyer is exposed to a potential foreign exchange gain or loss. Additionally, the domestic buyer may still want information about the reliability of the foreign supplier, for which it can again turn to its bank or lawyer or accounting firm.

Establishing an Internal International Accounting Capability

As the firm becomes increasingly involved in trade, the international accounting activity increases, and so too do the costs of using outside expertise. At some point it becomes feasible for the company to develop the international capabilities of its own staff, including its own accountants.

The next major development which is likely to necessitate increased international accounting skills is the creation of a separate organization within the company to handle international trade. In its least complicated form, this may be an international division. In more complicated forms, it may be a special export company such as a domestic international sales corporation (DISC), which receives special tax treatments under U.S. tax law. (For more on these organizational forms, see Chapters 11 and 12.) Special accounting systems and procedures must be established for these new organizational firms in control, reporting, and possibly taxation areas.

The next step is the establishment of a foreign operation of some sort. In the minimal case, the company may decide to license a foreign manufacturer to produce its product or some part of its product. This involves selecting a potential licensee, analyzing its reliability and capability, and drawing up a contract. It also involves developing an accounting system to monitor contract performance and royalty and technical payments and to handle the foreign money flows into the company's tax and financial statements.

In the maximum case, the development could entail establishing a wholly owned subsidiary in a foreign country. Accounting for the foreign subsidiary would include (1) meeting the requirements of the foreign government, which would be based on procedures and practices different from those in the parent company's country, (2) a management information system to monitor, control, and evaluate the foreign subsidiary, and (3) a system to consolidate the foreign subsidiary's operating results with those of the parent for financial and tax reporting purposes.

In between these extremes are a host of other alternatives: setting up a sales office, setting up a warehouse, forming a joint venture with another company, acquiring an existing company. Each brings with it new international dimensions and requirements for management and, more specifically, for the company's accountants. And it should be pointed out that before any of this takes place, a thorough study of market conditions—legal, economic, political, and sociocultural— should be made, including detailed feasibility studies and risk analysis. All these steps require the collection and appropriate analysis of information in both quantitative financial terms and qualitative terms.

In its first venture into any of these more advanced areas, the international expertise of outside groups is all but indispensable because of the money and risks involved in international trade. However, using outside international experts in no way lessens the need to develop in-house international capabilities, not only in accounting but in other functional areas as well.

Finally, some knowledge of international accounting may be necessary even if a firm is *not* involved in international business per se—for example, if the firm wishes to borrow money or to buy or sell stocks or bonds outside its home country. In some cases, it may be cheaper to borrow money or issue stocks or bonds abroad because interest rates are lower or exchange rate movements are favorable. In order to take advantage of these situations, the firm needs to know not only the relevant foreign laws, regulations, and customs, but also the domestic, legal, tax, and accounting treatments of any of these transactions. Alternatively, there may be better investment opportunities abroad for short-term liquid funds, due to higher returns, predicted exchange rate movements, or both.

From an investment standpoint, the firm must know exactly what it is doing and must also know all the attendant risks. This entails an understanding of the financial statements, the terms of the foreign offer, and foreign currency movements. And as was the case with raising capital abroad, the investing firm must understand both the foreign and domestic laws and the tax and accounting treatments of the transaction being considered.

Thus there are potentially many situations which may require some understanding of international accounting. As the world's economies become increasingly interdependent, the frequency and importance of these occasions will also increase. What is more, there will be a greater need for public accountants to provide international accounting services to companies with international operations. There will also be a need for almost all users of financial statements to understand something about international accounting in order to understand the financial reports of these companies. In sum, virtually everyone who prepares, audits, or uses financial statements of companies with international operations will need to know more and more about international accounting. Hence the importance of international accounting. Hence the importance of this book.

DESCRIPTION OF REMAINING CHAPTERS

To provide a background for more detailed discussion of the problems, issues, and dimensions of international accounting, Chapter 2 describes the major environmental influences that determine the ways in which accounting systems and practices develop. A conceptual framework is first presented with illustrative examples. This framework is applied on a simplified comparative basis to Egypt, Brazil, and The Netherlands and then, on a more detailed basis, to Japan and France. The chapter concludes with a discussion of some commonalities among accounting systems and practices, using various forms of cluster analysis.

Chapter 3 covers international harmonization—the process of eliminating international differences in accounting. The forces pushing for and against harmonization are described, as well as the major organizations involved in the process: what they have accomplished and the prospects for future success.

Chapter 4 describes the international monetary system and the nature of currency exchange rates and movements. This constitutes a background for Chapters 5 through 7, each of which deals with accounting problems related to changes in foreign currency exchange values. More specifically, Chapter 5 deals with accounting for foreign exchange denominated transactions and introduces the process of translating foreign financial statements; Chapter 6 deals with contemporary issues involved in translating and consolidating foreign financial statement translations (consolidations); and Chapter 7 discusses managing foreign exchange risk. All three chapters cover both U.S. approaches and those of selected foreign countries.

Chapter 8 concerns inflation, the related accounting problems and issues, and how various countries have attempted to reflect the impact of inflation on accounting statements.

Chapter 9 is on accounting information disclosure: what kind of information should be disclosed about international operations and results—and why and in what form—and what is actually being done in the United States and elsewhere.

Chapter 10 deals with transfer pricing: the pricing of goods and services that move among members of a global corporation. The chapter discusses the nature of these transfers, the considerations used in setting prices, and the complications in terms of accounting and other matters.

Chapter 11 describes international taxation: the bases and methods for taxing international income and the related accounting implications. While the major focus is on the U.S. system of taxing foreign source income, much of the discussion compares how selected other countries do it.

Chapter 12 concerns international information systems, organization, and control: the peculiar needs of a multinational enterprise in these areas, and how systems can be designed and implemented to satisfy these needs, given the complex nature of the operational environment.

Chapter 13 deals with auditing in an international context: differences in auditing standards and professional groups in various countries and the problems these differences cause for multinationals and auditors. The chapter also focuses on the U.S. Foreign Corrupt Practices Act and its implications for both internal and external auditors.

Finally, Chapter 14 looks to some of the major issues that will confront accountants in the future. Some are historic, but will assume new intensity, and others will be new altogether.

STUDY QUESTIONS

1–1. In one sense accounting is a kind of language, a basic form of communication. But, while verbal languages date back to early history, accounting itself did not develop until much later. Why not?

1–2. Discuss the importance of the Industrial Revolution on the development of accounting practices.

1–3. Discuss how changes in the forms of business organizations (proprietorships, partnerships, corporations, etc.) have affected accounting practices.

1–4. Discuss the changes in accounting that were necessitated by multinational corporations.

1–5. Discuss the major reasons why accounting systems differ among individual countries in the world.

1–6. Leadership in accounting development often follows dominance in world economic activity. That is, a country that leads the world in business activity often also leads the world in accounting development. Why would this occur?

1–7.   Even though international business has been conducted for centuries, it has become truly significant in terms of its importance in the twentieth century. Why?

1–8.   Discuss the changing accounting needs of a firm as it progresses from a strictly domestic company to a multinational company.

1–9.   It is sometimes argued that an understanding of international business is important only for multinational enterprises. Why would this argument be labeled as naive?

1–10.   The same type of argument is often made also with respect to the need for understanding international accounting. What reasons could you give to counter this argument?

2

Comparative Systems of Accounting

Like other business practices, accounting is to a large extent culture-bound. That is, it is shaped by and reflects particular characteristics which are unique to each culture. The list of these characteristics is virtually infinite, ranging from personal traits and values to institutional arrangements, and can even extend to climatic and geographical factors.

ENVIRONMENTAL INFLUENCE ON ACCOUNTING

In what has become a classic conceptual framework for analyzing differences in business practices, Farmer and Richman organized environmental characteristics into four major groups: educational, sociocultural, legal and political, and economic.[1] In effect, these characteristics become constraints on a firm's ability to operate effectively and efficiently. For example, a firm operating in a country with high political and economic instability will have a difficult time planning, meeting schedules, keeping workers' minds on their jobs, and so on.

The various elements in each of the four groups explain the way business organizations in a particular country operate and, to a certain extent, make it possible to predict how they will operate in a given situation. For example, in a country with a high degree of illiteracy (one of the educational characteristics), business must rely to a greater extent on picturegrams or audio methods for advertising, rather than printed

[1]R. Farmer and B. Richman, *International Business: An Operational Theory* (Homewood, Ill.: Irwin, 1966 and subsequent editions).

messages in newspapers. Similarly, in a country where people are not materialistically oriented (one of the sociocultural characteristics), businesses will rely more on nonmonetary forms of reward, such as titles or job security, to attract and motivate their employees. The Farmer-Richman conceptual framework is presented graphically in Figure 1.

This conceptual framework can also be used to explain differences in the ways business is conducted in one country compared to another. If the Farmer and Richman hypothesis is correct that national characteristics affect the way business is conducted—and there is general agreement that the hypothesis *is* correct—then differences in the national environments can be used to explain differences in business operations. For example, if one country has a law which prohibits firing employees after a certain length of service whereas another country has no such law, then—other things being equal—hiring and particularly firing practices are likely to be different in the two countries. Similarly, if there is an extensive private capital market (for example, a large stock exchange) in one country but none in another country, the principal methods of obtaining capital for a business venture are likely to be different.

In later modifications of the basic Farmer and Richman model, it was pointed out that several additional factors could have considerable effect on business practices. Perhaps most important, a firm need not passively adapt to the environment in which it operates.[2] The firm itself can modify or change the environmental characteristics of the country, thereby bringing about changes which would permit it to operate more efficiently and effectively. For example, if a law bans some desired business activity, the firm could bring about a change in that law by supporting candidates who would change it or by lobbying for the change.

Cultural Relativism

Two essential points should be drawn from this opening section on environmental influences. First, environmental analysis can be a valuable tool in explaining and understanding differences in the way businesses operate in different countries and—more specifically and appropriately here—the ways in which accounting principles and practices differ. The second point concerns *cultural relativism*, which means that the rationality of any behavior should be judged in terms of its own

[2]Anant Negandhi and Bernard Estafen, "A Research Model to Determine the Applicability of American Knowhow in Differing Cultures and/or Environments," *Academy of Management Journal*, December 1965, pp. 309–318.

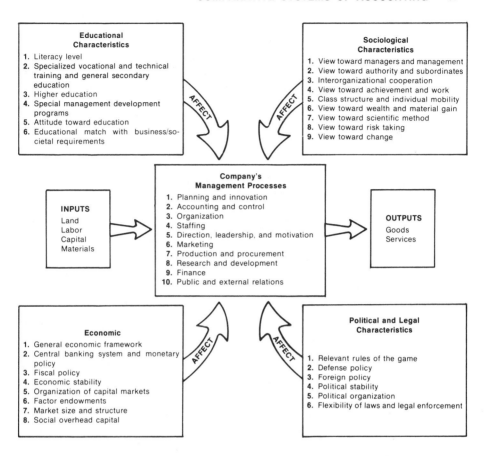

Figure 1. Environmental influence on the management process. (Source: Adapted from R. Farmer and B. Richman, *International Business: An Operational Theory,* Bloomington, Indiana: Cedarwood Press, 1974.)

cultural context, and not from an outsider's cultural context. Put another way, one cannot judge the rationality of behavior in Indonesia using U.S. mores and values.

There are many practices around the world which appear from a U.S. viewpoint to be illogical and irrational—and, we should add, vice versa. Yet when we understand the culture in which the behavior takes place, we will usually find that the seemingly irrational behavior is in fact quite rational. More important, it may be the only truly rational way of doing things in that country.

Too often the incorrect assumption is made that the other people simply don't know any better, that our own ways are better than theirs, and that our ways, if transplanted to that country, would be more successful than theirs. In case after case, this assumption has been proven false, at considerable financial loss to the companies involved.[3]

Let us now examine in greater detail how some of the environmental characteristics of a country affect the way accounting develops and is practiced.

Educational Factors

The educational characteristics of a country have a significant effect on accounting practices. These educational characteristics encompass (1) the degree of literacy, including the ability to use simple mathematics, (2) the percentage of people who have received formal schooling at various levels (elementary school, high school, college), (3) the basic orientation of the educational system (religion, vocational, liberal arts, scientific, professional), and (4) the educational match—the appropriateness of the educational system's output for the country's economic and societal needs.

Because accounting takes a written and numerical form, it has relatively little use or significance in a society that is predominantly illiterate. Meticulous preparation and widespread circulation of corporate financial reports in such a society obviously would not be a judicious use of corporate time, money, and effort. Internally, the accounting planning and control system would be more difficult to use effectively because of the limited ability of employees to prepare and understand budgets and reports. At the same time, the need for budgeting and control tends to be greater in developing countries (which have the highest level of illiteracy). Hence the accountant is hard put to design an accounting system for either external or internal use.

As the educational level of the population improves, most of these accounting problems decrease, and more extensive and sophisticated accounting systems and reports become feasible. Whether they are put into practice depends on other factors to be discussed later.

It should also be pointed out that even in countries with a largely illiterate population there can be relatively sophisticated accounting systems. This paradox occurs most often when the industrial sector and government are run by well-educated individuals and the major external user of the accounting reports is the government—or where the government itself is the principal owner/management of the firms. Egypt is an example of this situation. Egypt's literacy rate is not high, but its accounting system for large enterprises is relatively sophisticated because most of the major enterprises are government owned.

[3]D. Ricks, M. Fu, and J. Arpan, *International Business Blunders* (Columbus, Ohio: Grid Inc., 1974).

The orientation of the educational system also plays a part in determining accounting practices. Perhaps the most obvious relationship is whether mathematics is taught sufficiently to permit compilation and analysis of numerical data. Further, the extent to which accounting itself is taught in the educational system will influence the number of people who have some training in and understanding of bookkeeping, budgeting, financial analysis, and auditing. And more specifically related to accounting, does an accounting curriculum exist, and if so, what does it entail? Is there a degree in accounting, and for what type of work does the degree qualify someone? More subtly, the teaching and acceptance of the scientific method (the basic law of causality) influences people's acceptance of, and adherence to, the process of planning, budgeting, and control. Stated another way, if people in the organization are fatalistic—if they believe that whatever happens will happen, regardless of their activities or efforts—they will not perceive any need for planning, budgeting, and control.

Finally, the educational match influences accounting system development to the extent that accountants and information users grow in number and sophistication as the economic and social system need greater and more complex accounting information and procedures. In other words, as the country industrializes, there are more and bigger firms, more complex business arrangements (credit, leases, poolings, mergers), and usually an increased need for outside capital. Each requires more complex accounting procedures and more people who can use and understand them. The issue is whether the educational system is cranking out enough of these people at each stage of development.

Cultural Factors

Hundreds of cultural factors influence accounting practices. Among the most important are the society's degree of conservatism, secrecy, distrust, and fatalism, coupled with the people's attitudes toward business and the accounting profession itself.

The society's degree of conservatism influences a number of accounting principles and practices, especially valuation and profit determination. For example, the use of historical cost reflects a degree of conservatism, as do the lower-of-cost-or-market principles, the recording of contingent liabilities, the over-allowance for bad debts, and the practice of using a wide variety of special reserves. These last two practices also generally result in lower reported profits, reflecting a higher level of conservatism, and often a desire to appear weaker than one actually is.

The society's degree of secrecy most directly affects the amount of disclosure an enterprise is willing to make in its external reporting: the greater the level of secrecy or distrust of outsiders, the lower the level of disclosure. Internally, a high level of distrust makes it more difficult to implement a system of internal control and performance evaluation, because no one wants to have his activities scrutinized. Secrecy also affects the audit function, making it more difficult to obtain necessary support information, verification, and corroboration of the accounting data supplied by the enterprise. Curiously, in certain circumstances a high degree of trust may cause similar problems. In Japan, for example, to question someone's word is to question his honor—a serious insult and definitely bad form. Thus an auditor who attempts to obtain proof of accounting information supplied by someone else will be in a difficult and uncomfortable position, and certainly one not likely to win friends.

Fatalism and its effect on accounting have already been described. Suffice it to say here that the stronger this conviction, the less important will be the role of accounting in the enterprise, the economy, and the society.

Societal attitudes toward business may range from distrust and antagonism to wholehearted support and trust. Distrust generates demands for more information and closer scrutiny of business operations, perhaps even regulation or nationalization. The information requested is likely to encompass far more than mere financial data, and include the enterprise's treatment of employees, societal and political activities and contributions, environmental impacts, and so on. However, whether firms actually make such disclosure depends largely on their need for public-source funds and their relationship with the government.

Government support of society's wishes can lead to establishing and regulating accounting procedures and practices. This appears to be the situation in countries such as Sweden and France, where *social accounting* is becoming the order of the day. At the other extreme, society and government may make few if any disclosure demands on enterprises. In this situation, accounting is likely to be more flexible and much more at the discretion of firms, resulting in considerably less pressure for disclosure. This was the case in the United States before the Great Depression and remains largely the case in Switzerland today.

Finally, the attitude toward the accounting profession affects the status of the profession, the type of person who enters it, its credibility, and the work that accountants perform. In many countries, accounting is still regarded as a low-status occupation filled with thieves and people fit for no meaningful job. As can be expected, the best and brightest people in these countries do not aspire to become accountants. This may be a self-fulfilling prophecy; perhaps only thieves and other undesirables become accountants in these countries. In other countries, accountants occupy a highly respected place in society, and accounting attracts high caliber individuals as a result. Accountants in these countries tend to lead the world in the development of accounting theory, procedures, and practices. Germany, The Netherlands, the United Kingdom, and the United States are representative examples.

Legal and Political Factors

At first blush the legal system may appear to have little influence on accounting systems. Yet in many countries law, particularly tax law, is the only reason accounting is done at all. In these countries, the accounting rules and practices are spelled out in laws, often called *companies' acts*, which also contain the general laws for all business operations and activities. In addition, tax laws in virtually all countries specify accounting procedures to be used in the tax area.

The Legalistic Approach

The countries where laws determine accounting practices are commonly grouped in what can be called the *legalistic approach*. Their governments play an active, even dominant role in the economic sector, and their accounting profession is relatively weak. In most of these countries, there is no difference between tax accounting and financial accounting: if a certain transaction is treated one way for tax purposes, it *must* be handled the same way for financial reporting purposes. From a U.S. perspective, the legalistic approach to accounting has several major drawbacks and disadvantages. One is that accounting standards and practices are set by legislators who generally have little accounting background or training. Hence they may be unaware of the accounting implications for practitioners of the accounting legislation they pass— such as the amount of work required to comply with the laws. Perhaps more important, the legislators may ignore the validity and efficacy of the accounting practice in terms of either accounting theory or sound business practice.

The legalistic approach to accounting is found to a certain degree in all countries of the world, regardless of their stage of economic development or the level of their accounting profession's development. In the United States, for example, tax laws and the regulations promulgated by the Securities and Exchange Commission are clearly representative of the legalistic approach to accounting. Thus the main distinctions among countries are the *pervasiveness* of the legal approach and whether other approaches are permitted.

In countries where the legalistic approach is dominant, the role and function of the auditor are also quite different from those in the United States and the United Kingdom, for example. The main function of the auditor in the legalistic approach is to certify that the accounting books and related statements are in accordance with the law, down to the last detail. No assessment or comment is generally made in the audit report that a true and fair picture is presented by the statements. In addition, there are separate classifications of auditors into two groups: statutory auditors and all others. Statutory auditors are the only ones allowed to perform the official audit, and generally they must meet stringent qualifications specified by law.

Apart from a legalistic approach to accounting (either in general or in the tax or securities area), certain laws not directly related to accounting may have definite accounting implications nonetheless. A recent U.S. example is the *Foreign Corrupt Practices Act*. Its main purpose is to prevent U.S. companies—or anyone acting on their behalf—from paying bribes to foreign government officials. Yet the accounting implications are considerable. The major accounting effect of the law is that U.S. multinational companies must establish a system of internal controls and an internal audit staff to make sure that bribes are not being made or being hidden. The outside auditor must also make sure that the internal control system is appropriately designed and implemented.

Political Factors

Certain political factors also can influence accounting systems and practices. In socialist countries it is often politically expedient and desirable to require certain information from companies about their social impact. For similar reasons, developing countries may require reports from companies on the balance of payments impact of their planned operations as a precondition to approving the investment. Changes in political direction—from left to right, for example—can bring about new accounting rules through new laws or, in the extreme case, can result in government takeovers. In this situation, the accountant may become involved in determining the fair value of the firm taken over, in hopes of receiving from the government fair compensation for the assets seized.

Economic Factors

A country's stage of economic development and basic economic orientation are two of the major economic factors which influence accounting development and practices. At extremely low levels of economic development, there is little economic activity and correspondingly little financial, tax, or managerial accounting. As the level of economic activity and the size of companies increase, there is a corresponding increase in accounting activity. This continues through each successive stage of development, albeit with certain lags. Direct wealth (income) taxation of both individuals and companies increases, managerial accounting develops, and so does financial reporting to creditors, investors, and so on. In addition, as business operations and relationships become more complex, new procedures are developed—accounting for mergers, acquisition, leases, foreign exchange gains and losses, and so on.

How Much Government Involvement?

The basic orientation of the economic system concerns the degree of government involvement in the economic sector. In *communist countries*, for example, the state owns all production facilities, makes most of the economic and business decisions, and controls virtually all operations through a central planning and control mechanism. These countries have a highly standardized and uniform accounting system to facilitate the government's planning and control function, and there are few users of accounting information other than the government. In *market-capitalist economies*, there is predominantly private ownership. With greater individual freedom in economic activity and decision making, a correspondingly greater diversity in accounting practices is permitted and practiced. There are also more users of accounting information—stockholders, auditors, suppliers, creditors—in addition to the government. Between these extremes are *market-socialist countries*, which have considerable but not total state ownership, and countries with predominantly private ownership but some central planning and regulation by the government. Their accounting systems and practices fall somewhere between the other two systems.

A related economic characteristic is the type of monetary and fiscal policies employed by the government and their degree of use. For example, in order to stimulate economic activity, many countries have developed investment tax credit systems which are accompanied by specific accounting rules. Other countries permit the accumulation of sizable reserves or permit *income smoothing*[4] to provide pools of funds as a cushion during adverse times or for expansion.

Sources of Funds

Another important economic characteristic is the source of funds for investment and working capital. First of all, the sources influence the degree of investor orientation vs. creditor orientation of the accounting system. That is, if the major source of funds is *loans* from banks, financial intermediaries, or even wealthy individuals, then accounting standards, principles, and procedures will tend to be more conservative and reflective of creditor preferences and requirements. This creditor orientation remains predominant in the world, at least in terms of number of countries. On the other hand, if the major source of funds is of an *equity-investor* orientation, then the accounting system will be similarly oriented and will include such important investor information as earnings per share and more extensive public disclosure. In countries where formally organized stock exchanges play an important role, even more

---

[4]Income smoothing is a method by which companies can report lower than actual income in good years and higher than actual income in bad years using inventory write downs or movement of funds in and out of reserves.

complicated investor-oriented accounting standards and procedures will be evident, such as the Securities and Exchange Commission's accounting regulations in the United States.

A company based in a creditor-oriented country that desires to raise equity funds in an investor-oriented country typically suffers considerable cultural shock in terms of the amount of disclosure it must make in order to sell stock. For many such companies, the disclosure required becomes, in effect, a deterrent to seeking equity funds. In still other countries, banks have considerable freedom to take equity positions in corporations in addition to their more traditional creditor relationship. In Germany, for example, the banks are major shareholders in German companies. In such countries, there is less public financial reporting and disclosure because the banks are the major investors and already have all the information they need from the companies because of their existing credit relationships with them.

Degree of International Activity

Another economic characteristic which influences accounting practices is the *degree of international economic activity*. The greater the amount of a country's international trade, the greater its need for accounting practices concerning foreign exchange transactions and translations.

Going a step further, the number and size of a country's multinational firms is directly related to the development of accounting rules for consolidation of foreign accounting reports, international transfer pricing, and taxation of foreign source income (income earned outside the parent company's country). As an example, the United States is the largest single trading country and also the one with the largest amount of foreign investment outside its own boundaries. As a result, the U.S. accounting system includes the most elaborate practices and requirements of accounting for foreign exchange gains and losses, global consolidation of financial reports, transfer prices, and taxation of worldwide income. At the other extreme, Afghanistan has little international trade or investment, no multinationals, and hence little if any accounting related to international business activity.

Inflation

Inflation is another economic characteristic which has an important influence on accounting practices in individual countries. While inflation appears to be a worldwide phenomenon, its severity varies from single-digit to triple- and even quadruple-digit annual levels—often referred to as *hyperinflation*. Particularly in hyperinflationary countries, the cumulative effect of inflation over a number of years can render all accounting information meaningless *unless* it is appropriately adjusted. Chapter 8 describes in greater detail various countries' approaches to inflation accounting. Suffice it to say here that countries such as the United States and Germany, with relatively low levels of inflation, have been slower to develop inflation accounting rules than hyperinflationary countries such as Brazil, Argentina, and Chile.

Ties to Other Countries

One other economic factor deserving mention in terms of its influence on accounting system development is economic ties to and relationships with other countries. Historically, the first of such arrangements was *colonialism*. The colonies adopted or were forced to adopt the accounting system of their colonial power, even though it may not have been particularly appropriate at the colony's stage of development. Thus the accounting systems in the British colonies were significantly influenced by British accounting, and the influence remains today, such as in the United States, Canada, Jamaica, the Bahamas. The same can be said for former French colonies, Spanish colonies, and so on.

A second economic relationship worthy of note is formal regional economic groups such as the European Economic Community (EEC), the Andean Pact group, and the Central American Common Market (CACM). As these groups move toward full integration of their economic and political systems, they have recognized the need to integrate their accounting systems as well. This process is commonly referred to as *harmonization*. To date only the EEC has expended much effort or made much progress toward harmonizing the accounting systems of its nine member countries. Nevertheless, formal regional economic groups can significantly affect accounting development and practices as harmonization requires countries to modify their historical ways.

One final type of intercountry economic relationship which can affect accounting is the *product cartel*, such as the Organization of Petroleum Exporting Countries (OPEC), the copper cartel, and the bauxite cartel. In attempting to standardize world export prices, and in some cases to ensure equitable returns to its members, cartels often try to devise uniform costing and pricing systems among their members in addition to specific production or export quotas.

THE ENVIRONMENTAL ANALYSIS APPLIED

Of all the environmental factors which influence accounting system development, a strong case can be made that the economic characteristics are the most influential. The reason is that in addition to their direct effects on accounting, they also have significant indirect effects in terms of their influence on the other environmental areas. Economic development affects many sociocultural attitudes and brings about changes in legal, political, and educational objectives and sophistication—each of which in turn can affect accounting practices. Yet even the pervasive economic influences do not determine *in isolation* the development and practices of a country's accounting system. One need only examine the accounting systems and practices of the three dominant market economies of the world—the United States, Germany, and Japan—to see that there are considerable differences in accounting among them despite great similarities in their economic sophistication and stature. Thus there is a need to consider *all* the environmental factors in analyzing a country's accounting system.

Egypt, Brazil, The Netherlands

To begin a more specific discussion of differences in accounting systems linked to environmental differences, let us briefly compare Egypt, Brazil, and The Netherlands. On a continuum of economic development, Egypt would be at one end (underdeveloped), Brazil in the middle (rapidly developing), and The Netherlands at the other end (highly developed). Most of Egypt's industrial sector—which is small compared to those of Brazil and The Netherlands—is owned, operated, and highly regulated by the government. Brazil too has many large government-owned companies and many regulations, but it also has a flourishing private sector. The Netherlands has a large, flourishing, private sector and comparatively little government ownership and regulation.

The population in Egypt has comparatively low levels of literacy and education, The Netherlands has a highly literate and well-educated population, and Brazil falls somewhere in between. Egypt has virtually no multinational companies, Brazil has a few, The Netherlands many. Finally, Egypt is a socialist country politically and economically; The Netherlands is basically democratic and capitalist; and Brazil, once again, is somewhere in between—it has a military junta but is capitalism-oriented.

The environmental differences among these countries can be seen clearly in their different accounting systems. Egypt has a uniform, highly standardized accounting system whose main purpose is to provide information to the government for necessary centralized planning and control. Because accounting skills are relatively low and not widespread, accounting practices must be spelled out in fine detail. Standardization also permits intraindustry and interindustry comparisons on the efficiency and effectiveness of operations. Because there is really no domestic capital market, there is less need for financial reporting compared to The Netherlands. On the other hand, Egypt's socialist orientation requires the reporting of certain social information which is not found to anywhere near the same extent in The Netherlands or Brazil.

At the other extreme, the Dutch accounting system is virtually tailored to each firm. So long as the accounting practices reflect sound business practice, they are essentially acceptable. The widespread, high levels of education and accounting skills in The Netherlands are the source of some of the most sophisticated examples of accounting practices—particularly in inflation accounting, for which many of the companies use replacement cost (current value) accounting. Because so many Dutch companies are multinational and need to tap international money and capital markets, Dutch financial reports are typically well disclosed and presented in segmented form and in several languages. The business community and the accounting profession are highly regarded and independent; and compared to Brazil and Egypt, they are left relatively to their own devices by the Dutch government.

As should be expected at this point, the Brazilian accounting system falls somewhere between the Egyptian and the Dutch. In a sense, Brazil has a two-tiered system of accounting—one for the large publicly owned companies, called *open companies* (many of which are subsidiaries of foreign companies), and a second one for virtually all other firms. The accounting system of the open companies is not much different from that of U.S. companies (for example, fair presentation, independent auditing), while that for other companies is considerably different. Privately held companies have much less disclosure and regulation, and generally their financial statements are not very reliable or indicative of their true financial position.

All major companies in Brazil share one special accounting aspect in common: both balance sheets and income statements must be adjusted for inflation, using official government indices. This requirement is necessitated by the rampant inflation in Brazil for the past several decades. Brazil's extremely rapid movement from underdevelopment to an emerging industrialized status required different rules for different purposes and different economic entities. Hence the two-tiered accounting system with certain commonalities.

As this perhaps oversimplified analysis shows, the differences in countries' environments are reflected in their accounting systems. One cannot say that any one system is absolutely or even comparatively better than the others. All that can be concluded is that each accounting system reflects and is tailored for the environment of which it is a part. To see in even more detail how the environment affects a country's accounting system, let us now focus on the environment and accounting practices of Japan and France.

Japan

The Japanese society is highly organized, disciplined, respectful, and perhaps above all cooperative and group-oriented. It has one of the world's highest literacy rates due to its strong emphasis on education for all its people. Japan is a classic example of what sociologists call a closed, geometric society, in which every person and organization is defined and fixed in position in relation to all others. The society is held together by a complex network of interrelationships and interdependencies based largely on an equally complex system of reciprocal obligations.

Japan's societal characteristics are mirrored in its economic and business system, which is a complex maze of interdependencies among firms, between firms and their employees, and between firms and the government, all in a reciprocally supportive and cooperative arrangement. While most evident in the older industrial sectors (steel, chemicals, automotives, textiles), and to a lesser extent in almost all sectors, the web of interrelationships and obligations that comprise Japan's economy remains one of its most descriptive characteristics.

The complex pattern of cross-ownership and lending among members of a Japanese business group (such as the Mitsubishi group) virtually defies control analysis. It is virtually impossible to say who really controls what and whom. A manufacturing concern may own stock in several supplying and purchasing companies (and even a bank or two), each of which may in turn own stock in the manufacturing company. Credit arrangements within the group can be equally complex and serve to further cement business relationships.

When any group member gets into financial trouble, it is the obligation of the other members and, if necessary, the government to provide assistance to the ailing company. This may mean extending additional credit or delaying collections or providing technical or managerial assistance. Thus short-term debt can become long-term, and long-term debt can become a form of equity investment in the company by its creditors. This is why the extremely high leverage of Japanese firms, which also has considerable tax advantages, is seldom as precarious and risky as it appears to an outsider.

With respect to business, the government adopts a sort of Calvin Coolidge philosophy: what is good for business is good for the country. The Japanese government plays an active supporting role in the economy, which has at its core the stable growth of enterprises and employment by means of domestic and international expansion of its companies. At times it has also pursued a stringent policy of protecting its domestic market from foreign business influences and activities. Yet overall, the government has sought ways to enhance the international competitiveness of its firms by encouraging and promoting mergers and consolidations, overseas market development, modernization of plants and equipment, and the development and implementation of new product and process technologies.

Accounting Practices

The influence of Japanese environmental characteristics can be clearly seen in its accounting practices. To facilitate the accumulation of funds in companies to achieve and maintain international competitiveness, the government permits a wide variety of reserve accounts. These reserves are for general purposes (bad debts, security price fluctuations, retirement allowances) and for specific purposes (overseas market development, export activities). The government also permits special depreciation allowances in excess of statutory limits for certain types of assets: computers, shipping vessels, company housing, antipollution equipment. The reserves and allowances are pre-tax deductions, thereby lessening or postponing taxes. They also permit income smoothing, which has the effect of stabilizing income and inspiring societal confidence in the firms.

The government provides a wide variety of tax credits, primarily for use by companies that are losing their international competitive position. These credits cover expenses for scrapping obsolete equipment, promoting mergers, and conducting experimental research and development. The tax credits can also have considerable impact on reported income and cash flows. Together with the use of reserves, Japanese companies generally show a lower level of profitability and pay less taxes than they would if they were operating under U.S. tax laws and generally accepted accounting principles.

Other environmental characteristics of Japan are reflected in still other accounting practices. The general public confidence and trust in the business-government partnership results in no great desire for significant disclosure of financial information by Japanese companies. For similar reasons, the audit function is largely perfunctory and ceremonial. Because Japanese society is oriented to both long-term growth and employment security, and because cross-ownership of firms is commonplace, there is little interest in such information as earnings per share or even current financial performance. Nor would either kind of information be particularly meaningful because of income smoothing. And while accountants enjoy a respected position in Japan, their role is largely passive: the government plays the dominant role in setting accounting standards, policies, and practices.

In recent years there have been noticeable changes in the Japanese accounting system, the most significant one concerning consolidation of corporate financial reports. Prior to the 1970s non-consolidation was the rule; financial reports were typically prepared on a parent-company-only basis. This practice often hid losses in subsidiary companies (which were not consolidated) and showed artificially high profits in parent company reports because intracompany sales and profits were not eliminated. Prior to 1975 some of the major Japanese companies were compelled to prepare consolidated financial statements according to U.S. generally accepted accounting principles in order to obtain funds from U.S. or other international sources. However, a law passed in 1976 requires consolidated reports for most of Japan's major companies, as well as considerably more disclosure in these reports.

France

Historically France was a nation of independent, self-reliant craftsmen, artists, and farmers who took pride in themselves and in their work. An elitist aristocracy governed France politically, and the aristocratic status quo orientation, combined with the society's Catholicism-based lower drive for achievement and materialism, caused France to fall behind as its neighbors and competitors industrialized.

Several forces made changes essential if France was to remain a world power. The agricultural revolution, which reduced employment in the agricultural sector from 44 percent in the 1940s to less than 10 percent in the 1970s, provided a large pool of labor for industry, new markets, and a middle class; but it also caused rising expectations and societal polarizations. The formation of the European Economic Community brought increased competition to France, as did the influx of American and other foreign investments into France and the EEC. It became evident that France's traditional business strucure and traditional ways of doing business were no longer viable. Yet the traditionalist and independent Frenchman was slow to recognize this and to make the necessary adaptations. The government therefore had to take action to restructure the policies, management, and activities of the French economy, industries, and firms.

The major thrust was a renewed and strengthened policy of economic and sectoral planning. Tax incentives and political suasion were used to induce firms to move in ways which would improve not only their own financial and competitive position, but also that of the economy in general. And when and where such inducements or efforts were not successful, the French government itself became involved directly in the ownership of French companies.

Accounting Practices

To facilitate economic planning and analysis, France revamped an old uniform plan of accounting. Historically, the uniform plan had for the most part been restricted to nationalized industries (iron, coal, steel, railroads) and to the few largest publicly held companies. By successive government acts, however, the plan was made more comprehensive and extended to more and more enterprises, both publicly and privately held.

The main advantage of the uniform plan is that it facilitates and permits better government decision making because all firms covered by the plan must follow identical procedures and formats for accounting reports. Thus interindustry and intraindustry comparisons are easier to make, and strengths and weaknesses, opportunities and bottlenecks are easier to identify. Once identified, the government can change the plan or change the inducements and more readily observe the impact of such changes.

The French government also embarked on a policy called *contracts de croissance*, which had as its objective the development of national champions in the major French industries. The *contracts de croissance* policy included tax incentives (allowances, credits) to nurture the development of the selected national champions. The uniform plan made it easier to identify the best candidate firms, to determine what inducements would be best, and to assess the program and success of the policy.

The growing socialist movement in France has also been felt in the accounting sector. The society has made increased demands on the government to require firms to make more disclosure about their activities, particularly those which relate to workers and working conditions. In 1977 the government passed new legislation requiring certain large companies to prepare a *Bilan Social*, or social report, showing what actions they had taken with respect to their workers and working conditions. More about this social accounting in Chapters 9 and 14.

In sum, the increased direct and indirect role of the French government in the economy of France strongly influenced the French accounting system even though the basic plan had existed for centuries. And as the economy and society changed in consequence of this intervention, new pressures brought about yet more changes in accounting. And the process goes on.

COMMONALITIES AND CLUSTERS

Up to this point we have seen some of the unique differences in national environments and their effects on accounting. If carried to the extreme, one might conclude that comparative accounting is a never-ending task of investigating minute differences in cultures and accounting practices, with little aggregation or generalization. Yet despite all the differences in cultures and accounting practices, there are major commonalities in both respects among the countries of the world. These commonalities permit the clustering of countries on the basis of similarities in their environments or in their accounting practices or both.

As a point of departure it should be said that all generalizations are patently false—including this one—and that for every generalization there are innumerable exceptions. Applied to the discussion that follows, this means that the generalizations and clusters have limited value and should not be construed otherwise. Yet generalizations and cluster analysis can serve a useful function in that they partially demark areas of common ground and highlight similarities and differences among groups. Finally, some generalizations and clusters are better than others, depending on their degree of specificity, the methods used to derive them, and their relevance to the area of interest being studied.

Accounting Clusters

The most basic cluster divides the world into two groups: those with a legalistic approach to accounting, and those with a non-legalistic approach. An illustrative legalistic cluster is made up of Germany, France, Switzerland, Japan, and most of the Latin American countries, whereas the British, Canadian, Australian, South African, U.S., and Dutch systems are more representative of the non-legalistic. The essential difference lies in whether the accounting practices are extensively legislated and hence a matter of law, or whether they are more a matter of individual choice—or, as the U.S. terminology goes, are *generally accepted*. Another major difference is that the legalistic cluster tends to be heavily tax- and creditor-oriented as opposed to investor-oriented. Among other things, this difference influences the degree to which accounting statements reflect the true or fair financial position of the entity—which is decidedly more true for the non-legalistic cluster.

An examination of audit statements reveals a good example of these differences. The German audit statement, representing the legalistic cluster, states: "According to our audit, made in conformity with our professional duties, the accounts, the annual financial statements, and the board of management comply with German law and the company's statutes." But the U.S. audit statement, representing the non-legalistic cluster, states: "In our opinion, the consolidated financial statements present fairly the financial position of the company and its subsidiary companies and the results of their operations and changes in financial position, in conformity with generally accepted accounting principles." principles."

Additionally, there is seldom any difference between tax and financial statements in the legalistic cluster because of the requirement that if a particular treatment is used for tax records it must also be used for book records, or financial statements. In the non-legalistic cluster, however, there are usually substantial differences between tax and financial statements, although the financial statements must usually reconcile any material differences. To cite a more specific example, there is seldom any interperiod tax allocation in the legalistic cluster, but there is in the non-legalistic cluster.

It should be acknowledged that there are degrees of complexity and thoroughness *within* each approach. The German system is more complex and thorough than the Swiss, which is more so than the Spanish, and so on. There are also hybrid systems, such as the British, which although codified and hence legalistic also presents a true and fair picture of the firm. So do the Canadian and South African systems. Thus while the distinction between legalistic and non-legalistic clusters is useful, it is not sufficient in most cases because there are sometimes as many accounting differences within the two groups as between them.

Gerhard Mueller, in his pioneering book on international accounting, divided the various approaches to accounting into four clusters: those with a macroeconomic orientation; those with a microeconomic orientation; those with an independent orientation; and those with a uniform orientation.[5]

The Macroeconomic Approach

In the macroeconomic orientation Mueller identified several postulates, among the more important ones being these two:

1. The business enterprise accomplishes its goals best through close coordination of its activities with the national economic policies of its environment.
2. Public interest is served best if business enterprise accounting interrelates closely with national economic policies.

What are the accounting implications of such a formulation? Postulating a policy of full employment, this approach implies sustained efforts toward economic and business stability. It also means administrative efforts to minimize the effects of business cycles or, better yet, to avoid pronounced swings in business cycles altogether. Accounting adaptation to such a policy would require some averaging of reported income for the firm over the length of the typical business cycle.

Another national policy might be the achievement of a predetermined rate of economic growth. Here, accounting might adjust its depreciation and amortization procedures with regard to firms or industries that are most likely to be significant contributors to the rate of economic growth in a given period. Moreover, accounting might incorporate measurements of a firm's contributions to gross national product or of changes in its rate of productivity. For example, accounting could encompass information on utilization of resources or, alternatively, the wasting of resources. Other specific examples of accounting practices under a macroeconomic orientation would include these:

1. Periodic income smoothing.
2. Revenues to include amounts of value created by a firm's construction, or development of assets intended for its own use plus amounts of value added to inventories of goods and materials.

[5]The following discussion of these four approaches was adapted from Gerhard G. Mueller, *An Introduction to International Accounting* (Englewood Cliffs, N.J.: Prentice-Hall, 1965).

3. Formal recognition of discovery values of natural resource deposits.
4. Accelerated write-offs of plant and equipment to achieve national objectives.
5. Inclusion of externalities such as pollution or access road construction in a firm's expenses and revenues.
6. Accounting for social impacts.
7. Human resources accounting.
8. Local community and national impact accounting.

Sweden has developed the single most comprehensive system of accounting along macroeconomic lines, but elements of this approach are found in many other countries.

The Microeconomic Approach

In the microeconomic approach, Mueller's more critical postulates included three points.

1. The main policy of the business firm is to ensure its continued existence.
2. Optimization in an economic sense is a firm's best policy for survival.
3. Accounting, as a branch of business economics, derives its concepts and applications from economic analysis.

The central accounting concept in a development pattern based on microeconomics is that the accounting process must hold constant in real terms the amount of capital investment in the firm. This is essential on three counts: (1) The firm cannot survive if its real capital base is eroded away by tax or dividend payments that fully or partly invade the real investment capital base. (2) The permanently invested capital is the economic root of the firm, and the capital investment must therefore receive key considerations as long as the firm itself is the focal point of business activities. (3) An effective separation of capital and income is prerequisite to evaluating and controlling the firm's business activities.

Specific accounting practices which could be included in a microeconomically oriented system are:

1. A valuation measurement system based on current value concepts, such as replacement costs.
2. A heavy managerial emphasis on all accounting reports, usually more often than annually.
3. Highly segmented reports of important financial indicators, by product and markets.
4. Detailed disclosure of production data and other internal corporate affairs.

Again, certain elements of this microeconomic approach can be found in many countries, but The Netherlands has developed the most comprehensive application.

The Independent Approach

In the independent approach, pragmatism is the dominant concept in business. Good business practices are those that succeed, over time, in generating new business and profit and in reducing uncertainty. These practices are largely introspective, often based initially on intuition, and become accepted through trial and error. As Mueller put it:

> If business is the main interest served by accounting and if accounting provides primarily an efficient and effective service to business, the inevitable question is, should not accounting and business practices have the same basis and follow the same pattern of development? If the answer to this question is affirmative, a case is made for regarding accounting as an independent discipline. If business can produce its own concepts and methods from experience and practice, the argument follows that accounting can (or should) do the same. If business can develop itself from within, why should accounting not be capable of doing the same?[6]

The accounting implications of the independent approach are as follows:

1. A cohesive and complete conceptual structure of accounting is difficult to construct.
2. A piecemeal, incremental approach to establishing accounting principles and standards is the only viable approach, given that there is no theoretical framework as a benchmark.
3. Income and other concepts are defined simply in terms of the pragmatic application, what is most useful in business.
4. Full and fair disclosure is extremely important because there is greater leniency to interpret and improvise what is generally accepted.

If all this sounds familiar to those who know the U.S. system of accounting, it should; the U.S. system is the most comprehensive application of this independent approach, followed closely by the United Kingdom.

---

[6]Ibid.

The Uniform Approach

The uniform approach concerns the quest to make accounting more scientific and more suitable for centralized administrative uses. The idea is to have all organizations collect, record, categorize, and report all data in an identical systematic and scientific manner. If successful, such a system can facilitate intercompany and interindustry comparisons and can make central economic planning and regulation more effective and efficient. In its most comprehensive form, on a national economic scale, it closely resembles the macroeconomic approach described earlier. That is, national economic policy considerations dominate technical and theoretical accounting considerations.

The centrally planned economies of Asia and Eastern Europe are the major users of this approach, but the French have also used it for many years in their *Plan Comptable*. However, the uniform approach is not restricted to the national level. It also has application on an industry level, such as for railroads or public utilities or, as in the case of Sweden's M Chart, for metal-working industries. Most systems of federal taxation are similarly uniform in approach.

Other Approaches

It should be clear that while many national accounting systems favor one of these four approaches, each also contains some elements of more than one approach. For example, in the United States the independent approach is dominant but the uniform approach is used for regulated industries such as public utilities; some elements of the macroeconomic approach are beginning to appear in such areas as social accounting and the micro approach is becoming evident in the form of current value accounting. Thus further refinements in clustering are needed.

In a later work, Mueller made just such an attempt.[7] Using the four variables of (1) stage of economic development, (2) stage of business complexity, (3) impact of political orientation, and (4) reliance on a particular set of laws, he used a judgmental approach to identify ten distinct clusters of business environments (see Table 2-1). And while his analysis did not specifically address accounting practices, there is a degree of correlation between the accounting practices and each of the economic clusters.

Going one step farther, H. M. Abu-Jbarah[8] used formal statistical analysis to cluster countries by dominant economic characteristics for

---

[7]Gerhard Mueller, "Accounting Principles Generally Accepted in the United States versus Those Generally Accepted Elsewhere," *International Journal of Accounting*, Spring 1968, pp. 83–94.

[8]Hani Mahmoud Abu-Jbarah, "A Subentity for Financial Reporting by Multinational Firms: A Cluster Analysis Approach," unpublished Ph.D. Dissertation (Madison: University of Wisconsin, 1972).

TABLE 2–1. Clusters of Business Environment

1. United States/Canada/The Netherlands
There is a minimum of commercial or company legislation in this environment. Industry is highly developed; currencies are relatively stable. A strong orientation to business innovation exists. Many companies with widespread international business interests are headquartered in these countries.

2. British Commonwealth (excluding Canada)
Comparable companies acts exist in all Commonwealth countries; administrative procedures and social order reflect strong ties to the mother country. Currencies are intertwined through the so-called sterling block arrangement. Business is highly developed but often quite traditional.

3. Germany/Japan
Economic growth has been rapid since World War II. Influences stemming from various U.S. military and administrative operations have caused considerable imitation of many facets of U.S. practices, often by grafting U.S. procedures to various local traditions. A new class of professional business managers has appeared. Relative political, social, and currency stability exists.

4. Continental Europe (excluding Germany, The Netherlands, and Scandinavia)
Private business lacks significant government support. Private property and the profit motive are not necessarily at the center of economic and business orientation. Some national economic planning exists. Political swings from far right to far left and vice versa have a long history in this environment. Reservoirs of economic resources are limited.

5. Scandinavia
Here we have developed economies, but characteristically slow rates of economic and business growth. Governments tend toward social legislation. Companies acts regulate business. Relative stability of population is the rule. Currencies are quite stable. Several business innovations (especially in consumer goods) originated in Scandinavia. Personal characteristics and outlooks are quite similar in all five Scandinavian countries.

6. Israel/Mexico
These are the only two countries with substantial success in fairly rapid economic development. Trends of a shift to more reliance on private enterprise are beginning to appear; however, there is still a significant government presence in business. Political and monetary stability seem to be increasing. Some specialization in business and the professions is taking place. The general population apparently has a strong desire for higher standards of living.

7. South America*
Economic, social, and educational underdevelopment are commonplace. The business base is narrow. Agricultural and military interests are strong and often dominate governments. There is considerable reliance on export/import trade. Currencies are generally soft. Populations are growing apace.

8. The developing nations of the Near and Far East*
Modorn oonoopto and othioc of bucinocc, which havo prodominantly woctern origins, often clash with oriental cultures. Business in the developing nations of the Orient largely means trade only. There is severe underdevelopment on most measures, coupled with vast population. Political scenes and currencies are most shaky. Major economic advances are probably impossible without substantial assistance from the industrialized countries. OPEC member countries are developing more rapidly since 1973.

(table continues)

TABLE 2-1 *(Continued)*

---

9. Africa (excluding South Africa)

Most of the African continent is still in early stages of independent development, and thus little native business environment exists. There are significant natural and human resources. Business is likely to assume a major role and responsibility in the development of African nations.

10. Communist nations

The complete control by central governments places these countries in a grouping all their own.

*These areas are obviously treated very generally; exceptions exist for a few given countries.

SOURCE: Gerhard Mueller, "Accounting Principles Generally Accepted in the United States versus Those Generally Accepted Elsewhere," *International Journal of Accounting,* Spring 1968, pp. 93–94.

purposes of recommending segmented financial reporting according to the resultant clusters. Here are the eight economic variables used by Abu-Jbarah:

1. Per capita national income.
2. Private consumption expenditure as a percentage of GNP.
3. Gross capital formation as a percentage of GNP.
4. Exports minus imports as a percentage of GNP.
5. Share of agriculture of all gross domestic products.
6. Rate of growth of real domestic products at factor cost.
7. Change in the foreign exchange rate.
8. Change in the consumer price index.

The end result was eight separate clusters of countries with significantly different degrees of economic homogeneity (see Table 2–2). Like Mueller, Abu-Jbarah did not specifically use accounting practices to form the clusters, although again the resultant economic clusters have some major commonalities in terms of accounting practices.

The only large-scale categorization of countries according to specific accounting practices or standards was done by Watt, Hammer, and Burge.[9] In this study the resulting clusters were derived from a review of published materials for 45 countries for the type of business organization most closely resembling the U.S. corporation (the AG form in Germany, the S.A. in France and Switzerland, and so on). One part of the study dealt with the categorization of audit requirements and resulted in four distinct clusters:

---

[9]George Watt, R. Hammer, and M. Burge, *Accounting for the Multinational Enterprise* (New York: Financial Executives Research Institute, 1977).

TABLE 2–2. Cluster of Countries According to Observed Economic Characteristics

CLUSTER NUMBER	NUMBER OF COUNTRIES IN CLUSTER	COUNTRIES IN CLUSTER	CLUSTER NUMBER	NUMBER OF COUNTRIES IN CLUSTER	COUNTRIES IN CLUSTER
1	20	Burma	3	18	Australia
		China (Taiwan)			Austria
		Costa Rica			Belgium
		Cyprus			Canada
		Egypt			Denmark
		Greece			Finland
		Guyana			France
		Ireland			Germany
		Jamaica			Iceland
		Mauritius			Italy
		Nicaragua			Japan
		Panama			Luxembourg
		Peru			Netherlands
		Portugal			New Zealand
		South Africa			Norway
		Spain			Sweden
		Syria			Switzerland
		Thailand			United Kingdom
		Trinidad and			
		Tobago	4	7	Ethiopia
		Tunisia			Ghana
					India
2	19	Bolivia			Nigeria
		Cameroon			Pakistan
		Ceylon			Sudan
		Colombia			Tanzania
		Dominican			
		Republic	5	5	Jordan
		Ecuador			Korea
		El Salvador			Malawi
		Guatemala			Singapore
		Honduras			Viet Nam
		Iran			
		Ivory Coast	6	4	Argentina
		Kenya			Brazil
		Malaysia			Chile
		Mexico			Uruguay
		Morocco			
		Paraguay	7	3	Iraq
		Philippines			Venezuela
		Sierra Leone			Zambia
		Turkey			
			8	3	Israel
					Malta
					Puerto Rico

SOURCE: Hani Mahmoud Abu-Jbarah, "A Subentity Basis for Financial Reporting by Multinational Firms: A Cluster Analysis Approach," unpublished Ph.D. dissertation, University of Wisconsin, 1972, p. 98.

Group A. The financial statements of all or most public companies are required to be examined by independent public accountants.

Group B. All or most companies must appoint one or more statutory examiners, and some companies—because of size, type of business, or sale of securities to the public—must be examined by independent public accountants.

Group C. All or most companies must appoint one or more statutory examiners who need not be independent accountants.

Group D. There are no requirements, or only a limited number of companies—such as banks, insurance firms, or listed companies—are subject to audit requirements.

In the *A* group were 19 countries (20 if one includes the United States); it was dominated by British accounting tradition. The *B* group included eight countries, the *C* and *D* groups nine countries each. Table 2–3 lists the countries in each group. Bear in mind that no representation has been made as to the degree of comparison between the foreign auditing standards and the auditing standards generally accepted in the United States.

In a second part of the study, a categorization was made on the "probability of fair presentation," based largely on the US-UK definition of fair presentation (see Table 2–4). The resulting five clusters were:

1. Those countries with fair presentation broadly equivalent to U.S. standards, with some differences in principles to be dealt with, but with fewer differences of less serious dimensions (17 countries).
2. Fair presentation based on standards from Canada, the United Kingdom, or the United States, but greater differences in number and extent than those in Cluster 1 (5 countries).
3. Statutory requirements approaching U.S. standards in many aspects but some valuation principles being *not* acceptable in the United States (3 countries).
4. Fair presentation recognized in principle but not found consistently in practice (7 countries).
5. Statutory requirements do not approach U.S. standards (2 countries).

The authors of this project limited their analysis to 45 countries and largely to countries of some significance in terms of world economic activity and interest. A more exhaustive examination of the other 80 or so countries in the world would result in a much larger number of countries in Group D in the Audit area and in Group 5, the Presentation area. In fact, these two clusters would probably be greater in total number than all the other clusters *combined.* Nonetheless, the Watt,

TABLE 2–3. Categorization of Audit Requirements in 45 Foreign Countries

A. The financial statements of all or most public companies are required to be examined by independent public accountants.

Australia	Netherlands
Canada	New Zealand
Colombia	Pakistan
Denmark	Peru
Germany	Philippines
Hong Kong	Rhodesia
India	Singapore
Israel	South Africa
Jamaica	United Kingdom
Kenya	

B. All or most companies must appoint one or more statutory examiners and some companies, because of size, type of business, or sale of securities to the public, must be examined by independent public accountants.

Argentina	Mexico
Brazil	Norway
Greece	Sweden
Japan	Venezuela

C. All or most companies must appoint one or more statutory examiners who need not be independent public accountants.

Belgium	Italy
Chile	Lebanon
France	Spain
Guatemala	Switzerland
Honduras	

D. There are no requirements or only a limited number of companies, such as banks, insurance firms, and listed companies, are subject to audit requirements.

Bahamas	Nicaragua
Bolivia	Panama
Cayman Islands	Paraguay
Indonesia	Uruguay
Netherlands Antilles	

SOURCE: G. Watt, R. Hammer, and M. Burge, *Accounting for the Multinational Corporation,* New York: Financial Executives Research Institute, 1977, pp. 214–215.

NOTE: The above, which is based on a review of published material in 1975, lists the general audit requirements in 45 foreign countries for the form of business organization most closely resembling a U.S. corporation. Other forms of business entities may be subject to the same or less stringent requirements. No representation is made as to the degree of comparison between local auditing standards and auditing standards generally accepted in the United States.

TABLE 2–4. Probability of Fair Presentation in 45 Foreign Countries

Fair presentation is broadly equivalent to U.S. standards;[1] differences in principles must still be dealt with, but there are a fewer number of such differences with less serious dimensions.

Argentina[2]	Netherlands
Australia	New Zealand
Bermuda	Peru
Canada	Philippines
Denmark	Rhodesia
India	South Africa
Ireland	United Kingdom
Jamaica	Venezuela
Mexico	

Fair presentation is based on standards imported from Canada, the United Kingdom, or the United States.

Bahamas	Panama
Barbados	Trinidad and Tobago
Nigeria	

Statutory requirements approach U.S. standards in many respects, but some valuation principles would not be acceptable in the United States.

Chile	Japan
Germany	

Fair presentation is recognized in principle but not found consistently in practice.

Brazil	Malaysia
Colombia	Pakistan
Ethiopia	Singapore
Kenya	

Tax legislation is the predominant influence

Austria	Luxembourg
Belgium	Paraguay
Bolivia	Portugal
France	Sweden
Greece	Uruguay
Italy	

Statutory requirements do not approach U.S. standards

Spain	Switzerland

Source: G. Watt, R. Hammer, and M. Burge, *Accounting for the Multinational Corporation,* New York: Financial Executives Research Institute, 1977, p. 187.

Note 1: For this schedule, failure to require consolidation or the equity method of accounting for investments was not considered a block to fair presentation.

Note 2: Because of the extreme rate of inflation fair presentation is dependent on the submission, together with historical-cost-based financial statements, of supplemental financial data restated for price-level changes. The same requirement applies in other countries where inflationary conditions are similar.

Hammer, and Burge study represents the most comprehensive attempt to cluster countries of the world in terms of specific accounting criteria.

CONCLUSIONS

As we have seen, a host of environmental variables affect any nation's accounting system and its specific accounting principles, procedures, and practices. Because no two countries share identical environmental characteristics, no two countries do accounting in identical ways. Even within a single country, accounting rules and practices often differ for certain kinds of companies or for specific geographic or cultural areas. Thus you should be careful about assuming that accounting is done the same way or has the same purpose in countries other than your own.

At the same time, some accounting similarities among certain countries are based largely on similarities in environmental and economic characteristics. In this sense, there are generally more commonalities in accounting among the industrialized countries and among the lesser developed countries than between these two groups. Yet even then, in some less-developed countries, accounting is similar to highly developed countries, and significant accounting differences exist even among the most highly developed countries.

STUDY QUESTIONS

2–1. What is meant by the statement that accounting is culture-bound?

2–2. What accounting functions and practices would be affected by:
    a. a very low level of literacy in the population;
    b. a high degree of distrust in the society;
    c. a high degree of international business activity;
    d. a high degree of government planning and regulation.

2–3. Explain how the perceived status of accountants in a country affects the development of the country's accounting standards and practices.

2–4. Even though The Netherlands and France are neighbors in a geographic sense, their accounting systems are quite different. What factors explain their differences?

2–5. The United States, United Kingdom, Canada, and Australia are geographically distant, yet have many similarities in their accounting systems. What factors explain their similarities?

2–6. Most of the accounting practices in Latin America are not as sophisticated as those in the United States or Canada, yet several Latin American countries have inflation accounting procedures that are as or more sophisticated than those in the United States or Canada. Explain the apparent paradox.

2–7.   Explain how the Japanese accounting system contributes to Japan's international economic competitiveness.

2–8.   Among the most important environmental influences on accounting are the country's stage of economic development, and companies' needs for external financing. Why are these factors so influential?

2–9.   Inflation is a common problem in most countries. Explain how one country might learn something of benefit from studying how another country handles inflation (in an accounting sense).

2–10. What benefit can be derived from learning about other countries' accounting systems—

    a.   for an accountant of a multinational firm?

    b.   for an accountant *not* employed by a multinational?

CASES

HOWE'S DILEMMA

Ross Howe stared at the two piles of documents on his desk and threw his hands up. He had been given the assignment of ascertaining the creditworthiness of two companies in the same industry, normally an easy task: simply apply the standard financial analysis ratios he had learned and see which company was in better financial shape. However, these companies were foreign—one Egyptian and one Dutch—and Ross knew that his trusted and reliable methods were not necessarily going to work.

First of all, the Egyptian statements were in Arabic and the monetary values were expressed in Egyptian pounds. Second, once he had obtained a translation, he realized that he had never seen such a confusing format. Nothing seemed to be in the right order, many accounts appeared to have no direct U.S. equivalents, and he was not sure of the meaning of the account numbers listed in the margin beside each account. Finally, the few notes to the statements generally did not help explain anything he was unsure about. Even the auditors' statement was not much help, since it merely referred in general to compliance with Egyptian legal statutes and codes.

The Dutch company's statements, by contrast, initially seemed easier and more straightforward, as the company's annual report was available in English and U.S. dollar equivalents. Even after Ross had realized that the Dutch balance sheet was upside down by U.S. standards (increasing order of liquidity rather than decreasing), he noticed several major similarities between U.S. and Dutch accounting terms. However, his early euphoria was dampened by the realization that Dutch accounting principles were quite different from those in the United States. He was also bothered by the fact that the company's financial statements were prepared according to "sound business practice," a term unfamiliar to him. He also noticed that replacement cost values were used throughout the statements and wondered about their objectivity and verifiability. On the other hand, Ross was impressed by the tremendous amount of disclosure in the company's report, which was even more extensive than U.S. reports.

Questions

1. Why do you suppose there were such significant differences between the Egyptian and Dutch companies' reports?
2. What suggestions or sources of information would you give Ross to help him to a better understanding of the foreign statements?
3. If both companies' statements showed the same net income, in which would you place more confidence? Why?

THE JAPANESE PARADOX

David Sparks was puzzled. He had just completed a standard financial ratio analysis of the translated financial statements of a major Japanese steel company. He knew that it was an acknowledged leader in its industry and one of the largest and most successful in terms of world market share. What puzzled him was that the company appeared to be on the verge of bankruptcy—at least according to his calculations of the various financial ratios and indicators commonly employed in the United States. As shown in the accompanying table, the company's debt to equity ratio was 9 to 1, its long-term debt as a percentage of total assets was nearly 50 percent, and its times-interest earned topped 2.5. If this wasn't disconcerting enough, the company's quick ratio was .52 and its current ratio was .92. It didn't appear that the company would be able to repay its short-term debt, and even its ability to repay its long-term debt looked questionable.

Accounts receivable to average days sales was an incredible 185, and the company's inventory was turning only slightly more than four times. Furthermore, the company's net income before taxes, expressed as a percentage of sales, was only 4 percent for the past two years. In fact, it was somewhat surprising that this percentage had remained approximately 4 percent for the past seven years. Finally, there were few notes to the statements and little mention of the company's overseas subsidiaries' operation except in the president's narrative.

While Dave knew that there were considerable differences between U.S. and Japanese cultures, he was not certain how these differences might affect the Japanese company's financial statements. Either something was wrong with his use of the standard financial rates analysis, or this Japanese company was dangerously illiquid and about to go under.

Financial Ratios	
Quick	.52
Current	.92
Long term debt/total assets	50%
Total debt capitalization	90%
Time interest earned	2.6
Sales/total assets	.50
Sales/inventory	4.1
Accounts receivable/average days sales	185

Accounts receivable
    not yet due
    1 to 30 days past due
    31 to 60 days past due
    61 to 90 days past due
    over 91 days past due
	
	20
	20
	20
	20
	20

Net income before taxes/sales	4.0%
Net income after taxes/sales	2.2%
Net income after taxes/equity	6.5%
Net income after taxes/total assets	1.3%

Questions

1. In general, what are the problems with applying one country's standard financial analysis techniques to the analysis of financial statements of a company from another country?
2. In this specific case, what conditions or factors in Japan might be causing the distorted financial analysis results?
3. What might Dave do to assess the true financial position of this company?

3

Harmonization of International Accounting Systems and Standards

As the pace of international trade quickens, and as regional economic groups grow in number and in sophistication, the multiplicity of accounting methods becomes a stumbling block. This explains the global and regional efforts to eliminate the differences in accounting systems and standards, a process called *harmonization*.

There are many good underlying reasons for international harmonization, as well as a host of related benefits. At the same time, there are some legitimate arguments against it. This chapter identifies the forces pushing for and against harmonization, identifies the organizations which are pursuing harmonization, and assesses what progress has been made and what the future holds.

THE FORCES AND THE ARGUMENTS

Growth of International Trade

The dominant force behind harmonization is the growing internationalization of the world's economies. As was pointed out in Chapter 1, virtually every economy in the world has become more dependent on international trade and investment flows. This means that more of their businesses are involved in one form or another of international activities. In a domestic context, we know that decision making is facilitated and improved with access to information prepared in similar if not identical ways. For example, potential investors in the United States can obtain 10-K reports, which must meet certain uniform standards, of companies listed on the New York Stock Exchange. Investment decisions are facilitated by the common appearance, content, and method of derivation of these 10-K reports.

Another example involves buyer-seller relationships. A prospective purchaser can examine the financial statements of a seller in order to assess the risk of the seller's going bankrupt before the product is delivered. A similar situation involves the extension of credit from the seller to the buyer. In both cases, having all financial statements based on the same accounting procedures clearly facilitates and improves decision making.

This is true for domestic transactions and decisions. Shouldn't it also be true for international transactions and decisions? The answer is clearly yes. International transactions and decisions would be facilitated by uniform accounting terminology and procedures. This would be true for governments and businesses as well as for individuals, whethr ˜ they were investors, creditors, buyers, suppliers, or just interested spectators.

One worldwide accounting system would also improve country and company efficiency by putting to more productive use the personnel, time, and money currently required to translate and interpret financial statements and accounting records prepared under disparate accounting principles and procedures. International financial markets would become more efficient as well. Pricing and resource allocation decisions would become easier and more accurate, and economic and political integration would be facilitated.

Need for Capital

Another major force behind harmonization is the need for companies to raise outside capital. For decades, companies enjoyed comparatively higher levels of protection than they do now in terms of both trade and investment. In addition, formal oligopoly and cartel arrangements made the environment significantly less competitive than it is today.

Over the past two decades, however, international competition has increased dramatically. The formation of the European Economic Community brought about increased competition among European companies. It also brought a surge of investment into the EEC from the United States, Canada, and Japan, further increasing competition. This higher level of competition in the EEC, along with the increased growth and maturity of European companies in their own right, led to a flow of European investments into the United States and other parts of the world. And finally, competition was increased by the entry of new countries such as Taiwan, South Korea, Mexico, and Brazil into the international business arena.

The new era of international competition made it necessary for firms to strengthen their competitive abilities if they wanted to survive, let alone grow. The main keys to success were large-scale operations, enhanced research and technology, and better management of resources, virtually all of which required additional funds. When the environment was less competitive, companies could finance their growth by means of retained earnings or local borrowings because the sums needed were moderate and there was less competition for funds.

In today's environment, however, this is not nearly as feasible. Today, few companies have sufficient retained earnings to finance the projects needed to maintain or enhance their competitiveness. They must instead turn to borrowing or selling stock, but these opportunities have also decreased. U.S. companies borrowing in Europe reduce the availability of European loans for European-owned companies and vice versa. The same sort of thing happens when Japanese companies sell stock in the United States and vice versa.

The growing competition for domestic and international funds has forced a certain amount of accounting harmonization to take place because the suppliers of funds have required it. That is, lenders and investors have a wide variety of requests for their funds from companies of an equally wide variety of countries. In order to make the best investment or loan decision, these suppliers require standardization of financial reports. A company whose financial statements are highly detailed and disclosed, and represent fairly its financial position, is more likely to get funds from the suppliers than is the one whose financial statements are incomplete, poorly disclosed, and not truly reflective of its financial position. In many cases, companies are not allowed to sell stock or float bonds unless their statements meet certain uniform, rigid formats. This is true for any company seeking to sell its shares on the New York Stock Exchange, for example.

Even when uniformity is not required, such as in the Eurodollar or Eurobond market, companies have found it necessary to provide financial statements in forms comparable to those of major U.S. multinationals. This does not mean there is international consensus that U.S. accounting is the best. But it does reflect the fact that the United States is the largest single financial market and its companies are the largest borrowers and investors on a global scale; hence they tend to set the standards. It also reflects the influence of the major international accounting firms, which typically provide the company audit before a major international funding is attempted. These accounting firms have their historic roots in the United Kingdom and the United States, and they tend to force a certain harmonization of accounting reports along U.S.–U.K. lines as a consequence. More about their harmonization influence later.

The same increased need for capital pushes countries toward harmonization in order to obtain funding for large-scale national or regional projects, such as infrastructure developments. They too must compete for funds with multinationals and other governments seeking funds. Organizations such as the International Bank for Reconstruction and Development generally require a certain uniform format and underlying accounting system in order for a proposal to be considered.

Impediments to Uniformity

What all this means is that economic forces and fund suppliers' preferences have exerted significant pressures for harmonization. Combined with the earlier cited advantages, they offer what appears to be a compelling argument in favor of harmonization.

All well and good, you say. So why hasn't it happened? Who would stand in the way of achieving such a desirable condition? The answer lies in the differences in environments and predilections of the countries of the world. The same environmental differences which cause each country's accounting system to be different also act as impediments to eliminating the differences in accounting. Differences in industrialization, education, societal goals, and aspirations pose significant difficulties in achieving consensus on accounting standards and their feasibility of application.

Nationalism, egotism, and pride also impede progress: the French would like to have the new global system patterned after the French system, the Germans after the German system, the Americans after the American system. Each country believes its system is the best and is reluctant to adopt a system it perceives to be inferior or unsuitable.

Some countries, companies, and individuals prefer to retain the imperfections and inefficiencies caused by the differences in accounting in order to take advantage of them. The *secrecy* offered by the Swiss banking and accounting system is one example. Another is *dumping:* the aggressive pricing of goods for export without regard for real prices (costs) for factor inputs. While secrecy or dumping may not be grounds for sustaining differences in accounting systems, environmental differences may be valid and justifiable grounds.

It is difficult to imagine one single, uniform system of accounting for all companies of all countries. After all, the American accounting profession has argued since its inception that uniformity is not desirable or possible even for the United States alone. Flexibility and adaptability, the cornerstones of such reasoning, are not totally out of the line of logic.

What is likely to develop is blocs of accounting uniformity. That is, certain economic groups or blocs will establish uniform accounting procedures among their members—for example, regional economic groups and resource cartels.

Yet regardless of the level at which harmonization is desirable and feasible, attaining it requires specific action. Some persons or groups must lay the groundwork, do the homework, lobby for the change, and, if necessary, provide the skills and knowledge. It is to these that we now shift our attention.

THE ACTORS AND THE ACTION

Even a partial list of the actors in this evolving drama of international accounting harmonization looks like a bowl of alphabet soup: ICCAP, IEAC, IASC, ICAC, AISG, IAA, VEC, CAPA. Virtually all of them have similar objectives and motivations. The differences are in the scope and scale of their efforts and the likelihood of their success.

The ICA, ICCAP, and IFAC

Paying homage to age, we begin with the International Congress of Accountants (ICA), which was founded in 1904. Its general objective is to increase interaction and the exchange of ideas between accountants of different countries. Meetings are held every five years, at which general interest papers are presented at plenary sessions, international summary reports emerge from technical sessions, and a host of small discussion groups consider items of special interest. During ICA's first 75 years these meetings were essentially independent one from the other: there were no specific, formal tie-ins, no follow-up, no permanent technical research staff or on-going formal research projects.

To improve continuity, in 1972 the ICA formed the International Coordination Committee for the Accounting Profession (ICCAP). Its objectives were to conduct specific studies of professional accounting ethics, education and training, and the structure of regional accounting organizations. The original membership came from 12 countries: Australia, Canada, France, India, Ireland, Japan, Mexico, The Netherlands, Philippines, United Kingdom, United States, and West Germany. In 1976, in what remains a rarity for organizations, the ICCAP dissolved itself, and was reconstituted as the International Federation of Accounting Committee (IFAC).

The IFAC remains a coordinating organization whose goal is to develop international guidelines such as ethical standards for the accounting and auditing profession and for accounting education. It also seeks reciprocal recognition of qualifications or practice and promotes the development of both regional organizations and broad agreements on common aims for the accounting profession. IFAC's Twelve Point Program is listed in Table 3-1. To date, the IFAC has issued one standard:. *International Auditing Guideline No. 1: Objective and Scope*

TABLE 3–1. IFAC's 12 Point Program

1. Develop statements that would serve as guidelines for international auditing practices.
2. Establish a suggested minimum code of ethics to which it is hoped that member bodies would subscribe and which could be further refined as appropriate.
3. Determine the requirements and develop programs for the professional education and training of accountants.
4. Evaluate, develop and report on financial management and other management accounting techniques and procedures.
5. Collect, analyze, research and disseminate information on the management of public accounting practices to assist practitioners in conducting their practices more effectively.
6. Undertake other studies of value to accountants such as, possibly, a study of the legal liability of auditors.
7. Foster close relations with users of financial statements, including preparers, trade unions, financial institutions, industry, governments and others.
8. Maintain close relations with regional bodies and explore the potential for establishing other regional bodies as well as for assisting in their organization and development, as appropriate. Assign appropriate projects to existing regional bodies.
9. Establish regular communication among the members of IFAC and with other interested organizations through the medium of a newsletter.
10. Organize and promote the exchange of technical information, educational materials, and professional publications and other literature emanating from member bodies.
11. Organize and conduct an International Congress of Accountants approximately every five years.
12. Seek to expand the membership of the IFAC.

Source: Joseph P. Cummings and Michael N. Chetkovich, "World Accounting Enters a New Era," *The Journal of Accountancy*, 145, April 1978.

of the Auditing of Financial Statements. It has also issued exposure drafts on audit engagement letters, basic principles governing an audit, and planning an audit. The auditing aspects of the IFAC are discussed in greater detail in Chapter 13. The success of the ICA and the IFAC has been mainly in fostering the interchange of ideas and people, a necessary prerequisite to the actual harmonization of principles and practices. But neither group has actually achieved much harmonization.

The IASC

Perhaps the most successful international organization in achieving some harmonization of standards has been the International Accountants Standards Committee (IASC). Founded in 1973, IASC's main objective has been to formulate standards to be observed in the presentation of audited financial statements, and to promote their acceptance and adherence.

The formal IASC objectives follow:

1. To establish and maintain an International Accounting Standards Committee with a membership and powers set out below whose functions are to formulate and publish, in the public interest, standards to be observed in the presentation of audited financial statements and to promote their worldwide acceptance and observance.
2. To support the standards promulgated by the Committee.
3. To use their best endeavors
    a. To ensure that published financial statements comply with these standards or that there is disclosure of the extent to which they do not, and to persuade governments, the authorities controlling securities markets, and the industrial and business community that published financial statements should comply with these standards.
    b. To ensure (1) that the auditors satisfy themselves that the financial statements comply with these standards or, if the financial statements do not comply with these standards, that the fact of non-compliance is disclosed in the financial statements, (2) that in the event of non-disclosure reference to non-compliance is made in the audit report.
    c. To ensure that, as soon as practicable, appropriate action is taken in respect of auditors whose audit reports do not meet the requirements of (b) above.
4. To seek to secure similar general acceptance and observance of these standards internationally.[1]

The actual workings of the IASC are similar to those of the Financial Accounting Standards Board (FASB) of the United States. Both organizations conduct research studies, make exposure drafts, do interim studies, and promulgate standards. As of August 1980, the IASC had adopted thirteen standards, had four exposure drafts outstanding, and was considering drafts on additional topics. Table 3-2 lists the topics these standards, exposure drafts, and studies are concerned with.

The founding members of the IASC were Australia, Canada, France, Japan, Mexico, The Netherlands, United Kingdom and Ireland, United States, and West Germany. As shown in Table 3-3, an additional 32 countries or organizations have subsequently joined as associate members. On a comparative basis, the IASC has been successful. How-

---

[1]International Accounting Standards Committee, *Work and Purpose of the International Accounting Standards Committee* (London: IASC, 1973).

TABLE 3–2. Adopted Standards and Exposure Drafts of the IASC as of 1980

STANDARDS

IAS–1   Disclosure of Accounting Policies
IAS–2   Valuation and Presentation of Inventories in the Context of the Historical Cost System
IAS–3   Consolidated Financial Statements
IAS–4   Depreciation Accounting
IAS–5   Information to Be Disclosed in Financial Statements
IAS–6   Accounting Responses to Changing Prices
IAS–7   Statement of Changes in Financial Position
IAS–8   Unusual and Prior Period Items and Changes in Accounting Policies
IAS–9   Accounting for Research and Development Activities
IAS–10   Contingencies and Events Occurring after the Balance Sheet Date
IAS–11   Accounting for Construction Contracts
IAS–12   Accounting for Taxes on Income
IAS–13   Presentation of Current Assets and Liabilities

EXPOSURE DRAFTS

E–15   Reporting Financial Information by Segment
E–16   Accounting for Retirement Benefits
E–17   Information Reflecting the Effects of Changing Prices
E–18   Accounting for Property, Plant, and Equipment in the Context of the Historical Cost System

TABLE 3–3. Founder and Associate Members of IASC

FOUNDER MEMBERS

Australia	The Institute of Chartered Accountants in Austria, Australian Society of Accountants
Canada	The Canadian Institute of Chartered Accountants in conjunction with the General Accountants' Association and The Society of Industrial Accountants of Canada
France	Ordre des Experts Comptables et des Comptables Agrees
Germany	Institut der Wirtschaftsprufer in Deutschland e.V. Wirtschaftspruferkammer
Japan	The Japanese Institute of Certified Public Accountants
Mexico	Instituto Mexicano de Contadores Publicos, A.C.
Netherlands	Nederlands Instituut van Registeraccountants
United Kingdom and Ireland	The Institute of Chartered Accountants in England and Wales, The Institute of Chartered Accountants of Scotland, The Institute of Chartered Accountants in Ireland, The Association of Certified Accountants, The Institute of Cost and Management Accountants, The Chartered Institute of Public Finance and Accountancy
United States	American Institute of Certified Public Accountants

(table continues)

TABLE 3–3 *(Continued)*

ASSOCIATE MEMBERS

Bangladesh	The Institute of Chartered Accountants of Bangladesh
Belgium	College National des Experts Comptables de Belgique, Institut des Reviseurs d'Entreprises, Institut Belge des Reviseurs de Banques
Brazil	Instituto dos Auditores Independentes do Brazil
Cyprus	The Institute of Certified Public Accountants of Cyprus
Denmark	Foreningen Af Statsautoriserede Revisorer
Fiji	The Fiji Institute of Accountants
Finland	KHT-Yhdistys—Foreningen CGR
Ghana	The Institute of Chartered Accountants (Ghana)
Greece	Institute of Certified Public Accountants of Greece
Hong Kong	Hong Kong Society of Accountants
India	The Institute of Chartered Accountants of India, The Institute of Cost and Works Accountants of India
Israel	The Institute of Certified Public Accountants in Israel
Jamaica	The Institute of Chartered Accountants of Jamaica
Korea	Korean Institute of Certified Public Accountants
Luxembourg	Ordre des Experts Comptables Luxembourgeois
Malaysia	The Malaysian Association of Certified Public Accountants
Malta	The Malta Institute of Accountants
New Zealand	New Zealand Society of Accountants
Nigeria	The Institute of Chartered Accountants of Nigeria
Norway	Norges Statsautoriserte Revisorers Forening
Pakistan	The Institute of Cost and Management Accountants of Pakistan, The Institute of Chartered Accountants of Pakistan
Philippines	Philippine Institute of Certified Public Accountants
Rhodesia	The Rhodesia Society of Chartered Accountants
Sierra Leone	The Association of Accountants in Sierra Leone
Singapore	Singapore Society of Accountants
South Africa	The National Council of Chartered Accountants (S.A.)
Spain	Instituto de Censores Jurados de Cuentas de Espana
Sri Lanka	The Institute of Chartered Accountants of Sri Lanka
Sweden	Foreningen Auktoriserade Revisorer
Trinidad and Tobago	The Institute of Chartered Accountants of Trinidad and Tobago
Yugoslavia	Yugoslav Association of Accountants and Financial Experts, Social Accounting Service of Yugoslavia
Zambia	Zambia Association of Accountants

ever, it is evident that adherence to the existing standards, even by the founding member countries, has been far from complete or comprehensive. In his now classic article on international accounting standards, Sir Henry Benson, former president of the Institute of Chartered Accountants in England and Wales, summarized some of the major reasons:

Some of the members of the IASC have not arranged compliance with the new Standards by their individual members sufficiently firm, and sometimes not at all. My own country has been staunch in this respect. The members of the accountancy bodies in the United Kingdom have been informed that they are under an obligation to comply with international accounting Standards in the same way that they are under an obligation to comply with our own local U.K. Standards, and members have been told that failure to comply can lead to an appropriate enquiry. Other members of IASC, both founder and associate members, have taken similar action. But some founders and associates have not yet done so.

There are various reasons for this. Some countries take the view that they cannot require compliance locally until they are satisfied that the Standards are internationally acceptable. Some see local legislation as an obstacle to the introduction of international Standards. Some accounting bodies do not have the power to discipline over their members, and cannot therefore impose compliance with either national or international Standards. Some countries have not yet overcome stubborn local resistance from the business community. But all these impediments must be broken down, and there should be no delay in starting this process.

But the ultimate objective is more far-reaching. It is one step to write international Standards; it is another step forward for professional bodies to notify their members that they are to observe them. The ultimate goal is to make reasonable efforts to see that the members do, in fact, observe them. Although progress is being made here and in other countries, I am sure that no other accountancy body anywhere in the world has yet done enough to ensure that either its own local Standards or international Standards are, in fact, being applied by its members in the conduct of their professional practice or in their capacity as directors of business enterprises.[2]

Thus, while there has been explicit formal acceptance of the IASC Standards, there remains considerable discrepancy between what some countries say they do and what they actually do. Despite this shortcoming, the IASC has been the most successful of any of the *large*-scale international efforts toward harmonizing accounting standards. However, the prospect for full harmonization of account standards among IASC members is tenuous.

---

[2] Sir Henry Benson, "The Story of International Accounting Standards," *Accountancy*, July 1976, pp. 34–39.

The UN

Another major actor on a world scale is the United Nations, by way of its Commission and Center on Transnational Corporations. In addition to proposing a code of conduct for multinational companies, the UN has undertaken a massive data collection project on multinational activities and is moving toward establishing international standards of accounting and reporting with particular emphasis on increased disclosure in corporate reports. The commission envisioned establishing a minimum list of standards which corporations could use on an experimental basis to supplement information they already provide. The experience of corporations in using the minimum list would then be used in the formulation of a more comprehensive accounting and reporting system. Possible items in the minimum list are categorized into five broad headings:

1. Information to be disclosed in financial statements.
2. Accounting policies to be disclosed in financial statements of transnational corporations.
3. Financial information on the members of transnational corporation groups.
4. Reporting on segments of a transnational corporation.
5. Nonfinancial information to be presented in annual reports.[3]

While much of the UN proposal follows the exposure draft standards of the International Accounting Standards Committee (particularly IASC exposure drafts 1, 3, 5, and 7) the UN proposals go well beyond those of the IASC. The UN Commission issued a formal proposal in 1979, but action was deferred until a committee could reconsider the many objections which were raised by multinational firms and national governments.

The OECD

A related activity has taken place within the Organization for Economic Cooperation and Development (OECD). It too has proposed a code of conduct for multinational enterprises which deals in part with accounting. More specifically, one provision of the code contains guidelines for financial disclosure. The major elements of this provision are listed below.

Enterprises should publish within reasonable time limits, on a regular basis, but at least annually, financial statements and other pertinent

---

[3] United Nations Economic and Social Council Commission on Transnational Corporations, *Towards International Standards of Accounting: Reporting for Transnational Corporations* (United Nations, E/C.10/AC.1/2, 28 July 1976).

information relating to the enterprise as a whole, comprising in particular:

- the structure of the enterprise, showing the name and location of the parent company, its main affiliates, its percentage ownership, direct and indirect, in these affiliates, including shareholdings between them;
- the geographical areas (1) where operations are carried out and the principal activities carried on therein by the parent company and the main affiliates;
- the operating results and sales by geographical area and the sales in the major lines of business for the enterprise as a whole;
- significant new capital investment by geographical area and, as far as practicable, by major lines of business for the enterprise as a whole;
- a statement of the sources and uses of funds by the enterprise as a whole;
- the average number of employees in each geographical area;
- research and development expenditure for the enterprise as a whole;
- the policies followed in respect of intra-group pricing;
- the accounting policies, including those on consolidation, observed in compiling the published information.[4]

It should be pointed out that both the UN and OECD codes are suggestive. Company and country compliance with them is voluntary, and neither organization has any real power to enforce adoption or adherence. Nevertheless, these two international organizations do carry certain clout and powers of suasion not found in the other international groups discussed earlier. This fact, and the fact that both groups tend to be more political than accounting in nature and composition, has caused some alarm in national professional accounting groups. Yet, until the latter can make more substantial progress on their own or collectively toward international accounting harmonization, the UN and OECD are certain to persist in their respective courses of action.

The major problem facing all large-scale international harmonization efforts is the number and heterogeneity of the countries encompassed. Prospects are better for harmonization among smaller, less heterogeneous groups, such as those on a regional level, whose efforts are discussed next.

Regional Organizations

Three of the major regionally organized accounting groups are the Inter-American Accounting Association (IAA), the Conference of Asian

---

[4] Organization for Economic Cooperation and Development, "Declaration on International Investment and Multinational Enterprises," *The OECD Observer*, No. 82 (July/August 1976), p. 14.

and Pacific Accountants (CAPA), and the Union Européenne des Experts Comptables Economiques et Financiers (UEC). Their constituents and their geographical focus are evident from their names. There is one other major difference: the UEC has been significantly more active and effective. It has the largest permanent staff: a dozen standing committees which prepare reports and present resolutions to the executive committee. The UEC also generates recommendations on accounting and auditing matters; and it publishes an excellent journal, an accounting dictionary covering eight languages, an auditing handbook, and numerous brochures and studies.

The EEC

Even more active and with even greater prospects for being effective in achieving regional accounting harmonization is the European Economic Community (EEC). The EEC has moved toward full economic and political integration of its member countries along a planned schedule. Significant strides have already been made by eliminating internal trade restrictions and establishing an EEC parliament. The parliament has also made progress toward establishing EEC-wide laws, including business law; and several steps have been taken by an EEC commission to harmonize the accounting systems of the nine member countries. More specifically, the commission has proposed directives regarding the presentation and content of limited liability companies' annual reports or financial statements, the method of valuation and consolidation used to derive them, and their audit and publication. Of the many proposed directives issued by the commission, the Fourth, Fifth, and Seventh Directives most directly concern accounting harmonization.

The Fourth Directive

The Fourth Directive was proposed in 1971, revised and reissued in 1974, and formally adopted in 1978.[5] Articles 1 and 2 specify the types of companies covered by the directive (essentially the European equivalents to U.S. corporations) and the general reporting requirements. Articles 3–27 pertain to the format of the annual reports, and Articles 28–39 concern the rules for valuation. Articles 40–43 deal with the content of the notes to the accounts, Articles 44–50 with publication requirements, and Articles 51–52 with the procedural, statutory changes in national laws which would be necessary for compliance.

The main features of the EEC-wide system of financial reporting are

---

[5] Commission of the European Communities, *Amended Proposal for a Fourth Council Directive for Co-ordination of National Legislation Regarding the Annual Accounts of Limited Liability Companies* (Brussels, 1974).

the true and fair presentation concept, the going concern and matching concepts, valuation at replacement cost of limited life tangible fixed assets, disclosure of differences in inventory values determined by FIFO and any other specified method used (if internal), and considerable improvements in disclosure in general including a great deal of segment reporting.

The Fifth Directive

The proposed Fifth Directive dealt with the structure, management, and external audits of limited liability corporations. However, significant difficulties in reaching agreement on this directive caused it to be withdrawn. The major disagreements centered on the management structure of these companies, which vary significantly among countries. Probably other EEC legislation on this topic will be needed before the Fifth Directive can be taken up again.

The Seventh Directive

The Seventh Directive, proposed in 1976, calls for consolidated financial statements—the largest single omission of the Fourth Directive.[6] The first group of articles describes who must prepare consolidated statements, and there are a few cases identified which differ from standards in the United States. One of the cases concerns enterprises under central or unified management but not necessarily a controlling degree of ownership—more specifically, an enterprise that (a) holds the major part of another enterprise's subscribed capital, (b) controls the majority of votes in another enterprise, and (c) can appoint more than half the members of another enterprise's administrative, managerial, or supervisory body.

There is also a requirement for consolidation of enterprises which are independent of each other but dominated in the sense of any of these three conditions by a common enterprise (such as the parent) domiciled outside the EEC. For example, General Motors would have to prepare and publish a combined statement limited to but encompassing all its subsidiaries and branches in the EEC countries and including any other subsidiaries dominated by its European subsidiaries.

Articles 9–20 cover the composition of consolidated accounts and the methods and principles of consolidation. Among other things, these articles specify that acquired assets be valued at fair market value, accounts of enterprises with different year-ends be consolidated on the basis of audited interim statements, the same accounting principles used for consolidation be used in preparing the individual annual accounts

---

[6] Commission of the European Communities, *Proposal for a Seventh Directive Concerning Group Accounts* (Brussels, 1976).

which were subsequently consolidated, and the equity method of accounting be applied to all intercorporate investments over which significant influence is exercised (more than 20 percent of ownership). The remaining articles deal with disclosure of items in the notes of consolidated statements and publication rules.

In assessing EEC efforts toward accounting harmonization, several things must be kept in mind. First, only the Fourth Directive had been adopted as of 1979. Second, most of the articles of the directives are devoted to matters of form rather than content. Third, many of the provisions call on member countries to *permit* companies to comply with the directives, rather than *require* their companies to comply. Fourth, there are no provisions concerning professional auditing because the Fifth Directive was withdrawn.

The major underlying reason for the less-than-hoped-for current status of the EEC Directives is that there remain essentially two dominant yet opposing accounting schools of thought within the EEC. The first school is that of France and Germany, basically a legalistic and highly codified approach; the other is that of the United Kingdom, Ireland, and The Netherlands, which is essentially a true and fair approach. In addition, professional auditing standards vary considerably among the nine member countries, as do existing accounting principles and especially accounting practices. Finally, significant environmental differences remain among the EEC nations, and these differences continue to impede both accounting harmonization and full economic and political integration. Thus the EEC's movement toward accounting harmonization still has a long way to go. Nonetheless, the effort is both commendable and exciting, and it does demonstrate that harmonization is feasible, albeit slow.

Supporting Roles

The previous sections have identified the major actors in the unfolding drama of global harmonization. However, several other groups deserve mention for their supporting roles. By and large, these groups are smaller in size, scope, and clout, yet they have played important roles.

University-based Organizations

The Center for International Education and Research in Accounting, housed at the University of Illinois, conducts seminars, publishes one of the few scholarly journals dealing with international accounting (*The International Journal of Accounting*), and periodically issues research monographs. Its counterpart in Europe is the Center for International Research in Accounting at England's University of Lancaster. The Lancaster center's activities include the sponsorship of international accounting research studies and conferences and the publication of related monographs. Similar activities are conducted at the University of Washington's International Accounting Studies Institute (INTASI), the Center for International Accounting Development at the University of Texas at Dallas, and the Center for International Accounting Studies at California State University at Northridge. Of particular interest to international accountants is the periodic publishing of an international accounting bibliography compiled by INTASI.

The AISG

Although recently disbanded, one of the earliest groups to strive for accounting harmonization was the Accountants International Study Group (AISG). The AISG focused its activities on accounting and auditing subjects in the United States, United Kingdom, and Canada. Among the AISG completed studies were *Auditor's Reporting Standards* (1969), *Consolidations* (1972), *Published Profit Forecasts* (1974), *Interim Financial Reporting* (1975), *Comparative Glossary of Accounting Terms* (1975), and *Accounting for Pension Costs* (1977). When deemed appropriate, the AISG also made recommendations to the sponsoring national institutes, based on the research studies. See Table 3–4 for a list of completed AISG studies.

TABLE 3–4. Studies Produced by AISG

1. Accounting and Auditing Approaches to Inventories in Three Nations—1968
2. The Independent Auditor's Reporting Standards in Three Nations—1969
3. Using the Work and Report of Another Auditor—1969
4. Accounting for Corporate Income Taxes—1971
5. Reporting by Diversified Companies—1972
6. Consolidated Financial Statements—1972
7. The Funds Statement—1973
8. Materiality in Accounting—1974
9. Extraordinary Items, Prior Period Adjustments, and Changes in Accounting Principle—1974
10. Published Profit Forecasts—1974
11. International Financial Reporting—1975
12. Comparative Glossary of Accounting Terms in Canada, the United Kingdom, and the United States—1975
13. Accounting for Goodwill—1975
14. Interim Financial Reporting—1975
15. Going Concern Problems—1975
16. Independence of Auditors—1976
17. Audit Committees—1976
18. Accounting for Pension Costs—1977

The ICAC

The International Committee for Accounting Cooperation (ICAC) was established in 1966 to facilitate the development of accounting in developing countries. It was based on the notion that the lack of a modern accounting system (or unfamiliarity with it) serves as an impediment to economic development. This is particularly true when these countries seek international loans or equity capital from foreign sources and cannot provide the required reliable and accurate accounting data. Among the members of the ICAC are the U.S. Agency for International Development, the Inter-American Development Bank, the International Finance Corporation, the AICPA, the Canadian Institute for Chartered Accountants, and the Mexican Institute of CPA's. The first and most ambitious ICAC project involving a plan for intensive accounting development in Colombia was never fully implemented. Since that time (late 1960s), the organization has pursued far less ambitious projects, concentrating on faculty and student exchanges and occasional publications.

U.S. Organizations

Several other U.S. organizations have fostered international accounting research, discussion, and interchange, among them (1) the American Institute of Certified Public Accountants, through its International Practice Division; (2) the American Accounting Association, through its International Accounting Section; (3) the Securities and Exchange Commission, through its Office of International Operations; (4) the international divisions of the Internal Revenue Service and the Government Accounting Office; (5) the National Accountants Association; and (6) the Financial Executives Institute.

Of these groups, the International Section of the AAA has been the most active and has had the widest range of interests and activities. Its more than a dozen committees focus on such topics as international accounting education and research, financial and managerial accounting for developing nations, international programs, the internationalization of accounting curricula, and continuing education and professional development programs of an international nature.

Examples of organizations in other countries which have played roles somewhat similar to those of the U.S. organizations include the Canadian Institute of Chartered Accountants; the Chartered Accountants Institute in England, Scotland, and Wales; and NIVRA (the Dutch Institute of Certified Accountants).

International Accounting Firms

Finally, as was alluded to earlier, the large international accounting firms have played an active supporting role in the process of international accounting harmonization.

To provide accounting services to clients with international activities, the larger accounting firms followed their clients abroad, opening offices in many countries. Other firms established formal relationships with local accounting firms in other countries. Regardless of the methods followed in expanding internationally, they had to establish some uniformity in the work they performed, or had performed for them, around the world. This uniformity was necessary so that the accounting firm could be confident of the work's quality, reliability, and verifiability.

As most of the international accounting firms discovered, a great deal of work was necessary *before* this desired uniformity could be achieved: their employees had to be trained in the idiosyncrasies of other countries' accounting practices and the intricacies of international accounting. The foreign employees also had to become knowledgeable about U.S. or U.K. accounting practices and procedures; and so forth.

To solve these problems, the large international accounting firms embarked on a series of programs involving international exchanges of personnel and international training seminars. Through these programs, their employees in the countries where they had representation acquired the background, perspective, and experience necessary to perform international accounting services on a much higher level of uniformity, consistency, and sophistication. These efforts were not oriented primarily toward achieving international harmonization, but the exchange of information, personnel, and experience resulted indirectly in an atmosphere more conducive to harmonization.

CONCLUSIONS

In assessing the overall effectiveness of the combined harmonization efforts of all these groups, one must conclude that their efforts have been commendable, but their results have remained disappointing. In all fairness, however, one must also recognize that the obstacles they face are considerable. The rocky and tortuous path to international accounting harmonization is not for those with weak hearts and limited patience. And while it is doubtful that Chairman Mao had international accounting harmonization in mind when he said it, his adage (loosely translated) that "every march of a million miles must begin with the first step" certainly would apply to harmonization. Or, to adapt Martin Luther King, Jr.'s famous slogan, perhaps some day we shall overcome.

STUDY QUESTIONS

3–1.   Identify and explain the major arguments for and against the international harmonization of accounting systems and standards.

3–2.   Identify and explain the major forces behind the movement toward harmonization and those that are impeding its progress.

3–3.   Identify the major international organizations working for accounting harmonization. What is the major purpose of each and what successes has each had?

3–4.   List the major reasons why some groups have been more successful than others in achieving harmonization.

3–5.   Could it be argued that harmonization would be easier to achieve at the principles level compared to the procedural or practices level? Why or why not?

3–6.   Discuss the role that the major international accounting firms have played in moving the world toward greater harmonization of accounting standards and practices.

3–7.   Discuss how international accounting courses, conferences, and exchange programs might affect the process of harmonization.

3–8.   How might multinational enterprises cause pressures for governments to seek harmonization of accounting systems.

3–9.   How might the multinational enterprise itself be an instrument for accounting harmonization?

3–10.   How would you assess the prospects for achieving global harmonization in the next decade? What about regional harmonization?

CASE

THE PRESENTATION

Roy Burgher, a junior staff member of one of the large international accounting firms, had been given a rush assignment. The senior partner of his firm had been asked to present a paper on the progress of international accounting harmonization to a group of accountants from several countries who would be visiting the city in a few days. The presentation was to cover the origins of the harmonization efforts, the problems it had encountered, and what prospects there were for success any time soon. In a quick trip to the local university's library Ray had swept together a potpourri of information about the topic but nothing that outlined in any systematic form the details sought by his boss. Ray knew that he did not have much time to prepare a suitable presentation, but as a junior staff member he knew he had better come up fast with something good.

Assignment

Write a two page description and analysis of the major efforts to harmonize differences in international accounting which Roy's boss could use for his presentation.

4

The World of Foreign Exchange

During 1978 the U.S. dollar plunged dramatically against several foreign currencies, among them the Japanese yen (21.6 percent), Swiss franc (25.7 percent), and West German mark (13.6 percent). The dollar recovered somewhat in 1979 and surged forward in early 1980 as U.S. interest rates rose to astronomical levels. However, as interest rates began to fall, so did the dollar—16 percent against the yen, 12 percent against the Swiss franc, and 10 percent against the German mark during April. Mid-1980 saw a repetition of 1978: central banks were trying desperately to support weak currencies in order to keep exchange rates from fluctuating too widely, the U.S. government was groping for ways to alter the fundamental forces weakening the dollar, and corporate treasurers were frantically shifting liquid assets to protect against potential foreign exchange losses.

In order to understand the complexity surrounding the controller and treasury functions of the multinational enterprise, one must first understand the organization and dynamics of the foreign exchange market. This chapter explains the terminology of foreign exchange, describes the spot and forward markets, explains the forces that determine rates, and traces the history of currency movements up to the present time. It focuses more on foreign exchange from the corporate and banking perspective than from a theoretical viewpoint. The usage of foreign exchange is fully developed in subsequent chapters on foreign currency transactions, translation of financial statements, foreign exchange risk management, and performance evaluation and control.

BASIC MARKETS

An *exchange rate* is the amount of one currency that must be given to acquire one unit of another currency. If the rate is quoted for current currency transactions—usually for delivery to be made two business days later—it is called the *spot rate*. Most currency transactions take place in the spot market. The forward market is for transactions that are to be completed at a later date. The majority of the transactions in the forward market are 30 to 180 days into the future, but contracts of other maturities are possible. The *forward rate* is a contractual rate between the foreign exchange trader and his client. It is seldom the same as the spot rate on the day the contract is made, and it may or may not be the same as the spot rate in effect when the forward contract is completed.

Spot Market

As is noted later in the chapter, most foreign currency transactions take place with the foreign exchange traders of banks. Therefore, rates are quoted from the trader's perspective. Ordinarily, the trader will offer two quotes—the bid and offer price of a foreign currency. For example, the quote for British pounds sterling may appear as follows:

$2.0400/10

which means that the trader will buy pounds for $2.0400 (bid) and sell pounds for $2.0410 (offer or ask). The difference between the two quotes is the profit margin for the trader and is often referred to as the *points* (10 points in the above example).

Exchange rate quotes can be obtained from a number of sources, such as the *Wall Street Journal*. In Table 4–1 are quotes of a few currencies. Note that the rates listed in the table are the offer rather than bid price. Also note that two different rates are quoted for each day. The first two columns contain a *direct quote*, which is the amount of local currency equivalent to one unit of the foreign currency. Since the quote was made in the United States, the dollar is the local currency. The second two columns contain an *indirect quote*, which is the amount of foreign currency required for one unit of the local currency. For example, in Table 4–1 the exchange rate for U.S. dollars and Brazilian cruzeiros was as follows:

$.0197 or 2¢ per cruzeiro (direct) or

NC 50.76 per U.S. dollar (indirect).

Obviously, what is a direct quote in the United States would be considered an indirect quote in Brazil. Even if the direct quote were the only

TABLE 4–1. New York Foreign Exchange Selling Rates

COUNTRY	U.S. DOLLAR EQUIVALENT		CURRENCY PER U.S. DOLLAR	
	THUR.	WED.	THUR.	WED.
Brazil (cruzeiro)	.0197	.0201	50.76	49.93
Britain (pound)	2.3350	2.3225	.4282	.4305
30-day futures	2.3210	2.3077	.4308	.4333
90-day futures	2.2960	2.2832	.4355	.4380
180-day futures	2.2705	2.2575	.4404	.4429
Canada (dollar)	.8649	.8632	1.1562	1.1585
30-day futures	.8623	.8611	1.1597	1.1612
90-day futures	.8606	.8597	1.1620	1.1631
180-day futures	.8603	.8598	1.1624	1.1630
Japan (yen)	.004562	.004505	219.20	222.00
30-day futures	.004555	.004494	219.55	222.50
90-day futures	.004548	.004486	219.90	222.90
180-day futures	.004551	.004486	219.75	222.90
Mexico (peso)	.0439	.0439	22.80	22.80
Switzerland (franc)	.6076	.6064	1.6460	1.6490
30-day futures	.6096	.6084	1.6405	1.6437
90-day futures	.6141	.6134	1.6285	1.6302
180-day futures	.6204	.6200	1.6120	1.6130
West Germany (mark)	.5639	.5629	1.7733	1.7765
30-day futures	.5641	.5631	1.7727	1.7759
90-day futures	.5645	.5637	1.7715	1.7740
180-day futures	.5662	.5654	1.7663	1.7687

SOURCE: Wall Street Journal, June 6, 1980. Reprinted by permission. © Dow Jones & Company, Inc. All rights reserved.

NOTE: These rates apply to trading among banks in amounts of $1 million and more, as quoted at 3 P.M. Eastern time by Bankers Trust Co. Retail transactions provide fewer units of foreign currency per dollar.

one provided, one could derive the indirect quote by taking the reciprocal of the direct quote. For example:

$$\frac{1}{\$.0197} = 50.76$$

The discussion thus far has centered on exchange rates between the U.S. dollar and other currencies. Rates are generally quoted this way because most foreign currency transactions take place in dollars, even when two currencies other than the dollar are directly involved. For example, a Japanese company selling goods to a Peruvian company may denominate the sale in dollars such that the Peruvian importer converts soles into dollars, and the Japanese exporter converts dollars into yen. Sometimes, however, *cross rates* are quoted. This establishes the relationship between two non-dollar currencies. For example, in Table 4–1 the spot rates for German marks and Swiss francs were:

$.5639 marks
$.6076 francs

The mark/franc cross rate would be:

$$\frac{.5639}{.6076} = .928$$

which means that one mark equals .928 francs. The cross rate is often stated as 92.8. Germans and Swiss keep track of the cross rate since they trade extensively with each other. Any material shifts in the cross rate could change the local currency equivalent of foreign goods and thus alter trade flows. For example, at a cross rate of .928 a German product being sold to a Swiss wholesaler for 100 marks would cost 92.8 francs. If the cross rate were to move to .950 the same product would cost 95 francs, which may be higher than the market is willing to bear.

Forward Market

As mentioned earlier, the forward rate is a contract rate between a foreign currency trader and customer for future sale or purchase of foreign currency. During a period of foreign exchange stability, there may be no difference between the current spot and forward rate. However, there normally is a difference, known as the *spread,* between the spot and forward rate. In Table 4–1, for example, forward (or futures) rates are quoted for several currencies. The spot and 90-day forward rates quoted for pounds and marks are as follows:

	SPOT	90-DAY FORWARD
British pounds (£)	$2.3350	$2.2960
German marks (DM)	$ .5639	$ .5645

The spread in pounds is .0390 [$2.3350 − $2.2960] or 390 points. Because the forward rate is less than the spot rate, the pound is selling at a *discount* of 390 points. The spread in marks is .006 or 6 points. Because the forward rate exceeds the spot rate, the mark is selling at a *premium* of 6 points.

The premium or discount is normally quoted at the number of points above or below the spot rate, but it could also be expressed in annualized percentage terms. The formula used to determine the percentage is as follows:

$$\text{Premium (discount)} = \frac{F_0 - S_0}{S_0} \times \frac{12}{N}$$

where F_0 is the forward rate on the day that the contract is entered into, S_0 is the spot rate on that day, and N is the number of months forward. Using the example of pounds given above,

$$\text{Discount} = \frac{\$2.2960 - \$2.3350}{\$2.3350} \times \frac{12}{3}$$

$$= .0668 \text{ or } 6.7\%$$

Using the mark example,

$$\text{Premium} = \frac{\$.5645 - \$.5639}{\$.5639} \times \frac{12}{3}$$

$$= .0043 \text{ or } .43\%$$

FOREIGN EXCHANGE MARKETS AND INSTRUMENTS

Before discussing the major determinants of spot and forward rates, it would be useful to consider the actual market in which foreign currency is traded. The volume of foreign exchange transactions is unknown because accurate, centralized statistics do not exist. However, it has been estimated that the total in 1977 was approximately $25 trillion, nearly twenty times the volume of world trade.[1] What is the nature of this trading, and where does it take place?

Most foreign exchange trading worldwide is carried on by the foreign exchange traders of commercial banks. In some countries, tourists can exchange money at hotels and elsewhere, but the volume is obviously small. In other countries the government is the sole official trader of currency, and it normally operates through the nationalized banking sector. The black market is also a source. What traveler to a developing country has not at least once been approached on the street by someone seeking to buy a relatively stronger currency at very favorable exchange rates? In the United States, the International Money Market Division of the Chicago Mercantile Exchange is another place where currencies—

---

[1] Ian H. Giddy, "Measuring the World Foreign Exchange Market," paper presented at the Northeast Regional Meeting of the Academy of International Business in New York City, November 1978, p. 3.

especially forward contracts—can be bought and sold. However, the commercial banking sector is the major source of trading.

Worldwide, it is estimated that 95 percent of all foreign exchange trading is *interbank*—that is, between large commercial banks.[2] This trading is often facilitated through foreign exchange brokerage houses that try to match interbank trade. These brokers earn a commission on their transactions and greatly facilitate the flow of money. The trade can be between domestic banks of the same country or between banks of different countries. The remainder of the transactions would be between the bank trader and his clients—primarily corporate clients.

Speculators play an important part in the psychology of the market as they attempt to profit on anticipated future trends. For example, a speculator who holds dollars and expects the German mark to strengthen vis-à-vis the dollar in the near future may sell dollars for marks. As the mark strengthens to a higher level in the future, the speculator will sell the marks for more dollars and earn a profit on the transaction. If enough speculators move into the market, they may play an active role in causing the exchange rates to change.

Nearly 80 percent of foreign exchange trading is in the spot market rather than the forward market.[3] However, the use of the forward market appears to have increased owing to the continued volatility of exchange rates and the desire of banks and corporations to protect against future changes in foreign exchange. Although the U.S. dollar is the most important trading currency and the U.S. market is increasing in size and importance, Europe is by far the most important center in foreign exchange trading. Approximately 87 percent of all foreign exchange trading takes place in Europe, with London, West Germany, and Switzerland as the three most important markets. The trading volume for each of these markets is more than twice that of the United States.[4]

The International Money Market Division (IMM) of the Chicago Mercantile Exchange specializes in trading currency futures. The IMM was initiated in 1972 in response to the uncertainty prevalent in foreign exchange markets and the demand of speculators and businessmen for a futures market. The IMM currently offers contracts in the British pound, Canadian dollar, Dutch guilder, West German mark, Japanese yen, Mexican peso, French franc, and Swiss franc. Contracts are of set sizes and maturity dates. For example, one British pound contract is for £25,000 with major delivery months of March, June, September, and December. One Japanese yen contract is for 12 million yen and the same delivery dates as pounds. Users of the IMM buy or sell one or more contracts in a particular currency.

[2] Ibid., p. 6.
[3] Ibid.
[4] Ibid., p. 3.

Instruments of Payment

How does an importer transfer payment in foreign currency to an exporter in a foreign country? Most corporations do not keep large foreign currency deposits in each of their banks around the world; instead, they utilize commercial banks. The importer could receive a check in foreign currency from its bank, drawn on the bank's foreign branch or correspondent. Then the importer could mail the check directly to the exporter. Or the importer may simply give instructions to the bank and allow the bank to effect payment. Or the bank could Telex instructions to its foreign branch or correspondent to effect payment, or it could send instructions by airmail.

In order to facilitate the flow of money, the exporter may send instructions to the importer in the form of a *commercial bill of exchange*. This instrument tells the importer how payment should be made. Normally, payment is made to the exporter's bank and added to the exporter's account. Payment can be required either at sight (when the importer receives the bill of exchange) or *on time* (a specified time after the importer is presented the bill of exchange). The importer then instructs his bank on how to transfer funds to the exporter.

A more formal document to facilitate the flow of money is a *letter of credit*. The importer may instruct his bank to issue a letter of credit to the exporter assuring that the bank will effect payment. If the letter of credit is *irrevocable*, the importer's bank will honor the bill of exchange even if the importer defaults. If the letter of credit is *confirmed irrevocable*, the exporter's bank will honor the bill of exchange even if the importer's bank defaults. Thus the letter of credit can be used to ensure that the bill of exchange is honored.

DETERMINATION OF RATES

Spot Rate

The spot and forward markets are separate but related. Since the dynamics of the spot market and its future expectations have an impact on the forward market, let's look at the spot market first.

The foreign exchange market has developed in recent years into a highly competitive market based primarily on the forces of supply and demand. The major actors in the market are foreign exchange traders of commercial banks, corporate treasurers, speculators, and national central banks. Their desire to buy or sell foreign currency is a combination of foreign currency balances they currently hold, anticipated changes in the spot rate, and anticipated future needs for foreign currency. Actors buy and sell foreign exchange for routine business transactions—trade, investment, working capital needs—as well as for profit-seeking. According to a study cited earlier, approximately 82 percent of foreign exchange transactions are profit-seeking, rather than for normal business purposes.[5] What, then, causes these rates to change?

Trade flows are important in determining supply and demand for foreign exchange. If a country persistently runs a balance of trade deficit—as the United States has since 1971—the supply of its currency begins to increase abroad. The opposite will occur for countries like Japan and West Germany that are experiencing a trade surplus. Among the economic forces that affect these trade flows are changes in consumer tastes and preferences; changes in levels of income and therefore in consumption patterns; levels of economic development which may force developing countries to import expensive capital-intensive products; changes in the technology gap; and relative levels of inflation.

Inflation is critical because it affects not only the relative costs and therefore competitiveness of goods worldwide, but also the confidence that actors have in the government of a country. Confidence in a government and therefore in its currency is partly a function of how well the government manages the economy. Confidence is low when the government piles up huge budget deficits, cannot control inflation, and does not seem to have the general support of the populace. This can make actors nervous about a currency and cause the value of the currency to decline.

In addition to the basic economic forces and confidence in leadership a number of *technical factors* influence exchange rates, such as the release of national economic statistics, seasonal demands for a currency, and a slight strengthening of a currency following a prolonged weakening or vice versa. *Arbitrage* is another factor that causes rates to change. Arbitrage in the spot market occurs where a speculator is able to make a profit by buying and selling currencies simultaneously in different markets. For example, assume the following rates in the following markets:

	ACTUAL RATES	EQUILIBRIUM RATES
United States	$.5366/DM	$.5366/DM
West Germany	DM3.70/£	DM3.8021/£
United Kingdom	$2.0500/£	$2.0402/£

At the equilibrium rates, a speculator could trade $1,000 for deutsche marks in the United States, trade marks for pounds in West Germany, trade pounds for dollars in the United Kingdom, and still end up with $1,000. If the *actual* rates were quoted as listed, he could obtain a profit of $32.53 as shown below:

United States $1,000 ÷ $.5366 = DMl,863.5855
West Germany   DM1,863.5855 ÷ 3.70 = £503.67175
United Kingdom   £503.67175 × $2.0500 = $1,032.53
Profit $1,032.53 − $1,000 = $32.53

However, the market would soon recognize such differences in rates, and as funds flow from one country to another, rates would quickly move back to an equilibrium position.

Foreign exchange traders are the ones who actually quote the rates that make up the spot market. What do they consider? Some of the major factors are (1) the price and size of recent transactions in the market, (2) trends by direction and time, (3) impending events concerning the economy and political stability of a country as brought out in news releases and elsewhere, (4) information from other currency centers when the market is especially volatile, (5) the time of day and day of the week, and (6) the currency position of the trader.[6] These factors are all related closely to the issues mentioned earlier.

Pressures can mount against a currency, and when they do, a number of things can occur. A country may move to correct the fundamental imbalances in its economy by slowing down inflation and encouraging the development of export industries. The country may attempt to correct a run on its currency by rationing foreign exchange through licensing or through multiple exchange rates. In Brazil, for example, the government required that firms apply for a license to receive foreign exchange to pay for imports and then required that the firms deposit an amount equal to the FOB value of the imports in an interest-free account in the central bank for one year before receiving the foreign exchange. *Multiple rates* involve a government's allowing some transactions to occur at a preferential exchange rate (such as for essential imports) and others at a less desirable rate (such as for luxury imports). Some countries, such as the United States and the United Kingdom, allow full *convertibility* to their currency by anyone. Others, such as Peru, have only partial convertibility, granting nonresidents free convertibility and giving residents only limited convertibility. Various ranges of convertibility also exist.

In addition to these solutions, a government may simply allow its currency to *float* within certain limits in the open market to seek an equilibrium level. Few countries allow total market control over their currency. Generally a central bank will support its currency to keep it from falling too far by buying the currency in the open market, thus creating a demand and causing the price to stabilize or rise. The opposite action could be taken for a strengthening currency. Central bank inter-

[6] For a more detailed discussion of this issue, see "An Inside View of the Foreign Exchange Market," Chase Manhattan Bank N.A., 1976, pp. 11–12.

vention has led to the terms *dirty float* and *managed float* to describe how today's system actually operates.[7]

Forward Rate

Someone who wants to buy or sell foreign currency in the future at a predetermined price can do it with a *forward contract*. Most forward contracts are entered into with a commercial bank at a contractual exchange rate called the *forward rate*. The accounting for and use of forward contracts are discussed in detail in subsequent chapters; however, one example of a contract would be useful at this point.

Assume that the British subsidiary of a United States company declares a dividend which will be paid to the parent in ninety days. The parent company, which deals in dollars, is concerned because the dividend will be received in British pounds. If the parent does nothing, the dollar equivalent of the dividend may fall over the next ninety days if the exchange rate changes. The parent could enter into a forward contract to deliver pounds to the bank in ninety days in return for dollars at a set forward contract rate. Thus a fixed amount of dollars will be received no matter what the actual spot rate is when the dividend is received.

Forward markets do not exist for all currencies, and factors influencing the setting of rates vary from currency to currency. *The Wall Street Journal* lists forward rates for the British pound, Canadian dollar, French franc, Japanese yen, Swiss franc, and West German mark. Markets can be found for other currencies as well, but it could be that only the central banks of the specific countries will quote on them, not commercial banks.

One of the most important determinants for the forward rate is the *interest rate differential*, as illustrated in the following example. Assume that the spot rate for pounds is $2.0402, the interest rate on a 90-day United States treasury bill is 10 percent per annum, and the interest rate on a British debt instrument of similar risk and maturity is 11 percent. If investors were positive that the exchange rate would not change, they would always invest in the U.K. debt instrument since it has a higher yield. But as more dollars were invested in the United Kingdom, it would become clear that in ninety days there would be a surplus of pounds on the market as the investors liquidated their British pound investments back into dollars.

This surplus of pounds would cause the spot rate to decline, and each investor would face the prospect of getting fewer dollars back for each pound invested. Of course, no one knows precisely what the future spot

---

[7] John D. Daniels, E. W. Ogram, and Lee H. Radebaugh, *International Business: Environments and Operations*, 2nd ed. (Reading, Mass.: Addison-Wesley, 1979), chapter 10 for a more detailed discussion of the forces influencing exchange rate changes.

rates will be, and thus the uncertainty and risk might prevent someone from investing in the U.K. instrument.

This is where the forward rate comes in. At least in theory, the forward rate in the example would be the rate which exactly neutralizes the difference in interest rates between the United States and United Kingdom. This forward rate would be computed by the foreign trader as shown in Table 4–2.

TABLE 4–2. Determination of Forward Rates

$r_{us} = 10\%$ $S_0 = \$2.0402$
$r_{uk} = 11\%$ $F_0 = ?$

N = number of months for the T bill

$$r_{us} - r_{uk} = \frac{F_0 - S_0}{S_0} \times \frac{12}{N}$$

$$S_0(r_{us} - r_{uk})\left(\frac{N}{12}\right) + S_0 = F_0$$

$$2.0402(.10 - .11)\left(\frac{3}{12}\right) + 2.0402 = F_0$$

$$\$2.0351 = F_0$$

At this forward rate, there is no incentive for someone to invest in the United States as opposed to the United Kingdom or vice versa. For example, if someone were to invest \$1,000 in the United States for three months, the yield would be:

$$\$1,000 + \$1,000\,[.10 \times 3/12] = \$1,025$$

A similar investment of \$1,000 in the United Kingdom would yield \$1,024.93 as shown in Table 4–3.

If investors were to move out of dollars and into pounds, for whatever reason, the demand would cause either interest rates or exchange rates to move to a new equilibrium level. Thus the forward rate allows investors to freely trade currencies for future delivery at no exchange risk and without any differential in interest income. If a difference were to exist, traders would engage in *interest arbitrage*. This means that they would sell one currency for another and invest in the latter currency if the difference in interest rates exceeded the difference in exchange rates. Assume the same information as in the previous example except that the forward rate is \$2.05. Table 4–4 illustrates the possible yields of \$1,000 for a U.S. investor. In this situation it is obvious that investors would rather invest in the United Kingdom than in the United States. However, the flow of

TABLE 4–3. Investment Yields I

1. Convert dollars to pounds at the spot rate	$1,000 ÷ $2.0402 = £490.148
2. Invest the pounds at 11 percent for three months	490.148 + 490.148 (.11 × 3/12) = 503.627
3. At the same time, enter into a forward contract to deliver £503.627 for dollars	
4. At the end of three months, deliver the pounds and receive dollars at the forward rate	£503.627 × $2.0351 = $1,024.93

funds would cause the spot rate, the forward rate, or the interest rates to change to the equilibrium position.

Although the interest rate differential is the critical factor for a few of the most widely traded currencies, the expectation of future spot rates is also very important. Normally, a trader will automatically compute the forward rate through the interest rate differential and then adjust it for future expectations where deemed necessary. Some forward rates are quoted strictly on future expectations rather than interest rate differentials. This would especially be true for currencies not traded very widely and for which total convertibility does not exist, such as the Chilean escudo or Indian rupee.

TABLE 4–4. Investment Yields II

UNITED STATES
Invest $1,000 at 10% per annum for 90 days (¼ year)

$$1,000 + 1,000\left(\frac{.10}{4}\right) = \$1,025$$

UNITED KINGDOM
1. Convert $1,000 into pounds at the spot rate

$$1,000 \times \frac{1}{2.0402} = £490.15$$

2. Invest the pounds for 90 days

$$490.15 + 490.15\left(\frac{.11}{4}\right) = 503.63$$

3. Sell pounds forward for 90 days to cover the principle and interest

$$£503.63 \times \$2.05 = \$1032.44$$

FOREIGN EXCHANGE AND
THE BALANCE OF PAYMENTS

The *balance of payments* of a country summarizes the international transactions that take place in a given year. These transactions involve the flow of goods, services, and financial claims, and they affect and are affected by the value of currencies. Table 4–5 summarizes the major categories of statistics collected annually for U.S. purposes.

Exports and imports are divided into two categories: merchandise trade and other goods and services. The first category features the trade most people are familiar with, such as grain exports and television imports. *Services* involve a variety of transactions such as foreign travel expenses, fees and royalties (such as earnings from showing U.S. movies and television shows abroad), and income from foreign investments. *Unilateral transfers* result from sending money or goods abroad without receiving anything in return, such as sending relief supplies to a country devastated by an earthquake. The transactions under *U.S. assets abroad* include changes in U.S. official reserve assets (such as gold, special drawing rights, and foreign currencies), foreign direct investment, and the purchase of foreign securities. The *foreign assets in the U.S.* category refers to foreign investment in the United States, the purchase of U.S. securities, and so on.

As can be seen from Table 4–5, merchandise exports were less than imports, resulting in a deficit of approximately $29 billion ($211.524 billion − $182.074 billion). Since U.S. residents bought more than they sold abroad, how were their transactions financed? If purchases were in foreign currencies, buyers would convert dollars into foreign currencies at their banks, which would eventually run down our foreign currency assets. Alternatively, purchases could be made in dollars, which would increase our official liabilities abroad.

As more and more dollars flow abroad to finance the transactions, foreign central banks become reluctant to hold dollars, and pressure

TABLE 4–5. Selected Balance of Payments Data—1979 (millions of dollars)

Exports of goods and services		$286,312
merchandise trade	$182,074	
other goods and services	104,238	
Imports of goods and services		−280,980
merchandise trade	−211,524	
other goods and services	−69,456	
Unilateral transfers, net		−5,648
U.S. assets abroad, net		−63,423
Foreign assets in the U.S., net		33,902

SOURCE: Christopher L. Bach, "U.S. International Transactions, Fourth Quarter and Year 1979," *Survey of Current Business,* Department of Commerce, March 1980, p. 45.

begins to build. If the pressure gets strong enough, action may need to be taken. For example, fundamental economic forces leading to the trade imbalance (such as inflation) could be corrected. In the short run, a country may resort to capital flow restrictions (such as not allowing money to flow abroad for foreign investment) or import controls. In the case of the United States, these actions could result in a reduction in the supply of dollars abroad.

In today's world, where exchange rates float relatively freely with respect to each other, the pressure may cause the value of a currency to change. In the face of excess supply, the value of a country's currency would fall, and in the face of excess demand, the value would rise. Thus the balance of payments formally records the transactions that eventually put pressure on a currency, as discussed earlier in the chapter.

GLOBAL COORDINATION OF FOREIGN EXCHANGE

Many people would argue that the heading for this section should be a question rather than a statement, and they are probably correct. Stability and order are elusive in world money markets, but two institutions and one market *are* worth mentioning: the International Monetary Fund, the European Monetary System, and the Eurodollar market.

The International Monetary Fund

Although foreign currencies are traded quite freely, there is a form of supranational influence that tries to encourage a certain amount of order. The *International Monetary Fund* (IMF) was created in 1944 with the primary objective of promoting exchange stability. At that time, the currencies of 133 member countries were assigned a fixed exchange rate or par value based on gold and the U.S. dollar; gold was worth $35 an ounce, and currencies were quoted on that basis. Currencies were allowed to float freely in a band of 1 percent on either side of par value. However, stability did not last forever, and major changes began in the 1970s. Countries like Brazil were constantly devaluing their currency, permanently decreasing the par value in terms of gold and the dollar. Others were experiencing periodic changes, such as the British pound in 1967. But the major trading currencies were still adhering fairly well to par values. In December 1971 the IMF allowed the U.S. dollar to formally devalue and also allowed currencies to float 2¼ percent on either side of par value without a formal devaluation or revaluation.

Continued pressure on the dollar in early 1973 forced another devaluation, with subsequent instability finally forcing the major trading countries of the world to break loose from the fixed rate system and allow their currencies to float freely against each other, subject to the influence of central bank intervention. Currently, the IMF permits a country to select one of three systems to value its currency. The first is to *peg* (or fix) the value of its currency to another currency. Some Latin American countries, for example, peg the value of their currency to the U.S. dollar. Thus their currency may float relative to other currencies in the world, but it remains fixed to the dollar. The second is to peg a currency to the value of a *basket of currencies*. The European Monetary System, as explained in the next section, is an example of a basket of currencies. The third alternative is to allow a currency to float freely against other currencies. Thus the currency may strengthen against some and weaken against other currencies. In spite of this apparent freedom, the IMF is still

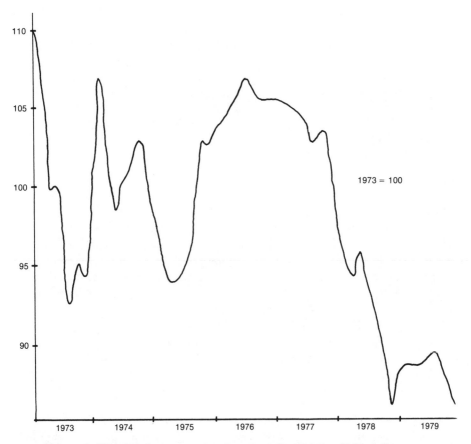

Figure 2. Weighted average exchange value of the U.S. dollar, March 1973 = 100. Index of weighted average exchange value of the U.S. dollar against currencies of Germany, Japan, France, United Kingdom, Canada, Italy, Netherlands, Belgium, Sweden, and Switzerland. (Source: Various issues of the *Federal Reserve Bulletin.*)

concerned with promoting measures to enhance exchange rate stability worldwide.

The U.S. dollar has been floating freely against major world currencies, subject to central bank intervention, since 1973. Figure 2 illustrates how the dollar has fluctuated against ten major trading partners. As can be seen, the dollar hit peaks in early 1973, 1974, and 1976, and it has declined steadily since the second quarter of 1977. Figures 3 and 4 show the performance of the dollar against the Canadian dollar and the German mark to illustrate the diversity in currency movements.

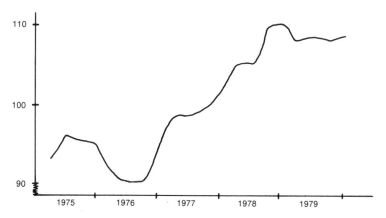

Figure 3. Canadian dollar price of the U.S. dollar, May 1970 = 100 (Source: Various issues of the *Survey of Current Business.*)

The European Monetary System

The instability in the foreign exchange markets has been especially damaging to European countries that rely heavily on foreign trade. In addition, intrazonal trade among the nine members of the European Economic Community (West Germany, France, Italy, United Kingdom, Belgium, Netherlands, Luxembourg, Denmark, and Ireland) exceeds 50 percent of their total foreign trade. The EEC members therefore created the *European Monetary System* (EMS) in March 1979 in hopes of stabilizing their own exchange rates. The EMS links together the currencies of all EEC members except the United Kingdom in two ways: through a *European currency unit* (ECU) and a parity grid. The ECU is a basket of all nine EEC currencies weighted by the importance of each economy. The percentage weight that each currency has in one ECU is the following:[8]

---

[8] *The Economist*, 17 March 1979, p. 75.

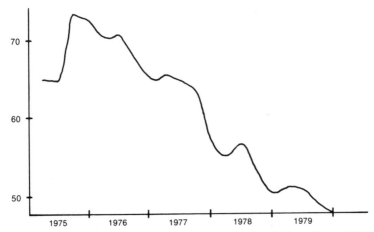

Figure 4. West German mark price of the U.S. dollar, May 1970 = 100.
(Source: Various issues of the *Survey of Current Business*.)

33.0%	D-mark (West Germany)
19.8%	Franc (France)
13.4%	Sterling (United Kingdom)
10.5%	Guilder (Netherlands)
9.5%	Lira (Italy)
9.2%	Franc (Belgium)
3.1%	Krone (Denmark)
1.15%	Pound (Ireland)
.35%	Franc (Luxembourg)
100.0%	

Each currency is given a par value in ECUs and is allowed to fluctuate around that value in certain limits determined by the central banks involved. The limits vary by currency, so a strong currency like the deutsche mark would not be allowed to vary much.

The second part of the attempt at stability in the EMS involves a *parity grid*. According to the grid, each currency (except the Italian lira) is allowed to float 2¼ percent above or below a central exchange rate fixed between that currency and every other currency in the EMS. The central rate is determined in ECUs. The lira is allowed a fluctuation of plus or minus 6 percent. The British pound sterling is the only EEC currency that did not join the EMS initially.

In order to help stabilize exchange rates so that they will remain within the upper and lower limits, the EMS members have established a *European monetary cooperation fund* that will have resources to be used for intervention and support, should a crisis arise. The hope is that the EMS will stabilize exchange rates among member nations so that trading relationships are not disrupted by disorderly foreign exchange markets.

The Eurodollar Market

A currency banked outside its country of origin is considered a *Eurocurrency*. Since the largest market is in Europe and the greatest volume is in dollars, the market has come to be termed the *Eurodollar market*. In many respects, the Eurodollar market is parallel to the various domestic markets since dollars can be deposited or invested in the United States or in Europe. The Eurodollar market is not regulated by a specific government or organization like the World Bank and is therefore free to operate according to supply and demand.

The Eurodollar market, estimated in size to be between $700 billion and $1 trillion, is an important source of funds that has been around since the late 1950s. There are three major uses of the Eurodollar market: as a source of short-term financing, as a medium-term market through Eurocredits, and as a long-term source of funds through Eurobonds. The short-term *Eurocurrency market* is the largest of the three and is an important source of funds for multinational corporations. Loan maturities range from thirty days to three or five years, with interest rates often quoted on a floating rather than fixed basis. This allows banks to protect their profits in a dynamic market. Medium-term *Eurocredits* are of a longer maturity, five to seven or eight years, and are popular with countries experiencing severe balance of payments problems arising in recent years from large increases in the price of oil. A *Eurobond* is a bond sold in a currency different from the country of issue. For example, the French subsidiary of a U.S. multinational corporation may raise Eurofrancs by issuing a French franc bond in Luxembourg. Most Eurobonds are denominated in dollars, however.

The Eurocurrency market exists because of capital restrictions in other countries, because of the large volume of U.S. dollars banked outside the United States, and because the market itself is free of regulations and restrictions. Firms find that funds are cheaper and more accessible in the market than elsewhere.

The Eurodollar market is significant in international accounting because it is an important source of debt that can be used to expand operations and balance foreign exchange exposure. Because it is part of an important international capital market, its informal requirements for reporting could have an obvious impact on internationalizing good accounting and reporting practices in countries whose companies deal extensively in the market.

CONCLUSIONS

Because the multinational enterprise operates in a variety of countries with different national currencies, foreign exchange poses unique problems. As businesses negotiate foreign purchases and sales, they must be cognizant of the spot exchange rate in order to determine their yield. In addition, exchange controls may keep them from receiving payment at *any* exchange rate, which adds another dimension to business risk.

As a firm plans future flows, it must anticipate the future rate, using the forward rate or models and business judgment as predictors of future spot rates. Because the forward rate is contractual, the firm may enter into a forward contract with a bank to ensure a precise inflow or outflow of its reporting currency.

That foreign exchange markets are far from stable puts added strain on a firm dealing heavily in foreign exchange. With respect to transactions, firms will rely increasingly on forecasting to predict future spot rates and on forward contracts to hedge (protect) future cash flows. Most companies try to denominate their sales in their own currency, so U.S. companies selling in dollars will not have any foreign exchange risk. As the dollar continues to fall in value relative to the currencies of our major trading partners, foreign importers will find that they need to generate less of their currency to buy U.S. dollars—a definite advantage to them. But U.S. importers will need to generate more dollars for each unit of the stronger foreign currency, which could create problems for them. This and related issues are covered in Chapter 7. Chapters 5 and 6 deal with the accounting implications of each of these issues.

The major countries of the world need to resolve their fundamental economic imbalances if foreign exchange markets are to stabilize. If the markets become increasingly chaotic, the uncertainty may cause a reduction in trade and a return of the isolationism that characterized the 1930s.

STUDY QUESTIONS

4–1. If the quote for U.S. dollars is given as FF4.1070/74, how much will a trader pay for $100? What would the profit be if the trader sold the $100 for French francs?

4–2. The spot rates for Danish krone and Indian rupees are:

$.1921 krone
$.1230 rupees

What are the direct and indirect quotes in terms of krone? In terms of rupees?

4–3. The spot and forward rates for the British pound and the Japanese yen are:

	Spot	180-day Forward
British pound	$2.1615	$2.1353
Japanese yen	$.004010	$.004121

a. What is the annual percentage premium or discount for each?

    b.   If the pound were selling 180 days forward at a 5 percent premium, what would the forward rate be?

    c.   If the yen were selling 180 days forward at a 5 percent discount, what would the forward rate be?

4–4.   What is the difference between a commercial bill of exchange and a letter of credit?

4–5.   Discuss the underlying factors which help to determine spot and forward rates. Explain why the spot and forward rates generally aren't equal.

4–6.   Assume the following exchange rates:

	Actual Rates		
Location	$/£	$/FF	FF/£
New York	2.1615	.2435	—
Paris	—	.2500	FF8.8768
London	2.1000	—	FF8.9000

What is the maximum profit in French francs that an arbitrager could earn by trading FF1,000? Why is this a riskless profit?

4–7.   Given the following rates:

spot	$.2435/FF
60-day forward	$.2450/FF
interest-U.S.	12 %/yr
interest-France	9%/yr

For someone who had $1,000, what steps would be involved in interest rate arbitrage? What is the total profit, assuming no transactions costs? Why is this a riskless profit? What is the equilibrium forward rate? What is the equilibrium U.S. interest rate?

4–8.   What is the difference between exchange rate arbitrage and exchange rate speculation?

4–9.   Using a recent copy of U.S. balance of payments data, find out which balances might indicate future pressure on the dollar to appreciate or depreciate. Explain why.

4–10.   Pick a major world currency and do the following:

    a.   Using a statistical source such as the *Federal Reserve Bulletin* or *International Financial Statistics*, trace the movement of that currency vis-à-vis the U.S. dollar over the past five years.

    b.   Identify some of the facts of the political and economic environment that currently have an impact on that country's currency. Use sources such as *Euromoney*, the *Economist*, the *Financial Times*, or the *Wall Street Journal*.

4–11.   How do the following institutions directly or indirectly affect the activities of a multinational enterprise?
   a.   International Monetary Fund
   b.   European Monetary System
   c.   Eurodollar market
4–12.   Should businesses use the black market to obtain foreign currency?
4–13.   Check the foreign exchange rates report in a recent *Wall Street Journal*. Which currencies are appreciating relative to the U.S. dollar? Which are depreciating?

CASE

A FINANCIAL SAMBA

Jerry King propped his feet up on the desk and looked out of his fifteenth floor office window at Copacabana Beach not far away. He had been in Brazil for a little over a year and was concerned about the future of the economy—especially the currency. Jerry was director and vice-president of the Brazilian subsidiary of a large U.S. multinational manufacturer. It was November 15, 1979, and the regional controller was due for a visit on December 2.

Brazil started its economic miracle in the late 1960s as the military dictatorship brought in a group of high-powered technocrats to transform the country into an economic power. Brazil, which contains half the population of South America, began its growth spurt in 1968, and in the following five years it grew at an annual rate of 11 percent. In 1971 its growth rate of 11.3 percent was the highest in the world. The government had succeeded in reducing inflation from 150 percent in the early 1960s to 16.7 percent by 1972.

The exchange rate policy had changed from one of steep, infrequent devaluations to one of mini-devaluations with the cruzeiro devalued by an average of 1–2 percent every four to six weeks. The stated policy was to devalue the cruzeiro by the difference between Brazilian inflation and U.S. inflation. This made it easier for businessmen to plan their currency flows. The sense of euphoria at the progress made during that period caused one Brazilian banker to predict that Brazil would be one of the five great powers of the world by 1982.

All that was before the oil price increases generated by OPEC in 1973 and 1974. Because Brazil imports all its oil, the economy was thrown into disarray. Inflation began to creep back up, the balance of trade deteriorated, and Brazil was forced to borrow heavily to finance its oil imports and pay off past debt obligations.

Jerry was a little worried because his economic staff couldn't seem to make any predictions; they just kept feeding him data. When he arrived in Brazil in 1978, all the U.S. multinationals were concerned about a pending devaluation. As late as December, managers were getting out of dollar debt and borrowing cruzeiros in anticipation of a major devaluation that they thought would hit by

March. Jerry couldn't figure out what all the fuss was about, so he decided to stay put and conduct business as usual. The cruzeiro wasn't devalued, and it has kept right on changing at 1 to 2 percent every four to six weeks. However, the talk of devaluation is still in the air, and Jerry has to say something to the controller on December 2. He is also worried about the latest stream of data, as shown in the table, just given to him by his economic staff.

	Consumer Price Index Brazil	Consumer Price Index U.S.	Exchange Rate (Cr./$)	Exports	Imports
				(millions of $US)	
1972	16.7%	3.3%		3.991	4.783
1973	12.6	6.2	6.220	6.199	6.999
1974	27.6	10.9	7.435	7.951	14.168
1975	28.9	9.2	9.070	8.670	13.592
1976	41.9	5.8	12.345	10.128	13.592
1977	43.7	6.5	16.050	12.120	13.726
1978	38.7	7.5	20.920	12.651	13.257
1979 (est.)	70–75	10–11	?	15.000	15.054
1st Q			23.130		19.500
2nd Q			25.655		
July			26.115		
August			27.775		
September			29.825		
October			30.415		

Jerry's economists also pointed out that Brazil's external debt was expected to be about $50 billion by the end of 1979 and that its ratio of net debt to total exports had climbed from less than 1 in 1973 to 2½ by 1978.

Questions

1. What is your opinion of the way that Jerry made his "decision" in 1978 concerning a probable devaluation?
2. According to the indicators provided by Jerry's economists, what do you think will happen to the cruzeiro?
3. If you were trying to figure out what would happen to the cruzeiro, what other information (if any) would you look at?
4. What recommendations would you give Jerry concerning his economic staff?
5. Given Brazil's balance of trade position and the history of the value of its currency, what are some other exchange rate policies you would expect the Brazilian government might implement?
6. Would you expect to find a Black Market for hard currency in Brazil? Why?

5

Accounting in Foreign Currency: Transactions and Translation

In 1978 Exxon suffered foreign exchange losses of $316 million, which were larger than the profits of Chase Manhattan Corporation or U.S. Steel or Goodyear Tire and Rubber Company. The total sales of the firm at the bottom of *Fortune's* 500 list for 1978 barely exceeded Exxon's foreign exchange losses. Thus, changing exchange rates can have a dramatic impact on earnings. Chapter 4 focused on exchange rates and the major economic influences on those rates. How do accountants fit in? One recent article posed the questions: "Are the gnomes of Zurich really just a bunch of accountants? Is the weakness of the U.S. dollar at least partly attributable to an asinine accounting rule?"[1] The rule referred to—Statement 8 of the Financial Accounting Standards Board of the United States—determines how firms must account for foreign currency transactions and the translation of financial statements. The concern mirrored in the quote is that accountants may be making decisions that influence exchange rates. Although this may be all but impossible to prove, one thing is sure: the U.S. firms that are required to use FASB 8 have indeed been affected.

FOREIGN CURRENCY TRANSACTIONS

A domestic corporation can enter into a variety of business transactions including exports of goods and services and foreign borrowing or lending. Transactions cover merchandise trade; the sale or purchase of services

[1]"Are There Gnomes in Connecticut?" *Forbes*, 5 March 1979, p. 104.

such as banking, insurance, and management consulting; and the payment or receipt of dividends, royalties, and management fees.

No accounting problem arises as long as the transactions are denominated in the firm's domestic currency. However, when a transaction is denominated in a foreign currency, the firm needs to resolve four accounting problems. The first is the initial recording of the transaction; the second is the recording of foreign currency balances at subsequent balance sheet dates; the third is the treatment of any foreign exchange gains and losses; and the fourth is the recording of the settlement of foreign currency receivables and payables when they come due. These issues are obviously interactive. In addition, a firm may look at its transactions from two major perspectives. How these four issues are resolved depends on the perspective the firm chooses.

One-Transaction Perspective

A succinct description of a *one-transaction perspective* is as follows: "A transaction involving purchase or sale of goods or services with the price stated in foreign currency is incomplete until the amount in dollars necessary to liquidate the related payable or receivable is determined . . . an exchange gain or loss related to the transaction should be treated as an adjustment of the cost of imports or revenue from exports."[2]

To illustrate how to account for foreign currency transactions using the one-transaction perspective, assume that a U.S. firm, XYZ Corporation, imports merchandise from West Germany on December 1 for DM 1 million when the exchange rate is $.54. Payment in marks does not have to be made until January 31. Assume that the exchange rate moves to $.56 on December 31 and back to $.55 on January 31. The following entries would be made:

December 1	Purchases	540,000	
	Accounts payable		540,000
	DM1,000,000 × $.54		
December 31	Purchases	20,000	
	Accounts payable		20,000
	DM1,000,000 × ($.56 − $.54)		

The movement in the exchange rate causes the liability to increase to $560,000. The resulting difference, normally considered a foreign exchange loss, is treated as an adjustment of purchases.

---

[2]Financial Accounting Standards Board, *Statement of Financial Accounting Standards No. 8* (Stamford, Conn.: FASB, October 1975), paragraph 113.

January 31	Accounts payable	10,000	
	Purchases		10,000
	DM1,000,000 × ($.56 − $.55)		

	Accounts payable	550,000	
	Cash		550,000
	DM1,000,000 × $.55		

The movement of the exchange rate to $.55 means that XYZ Corporation must pay $550,000 in order to get the DM1,000,000 necessary to liquidate the obligation. The exchange gain is considered once again as an adjustment of purchases.

The result of the one-transaction perspective is that the impact of an exchange rate change is not recognized until the inventory is sold, and the gain or loss is considered a part of cost of goods sold instead of being treated as a separate financial item. Although this method is not accepted in the United States, it is common practice in a number of other countries.

Two-Transaction Perspective

The *two-transaction perspective* treats foreign currency receivables and payables as separate from the sale or purchase that gave rise to them. Thus the foreign exchange gain or loss that arises from translating the receivable or payable at the current exchange rate is not used to adjust the revenue of the export or the cost of the import.

Under the two-transaction perspective, the foreign exchange gain or loss could be handled one of two ways. One possibility is to defer the gain or loss until it is actually realized when the payable or receivable is liquidated. The other possibility is to take the gain or loss directly to the income statement in the period incurred. This is the approach required by Statement of Financial Accounting Standards No. 8 (FASB 8) of the Financial Accounting Standards Board (FASB) in the United States and is also the approach being considered in the possible revision to FASB 8, which was issued in exposure draft form in August 1980.

Table 5–1 illustrates the difference between these two approaches. Assume the same transaction and exchange rates given in the one-transaction approach.

The first column is consistent with the idea that gains or losses not deferred in the annual financial statements should not be deferred in the interim statements. Also, interim period recognition reflects the impact of the economic event (the exchange rate change) that occurred during the period.

The second column acknowledges that the event occurred but prefers

TABLE 5–1. Difference Between Recognition and Deferral of Gains and Losses

		IMMEDIATE RECOGNITION OF GAIN OR LOSS		DEFER GAIN OR LOSS UNTIL REALIZED	
Dec. 1	Purchases Accounts payable	540,000	540,000	Same	

Dec. 31	Loss
	  Accounts payable
		20,000	20,000	Deferred loss
				  Accounts payable
					20,000
					20,000

Jan. 31	Accounts payable
	  Gain
		10,000	10,000	Accounts payable
				  Deferred gain
					10,000
					10,000

	Accounts payable
	  Cash
		550,000	550,000	Loss (net)
				Accounts payable
				  Cash
				  Deferred loss (net)
					10,000
					550,000
					550,000
					10,000

to allow the gain and loss from the two periods to offset each other and be realized in the income statement only when the receivable or payable (as in the above example) is liquidated.

Table 5–2 summarizes the differences between the one- and two-transaction perspective.

As noted, the three situations reflect the exchange rate changes but in different places in the financial statements and in different periods. The difference in the final value of the purchase is $10,000, the same as the net foreign exchange loss. Therefore, the one-transaction perspective recognizes the foreign exchange loss when the inventory is sold in some future period in the form of higher cost of goods sold. If the asset is not inventory, the loss is recognized as a higher depreciation charge each period. In the second and third situations summarized above, the issue is simply one of the timing. The net loss is the same in both situations and is treated as a foreign exchange loss but in different periods.

TABLE 5–2. Difference Between One- and Two-Transaction Perspective

	ONE TRANSACTION	TWO TRANSACTIONS RECOGNIZE GAIN/LOSS	TWO TRANSACTIONS DEFER GAIN/LOSS
Final value of purchase	$550,000	$540,000	$540,000
Total cash disbursed	550,000	550,000	550,000
Gain (loss) on December 31	—	(20,000)	—
Gain (loss) on January 31	—	10,000	(10,000)

Having looked at all possibilities, it would be useful at this point to reiterate the position of FASB 8 as required in the United States.[3]

1. At the transaction date, all assets liabilities, revenues or expenses resulting from the transaction shall be translated into dollars at the exchange rate on that date.
2. At subsequent balance sheet dates, foreign currency receivables and payables resulting from the transaction will be translated at the exchange rate on that date.
3. At subsequent balance sheet dates, assets (such as merchandise purchased) carried at historical cost should be translated at the historical exchange rate; assets carried at market should be translated at the exchange rate in effect on the balance sheet date.
4. Foreign exchange gains and losses must be recognized in income in the period in which the rate changes.

As mentioned earlier, this position would remain essentially the same under possible changes being considered in FASB 8.

Forward Contracts

The transactions described so far relate to the principal activities of a firm, such as buying and selling merchandise. These transactions give rise to a real cash flow as foreign currency is converted into dollars and vice versa. As illustrated earlier, the final cash flow in dollars will be different from the initially anticipated flow if the exchange rate between the dollar and the foreign currency changes. In order to protect against possible losses on these flows, firms often become heavily involved in foreign exchange risk management, the subject of Chapter 7. One of the tools frequently used is the *forward contract.* In the previous chapter we considered the difference between forward and spot exchange rates and learned how to compute the premium or discount on a forward contract. Now let us consider how to account for a forward contract. There are several reasons for entering into forward contracts, but our focus is on two: to hedge (protect or cover) an identifiable foreign currency commitment and to hedge a receivable or payable denominated in a foreign currency and arising from a transaction.

The Cost of a Forward Contract

The costs of the contracts—excluding transactions costs that the foreign exchange trader may charge—require knowledge of four exchange rates: the spot rate on the date the contract is entered into (S_0), the forward

---

[3]Ibid., paragraph 7.

contract rate (F_o), the expected spot rate when the contract is to be completed (ES_c), and the actual spot rate when the contract is completed (S_c). These rates are necessary when trying to determine whether to enter into a contract and in evaluating the contract decision once it is completed. In addition to these rates, the spot rates in effect at each financial statement date are used to determine the gains or losses on the contracts.

In trying to decide whether to enter into a contract, the financial manager may look at two different costs, the premium or discount and the opportunity cost (ex ante). The *premium* or *discount* is simply $F_o - S_o$. If German marks are selling at $.5366 spot and $.5455 90 days forward, then the cost would be

$$\frac{\$.5455 - \$.5366}{\$.5366} \times \frac{12}{3} = 6.6\% \text{ premium}$$

on an annual basis. The financial manager might perceive this as fairly inexpensive insurance against a potential loss.

The *opportunity cost (ex ante)* is the difference between the forward rate and the expected spot rate $(F_o - ES_c)$. Although one would expect the forward rate to equal the expected spot rate, this may not be true in the short run, thus affecting the decision of the financial manager to enter into a contract.

Another type of opportunity cost may be used to evaluate a contract after completion. The *opportunity cost (ex post)* is the difference between the forward rate and the actual spot rate in effect when the contract is completed $(F_o - S_c)$. Here the manager can evaluate what would have happened if no contract had been entered into. The first two costs are relevant for deciding whether to enter into a contract, and the third cost is for postevaluation.

In a study of 156 multinational corporations, it was determined that 47.5 percent of them computed the cost of a forward contract as the difference between the forward and current spot rates $(F_o - S_c)$, 36.5 percent computed the cost as the difference between the forward rate and the spot rate on the day the contract matures, and 6.4 percent used both methods.[4]

In spite of these costs, the only costs to be accounted for in the financial statements are the premium or discount and the contract gains or losses that arise from subsequent changes in the spot rate. The treatment of these items depends on the purpose of the contracts. Table 5–3 summarizes the treatment.

Before going into the accounting treatment of forward contracts as hedges against foreign exchange losses, it should be pointed out that a

[4]Thomas G. Evans, William R. Folks Jr., and Michael Jilling, *The Impact of Statement of Financial Accounting Standards No. 8 on the Foreign Exchange Risk Management Practices of American Multinationals: An Economic Impact Study* (Stamford, Conn.: FASB, 1978), p. 179.

TABLE 5-3. Forward Contract Treatment

PURPOSE OF FORWARD CONTRACT	TREATMENT OF GAIN OR LOSS	TREATMENT OF DISCOUNT OR PREMIUM
Hedge of identifiable foreign currency commitment	Deferred	Deferred
Hedge of foreign currency receivable or payable	Recognized currently	Amortized to operations over life of contract

SOURCE: Adapted from Ernst & Ernst, *Accounting for Foreign Currency Translation*, Financial Reporting Developments, Retrieval No. 38409, February 1976, p. 13.

forward contract is an *executory contract,* in which two parties agree to do something in the future. For example, a bank agrees to deliver foreign currency to a corporation, and the corporation agrees to deliver dollars to the bank in the future. Because neither party has fulfilled the commitment when they enter into the arrangement, this forward contract is recorded as a memorandum entry that is not reflected in the financial statements. The correct way to record a forward contract as an executory contract is given in Appendix 1 to this chapter. The illustrations that follow assume that the forward contract *is* recorded in the financial statements. The eventual cash flows are the same under either approach, but the method given in the appendix is a little more complex. It should also be noted that the concepts discussed below and in the appendix are the same for FASB 8 as for the exposure draft on a new standard to replace FASB 8.

Hedging Commitments

When a U.S. firm takes on a commitment it enters into a contract to buy merchandise from a foreign supplier with delivery to be made some time in the future. At that point, no transaction is recorded on the books because neither party has fulfilled any part of the contract; delivery has not taken place and payment has not been made. This is an executory contract.

FASB allows the gain or loss from the contract and the premium or discount to be deferred until the transaction is recorded, and they are used to adjust the cost of the purchase or the revenue from the sale, if certain conditions are met.[5]

[5]The conditions are outlined in detail in paragraph 27 of FASB 8 and in *Statement of Financial Accounting Standards No. 20—Accounting for Forward Exchange Contracts* (Stamford, Conn.: FASB, 1978). Basically, the contract must extend from the commitment date to the transactions date

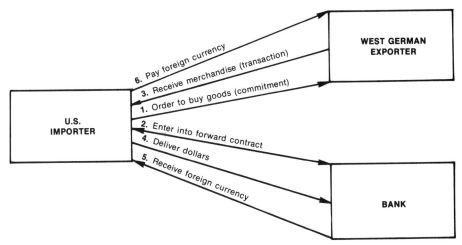

Figure 5. Financial flows in foreign exchange contracts

Before considering a numerical example we need to understand the actual goods and financial flow. Assume that a U.S. importer enters into a commitment to purchase merchandise from a West German supplier and is to pay the supplier in marks on the transaction date. In order to *hedge* against a potential loss, the importer enters into a forward contract with its bank to deliver dollars for marks on the transaction date. Figure 5 illustrates how the flow might take place in six sequential steps.

Since the commitment is an executory contract, it is not officially recorded on the books until it becomes a transaction. The same is true of the forward contract as described above.

Assume in the illustration provided in Figure 5 that the importer agrees to pay DM1 million for the merchandise on the transaction date. The relevant exchange rates, journal entries, and explanations are as follows:

$.3903 S_0 March 1

$.3923 F_0 rate for contract due on April 30

$.3860 S_c April 30 (the rate changed to $.3860 on March 21; the change is reflected when a statement is prepared on March 31)

These exchange rates represent actual spot and forward rates in existence at one time for the mark and the dollar. Normally, you would expect to see the future spot rate (S_c) moving from the initial spot rate in the same direction as the forward rate. For example, S_c might be $.3920 (greater

---

or longer, it must be in the same currency as the commitment and for no more than the amount of the commitment unless related tax effects are an issue (see FASB 20 for details), and the commitment must be firm and uncancelable.

than the initial spot but less than the forward rate) or $.3930 (greater than the forward rate). In times of uncertainty in the foreign exchange market, what you anticipate doesn't always happen. For that reason the rates of S_o = $.3903, F_o = $.3923, and S_c = $.3860 were chosen.

March 1	Contract receivable (DM)	390,300	
	Deferred premium expense	2,000	
	Contract payable ($)		392,300

This entry represents step 2 in Figure 5. The importer will pay the bank in dollars at the forward rate (DM1,000,000 × $.3923) and will receive DM1,000,000. The DM receivable is translated at the spot rate ($.3903) on the commitment date, consistent with the idea stated earlier that foreign currency receivables and payables are always translated at the spot rate on each balance sheet date. The premium expense (DM1,000,000 × [$.3923 − $.3903]) is deferred until the transaction date.

Note that the dollar portion of the contract is *always* recorded at the forward rate and the foreign currency portion at the spot rate.

| March 31 | Deferred loss | 4,300 | |
| | Contract receivable (DM) | | 4,300 |

The contract receivable drops to a dollar equivalent of $386,000 (DM1,000,000 × $.3860) when the exchange rate changes, yielding a loss of $4,300. The loss is deferred until the transaction date.

| April 30 | Purchases | 386,000 | |
| | Accounts payable | | 386,000 |

This recognizes that the commitment has actually become a transaction as title of the goods passes to the importer, who now must pay DM1,000,000 ($386,000 at the spot rate of $.3860). This is step 3 in Figure 5.

| | Contract payable ($) | 392,300 | |
| | Cash | | 392,300 |

This is step 4 in Figure 5.

| | Foreign currency | 386,000 | |
| | Contract receivable (DM) | | 386,000 |

This is step 5 in Figure 5 and represents the spot rate value of the DM1,000,000 received from the bank.

| | Accounts payable | 386,000 | |
| | Foreign currency | | 386,000 |

The latter is step 6 and reflects the liquidation of the payable to the exporter.

Purchases	6,300	
Deferred premium expense		2,000
Deferred loss		4,300

This final entry closes the deferred accounts to purchases, as allowed in FASB 8.

These entries show that the forward contract establishes the value of the merchandise purchased and the cash given up for the merchandise. If the importer had not entered into the contract, he would have had to pay only $386,000, or $6,300 less than the contract price of $392,300. The $6,300 additional cost is in one sense similar to an insurance premium in that it fixed the maximum price in dollars that the buyer would have to pay for the merchandise. This opportunity cost is reflected in the income statement as the higher cost of inventory flows through the cost of goods sold. Therefore, the premium expense and contract loss are treated as product costs rather than period costs.

Hedging Receivables or Payables

This situation differs from the previous one in that a transaction has taken place which gives rise to a foreign currency receivable or payable. The event could be the sale or purchase of goods or services, the payment or receipt of dividends, or the payment or receipt of principal and interest on financial obligations. FASB 8 requires that foreign currency receivables or payables be translated at the current exchange rate at each balance sheet date, with the resulting gains or losses reflected in current income. For forward contracts entered into as a hedge for foreign currency receivables or payables, FASB 8 requires that the premium or discount be amortized over the life of the contract and that gains or losses on the contract be taken directly to income.

As an illustration, assume that a company purchases merchandise on March 1 for DM1 million with payment to be made on April 30. The relevant exchange rate and journal entries are as follows, with the explanation following each entry:

$.3903	S_0	March 1
$.3923	F_0	rate for contract due on April 30
$.3860	S_c	April 30 (the rate changed to .3860 on March 21; the change is reflected when a statement is prepared on March 31)

| March 1 | Purchases | 390,300 | |
| | Accounts payable | | 390,300 |

To record the initial transaction at the spot rate.

	Contract receivable (DM)	390,300	
	Deferred premium expense	2,000	
	Contract payable ($)		392,300

To record the forward contract that comes due at the same time as the accounts payable; the DM received from the bank will be used to pay the German exporter.

| March 31 | Accounts payable | 4,300 | |
| | Foreign exchange gain | | 4,300 |

To reflect the impact of the rate change ($.3903 to $.3860) on the foreign currency payable.

| | Premium expense | 1,000 | |
| | Deferred premium expense | | 1,000 |

To reflect the amortization of half the premium expense.

| | Foreign exchange loss | 4,300 | |
| | Contract receivable | | 4,300 |

To reflect the impact of the rate change on the forward contract; note that the loss is taken directly to income rather than deferred and that it offsets the gain on the payable so that the only income statement effect is the premium expense.

April 30	Contract payable ($)	392,300	
	Cash		392,300
	Foreign currency	386,000	
	Contract receivable (DM)		386,000

As the contract comes due, the importer delivers dollars to the bank and receives marks in return. The next entry reflects the settlement of the obligation with the exporter.

	Accounts payable	386,000	
	Foreign currency		386,000
	Premium expense	1,000	
	Deferred premium expense		1,000

To reflect the amortization of the remaining premium amount.

From these entries we can see that a forward contract establishes the amount of cash given up for the merchandise ($392,300) but not the *value* of the merchandise ($390,300). The difference between these two ($2,000) is reflected as a premium expense in the income statement. The opportunity cost $(F_o - S_c)$ of $6,300, which is the difference between what the importer paid for the merchandise ($392,300) and what he would have paid if he had not entered into a forward contract ($386,000), is not reflected anywhere in the financial statements. Part of that amount, $2,000, goes directly to income, but the remaining $4,300, is canceled out. There is a definite cash flow impact of the forward contract which is only partially recognized in income. The procedure for recording the forward contract as an executory contract is outlined in Appendix 2 in this chapter.

Table 5–4 compares the final balance sheet and income statement effects of forward contracts for a hedge of an identifiable foreign currency commitment and a hedge of a payable denominated in a foreign currency. In the case of the commitment, the contract establishes a higher value of inventory and therefore a higher cost of goods sold and lower gross profit than for the hedge of accounts payable. In the latter case, the contract results in lower earnings because of the premium expense. The result is the same, but the timing and location of the effect will differ.

A third reason for entering into a forward contract is to hedge an exposed balance sheet position of a foreign branch or subsidiary. The reason for this exposure is treated in the next section, and the method of accounting for forward contracts to hedge this type of exposure is explained in Appendix 3 to this chapter.

The situations just described involve forward contracts as a protection against a possible foreign exchange loss. However, a forward contract could be entered into as a result of speculation. A good example of the use of forward contracts for speculation involves Bankhaus I.D. Herstatt AG, a large West German bank that went bankrupt in June 1974. Apparently, Herstatt traders sold marks forward in late 1973 or early 1974 under the assumption that the mark would weaken relative to the dollar. When the contracts matured, Herstatt would take its stronger dollars and buy back

TABLE 5–4. Summary of Forward Contract Effects

	VALUE OF ASSET	CASH PAID	TOTAL EARNINGS EFFECT
Hedge of a commitment	$392,300*	$392,300	0
Hedge of accounts payable	$390,300†	$392,300	($2,000)‡

*Forward rate $.3923 × DM1,000,000
†Initial spot rate $.3903 × DM1,000,000
‡Premium expense $(F_o - S_o)$ ($.3923 − $.3903) × DM1,000,000

marks at a profit. However, the mark strengthened vis-à-vis the dollar by the time the contracts matured, so Herstatt had to pay more marks for dollars to fulfill the contracts than it could earn by reselling the dollars for marks. It ended up losing a sum estimated at more than $200 million, approximately six times its capital and reserves.[6]

TRANSLATION OF FOREIGN CURRENCY FINANCIAL STATEMENTS

The previous section dealt with amounts payable or receivable in foreign currency where conversion would eventually take place. *Conversion* implies that one currency is changed into another currency, usually through the foreign currency section of the commercial bank that the firm deals with. *Translation* implies that one currency is expressed or restated in terms of another currency. For example if a U.S. firm has an accounts receivable of DM1 million when the exchange rate is $.3903/DM, the account would be *translated* into dollars and carried on the financial statements at $390,300. If the firm were to receive DM1 million and *convert* them into dollars, it would record cash of $390,300.

The situation becomes more complex when a firm's financial statements are expressed in one currency but need to be restated in another. Why should translation occur in the first place? Sometimes financial statements are restated or translated from one currency into another to assist the reader of the financial statements. For example, a U.S. investor desiring to invest in a British company may want to see the financial statements in dollars rather than pounds. The management of a multinational enterprise may wish to see the results of a foreign operation stated in the parent currency in order to facilitate cross-national comparisons. If a multinational enterprise is to prepare consolidated financial statements, it needs to express the statements of its different operations in a common currency before combination or consolidation can occur.

In the remainder of this chapter, two terms are used extensively: parent currency and local currency. The *parent currency* is the currency of the country where the parent company or headquarters is located. For example, the parent currency of U.S.-based multinationals is the dollar, and the dollar is used as the parent currency in all examples. The parent currency is sometimes referred to as the *reporting currency*, the currency in which the parent company reports its results to primary users of the financial statements. The *local currency* is the currency where the foreign operation is located, such as the French franc for a subsidiary or branch located in France.

The translation of financial statements involves dealing with two key

[6]*The Wall Street Journal*, 27 June 1978, p. 5.

issues: the exchange rates at which various accounts are translated from one currency into another (translation methods) and the subsequent treatment of gains and losses.

Translation Methods

In the process of translation, all local currency balance sheet and income statement accounts are restated in terms of the parent currency by multiplying the local currency amount times the appropriate exchange rate. The four ways to determine the appropriate translation procedure are: current-noncurrent, monetary-nonmonetary, temporal, and current rate. In addition, there are slight variations of the first two approaches. No single method is used universally, and all have been used in one or more countries around the world at one time. A brief description of each approach follows; the approaches required or recommended in several countries are considered more extensively in the next chapter.

Current-Noncurrent Method

Under the current-noncurrent method, as shown in Table 5–5, current assets and liabilities are translated at current exchange rates (the rates in effect at the balance sheet date) and noncurrent assets and liabilities and owners' equity are translated at historical exchange rates (the rates in effect when each transaction occurred). The current-noncurrent method was generally accepted in the United States from the early 1930s until FASB 8 and was the most widely used approach, even though a number of variations were being used by U.S. firms.

This method was based on the assumption that accounts should be grouped according to maturity. Anything due to mature in one year or less should be translated at the current rate, whereas everything else

TABLE 5–5. Exchange Rates Used to Translate Selected Assets and Liabilities

	CURRENT-NONCURRENT	MONETARY-NONMONETARY	CURRENT RATE	TEMPORAL
Cash, current receivables and payables	C	C	C	C
Inventory	C	H	C	C or H
Fixed assets	H	H	C	H
Long-term receivables and payables	H	C	C	C

NOTE: C = current exchange rate; H = historical exchange rate.

should be carried at the rate in effect when the transaction was recorded—the historical rate.

Monetary-Nonmonetary Method

The mood began to change in the 1950s as Hepworth[7] suggested that accounts be translated according to their nature rather than the date of maturity. He suggested that accounts be considered as either monetary or nonmonetary rather than current or noncurrent. Under this method, monetary assets and liabilities are translated at current rates, and non-monetary assets and liabilities and owners' equity are translated at historical rates. The monetary-nonmonetary method was endorsed by the National Association of Accountants in 1960. This approach is a radical departure from the current-noncurrent method in the areas of inventory, long-term receivables, and long-term payables.

The philosophy behind the monetary-nonmonetary approach is that monetary or financial assets and liabilities have similar attributes in that their value represents a fixed amount of money whose parent currency equivalent changes each time the exchange rate changes. Those accounts should therefore be translated at the current exchange rate. In the current-noncurrent method some current assets are monetary (cash) and some are nonmonetary (inventory), and yet all are translated at the current rate. The proponents of the monetary-nonmonetary method consider it more meaningful to translate assets and liabilities on the basis of attributes instead of time. In 1965 the Accounting Principles Board of the American Institute of CPAs partially acknowledged this in APB 6 by allowing long-term debt to be translated at current rates. Under current generally accepted accounting principles of historical cost accounting in the United States, the monetary-nonmonetary method provides essentially the same results as the temporal approach under FASB 8.

Variations

Before discussing the temporal and current rate methods, it would be well to look at some of the variations on the current-noncurrent and monetary-nonmonetary methods. Prior to October 1975 when FASB 8 required the temporal approach, the current-noncurrent method was recommended in the United States. However, the influence of the monetary-nonmonetary method caused many firms to design their own approach to translation.

As pointed out in Table 5–5, inventories and long-term receivables and payables are treated differently under the current-noncurrent and monetary-nonmonetary methods. Some firms, when surveyed about their translation methods, said they were using the current-noncurrent

---

[7]Samuel R. Hepworth, *Reporting Foreign Operations* (Ann Arbor: University of Michigan, 1956).

method with the exception that long-term receivables and payables were translated at current rates. Other firms said they were using the monetary-nonmonetary method with the exception that inventory was translated at current rates. These two variations yield fairly similar results. A third variation is to translate all assets and liabilities at current rates except for fixed assets, which are translated at historical rates.

Table 5–6 summarizes the balance sheet translation practices of a sample of firms with extensive international operations. According to the table, the current-noncurrent method was most popular during the period prior to FASB 8, but it is about the same as methods 2 and 4 combined. Those methods are essentially the same and are the most popular variation to the monetary-nonmonetary and current-noncurrent methods.

Temporal Method

The temporal method was originally proposed in Accounting Research Study 12 by the AICPA[8] and formally required in FASB 8. The purpose of this section is merely to explain how the method accomplishes translation; the evolution and problems of FASB 8 are treated in the next chapter.

According to the temporal principle, cash, receivables, and payables (both current and noncurrent) are translated at current rates. Other assets and liabilities may be translated at current or historical rates, depending on their characteristics. Assets and liabilities carried at past exchange prices are translated at historical rates. For example, a fixed asset carried at the local currency price at which it was purchased would be translated into the parent currency at the exchange rate in effect when the asset was purchased. Assets and liabilities carried at current purchase or sale exchange prices or future exchange prices would be translated at current rates. For example, inventory carried at market would be translated at the current rather than the historical rate.[9] Under historical cost accounting where nonmonetary assets are carried at past exchange prices and therefore translated at historical exchange rates, the temporal approach closely approximates the monetary-nonmonetary method.

The attractiveness of the temporal approach lies in its flexibility. If the United States were to change to current value accounting the temporal method would automatically translate all—even nonmonetary—assets and liabilities at current rates. Critics of the temporal approach point out that firms would intuitively do that anyway and that we don't have to adopt another term (temporal) to cover the situation. Table 5–7 more

[8]Leonard Lorensen, *Accounting Research Study No. 12: Reporting Foreign Operations of U.S. Companies in U.S. Dollars* (New York: AICPA, 1972).
[9]FASB 8, paragraphs 11 and 12.

TABLE 5–6. Translation Methods Used by U.S. Multinational Corporations Prior to the Issuance of FASB 8

TRANSLATION METHODS	RESPONDENT FIRMS	
	NUMBER	PERCENT
1. Current-noncurrent method	54	34.6
2. Current-noncurrent method with noncurrent receivables and payables translated at the current rate	10	6.4
3. Monetary-nonmonetary method	22	14.1
4. Monetary-nonmonetary method with inventories translated at the current rate	41	26.3
5. Temporal method	7	4.5
6. Current rate method	4	2.6
7. Other	3	1.9
8. No response	15	9.6
Total	156	100.0

SOURCE: Thomas G. Evans, William R. Folks, Jr., and Michael Jilling. *The Impact of Statement of Financial Accounting Standards No. 8 on the Foreign Exchange Risk Management Practices of American Multinationals: An Economic Impact Study*, 1978, p. 147. Copyright by the Financial Accounting Standards Board, High Ridge Park, Stamford, Conn. 06905, U.S.A. Reprinted with permission. Copies of the complete document are available from the FASB.

precisely lists the rates at which various accounts would be translated under the temporal method.

Current Rate

The current rate method is the easiest to apply since it requires that all assets and liabilities be translated at the current exchange rate.

Only net worth would not be translated at the current rate. This approach is easier to use than the others since a firm would not have to keep track of various historical exchange rates. The current rate approach results in the local perspective, which implies that ratios and relationships existing in a local currency will be maintained after translation to the parent currency. For example, the ratio of net income to sales in local currency is rarely the same in the parent currency under other translation approaches because a variety of current, historical, and average exchange rates is used to translate the income statement. Since all accounts would be translated at a single current exchange rate under the current rate method, the ratio of net income to sales would remain the same in the parent currency. The proponents of this approach, which includes most of

TABLE 5–7. Rates Used to Translate Assets and Liabilities Under the Temporal Method

	TRANSLATION RATES	
	CURRENT	HISTORICAL
Assets		
Cash on hand and demand and time deposits	X	
Marketable equity securities:		
Carried at cost		X
Carried at current market price	X	
Accounts and notes receivable and related unearned discount	X	
Allowance for doubtful accounts and notes receivable	X	
Inventories:		
Carried at cost		X
Carried at current replacement price or current selling price	X	
Carried at net realizable value	X	
Carried at contract price (produced under fixed price contracts)	X	
Prepaid insurance, advertising, and rent		X
Refundable deposits	X	
Advances to unconsolidated subsidiaries	X	
Property, plant, and equipment		X
Accumulated depreciation of property, plant, and equipment		X
Cash surrender value of life insurance	X	
Patents, trademarks, licenses, and formulas		X
Goodwill		X
Other intangible assets		X
Liabilities		
Accounts and notes payable and overdrafts	X	
Accrued expenses payable	X	
Accrued losses on firm purchase commitments	X	
Refundable deposits	X	
Deferred income		X
Bonds payable or other long-term debt	X	
Unamortized premium or discount on bonds or notes payable	X	
Convertible bonds payable	X	
Accrued pension obligations	X	
Obligations under warranties	X	

SOURCE: Financial Accounting Standards Board, "Accounting for the Translation of Foreign Currency Transactions and Foreign Currency Financial Statements," *Statement of Financial Accounting Standards No. 8,* October 1975, p. 20. Copyright by the Financial Accounting Standards Board, High Ridge Park, Stamford, Conn. 06905, U.S.A. Reprinted with permission. Copies of the complete document are available from the FASB.

Europe, argue that the local perspective allows us to see in dollars the same relationships that exist in the local currency where revenues are earned and expenses paid. They maintain that it is ridiculous to treat transactions as if they occurred in dollars when in fact they did not.

The simple example in Table 5–8 illustrates the balance sheet effect of financial statement translation. Note the difference in net worth depending upon the chosen approach. The variation in the illustration is the monetary-nonmonetary method, with inventory translated at the current rate.

Translation of Income Statement

When translation methods were discussed, special attention was placed on balance sheet accounts. Translating the income statement involves a variety of problems. Except for the current rate method, which recommends that revenue and expense accounts be translated at current rates, all other methods have fairly consistently assumed that revenue and expense accounts should be translated at historical rates. Given the large volume of daily transactions flowing through the income statement, most firms try to approximate historical rates through the use of averages. Table 5–9 illustrates the pre-FASB 8 translation practices of firms covered in *Accounting Trends and Techniques*. As noted in the table, most firms translate all but depreciation at average rates. Depreciation expense is translated at the actual historical rate.

According to the temporal principle, expenses related to assets translated at historical rates, such as inventory and fixed assets, should also be translated at historical rates. In the case of cost of goods sold, beginning and ending inventory are usually translated at the average rates of the

TABLE 5–8. Balance Sheet Effect of Translation

	LOCAL CURRENCY	CURRENT-NON-CURRENT	MONETARY-NON-MONETARY	VARIATION	CURRENT RATE
Cash	LC100	$ 100*	$ 100*	$ 100*	$100*
Inventory	200	200*	400†	200*	200*
Fixed assets	600	1,200†	1,200†	1,200†	600*
	LC900	$1,500	$1,700	$1,500	$900
Current liabilities	LC250	250*	250*	250*	250*
Long-term debt	150	300†	150*	150*	150*
Net worth	500	900	1,300	1,100	500
	LC900	$1,500	$1,700	$1,500	$900

NOTE: Net worth is a plug figure.
*Translated at the current rate of 1LC = $1.
†Translated at the historical rate of 1LC = $2.

TABLE 5–9. Translation of Profit and Loss Accounts

	NUMBER	PERCENT
All accounts except depreciation at average rates	280	80.5
All accounts at average rates	38	10.9
Other methods	30	8.6
	348	100.0

SOURCE: *Accounting Trends and Techniques.* Copyright © 1975 by the American Institute of Certified Public Accountants, Inc.

period in which the inventory was accumulated, and purchases are translated at the average rates in existence when inventory was purchased. Depreciation would be translated at historical rates. Other revenues and expenses would be translated at average rates, weighted for sales volume. That means that greater weight is given to rates in effect when sales are higher. Usually, a firm translates the income statement monthly and simply adds together the translated statements each month.

It is interesting to note that the exposure draft of the new standard to replace FASB 8 adopts the current rate approach. However, it recommends that all revenues and expenses, including those related to fixed assets, be translated at a weighted-average exchange rate for the period, rather than at the current rate as one would expect.

Owners' Equity

The owners' equity section of the balance sheet usually contains capital stock and retained earnings. Capital stock is translated at the rate in effect when the stock was issued, but retained earnings is more complex. The beginning retained earnings figure is simply the ending balance of the previous period, so the parent currency amount from that period is used. Net income (or loss) is translated as described above, and dividends are translated at the rate in effect when the dividends are declared. The ending retained earnings balance, which is simply the beginning balance plus net income minus dividends in local currency, is a plug figure in the parent currency. That is because the balance sheet and income statement accounts are all translated at different exchange rates. The difference between the plug figure and what the ending balance would be by taking the beginning balance plus net income minus dividends in the parent currency is the foreign exchange gain or loss. This concept will make more sense in the example presented later in the chapter.

Foreign Exchange Gains and Losses

As mentioned above, the foreign exchange gain or loss that a firm experiences as a result of translating financial statements from local to parent currency is a plug figure used to derive the ending retained earnings balance so that translated assets equal liabilities and owners' equity. With reference to specific accounts, the gain or loss represents a gain or loss in command over the parent currency. For example, assume that a U.S. firm has a subsidiary in Mexico and that the subsidiary has a cash balance of 500,000 pesos when the exchange rate is peso 1 = $.04. The cash would be worth $20,000. If the exchange rate moved to peso 1 = $.044, the cash would be worth $22,000. Therefore, the parent would recognize a gain of $2,000 because the peso command over dollars increased from $20,000 to $22,000. The opposite would have occurred if the account had been notes payable instead of cash. The rate change would have yielded a loss since the dollar value of the liability would have increased to $22,000.

Gains or losses result from realized transactions, unrealized future transactions, and the translation of foreign currency balance sheets.[10] The first case might occur when a foreign currency receivable is collected and the cash converted into dollars at a rate different from that at which the receivable was recorded on the books.

The second situation arises when the foreign currency receivable is carried on the books but has not yet been collected and converted into cash. At each balance sheet date, the receivable must be translated into dollars at the new balance sheet rate. The conversion will eventually take place, so the receivable is part of an unrealized future transaction.

The final example involves translation of financial statements where no transaction (or conversion) is expected to take place between the local (foreign as stated above) and parent currencies.

Table 5–10 illustrates several options for dealing with gains and losses. The first approach requires the gain or loss to be taken directly to the income statement. Prior to FASB 8, many U.S. firms treated the gain or loss as an extraordinary item. FASB 8 requires that the gain or loss be treated as an ordinary item in the period in which it occurs—interim as well as year-end.

The second approach in Table 5–10 was widely used by U.S. firms in many ways. Some firms used the approach contained in Chapter 12 of Accounting Research Bulletin 43 of the AICPA by deferring all unrealized gains and recognizing unrealized losses and realized gains and losses. Other firms deferred all gains and losses. The deferrals were put into a reserve account, which had the effect of eliminating the earnings impact of foreign exchange gains and losses. The third approach is another attempt to eliminate the earnings impact by treating gains and losses as adjustments of stockholders' equity.

The fourth and fifth approaches in Table 5–10 involve a deferral of gains and losses and refer to special ways of dealing primarily with losses

---

[10]John K. Shank and Gary S. Shamis, "Reporting Foreign Currency Adjustments: A Disclosure Perspective," *The Journal of Accountancy*, April 1979, pp. 59–65.

TABLE 5–10. Translation Gain and Loss Treatment Used by U.S. Multinational Corporations Prior to the Issuance of FASB 8

	RESPONDENT FIRMS	
GAIN AND LOSS TREATMENT	NUMBER	PERCENT
1. Recognize in income currently	80	51.3
2. Defer based on certain criteria	58	37.2
3. Adjust stockholders' equity	1	0.6
4. Amortize over life of long-term debt	2	1.3
5. Adjust cost of nonmonetary assets or amortize over life of such assets	0	0.0
6. Other	7	4.5
7. No response	8	5.1
Total	156	100.0

SOURCE: Thomas G. Evans, William R. Folks, Jr., and Michael Jilling. *The Impact of Statement of Financial Standards No. 8 on the Foreign Exchange Risk Management Practices of American Multinationals: An Economic Impact Study,* Stamford, Conn.: *Practices of American Multinationals: An Economic Impact Study,* 1978, p. 148. Copyright by the Financial Accounting Standards Board, High Ridge Road, Stamford, Conn. 06905, U.S.A. Reprinted by permission. Copies of the complete document are available from FASB.

arising from the translation of long-term debt. In the fourth approach, the feeling is that foreign currency debt was entered into because of favorable interest rate differentials. Therefore, a foreign exchange loss resulting from translation should be viewed as an adjustment of interest expense and therefore be written off over the life of the debt. The fifth approach associates the cost of the debt with the acquisition of an asset which is translated at the historical rate. As the exchange rate changes, only the debt changes in value. The resulting gain or loss would be considered an adjustment of the asset purchased and amortized over the life of the asset.

Note from Table 5–10 that nearly half the U.S. firms surveyed had to alter their treatment of foreign exchange gains and losses to conform with FASB 8. The ramifications of this are discussed in more detail later.

Appropriate Exchange Rate

Irrespective of which translation method a firm decides to use, it must choose an appropriate exchange rate. At a given point in time, there may be several possible rates or multiple rates. An official rate may exist for certain types of transactions, whereas a free rate may be used for most financial transactions. In 1978 the Central Bank of Argentina established an official rate of $.0071/peso for *swap operations* (government-sponsored forward contracts), whereas the free market rate applying to dividends was $.00098/peso. Other exchange rates apply for other types of transactions. The government is able to control the multiple rate system by requiring a license to trade local for foreign currency. In Belgium, dividends can be remitted at an official rate if proper documentation is provided. Without such documentation, dividends would have to be remitted at the less favorable free market rate.

In many countries where the foreign exchange market is tightly controlled, a *black market* may exist where foreign currency can be bought and sold at a sizable premium. Many people look at the black market rate as reflecting what the exchange rate should be. Others feel that exchange rates are artificial and not appropriate for restating financial statements from one currency into another. They recommend a *purchasing power parity* that reflects the relationships among internal prices rather than focusing on a value that equates the supply and demand of currencies.

FASB 8 came out strongly in favor of using the dividend remittance rate for translating foreign currency financial statements. The rationale for the dividend rate is as follows:

> Use of that rate expresses results of operations in dollars in a more meaningful way than any other rate because the earnings can be converted into dollars only at that rate. Further, in translating an asset carried at a current price, the dividend rate measures the dollar amount that might be realized from sale of the asset and remittance of the proceeds and thereby establishes the asset's value in dollars. In translating an asset carried at cost, the dividend rate at the time the asset was acquired measures the sacrifice made by the parent in foregoing a remission of the local-currency cost of the asset and thus establishes the asset's dollar cost.[11]

The rationale, which adopts a liquidation mentality, is highly suspect. However, each exchange rate mentioned has both strengths and weaknesses.

In the case of foreign currency transactions, it makes sense to use the exchange rate at which obligations are to be settled. In a multiple rate system, for example, an importer would want to record its foreign currency payables at the rate at which the government requires such obligations to be settled.

The Translation Process Illustrated

The example in Tables 5–11 and 5–12 shows how the financial statements would be translated according to the temporal principle and the current rate method, the two methods most widely faced by multinational

[11]FASB 8, paragraph 227.

TABLE 5-11. Balance Sheet as of December 31, 1979

	LOCAL CURRENCY	TEMPORAL		CURRENT RATE	
		EXCHANGE RATE	U.S. DOLLARS	EXCHANGE RATE	U.S. DOLLARS
Assets					
Cash and current receivables	200,000	$2.10*	$ 420,000	2.10	$ 420,000
Inventory	250,000	2.08†	520,000	2.10	525,000
Fixed assets	800,000	1.97‡	1,576,000	2.10	1,680,000
Accumulated depreciation	(200,000)	1.97	(394,000)	2.10	(420,000)
Total	1,050,000		$2,122,000		$2,205,000
Liabilities and net worth					
Accounts payable	125,000	2.10	$ 262,500	2.10	$ 262,500
Notes payable—current	100,000	2.10	210,000	2.10	210,000
Bonds payable	200,000	2.10	420,000	2.10	420,000
Capital stock	450,000	1.95§	877,500	1.95	877,500
Retained earnings	175,000	—	352,000	—	435,000
Total	1,050,000		$2,122,000		$2,205,000

*The current or balance sheet rate on December 31, 1979.
†The average rate during the period in which inventory was accumulated.
‡The historical rate at which the fixed assets were purchased.
§The rate at which capital stock was issued.

TABLE 5-12. Statement of Income and Retained Earnings

	LOCAL CURRENCY	TEMPORAL		CURRENT RATE	
		EXCHANGE RATE	U.S. DOLLARS	EXCHANGE RATE	U.S. DOLLARS
Sales	1,400,000	$2.07**	$2,898,000	2.07	$2,898,000
Cost of goods sold					
Beginning inventory	275,000	2.03††	558,250	2.04§§	561,000
Purchases	450,000	2.06†‡	927,000	2.07	931,500
	725,000		1,485,250		1,492,500
Ending inventory	250,000	2.08	520,000	2.10	525,000
Cost of materials	475,000	2.07	965,250	2.07	967,500
Labor	400,000		828,000		828,000
Depreciation	90,000	1.97	177,300	2.07	186,300
Total cost of goods sold	965,000		1,970,550		1,981,800
Selling & administrative expenses	150,000	2.07	310,500	2.07	310,500
Foreign exchange loss (gain)	—		20,000		(74,250)
	1,115,000		2,301,050		2,218,050
Earnings before taxes	285,000		596,950		679,950
Taxes on income	170,000	2.07	351,900	2.07	351,900
Earnings after tax	115,000		245,050		328,050
Beginning retained earnings	150,000		295,950		295,950
Net earnings	115,000		245,050		328,050
	265,000		541,000		624,000
Less dividends	90,000	2.10	189,000	2.10	189,000
Ending retained earnings	175,000		$ 352,000		$ 435,000

NOTE: Assume that taxes were paid throughout the year and that dividends were declared at the end of the year. Also, the beginning retained earnings balance came from the previous year's statement.
**The average rate during the year. ††The average rate during which beginning inventory was accumulated. §§The rate at the beginning of the year.
†‡The average rate during which inventory purchases were made.

enterprises. The current rate method in Tables 11 and 12, which translates assets and liabilities at the current rate and revenues and expenses at the average rate, is the one proposed by FASB in their exposure draft. The foreign exchange loss produced by the temporal principle becomes a foreign exchange gain under the current rate method. They are included in net income in the example but could appear elsewhere in the financial statements, as is pointed out in the next chapter.

The foreign exchange loss obviously does not exist in the local currency, and there is no local income tax effect. Without the exchange loss, the after-tax earnings of the subsidiary would have been $265,050 under the temporal method. However, net earnings as derived from the statement of retained earnings was $245,050, as follows:

$352,000 ending balance (plug figure from balance sheet)
+189,000 dividends
_____
$541,000
−295,950 beginning balance (carried forward from previous year)
_____
$245,050

The difference between $245,050 and $265,050 is the foreign exchange loss which is recognized in the translated income statement.

CONCLUSIONS

Are the gnomes of Zurich really just a bunch of accountants? This hotly debated question probably will not soon be cleared up. As we have seen, different accounting conventions yield different results in accounting for foreign currency transactions and translating foreign currency financial statements. A variety of practices yields differences in the timing and location of foreign exchange gains and losses.

In the next chapter we extend the mechanics of this chapter into practices in a variety of countries and the controversies surrounding these practices. We have as yet made no attempt to judge which method is the more correct one for translating financial statements. Given the extensive discussion over the years in the United States and around the world, it is presumptuous to assume that we have all the answers. However, maybe we can ask some of the questions and try to come up with at least some of the answers.

STUDY QUESTIONS

Assume the following exchange rates for questions 1 and 2:

spot	January 1	$2.25/pound (£)
spot	January 31	$2.20/£
spot	February 15	$2.22/£

5–1. On January 1, XYZ Corporation purchased machinery from a British manufacturer for £500,000. XYZ closed its books at the end of the month, and on February 15 it paid the manufacturer for the machinery.
   a. What entries would you make on January 1, January 31, and February 15 under the one-transaction perspective?
   b. What entries would you make on the same dates under the two-transactions perspective where gains and losses are deferred?
   c. What entries would you make where gains and losses are recognized immediately in income?
   d. What are the differences in the timing and location of the foreign exchange gains and losses under the above approaches?

5–2. On January 1, XYZ Corporation sold machinery to a British importer for £500,000. XYZ closed its books at the end of the month, and on February 15 it received payment.
   a. What entries would you make on January 1, January 31, and February 15 under the one-transaction perspective?
   b. What entries would you make on the same dates under the two-transactions perspective where gains and losses are deferred?
   c. What entries would you make where gains and losses are recognized immediately in income?
   d. What are the differences in the timing and location of the foreign exchange gains and losses under the above approaches?

Assume the following exchange rates for questions 3 and 4:

spot	November 1	$.56/deutsche mark (DM)
spot	November 30	$.58/DM
spot	December 15	$.60/DM

5–3. On November 1, ABC Corporation sold machinery to a German importer for DM1,000,000. ABC closed its books on November 30 and received payment for the sale on December 15.
   a. What entries would you make on November 1, November 30, and December 15 under the one-transaction perspective?
   b. What entries would you make on the same dates under the two-transactions perspective where gains and losses are deferred?

    c.   What entries would you make where gains and losses are recognized immediately in income?

    d.   What are the differences in the timing and location of the foreign exchange gains and losses under the above approaches?

5–4. On November 1, ABC Corporation bought machinery from a German manufacturer for DM1,000,000. ABC closed its books on November 30 and paid the manufacturer on December 15. Answer parts a–d in question 3 given the assumptions listed above.

Assume the following exchange rates for questions 5–7:

spot	January 1	$.6076/Swiss franc (SF)
180-day forward	January 1	$.6323/SF
spot	March 31	$.6500/SF
spot	June 30	$.6300/SF

5–5. On January 1 a U.S. manufacturer enters into a commitment to manufacture goods for a Swiss importer for SF1,000 with delivery to be made on June 30 and payment to be received on that day. The manufacturer closes its books at the end of the quarter (March 31) only.

    a.   If the manufacturer hedges the commitment, what journal entries would be made on January 1, March 31, and June 30?

    b.   Compare the net revenue of the hedged versus unhedged commitment.

5–6. On January 1 a U.S. importer enters into a commitment to purchase goods from a Swiss chocolate maker for SF1,000 with delivery to be made on June 30 and payment to be made on that day. The importer closes its books at the end of the quarter (March 31) only.

    a.   Same as 5a.

    b.   Same as 5b.

5–7. On January 1 a company expects the June 30 spot rate to be $.6200/SF. In addition to the exchange rates listed above, assume that the 90-day forward rate on March 31 is $.6600/SF.

    a.   Given the forward rate on January 1 and the company's expectations of the future spot rate when the contract matures, would the company speculate by buying or selling U.S. dollars in the forward market? Why?

    b.   What journal entries would you make on January 1, March 31, and June 30?

    c.   What would have been the June 30 journal entries and net cash gain if the company's prediction had been correct?

Assume the following exchange rates for questions 8–10:

spot	March 1	$2.20/£
60-day forward	March 1	$2.15/£
spot	March 31	$2.14/£
spot	April 30	$2.17/£

5–8. On March 1, Athletic Imports buys £1,000 of athletic equipment from a British exporter with payment to be made on April 30. At the same time, AI enters into a forward contract to deliver dollars for pounds on April 30.

    a. What entries would be made on March 1, March 31, and April 30?

    b. Would AI have been better off not entering into the forward contract? Why?

5–9. On March 1, Athletic Exports sells athletic equipment to a British importer for £5,000 with payment to be received on April 30. At the same time, AE enters into a forward contract to deliver pounds for dollars on April 30.

    a. What entries would be made on March 1, March 31, and April 30?

    b. Would AE have been better off not entering into the forward contract? Why?

5–10. Assume that XYZ Corporation had a British subsidiary with an exposed liability position of £100,000 and that XYZ balances that position by entering into a contract to deliver dollars for pounds on April 30.

    a. What entries would be made on March 1 and April 30? (Assume that no statements are prepared on March 31.)

    b. What is the gain or loss of cash on the hedge?

5–11. Compare and contrast the timing and location of gains and losses resulting from forward contracts entered into for commitments versus transactions.

5–12. What is the major drawback on entering into a forward contract to hedge an exposed balance sheet position?

5–13. What are the ways to determine the cost of a forward contract? Which of the ways can be most helpful in deciding whether to enter into a contract, and which can be most helpful in evaluating the usefulness of the contract after it is completed?

5–14. What is the difference between translation and conversion?

5–15. What are the major differences among the various translation methods?

5–16. What are some of the reasons for and against the various treatments of translation gains and losses listed in Table 5–10?

5–17. Translate the French franc balance sheet to U.S. dollars at the spot rate of $.2435.

Cash	FF	2,000
Accounts receivable		2,000
Inventory		4,000
Net fixed assets		8,000
	FF	16,000

Accounts payable	FF	3,000
Notes payable		4,000
Owner's equity		9,000
	FF	16,000

Assume that $.2435 is the historical rate and that the rate changes to $.2200. Now translate the balance sheet using the current-noncurrent, monetary-nonmonetary, temporal, and all-current methods. What is the foreign currency net exposure and dollar translation gain or loss under each method?

5–18. On December 31, 1980, the trial balance of Bossa Nova S.A., a Latin music company, is as follows (in pesos):

Cash	40,000
Accounts receivable	100,000
Fixed assets (net)	200,000
Depreciation expense	40,000
Other expenses	80,000
	460,000

Accounts payable	75,000
Long-term debt	90,000
Capital stock	100,000
Retained earnings, January 1	45,000
Revenue	150,000
	460,000

The capital stock was issued five years ago to buy fixed assets; the exchange rate at that time was $1/peso. Revenue and other expenses were incurred evenly throughout the year. The other relevant exchange rates for the year were:

January 1	$1.15/peso
Average for the year	$1.20/peso
December 31	$1.35/peso

The balance in retained earnings at the end of the previous year was $35,000.

a. Prepare a trial balance for Bossa Nova S.A. under the temporal method.

b. Prepare a balance sheet for Bossa Nova as of December 31.

c. Prepare an income statement for Bossa Nova for the year.

5-19. Using the information given in question 18 prepare a trial balance, balance sheet, and income statement according to the current rate method.

APPENDIX 1

TREATMENT OF A FORWARD CONTRACT TO HEDGE A COMMITMENT AS AN EXECUTORY CONTRACT

Earlier in the chapter, two examples were given on how to account for forward contracts. The example below illustrates how a forward contract should be recorded properly as an executory contract in the case of a hedge of an identifiable foreign currency commitment.

March 1	Contract receivable	390,300	
	Premium expense	2,000	
	Contract payable		392,300
	Memo Entry		

The remaining entries are reflected in the books.

Deferred premium expense	2,000	
Deferred charge		2,000

March 31	Deferred loss	4,300	
	Deferred charge		4,300

April 30	Purchases	386,000	
	Deferred charge	6,300	
	Cash		392,300

To reflect the purchases at the spot rate and the cash paid for the purchases at the forward rate and to close out the deferred charge account.

Purchases	6,300	
Deferred premium expense		2,000
Deferred loss		4,300

The premium expense and loss on the contract are an adjustment of the cost of the asset purchased rather than considered as period adjustments.

In the final analysis, the value of the purchases and the cash given up remains the same whether one treats the forward contract as a memo entry or takes it directly into the accounts.

APPENDIX 2

TREATMENT OF A FORWARD CONTRACT TO HEDGE A PAYABLE AS AN EXECUTORY CONTRACT

The correct entries for treating the forward contract as a hedge for a foreign currency accounts payable are as follows:

March 1	Purchases	390,300	
	Accounts payable		390,300
	Contract receivable	390,300	
	Premium expense	2,000	
	Contract payable		392,300
	Memo Entry		
March 31	Accounts payable	4,300	
	Foreign exchange gain		4,300
	Loss on contract	4,300	
	Deferred charge		4,300
	Premium expense	1,000	
	Deferred charge		1,000
April 30	Premium expense	1,000	
	Deferred charge		1,000
	Deferred charge	6,300	
	Accounts payable	386,000	
	Cash		392,300

APPENDIX 3

ACCOUNTING TREATMENT OF A FORWARD CONTRACT TO HEDGE AN EXPOSED BALANCE SHEET

To show how to account for a forward contract used to hedge an exposed foreign currency financial statement, assume that a firm has a German subsidiary with a net exposed liability position of DM1 million. Therefore the firm enters into a forward contract to buy marks (thus offsetting the mark liability position with a mark asset in the form of a contract receivable). The relevant exchange rates and entries are:

$.3903	current spot rate on March 1
.3923	forward rate on March 31
.3860	actual future spot rate when contract comes due on March 31

March 1	Contract receivable (DM)	390,300	
	Premium expense	2,000	
	Contract payable ($)		392,300
March 31	Loss on contract	4,300	
	Contract receivable		4,300

DM1,000,000 (.3903 − .3860); at the same time, the exposed liability position in Germany would yield a gain of $4,300.

Contract payable	392,300	
Cash		392,300

To pay the bank for the contract.

Foreign currency	386,000	
Contract receivable		386,000

Receipt of foreign currency for the bank in fulfillment of the bank's part of the contract.

Cash	386,000	
Foreign currency		386,000

The sale of marks for dollars in the spot market.

As a result of the contract, the gain on the exposed position is offset by the loss on the contract so that the only income statement effect is the premium expense. The cash flow impact is a loss of $6,300 ($392,300 − $386,000), but only $2,000 (the premium expense) shows up in the income statement. This is why many financial managers feel that the cost of using a forward contract to hedge a potential foreign exchange loss is pretty high.

If the exposure draft to replace FASB 8 is adopted, one significant change would occur in the above example. Gains and losses on translating a foreign currency financial statement would generally not be taken to the income statement but would be included in a separate section in stockholders' equity. Therefore, any gains or losses from forward contracts entered into to hedge an exposed foreign currency financial statement, as in the example above, would also go to the stockholders' equity account rather than the income statement.

APPENDIX 4

ACCOUNTING TREATMENT OF A SPECULATIVE FORWARD CONTRACT

In order to account for a speculative contract, assume the following exchange rates for deutsche marks for the life of the contract:

Date	Spot Rate	90-Day Forward Rate	60-Day Forward Rate	30-Day Forward Rate
March 1	$.3903	$.3923		
March 31	.3937		$.3950	
April 30	.3944			$.3952
May 29	.3860			

According to FASB 8, a contract for speculative purposes requires current period recognition of gains or losses, which are computed as the amount of the contract times the difference between the forward rate available for the remaining maturity of the contract and the forward rate used to measure the gain or loss for an earlier period. On March 1, the speculator may decide that the DM is going to strengthen above the forward rate of $.3923, so he enters into a contract to buy DM1 million at the lower contract rate with the anticipation that he can sell the marks at the anticipated higher spot rate.

Journal entries for a speculative contract are as follows:

March 1	Contract receivable (DM)	390,300	
	Premium expenses	2,000	
	Contract payable ($)		392,300

| March 31 | Contract receivable | 3,400 | |
| | Gain on contract | | 3,400 |

To show the value of the receivable at the new spot rate of $.3937.
($.3903 − $.3937) × DM1,000,000

| | Loss on contract | 2,700 | |
| | Contract payable | | 2,700 |

To show the value of the contract in dollars at the new forward rate for contracts maturing on May 29.
($.3923 − $.3950) × DM1,000,000

| April 30 | Contract receivable | 700 | |
| | Gain on contract | | 700 |

New spot rate of $.3944.
($.3937 − $.3944) × DM1,000,000

| | Loss on contract | 200 | |
| | Contract payable | | 200 |

New forward rate of $.3952.
($.3950 − $.3952) × DM1,000,000

May 29	Contract payable	395,200	
	Cash		392,300
	Gain on contract		2,900

Even though the contract is recorded at $.3952 on the books, the firm still must pay the bank at the original contract rate of $.3923.

	Foreign currency	386,000	
	Loss on contract	8,400	
	Contract receivable		394,400

The loss reflects the write-down of the receivable to the new spot rate of $.3860.

| | Cash | 386,000 | |
| | Foreign currency | | 386,000 |

The final entry shows the conversion in the spot market of the marks received from the bank to fulfill the contract.

The speculative contract led to a net loss over the period of $6,300 ($2,000 premium expense and $4,300 as the net loss from restating the contract receivable at succeeding spot rates and the contract payable at succeeding forward rates). As noted earlier, the foreign currency portion of the contract is always stated at the spot rate, while the dollar portion of the contract is stated at the forward rate. Note that the loss is the same as the opportunity cost $(F_0 − S_c)$ or ($.3923 − $.3860) × DM1,000,000 = $6,300.

6

Translation of Financial Statements: Contemporary Issues

The mechanics of translating foreign currency financial statements are not inordinately difficult to master, as noted in Chapter 5. However, a number of difficult and possibly insoluble problems have arisen on the issue of translation, not only in the United States but worldwide. Most of the issues revolve around two fundamental questions: how do we translate foreign currency financial statements, and how do we dispose of the foreign exchange adjustments (normally referred to as gains or losses)? An investigation of specific practices in several countries should help us understand these issues a little better.

GENERAL PRINCIPLES WORLDWIDE

Price Waterhouse International published in 1979 a survey of accounting principles and reporting practices covering 64 countries. Principles and practices were evaluated for the countries and classified as: required (by pronouncement of a professional accountancy body or by law), insisted upon (lack of adherence would normally be expected to give rise to a qualified audit opinion even though there is no formal professional or statutory requirement), predominant practice, minority practice, rarely or not found, not accepted (converse of insisted upon), and not permitted (converse of required). A list of the countries included in the survey is shown in Table 6–1. This survey includes responses to 14 questions dealing with foreign currency transactions and the translation of financial statements and provides a good summary of principles and practices worldwide.

**TABLE 6–1. Countries Included in *International Survey of Accounting Princi-
ples and Reporting Practices***

Argentina	Honduras	Pakistan
Australia	Hong Kong	Panama
Austria	India	Paraguay
Bahamas	Iran	Peru
Belgium	Ireland	Philippines
Bermuda	Italy	Portugal
Bolivia	Ivory Coast	Senegal
Botswana	Jamaica	Singapore
Brazil	Japan	South Africa
Canada	Jersey, Channel Islands	Spain
Chile	Kenya	Sweden
Colombia	Korea	Switzerland
Costa Rica	Malawi	Taiwan
Denmark	Malaysia	Trinidad and Tobago
Dominican Republic	Mexico	United Kingdom
Ecuador	Morocco	United States
El Salvador	Netherlands	Uruguay
Fiji	New Zealand	Venezuela
France	Nicaragua	Zaire
Germany	Nigeria	Zambia
Greece	Norway	Zimbabwe Rhodesia
Guatemala		

Source: Price Waterhouse International, 1979.

In the beginning of Chapter 5 the basic concepts of accounting for
foreign currency transactions were discussed. According to the Price
Waterhouse survey, almost all countries initially record assets,
liabilities, revenues, and expenses arising from transactions at the exchange rate in effect on the transaction date. At subsequent balance
sheet dates it is required, insisted upon, or the predominant practice to
translate amounts receivable or payable in a foreign currency at the
current rate in most of the countries in the survey. A few notable
exceptions to this are Germany, Italy, Japan, Panama, Paraguay, Portugal, and Spain. In these countries, presumably, amounts are maintained at the original transaction rate. That practice is actually required
in Japan, whereas it tends to be the majority practice in the other
countries mentioned.

The treatment of exchange gains and losses on unsettled transactions
is not as clear-cut. Under the two-transactions perspective explained in
Chapter 5, a foreign currency receivable or payable would normally be
translated at each new balance sheet rate, giving rise to a possible gain
or loss if the rate were to change between balance sheet dates. It is
required or insisted upon in 8 of the 64 countries to take the exchange
gain directly to income. Canada and the United States (because of FASB
8) are the only major industrial countries that require this approach.

However, this is the predominant practice in 32 other countries. That leaves a sizable number of countries—24—that defer the gains until the transactions are actually settled. Such important industrial countries as Denmark, Germany, Italy, Japan, New Zealand, Norway, Portugal, Spain, and Sweden use this approach. All but ten of the 64 countries in the survey take losses directly to income, which is indicative of the principle of conservatism where unrealized gains are often deferred but unrealized losses are recognized. Note that taking losses directly to income is required in Japan and Germany, whereas gains are not permitted to be taken to income in Japan and are taken to income by a minority of firms in Germany.

As explained in Chapter 5, several translation methods have been used at one time or another in different countries. These methods can be broadly separated into two groups: (1) translation of all accounts at the current rate and (2) translation of accounts at a mixture of current and historical rates. The latter approach encompasses the current-noncurrent, monetary-nonmonetary, temporal, and hybrid methods. Table 6–2 summarizes the translation methods used worldwide. It is noteworthy that the United States and Canada are the only major foreign investors in the world that use something other than the current rate method. It is also noteworthy that only seven countries (including the United States and Canada) require or insist upon one specific method.

In order to understand the issues more specifically, let's look at translation methods from three sources: the International Accounting Standards Committee (IASC), the United States, and the United Kingdom.

THE INTERNATIONAL ACCOUNTING
STANDARDS COMMITTEE

As pointed out in Chapter 3, the IASC is an international organization composed of authoritative accounting bodies in more than forty countries. The representative of the United States is the American Institute of Certified Public Accountants rather than the standard-setting Financial Accounting Standards Board. In 1978 the IASC released Exposure Draft 11 (IED 11) on accounting for foreign currency financial statements. Because of uncertainty in the United States and other countries surrounding translation, the exposure draft has not been issued as a standard.

Concerning transactions, IED 11 generally requires that transactions be recorded at the spot rate initially, and that monetary items be adjusted to each subsequent spot rate until they are settled. Unlike FASB 8, however, IED 11 allows firms to carry the initial transaction

TABLE 6–2. Translation Methods Required, Insisted Upon, or Predominant Practice

MONETARY-NONMONETARY	TEMPORAL	CURRENT-NONCURRENT	CURRENT RATE
Bahamas	Argentina	El Salvador	Australia
Costa Rica	Austria*	Greece	Botswana
Guatemala	Bermuda*	Iran	Colombia
Honduras	Bolivia	Malawi	Denmark
Korea	Canada*	New Zealand	Fiji
Nicaragua	Chile	Pakistan	France
Philippines	Dominican Republic*	South Africa	Germany
Sweden	Ecuador	Zambia	Hong Kong
Taiwan	Jamaica*		India
	Panama		Ireland
	Peru		Ivory Coast
	United States*		Japan
	Venezuela		Jersey, Channel Islands
			Kenya
			Malaysia
			Netherlands
			Norway
			Paraguay
			Senegal
			Singapore
			Switzerland
			Trinidad and Tobago
			United Kingdom
			Uruguay*
			Zimbabwe Rhodesia

SOURCE: R. D. Fitzgerald, A. D. Stickler, and T. R. Watts, *International Survey of Accounting Principles and Reporting Practices,* Price Waterhouse International, 1979, 248–252.
*Required or insisted upon.

and resulting monetary items at the forward rate if the firm has entered into a forward contract as a hedge. Foreign exchange gains and losses would normally be taken directly to income. In the case of long-term monetary items, however, gains may be deferred until realized or taken directly to shareholders' equity and losses taken directly to income after they have offset previously deferred gains. This approach is allowed because of the uncertainty in future spot rates that long-term monetary items are subject to. IED 11 requires that firms disclose their policies for accounting for foreign currency transactions as well as the amount of gains and losses taken directly to income or shareholders' equity or deferred.

In the case of translation of financial statements, IED 11 is diplomatic. Rather than pick one approach, it identifies two equally acceptable approaches: the temporal method and the closing rate (current rate) method. The reasoning is that since there are irreconcilable views on the objective of translation, it is impossible to select one method that will have universal acceptance.

IED 11 also allows different ways to treat foreign exchange gains and losses. Under the temporal method, it points out that gains and losses are normally taken directly to income. For long-term monetary items, however, it allows firms to exclude from income all gains and losses or all gains on translation and losses to the extent of previously deferred gains. In the case of the closing rate method, gains and losses are normally taken to income, but deferral is allowed when future realization of the gains and losses is uncertain.

As you can see, IED 11 is all things to all people. As a result, disclosure is vital. IED 11 requires that firms clearly identify all accounting policies followed in translation and the disposition of resulting gains and losses. In addition, it requires the following amounts to be disclosed:

1.   The aggregate foreign exchange gain or loss originating in the current period, indicating the amount included in net income for the period and the amount reported as a change in shareholders' interests or deferred.

2.   The aggregate foreign exchange gain or loss included in net income for the period.

3.   The amount of a change either in shareholders' interests or a deferred gain or loss in respect of the translation of foreign monetary or nonmonetary items.

4.   The amount of any deferred gains or losses existing at the balance sheet date.

5.   The method of accounting for any accumulated deferred gains or losses on translation.[1]

Because the issue of translation is such an emotionally charged one in the United States and abroad, it would have been impossible for the IASC to recommend a single approach. As the individual countries come to a broader consensus as to what should be done, the IASC's task will be much easier.

THE UNITED STATES AND FASB 8

As the Accounting Principles Board faded away and the Financial Accounting Standards Board came on line, one of the first areas of business involved the translation of financial statements. Accounting Research

[1]"Accounting for Foreign Transactions and Translation of Foreign Financial Statements," *Accountancy*, January 1978, p. 49.

Study 12 had recommended the temporal method, but further action was suspended pending FASB action.

In December 1973 FASB issued its first statement: *Disclosure of Foreign Currency Translation Information.* The board stated that until it could resolve the translation issue with a uniform standard, it wanted firms to disclose their accounting policies as well as the following quantitative amounts:

1. The aggregate amount of exchange adjustments originating in the period, the amount thereof included in the determination of income and the amount thereof deferred.
2. The aggregate amount of exchange adjustments included in the determination of income for the period, regardless of when the adjustments originated.
3. The aggregate amount of deferred exchange adjustments, regardless of when the adjustments originated, included in the balance sheet (e.g., such as in a deferral or in a "reserve" account) and how this amount is classified.
4. The amount by which total long-term receivables and total long-term payables translated at historical rates would each increase or decrease at the balance sheet date if translated at current rates.
5. The amount of gain or loss which has not been recognized on unperformed forward exchange contracts at the balance sheet date.[2]

Obviously, this statement was intended to be a stopgap measure. Increased disclosure would allow investors to rearrange the numbers in order to make comparisons until a more comprehensive standard could be issued. A February 1974 discussion memorandum on translation outlined the issues and alternative solutions. After the public hearings and subsequent discussions, an exposure draft was issued in December. Comments on the exposure draft were received, further refinements were made, and a standard was issued in October 1975. It is *Statement of Financial Accounting Standards No. 8: Accounting for the Translation of Foreign Currency Transactions and Foreign Currency Financial Statements,* otherwise known as FASB 8.

FASB 8 requires the use of the temporal principle as outlined and illustrated in Chapter 5. It requires that foreign currency transactions be recorded at the initial spot rate and that resulting monetary receivables or payables be adjusted to subsequent balance sheet rates. Foreign exchange gains or losses should be taken directly to the income statement. This is fairly simple and straightforward. The controversy arises

[2]Financial Accounting Standards Board, *Statement of Financial Accounting Standard No. 1* (Stamford, Conn.: FASB, December 1973), pp. 6–7.

over translating foreign currency financial statements. Therefore, the balance of this section focuses on the specifics of FASB 8, the problems and controversies that have arisen, and the changes that are expected to occur.

According to FASB 8, the objective of translation is the following:

> For the purpose of preparing an enterprise's financial statements, the objective of translation is to measure and express (a) in dollars and (b) in conformity with U.S. generally accepted accounting principles (GAAP) the assets, liabilities, revenues, or expenses that are measured or denominated in foreign currency.[3]

Although our focus here is primarily on objective (a) above, it is important to note that translation cannot occur until the local financial statements are recast according to U.S. generally accepted accounting principles. Given that accounting principles and practices vary so much worldwide, this implies that local operations are going to have to keep at least two sets of books—one according to local GAAP and the other according to U.S. GAAP.

As brought out in Chapter 5, the temporal principle as outlined in FASB 8 requires the following approach to translation:

1. Cash, receivables, and payables are translated at the current exchange rate.
2. Assets and liabilities carried at past exchange prices are translated at historical exchange rates.
3. Assets and liabilities carried at current or future exchange prices are translated at current exchange rates.
4. Revenues and expenses are typically translated at average exchange rates, which approximate the actual historical rates at which the transactions occurred. However, revenues and expenses such as cost of goods sold and depreciation expense that relate to assets and liabilities translated at historical rates should also be translated at historical rates.
5. Foreign exchange gains and losses should be recognized in the income statement in the period in which they occur—interim as well as annual.
6. The dividend rate should be used to translate foreign currency financial statements into U.S. dollars.

Items 5 and 6 are unique to FASB 8 and are not required in order for the temporal principle to be followed, as noted in IED 11 of the IASC.

---

[3]Financial Accounting Standards Board, *Statement of Financial Accounting Standards No. 8* (Stamford, Conn.: FASB, October 1975), p. 3.

An interesting aspect of FASB 8 is the valuation of inventory according to the lower of cost or market. At the local subsidiary level, it is common to value ending inventory according to the lower of local currency cost or market. For translation purposes, however, the test is made in dollars. Thus cost translated at historical rates is compared with market translated at the current rate to determine the lower of cost or market in dollars. Table 6–3 illustrates in simplified fashion how the test is made.

In situation 1, market (450) is lower than cost (500) in local currency, so the carrying value in local currency is at market. Since translated cost ($1,200) is lower than translated market ($1,350), the carrying value in dollars on the translated financial statements is at cost. In situation 2, inventory is written down to the market value of $1,080, and the write-down is considered a part of cost of goods sold rather than an exchange loss.

Since its release, FASB 8 has generated a great deal of criticism. Early in 1976 the board acknowledged the criticism but decided that it had already considered the concerns expressed and did not feel the need to reconsider the statement.

The controversy escalated. In 1979 a 14-member task force was set up to advise the board on its reconsideration of FASB 8. Most of the criticism centers around the following points: the translation of inventory, the translation of long-term debt, the recognition of foreign exchange gains and losses in the quarterly and annual income statement, the appropriate translation method, and the responses of management and investors to the financial statement impact of FASB 8.

TABLE 6–3. Lower of Cost or Market Test

	SITUATION 1	SITUATION 2
Exchange rate at date of purchase	$2.40	$2.40
Cost expressed in units of foreign currency	500	500
Exchange rate at balance sheet date	$3.00	$1.80
Market at balance sheet date expressed in units of foreign currency	450	600
Carrying amount in untranslated foreign balance sheet	450 (market)	500 (cost)
Translated market (450 + $3.00 and 600 + $1.80)	$1,350	$1,080
Translated historical cost (500 × $2.40)	$1,200	$1,200
Carrying amount in translated balance sheet	$1,200 (cost)	$1,080 (market)

SOURCE: Ernst & Whinney, *Accounting for Foreign Currency Translation,* Financial Reporting Developments, Retrieval No. 38409, February 1976, p. 11.

Translation of Inventory

Under FASB 8, inventory carried at cost is translated at historical rates, and inventory carried at market is translated at current rates. Given the tendency to use FIFO for foreign inventories, and given worldwide inflation, inventory is likely to be carried at cost rather than at the higher market value. Firms complain about translating inventory at the historical exchange rate because they say that it is too complex to keep track of the local currency costs and exchange rates, and because they feel that inventory turns over quickly and should therefore be translated at current rates like cash and receivables.

Another problem is that relatively few multinationals translated inventory at historical rates prior to FASB 8, and the shift has changed their total accounting exposure position. Exposure is dealt with in more detail in the next chapter, but *accounting exposure* refers to accounts translated at current rates and thus subject to a change in dollar value when the exchange rate changes. Since inventory is roughly one-third of total assets of most manufacturing firms, whether inventory is exposed to an exchange rate change makes a big difference.

Translation of Long-Term Debt

Most of the arguments concerning long-term debt revolve around the disposition of the gain or loss rather than the method of translation. FASB 8 requires that firms translate long-term debt at current rates, a practice already followed by nearly half the U.S. multinationals prior to 1975. Since most of the foreign currency long-term debt in recent years has been in currencies that have strengthened vis-à-vis the U.S. dollar, U.S. firms have recognized sizable losses. Many firms feel that since the foreign currency debt is generally being liquidated by foreign currency earnings, there really is no dollar exposure. Also they argue that the fixed assets purchased by the debt are a natural hedge or protection against loss since they are constantly generating earnings. Thus they feel that they should be able to write off the losses over the life of the assets or treat the losses as an adjustment to interest expense.

Recognition of Foreign Exchange Gains and Losses

This issue has created a great deal of unfavorable reaction and strong debate. The question is, should gains and losses be taken directly to the income statement in the period in which they occur? Wide fluctuations in quarterly earnings have been experienced by a number of firms, causing executives to say that FASB 8 "distorts real operating results and provides misleading information . . . leads to uneconomic changes in financing methods . . . and results in non-productive activities."[4] Many firms have resorted to lengthy explanations in quarterly and annual reports about distortions in operating results created by foreign exchange gains and losses. FASB 8 requires that foreign exchange gains and losses be disclosed in the financial statements or footnotes. It also suggests that, where practicable, firms describe and quantify the effects of rate changes on operations, other than as mentioned above.

There are four major places in the annual report where a firm may choose to disclose the effect of foreign exchange gains and losses: the audited financial statements, the audited notes, the management notes and analysis, and the executive officers' message. The first two are the ones specified in FASB 8. In a study of the disclosure policies of 51 U.S.-based multinationals, it was found that 44 of the firms disclosed information on foreign exchange gains and losses in the footnotes and only 11 in the financial statements themselves.[5] (Obviously, some of the 51 firms disclosed the information in both places.)

In the same study it was determined that the most prevalent form of disclosure was the actual pretax gains and losses (41 of the firms). Although it was encouraging to note that 23 of the firms attempted to explain or describe the gains and losses, only 4 firms attempted to explain the effects of rate changes on operations.

To shed some additional light on what is meant by disclosure of exchange gains and losses, let us look at some relevant sections of a few actual corporate reports. The 1978 annual report of Armstrong Cork Company contains a good description of the details of the foreign exchange gains and loss for 1977 and 1978. (See Table 6–4.)

The 1978 Exxon report went considerably further by giving information by currency over time in the commentary prior to the financial statements. Figure 6 is the chart developed by Exxon; the accompanying commentary [reprinted with permission] follows:

> Exxon's earnings continue to be significantly affected by changes in exchange rates between the U.S. dollar and foreign currencies. These effects arise from translating into dollars those assets and liabilities denominated in foreign currencies for which year-end exchange rates are used in accordance with the Financial Accounting Standards Board's Standard No. 8.
>
> Under these presently prescribed accounting procedures, essentially all of Exxon's foreign liabilities, including short- and long-term debt obligations, are measured in terms of year-end exchange rates. As the dollar has weakened, these liabilities, translated at the year-end

---

[4]*Wall Street Journal,* June 20, 1978, p. 10.
[5]Robert Yocum, "Disclosures of Foreign Currency Adjustments in Financial Statements," unpublished MBA paper, Pennsylvania State University, 1979.

TABLE 6–4. Armstrong Cork Company

DETAILS OF FOREIGN EXCHANGE GAINS (LOSSES)	1978 (000)	1977 (000)
Realized, related to:		
Long-term debt	$ —	$ (45)
Other	(100)	(254)
Total before tax	(100)	(299)
Total after tax	(123)	(141)
Unrealized, related to:		
Long-term items	(8,325)	(8,969)
Less forward exchange contracts	2,263	—
	(6,062)	(8,969)
Other	59	(30)
Total before tax	(6,003)	(8,999)
Total after tax	(5,039)	(7,302)
Combined total before tax	$ (6,103)	$ (9,298)
Combined total after tax	$ (5,162)	$ (7,443)
Net earnings as reported	$61,132	$40,375
Earnings exclusive of foreign exchange losses	$66,294	$47,818

Unrealized foreign exchange losses, because of their significance, are reported in the Consolidated Statements of Earnings as separate items.

SOURCE: *Annual Report,* Armstrong Cork Company, 1978.

rates of exchange, are equivalent to greater U.S. dollar obligations. In contrast, a relatively small portion of the corporation's foreign assets—essentially only cash, marketable securities and receivables—are measured using year-end exchange rates. The balance of the corporation's foreign assets—mainly inventory, plant and equipment—are not included in this calculation and continue to be measured in terms of their equivalent dollar value at the time these assets were acquired. As a consequence of using the Standard No. 8 definition, Exxon continues to show a net liability exposure which creates currency translation losses during periods of U.S. dollar weakness.

While currency translation effects on financial assets and liabilities are readily determinable under Standard No. 8, it is not possible to quantify the overall effect on 1978 earnings of the substantial decline during the year in the foreign exchange value of the U.S. dollar. Undoubtedly, some portion of the increase achieved in operating

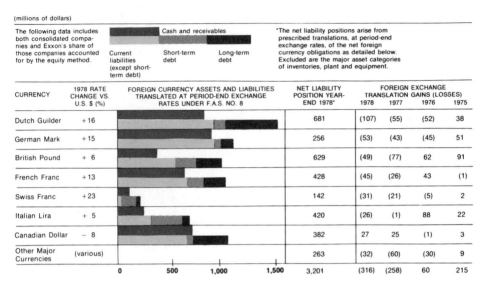

(millions of dollars)

The following data includes both consolidated companies and Exxon's share of those companies accounted for by the equity method.

Cash and receivables

Current liabilities (except short-term debt)   Short-term debt   Long-term debt

*The net liability positions arise from prescribed translations, at period-end exchange rates, of the net foreign currency obligations as detailed below. Excluded are the major asset categories of inventories, plant and equipment.

CURRENCY	1978 RATE CHANGE VS. U.S. $ (%)	FOREIGN CURRENCY ASSETS AND LIABILITIES TRANSLATED AT PERIOD-END EXCHANGE RATES UNDER F.A.S. NO. 8	NET LIABILITY POSITION YEAR-END 1978*	FOREIGN EXCHANGE TRANSLATION GAINS (LOSSES)			
				1978	1977	1976	1975
Dutch Guilder	+ 16		681	(107)	(55)	(52)	38
German Mark	+ 15		256	(53)	(43)	(45)	51
British Pound	+ 6		629	(49)	(77)	62	91
French Franc	+ 13		428	(45)	(26)	43	(1)
Swiss Franc	+ 23		142	(31)	(21)	(5)	2
Italian Lira	+ 5		420	(26)	(1)	88	22
Canadian Dollar	− 8		382	27	25	(1)	3
Other Major Currencies	(various)		263	(32)	(60)	(30)	9
		0 500 1,000 1,500	3,201	(316)	(258)	60	215

Figure 6. Foreign exchange translation effects (Reprinted with permission.)

earnings in 1978 resulted from the strengthening of a number of foreign currencies in which Exxon affiliates transact business.

The Financial Accounting Standards Board is currently reevaluating its position regarding foreign exchange translation procedures. In response to the FASB's request for comments, Exxon has suggested that present standards be modified to recognize the higher current U.S. dollar equivalent of foreign inventories when foreign currencies appreciate and to permit the translation difference calculated on long-term debt to be deferred and amortized over the life of the debt.

In 1978, currency translation losses reflected principally the weakening of the U.S. dollar relative to the British pound, the Dutch guilder, the German mark and the French franc, offset somewhat by gains which primarily reflect the strengthening of the U.S. dollar in relation to the Canadian dollar. Of the $316 million in reported unfavorable exchange translation effects, the major portion relates to foreign currency debt with maturities at various dates after 1978. This amount may be viewed over time as a net increase in borrowing costs.

[Figure 6] shows the major currencies which comprise Exxon's net liability position in foreign currencies at year-end 1978 under presently prescribed accounting procedures. The upper portion of each horizontal bar depicts assets which are translated at the year-end exchange rate, while the lower portion shows the liabilities which are similarly translated.

As mentioned earlier, only four of the firms in the survey chose to explain the effects of rate changes on operations. The reason why more firms did not attempt to do this was best explained by IBM:

> Effects of the (currency) rate changes on reported revenues, costs, and expenses cannot be quantified with any precision and accordingly are not reported. To quantify this effect would assume that all other factors involved in foreign operations are not affected by currency values and that no compensation changes are made. It doesn't consider the resulting economic effects of possible volume and price changes and expense level changes.[6]

As currently constituted, FASB 8 requires all gains and losses—whether realized or unrealized and related to transactions or translation—to be treated alike. This is confusing to the reader of financial statements who may not realize that these gains and losses are very different from each other and affect the cash flow of the business very differently.

The Appropriate Translation Method

Two translation methods have surfaced as the most important ones: the temporal method and the current rate method. Under the *temporal translation method*, foreign subsidiaries and affiliates are treated as an extension of the parent so that all transactions are accounted for as if they occurred in the currency of the parent. In the United States, the process of consolidation, by definition, tries to show the firm as an integrated entity rather than a collection of separate firms. Proponents of this concept say that the temporal method is the only one that makes sense.

Under the *current rate translation method*, foreign subsidiaries and affiliates are considered to be separate business entities in which transactions are carried on in the local currency. Therefore, foreign currency financial statements are the most meaningful way to present the results of operations. If those statements are translated into the parent currency at a single rate of exchange, then the local currency relationships are maintained and a relatively distortion-free view of the operations is retained.

There has also been discussion of a situational approach to translation where tightly controlled operations are translated by the temporal method and loosely controlled operations by the current rate method. FASB was not interested in leaving that much judgment to the firms,

---

[6]"The Nightmare of FASB-8," *Forbes*, 18 September 1978, 187.

even though such flexibility would be permitted by the IASC and is currently allowed in the United Kingdom.

Responses of Management and Investors

Table 6–5 illustrates the major sources of executive concern about FASB 8.

These issues have already been presented, but the major concern is that gains and losses be reflected in current income. In the same study it was found that 84 of 156 corporate executives felt that most investors were confused about the implications of translation gains and losses.[7] They may have been confused, but the confusion apparently did not carry over into the marketplace. In an economic impact study by Dukes, it was found that FASB 8 did not appear to have "significant detectable effects on the security returns of multinational firms."[8]

In spite of this result, corporate management has remained undeterred in its effort to change FASB 8. In the absence of change, management has sought to alter its exposure and enter into a variety of forward exchange and other money market contracts to hedge against potential losses. In some cases, firms have altered investment strategies because of the way foreign exchange gains and losses are determined and treated.

A New Standard

On August 28, 1980, FASB issued an exposure draft of a proposed statement of financial accounting standards entitled "Foreign Currency Translation." The exposure draft received substantial input from the United States business and academic community, the IASC, the United Kingdom, and Canada and is expected to become a standard replacing FASB 8 in 1981.

In contrast with FASB 8, the exposure draft states that the translation process should express in the reporting currency of the parent all assets, liabilities, revenues, and expenses that are measured or denominated in a foreign currency. In addition, it is stated in the exposure draft that the objectives of translation should allow the process to accomplish the following:

   a. Translation of foreign currency transactions and financial statements should preserve the financial results and relationships as measured

---

[7]Thomas G. Evans, William R. Folks Jr., and Michael Jilling. *The Impact of Statement of Financial Accounting Standards No. 8 on the Foreign Exchange Risk Management Practices of American Multinationals: An Economic Impact Study* (Stamford, Conn.: FASB, 1978), p. 133.
[8]Roland E. Dukes, *An Empirical Investigation of the Effects of Statement of Financial Accounting Standards No. 8 on Security Return Behavior* (Stamford, Conn.: FASB, 1978).

TABLE 6–5. Most Important Source of Concern Resulting from FASB Statement No. 8 at U.S. Multinational Corporations

MOST IMPORTANT SOURCE OF CONCERN	RESPONDENT FIRMS	
	NUMBER	PERCENT
The set of required translation practices (Feature 1)	44	28.2
The requirement that translation gains and losses be reflected in current income (Feature 2)	79	50.7
Feature 1 and Feature 2	6	3.8
Neither feature has been of concern	25	16.0
No response	2	1.3
Total	156	100.0

SOURCE: Thomas G. Evans, William R. Folks Jr., and Michael Jilling, *The Impact of Statement of Financial Accounting Standards No. 8 on the Foreign Exchange Risk Management Practices of American Multinationals: An Economic Impact Study,* 1978, 149. Copyright by the Financial Accounting Standards Board, High Ridge Park, Stamford, Conn. 06905, U.S.A. Reprinted with permission. Copies of the complete document are available from the FASB.

and expressed in the functional currency of each component entity of an enterprise.

b. Results of translating foreign currency transactions and financial statements should be generally compatible, in terms of direction of change and financial statement classification, with the expected effects of a rate change on an enterprise's exposure to foreign exchange risk.[9]

The treatment of foreign currency transactions would not change as a result of the exposure draft. However, the translation of financial statements could change dramatically. In most cases, firms would be able to translate all assets and liabilities into the parent currency at the current rate. Stockholders' equity would be translated at historical rates, and all revenues and expenses (including depreciation expense and cost of sales) would be translated at a weighted-average rate for the period. In most cases, revenues and expenses would be translated each month at the average rate for that month and added to the translated results of prior months.

The Board does allow some judgments to be made, however. The basic philosophy behind translating financial statements in the exposure draft is that accounts should be measured in their functional currency and expressed in the reporting currency. It is assumed that in most cases the functional currency would be the currency of the country in which

[9]Financial Accounting Standards Board, *Proposed Statement of Financial Accounting Standards,* "Foreign Currency Translation," (Stamford, Conn.: FASB, 1980), pp. 3–4.

the foreign operation is located—Brazilian cruzeiros in Brazil, pesos in Mexico, etc. Therefore, most balance sheet accounts would be translated at the current rate in order to preserve the relationships found in the functional currency. However, the temporal method could still be used if it were felt that the foreign operation was so inseparable from the parent operation that the parent currency was, in fact, the functional currency.

The approach recommended in the exposure draft would solve many of the problems mentioned in conjunction with FASB 8.

Concerning exchange gains and losses, the Board recommends in the exposure draft that gains and losses from foreign currency transactions be the only ones included in the income statement, and that the amount be disclosed in the income statement or the footnotes. Most gains and losses from translating foreign currency financial statements would be transferred to a separate section of stockholders' equity. The following information concerning this new section should be disclosed in the statements or footnotes:

   a. Beginning and ending cumulative amount,
   b. The aggregate adjustment for the period resulting from translation of foreign currency statements and gains and losses from hedging and investor-investee transactions,
   c. The amount of income taxes for the period that was allocated to stockholders' equity, and
   d. The amounts transferred from stockholders' equity and included in determining net income for the period as a result of substantial or complete liquidation.[10]

As noted in item d above, it might be necessary under certain circumstances to transfer to the income statement some of the foreign exchange losses previously included in stockholders' equity.

The exposure draft is obviously a radical departure from FASB 8. Most of the shortcomings in FASB 8 are corrected in the exposure draft, which recommends an approach more similar to that followed in the United Kingdom and continental Europe. If the exposure draft is adopted as a standard, it will have an impact on standards set by the IASC and in the United Kingdom.

THE UNITED KINGDOM

In 1977 the Accounting Standards Committee of the United Kingdom released Exposure Draft 21 (ED 21), which allows a company to choose between the temporal method and the closing rate method. The latter

---

[10]Ibid. p. 13.

approach is far more popular in the United Kingdom, and the ASC apparently included the temporal approach because of FASB 8 in the United States. In addition, the ASC appears reluctant to adopt only the closing rate method since that would be in conflict with IED 11, which allows both the temporal and the closing rate methods.

If the closing rate method is used, foreign exchange gains and losses may be taken to reserves or to income, depending on the situation. Exchange gains and losses relating to fixed assets are normally taken to balance sheet reserves. Those arising from net borrowings are normally taken to profit and loss. However, the gains and losses are treated as a separate item after profit and loss from ordinary operations. FASB 8 treats the gains and losses as a component of operating income. If the temporal method is used, gains and losses should be taken to income and distinguished between operating and extraordinary items. In the United States, foreign exchange gains and losses cannot be treated as extraordinary items. ED 21 also requires disclosure of the accounting policies for translating statements and dealing with foreign exchange gains and losses as well as the amount of change in the reserve account due to foreign exchange gains and losses. The reserves referred to here are similar to retained earnings in the United States.

There is considerable controversy in the United Kingdom over ED 21 since two different methods are allowed. The comments received on ED 21 were initially unanimously in favor of the closing rate method, and ED 21 clearly prefers it as well. However, many experts feel that it would be difficult to adopt one method when IED 11 would allow two methods and the United States requires the temporal method. This is another reason why the resolution of FASB 8 is so important in terms of standards in other countries.

TRANSLATION FOR CONSOLIDATION

The broader issue of consolidation is treated in the chapter on disclosure. However, given that consolidation must take place, what are some of the key issues that are peculiar to operations reported in a foreign currency? A parent firm can operate abroad through a subsidiary, affiliate, or branch. A *subsidiary* is a foreign corporation in which the parent owns more than 50 percent of the voting stock; an *affiliate* is a foreign corporation in which the parent owns less than a majority interest; and a *branch* is an enterprise in a foreign country that is an extension of the U.S. parent rather than a foreign corporation owned by the parent.

Three issues need to be resolved: the initial startup or acquisition of the foreign operation, the subsequent activity (net income or loss), and the presentation of this information on parent and consolidated financial statements. The parent books reflect the operations of the parent itself and treat all its investments worldwide as investments on the assets side of the balance sheet. Consolidated accounts treat the parent and its investments worldwide as one entity, so the financial statements are blended together into one set of financial statements.

Initial Acquisition

Under FASB 8, assets carried at historical cost must be translated at the historical rate. The question is, what is historical from the standpoint of acquisition? If a parent acquires an existing foreign corporation and accounts for the acquisition by the pooling of interests method, the historical rate is the one in effect when the original firm purchased the assets. For example, assume that Franco S.A. bought fixed assets in 1970 and was then acquired by a U.S. corporation in 1978. If the acquisition were treated as a pooling of interests, the fixed assets would be translated by multiplying the historical cost times the rate in effect in 1970.

If the acquisition were accounted for by the purchase method, the assets would be restated to fair market value in local currency at the time of acquisition and translated into dollars at the current rate. In our example, the rate in effect at the acquisition date in 1978 would be used to translate the fixed assets. From that time forward the value of the assets in local currency and the exchange rate at the date of acquisition would become the historical cost and historical rate.

This distinction becomes a moot point in the exposure draft of FASB since all assets and liabilities are translated at the current rate, irrespective of when they were initially acquired.

Subsequent Activity

As the foreign operation earns income, the income must be reflected in the books of the parent. There are two ways to reflect the income: the cost and equity methods. The *cost method* is very conservative and recognizes income only when dividends are declared. For example, assume that a foreign subsidiary recognizes net income after tax of LC1 million and declares a dividend to its U.S. parent of LC500,000 when the exchange rate is $.50/1LC. The entry on the parent books would be

Dividend receivable	$250,000	
Dividend income		$250,000

The cost method may be used in the United States only when the U.S.

parent owns less than 20 percent of the voting stock and when the initial acquisition is accounted for by the purchase method.

The other approach is the *equity method*, which is more complex. In the equity method, income of foreign operations increases the investment by the parent in the foreign operation, and dividends reduce the investment account. In order to determine income, the financial statements need to be translated into dollars. Using our example and assuming that the translated value of net income is $375,000 and that the foreign subsidiary is wholly owned by the parent, the entries would be as follows:

Investment in subsidiary	$375,000	
Equity in subsidiary income		$375,000
Dividends receivable	$250,000	
Investment in subsidiary		$250,000

In the equity method, therefore, income is recognized by the parent when earned by the subsidiary, not when declared as a dividend. The equity method may be used when the acquisition is recorded by the purchase or pooling method.

Parent and Consolidated Books

Table 6–6 summarizes the recognition of income on parent and consolidated financial statements. On the parent statements, the subsidiaries and affiliates are carried as investments. Therefore, income is recognized either when it is earned (the equity method) or when it is received as a dividend (the cost method). In the consolidated financial statements, affiliates are still carried as investments, so income is recognized by the cost or equity methods, just as in the parent financial statements. For subsidiaries, however, the investment account is eliminated and the financial statements of the parent and all subsidiaries are added together, line by line, to form the consolidated statements. Therefore, the balance sheet and income statement must be translated into dollars so that accounts can be added together in the same currency.

TABLE 6–6. Recognition of Subsequent Activity

	PARENT STATEMENTS	CONSOLIDATED STATEMENTS
Subsidiary	Equity	Line by line
Affiliate ≥ 20%	Equity	Equity
Affiliate < 20%	Cost	Cost

The principles are fairly simple for branch financial statements. After all intracompany transfers have been eliminated, the branch accounts are translated into dollars and combined with parent accounts for parent and consolidated financial statements.

CONCLUSIONS

Chapters 5 and 6 are difficult to separate, although they deal with the same subject at different levels. Clearly, there is a big difference between the mechanics of translation and the decision as to which method should be adopted by nations. The problems brought out in Chapter 3 on trying to harmonize financial statements are dramatically illustrated in the translation issue as well. It is all but impossible to harmonize standards across the world, leading to IED 11, which is really no standard at all. The difficulty facing national standard-setting bodies is also illustrated in the translation issue. The Americans have successfully fought what they consider to be a bad standard and will probably see it changed. The British are having difficulty in setting a standard because what the Americans require conflicts with what they would prefer to do.

The translation issue has also generated heavy discussion on the economic impact of accounting standards. Should accounting standards cause firms to change their behavior, as FASB 8 has done? Does the real issue lie in the fact that standards can cause firms to change their behavior as long as that behavior is consistent with economic reality? The force to change FASB 8 contends that the standard does not reflect economic reality and therefore creates uneconomic responses. It is difficult to refute or substantiate that point, but the argument is being echoed worldwide. Accountants cannot set standards in a theoretical vacuum. Thus what happens to FASB 8, IED 11, and ED 21 could have a material impact on standards set in other areas in the future.

STUDY QUESTIONS

6–1. What is the predominant practice used worldwide for initially recording foreign currency transactions and foreign currency receivables and payables at subsequent balance sheet dates? How are gains and losses recognized?

6–2. What translation methods are used most extensively worldwide?

6–3. How does the International Accounting Standards Committee require that foreign currency financial statements be translated and gains and losses recognized? Why does the committee allow such widely divergent approaches?

6–4.　What are the requirements for translating financial statements according to FASB 8?

6–5.　Discuss the major facets of any of the following issues relative to FASB 8:
a.　inventory
b.　long-term debt
c.　recognition of gains and losses
d.　appropriate translation method
e.　responses of management and investors

6–6.　What are some possible ways of modifying FASB 8? What are the strengths and weaknesses of these proposed modifications?

6–7.　How does ED 21 in the United Kingdom recommend that financial statements be translated? How does ED 21 differ from IED 11 and FASB 8? Why don't the British choose just one best approach?

6–8.　What is the difference in translating the accounts of a foreign operation acquired by the purchase or pooling of interest method according to FASB 8?

6–9.　How would you translate foreign income into dollars for the cost and equity methods?

6–10.　One of the problems of FASB 8 relates to the volatility of earnings. In response to that, Gerald I. White of Grace & White, Inc. said, "An accounting system which properly translates volatile exchange rates into volatile earnings is no more at fault than the bearer of bad news." What do you think about that statement?

6–11.　Many opponents of FASB 8 say that results are uneconomic in strong currency countries. As the foreign currency strengthens, the dollar equivalent of foreign assets should rise, and the dollar equivalent of future sales and dividends should also rise. However, a translation loss is recognized since most foreign subsidiaries have a net exposed liability position. Why would FASB 8 lead to a net exposed liability position, and what difference does it make? What do you think of the issue raised in this example?

6–12.　Rouse Co., a developer of major shopping-centers, built two shopping centers in Canada and financed more than 90 percent of the cost with a loan from Canadian lenders. The loan would be paid off with rental income from the shopping centers and no recourse to Rouse Co. Rouse translated its assets at historical rates and its long-term debt at current rates. Because the Canadian dollar was weakening against the U.S. dollar, Rouse was showing huge gains on its financial statements, in one case boosting the bottom line tenfold. Rouse was not able to get FASB to give it an exception in reporting its foreign exchange gain and was forced to sell its properties after two years.
a.　Explain how Rouse's situation constituted a natural hedge.
b.　Why would Rouse be upset about showing huge foreign exchange gains?

c.   Should FASB have allowed Rouse an exception? Why?

6–13. Starting with 1971, trace the development of the disclosure of foreign exchange gains and losses in Exxon's annual reports through 1979 and compare the disclosures with the requirements pre-FASB 1, FASB 1, and in FASB 8.

6–14. The following table is a hypothetical example (with actual exchange rates) of the First Quarter Report 1976 for Scholl, Inc.

	First Quarter 1975			First Quarter 1976		
	Pound Sterling	U.S. Dollar Equivalent Per Pound	U.S. Dollars	Pound Sterling	U.S. Dollar Equivalent Per Pound	U.S. Dollars
Net sales	£5,020	2.40	$12,050	£5,390	1.99	$10,730
Cost of sales	3,320	2.35	7,800	3,465	2.15	7,450
Gross profit	1,700		4,250	1,925		3,280
Operating expenses	1,170	2.40	2,800	1,315	1.99	2,620
Pre-tax results	530		1,450	610		660
Income taxes	310	2.40	750	315	1.99	630
Net earnings (under FASB 8)	£ 220		$ 700	£ 295		$ 30
Earnings if translated at quarter end rate	£ 220	2.41	$ 530	£ 295	1.92	$ 570

Analyze the effect of translation on reported sales and earnings from one year to the next and compare the dollar and pound changes. What are some reasons why the first quarter of 1976 looks so bad? Is it really that bad?

CASE

KAMIKAZE ENTERPRISES

Ray Addis, 63-year-old chairman of the Board of Ace Inc., a medium-size airplane manufacturing company, had called Frank Anderson into his office to talk about an investment made by Ace in Japan five years ago. Ray was really upset, because its Japanese affiliate, Kamikaze Enterprises, owned 40% by Ace and 60% by Mitsoo-hoo, was not doing well. He expected Frank, the CEO of Ace, to explain what was going on. Ray had been involved in marketing all his life, unlike Frank, who came up through the finance route.

"How are you doing, Frank?"

"Pretty good, I guess, Ray. I gather from your note that you're not too pleased with Kamikaze Enterprises."

"That's an understatement. In our last set of statements, I noticed that we picked up a dollar loss from Kamikaze for the fifth year in a row. I wouldn't mind it so much but that loss reduced our earnings by nearly 40 percent. Why can't we get that blasted operation in the black? I thought those Japanese were supposed to be cost-efficient. I feel like we're tapping money down a rathole."

"I can understand your concern, Ray, but we've gotten a healthy yen dividend from Kamikaze every year since we've been in operation. Because the yen keeps revaluing, the dollar equivalent of that dividend goes up every year."

"I realize that, Frank, but we report in dollars to our shareholders, and I have to explain those foreign exchange losses at the next annual meeting. What am I going to do? I understand that the book value of our investment has been written down to practically nothing because of those losses. Either that operation becomes profitable or we cut bait. Let me know in three weeks what our plan of action should be."

"O.K., Ray. I'll see what I can do."

"What a circus," thought Frank as he walked back to his office. "There's no way I can explain this situation so that he understands."

Ace Inc. had entered into the minority joint venture with Mitsoo-hoo to produce small corporate aircraft in Japan. Ace provided the technical expertise and some equity financing. However, Mitsoo-hoo provided most of the funds through debt financing with its bank. The investment was almost 90 percent debt financed.

Kamikaze Enterprises had actually been quite profitable, increasing yen profits by nearly 25 percent a year. Sales were growing at about the same rate. This growth and high profitability allowed Kamikaze to declare sizable dividends each year. When translated into dollars, however, the yen profits turned into losses which reduced Ace's equity investment in Kamikaze. Frank had spoken to the managers of Kamikaze, who didn't appear to understand the problem or want to do anything about it. Ace had been offered $50 million for its investment in Kamikaze, which seemed ironic since the book value on Ace's books was close to zero.

Questions

1. Explain what FASB 8 has done to allow this situation to arise.
2. What are some ways to correct this situation?
3. If you were Frank, what would you recommend to Ray and why?

7

Foreign Exchange Risk Management

Very little is certain in this world, particularly in the world of foreign exchange. Yet if anything is close to certainty it is that exchange rates will change—maybe up, maybe down, maybe a lot, maybe a little, but change they will, one way or another. As the chapter on the international monetary system pointed out, there are logical and illogical reasons for these changes, making their prediction at best difficult, at worst impossible. Yet the impact on a multinational's financial position of changes in the value of currencies is significant, as was demonstrated in Chapters 5 and 6. Thus the difficulties associated with changes in exchange rates cannot dissuade the multinational from attempting to minimize the negative impact of these changes on the company's earnings and financial position. To ignore them is to invite disaster.

The entire process of monitoring, predicting, and taking appropriate action with regard to changes in exchange rates is called *foreign exchange risk management*. This term suggests two important themes: there are risks involved, but there are ways to manage them. One set of risks was discussed in the previous chapters: the accounting losses which can result from changes in exchange rates. This chapter focuses on (1) the risks associated with trying to manage the risk of losses, and (2) the process of foreign exchange risk management.

THE OBJECTIVE OF FOREIGN
EXCHANGE RISK MANAGEMENT

The main objective of foreign exchange risk management is to minimize risk *and* minimize cost, subject to governmental and organizational constraints. There are three costs to be considered: (1) the direct costs of the financing and hedging operations; (2) the cost, expressed as a loss, caused by a change in a currency's value (net exposure times the change in currency value); and (3) the cost, expressed as opportunity cost (lost business), of changing the company's normal operating activities in order to reduce exposure. More about each later. There are also three risks involved: guessing wrong on the direction, magnitude, or timing of the currency change.

One of the most interesting aspects of foreign exchange risk management is that there is no single optimal solution to this dual minimization problem. Instead, the optimal solutions are virtually infinite. An *optimal solution* is defined as a solution when no other combination of policies has the same expected cost with a lower associated risk. Stated another way, no other combination of policies has the same level of risk with lower expected cost. What results is a *spectrum* of optimal solutions, ranging from the lowest risk/highest cost solution to the highest risk/lowest cost solution, with variations in between, as is shown in Figure 7. Once this array of optimal solutions has been generated, the decision maker must choose the solution that is consistent with corporate desires and capabilities and is acceptable in terms of government policies. For example, if a company is very risk-averse or not in a position to take much risk, the lowest-risk strategy would be selected. Alternatively, the company may not have sufficient funds to pursue the higher cost/lower risk strategies and may therefore need to select a lower cost/higher risk strategy. If all this sounds rather vague, it generally is less so in practice. Most companies have definite policies with regard to managing foreign exchange risk, ranging from aggressive to defensive. And within a company's guidelines, the corporate treasurer is usually constrained as to the acceptable level of risk and cost. In addition, government policies in the countries where the company has operations may preclude the use of certain otherwise optimal strategies. For example, the government may prohibit swap arrangements. Bearing in mind that there are numerous strategies and solutions to this problem of foreign exchange risk management, let us now turn to the specifics.

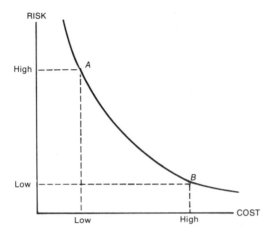

Figure 7. Spectrum of optimal solutions. (Source: Bernard Litaer, "Managing Risks in Foreign Exchange," *Harvard Business Review,* March–April 1970. p. 130.)

THE PROCESS OF FOREIGN EXCHANGE RISK MANAGEMENT

Foreign exchange risk management involves ten steps:

1. Determine a relevant planning period.
2. Forecast the change in relevant currencies during the planning period.
3. Prepare a company funds flow for the period, together with its expected effects on the company's financial position.
4. Determine the net accounting exposure and estimate the possible exchange rate gain or loss for the period.
5. If necessary or desired, rearrange the accounting exposure to minimize expected losses, bearing in mind the potential impact of this action on the firm's economic exposure.
6. Determine all the operational constraints which cannot be violated by hedging solutions.
7. Identify all the acceptable hedging and financial solutions and estimate their costs.
8. Plug all this information into a computer and generate the optimal solution spectrum.
9. Choose the solution most acceptable to the company.
10. Check to see that you have done everything correctly and accurately. Then pray.

Choosing the Planning Period

Choosing the planning period is largely a function of the reliability of the exchange rate forecast data, the corporate planning horizon, and the maturity period of the decisions and transactions. Because exchange rate forecasting becomes increasingly difficult and speculative as the time period under consideration becomes longer, time is the major constraint. Planning periods of over a year are rare and probably ill-advised. Since most companies operate from yearly plans and quarterly reporting periods, a yearly plan divided into quarterly segments makes sense for most companies. Shorter segments are often necessary or desirable if the exchange rate is particularly volatile and large sums are involved.

Predicting the Change in Exchange Rates

Knowing that exchange rates will change, the next step in the foreign exchange risk management process is predicting exchange rate movements. This prediction in itself involves three predictions of the movement: the direction, the magnitude, and the timing. The prediction of *direction* is obviously important, for the results are drastically different if the currency appreciates in value rather than depreciates. The *magnitude* of the change is also important not because the results are different from a gain versus loss standpoint but because the magnitude of the gain or loss is affected. The *timing* of the change is important because it affects the timing of the gains or losses and hence their realization and recognition. Finally, the direction, magnitude, and timing of the movement are important taken as a group because they jointly determine the direction, magnitude, and timing of the actions taken to manage the foreign exchange risk. For example, if a foreign currency is expected to move upward only slightly and only at the very end of the fiscal year, and if the company has no transactions in that currency, the company's strategy might be to do little or nothing and then only as the end of the year approaches because there is not much at stake in terms of gains or losses during most of the year. On the other hand, if the currency's rise in value is expected to be continuous and large, and the company has a great deal of payables in that currency, the foreign exchange risk management would be quite different and certainly more important, calling for exposure minimization and considerable hedging activities throughout the period.

Indicators of Change

As described in Chapter 4, a host of economic events can serve as indicators of potential changes in the exchange rates. A few of the more significant ones follow:

1. *Changes in international monetary reserves* (the country's total holdings of gold and hard foreign currencies). If the reserves are growing, there is likely to be upward pressure on the currency.
2. *Changes in the balance of payments* (the total sum of inflows and outflows of a nation's currency). If the balance of payments is positive (more inflow than outflow) there will be upward pressure on the currency. Changes in the balance of payments also obviously affect the amount of reserves.
3. *Changes in the balance of trade* (exports-imports). For many countries, the major determinant of balance of payments is net trade balance (because currency inflows and outflows for other reasons are very small). Thus a surplus (positive) balance of trade would exert upward pressure on the currency.
4. *Changes in inflation.* Because exchange rates essentially adjust for differentials in national price levels, a relative decline in the inflation rate in one country compared to its major trading partners should exert upward pressure on the first country's currency. Also of particular importance are inflation's effects on the prices of exports and imports as well as on prices in general.
5. *Changes in production costs.* Significant increases in wages and other costs of production can obviously affect prices and hence inflation. What must also be considered, though, are changes in productivity, which may offset or aggravate the effect on total production costs and prices and, ultimately, on exchange rates.
6. *Changes in agricultural yields* (crop harvests). For many developing countries, agricultural exports are the main source of foreign exchange. A bad harvest can put downward pressure on the currency.
7. *Changes in other currencies with close economic ties to the country of the currency in question.* Often, the value of a country's currency will change not because of problems in that country but because of changes in another country's currency. For example, because so much of South Korea's economy is related to exports to the United States, a decline in the dollar makes it more difficult for Korea to export to the United States. As a result, Korea may choose to let its own currency move downward with the dollar in order not to disrupt its trade pattern. To cite another example, when the British pound was devalued in 1967, 22 other countries also devalued their currencies. Someone who was analyzing economic and political conditions within only one of these other 22 countries might have been surprised when the currency devalued.
8. *Changes in monetary and fiscal policy.* The real issue here is whether the changes attack the causes or the symptoms of the economic problems. If they attack the causes, they may result in upward pressure on the currency; if they attack only the symp-

toms, the market may react with downward pressure on the currency.

9. *Changes in trade policy.* Somewhat like changes in monetary and fiscal policy, the reaction to changes in trade policy depends largely on whether the changes attack the symptoms or the causes of the trade imbalance. For example, a temporary surcharge on imports would probably not decrease downward pressure on the currency, but a major change in export incentives might. However, if a country were to move forward *extensive* protection (increasing tariffs and putting on quotas), it might help the value of the currency even though such a program attacks only the symptoms.

10. *Politics.* Government stability is often a key factor affecting exchange rates. Instability or lack of confidence in a government's ability to manage both its domestic and foreign affairs can cause downward pressure on the currency. This appears to have been a major factor influencing the dollar's declining exchange rate throughout the 1970s.

   While by no means all-inclusive, these ten factors can serve as key indicators of a currency's future movement—its direction, magnitude, and timing. Several models have been developed which attempt to quantify the predictive effects of these variables on exchange rate changes, but none of them can guarantee success (see Table 7-1). At best, they help clarify the importance of certain factors and put the whole process of exchange rate forecasting into a logical and coherent framework. Forecasting the probability of a currency change may be based on these models, on sophisticated guesswork, on pure intuition, or on divine guidance. It is not an exact science. However, an educated guess is better than an uneducated guess, which should be better than no guess at all. In more sophisticated foreign exchange risk management models, forecasts of the maximum likely change, minimum likely change, and most likely change are called for, which at least provides some form of sensitivity analysis.[1] To get really fancy, these forecasts should be done for the entire planning period and for each segment.

---

[1]For details of the more sophisticated models of foreign exchange risk management, see Alan Shapiro and David Rutenberg, "Managing Foreign Exchange Rates in a Floating World," *Financial Management*, Summer 1976, pp. 48–58; Bernard Litaer, "Managing Risks in Foreign Exchange," *Harvard Business Review*, March-April 1970, pp. 127–138; and *Financial Management of Foreign Exchange*, Cambridge: MIT Press, 1971; Laurent Jacque, *Management of Foreign Exchange Risk*, Lexington, Mass.: Lexington Books, 1978; and William R. Folks, Jr., "Decision Analysis for Exchange Risk Management," *Financial Management*, Winter 1972, pp. 101–112.

TABLE 7–1. Profiles of Econometric Forecasting Services

	CHASE ECONOMETRICS ASSOCIATES	DATA RESOURCES INCORPORATED
Idiosyncracies of forecasting agency	Initially a spinoff from the Wharton Econometric Forecasting Associates, Chase Econometrics has gone a long way toward establishing its identity in macroeconomic forecasting of both the U.S. and foreign economies.	A long timer in macroeconomic forecasting with respect to the U.S. economy. Research staff is primarily composed of statisticians as well as econometricians.
Nature of forecasts	Fourteen currencies are forecasted eight quarters ahead.	Fourteen currencies are forecasted eight to ten quarters ahead. Four currencies are forecasted independently (deutschemark, Japanese yen, pound sterling, and Canadian dollar). Balance of fourteen currencies are forecasted as a spinoff of the deutschemark. Quantitative unconditional forecasts are issued monthly. Weekly judgmental memoranda qualify and update monthly quantitative forecasts.
Econometric approach	Exchange rates are regarded as linkages between national economies.	Different equations are used for each currency; they are reviewed monthly and updated yearly. Structural equations are derived from standard balance of payments theory.
Informational inputs	Exogenous variables estimates are generated by other "in-house" macroeconomic forecasting models.	Exogenous variables estimates are generated by other "in-house" macroeconomic forecasting models.

SOURCE: Laurent Jacque, *Management of Foreign Exchange Risk,* Lexington, Mass.: Lexington Books, 1978, pp. 88-89.

PREDEX	FOREX RESEARCH
Predex is a subsidiary of Marketing Control, which in 1970 established the World Data Bank specialized in forecasting market conditions in 45 countries.	Forex Research is a subsidiary of Commodity Research Unit, a London-based advisory service specialized in speculative commodities.
Reseach staff is small.	The research staff is made up of economists (rather than econometricians) formerly associated with such major international institutions as the International Monetary Fund and the European Economic Community Commissions.
	These former professional linkages of Forex research staff should give it preferential and speedy access to both quantitative and qualititative information used as inputs to the forecasting models, thus avoiding the usual time lag associated with reliance on published information.
Fourteen currencies are forecasted four quarters ahead.	Monthly reports of up to four quarters ahead exchange rates outlook represent end-points to a detailed macroeconomic forecasts.
Monthly reports include both the equation-based forecast as well as judgmental qualification by Predex economists of the quantitative forecast.	For each currency, forecasts provide average quarterly exchange rates against U.S. dollar and pound sterling, as well as effective trade-**weighted exchange rates against fourteen export markets currencies.**
Subscribers can substitute their own assumptions about the future course of each exogenous variable through direct access via their own computer terminals to Predex Model (interactive use).	Subscribers are encouraged to consult with Forex's senior research staff for judgmental assessment of printed forecasts.
	Forex distinguishes between "actionable" and "nonactionable" forecasts depending on whether the spread between the forward and forecasted rates is more or less than 0.5 percent.
The same econometric specification is used for each currency except for those tied to the deutschemark (snake agreement).	Modeling approach emphasizes external payments analysis.
Forecasting equations are based upon a synthesis of both the "absorptionist" and "monetarist" approaches to balance of payments theory.	Forecasting model incorporates the behavior of central banks intervention through the assessment of an "option space"—that is, the extent of maneuverability allowed to central banks.
Cumulative trade balances, money supplies, and approximations of nominal incomes are used as independent variables.	
Data used by Predex comes monthly from such public sources as central banks, the International Monetary Fund, and the Organization for Economic Cooperation and Development. Hence a significant information lag that puts Predex at a disadvantage vis-à-vis other forecasting agencies that rely on "in-house" generated input data (Chase Econometrics Associates and Data Resources Incorporated)	Forex is able to avoid some of the publication lag by obtaining its statistical information directly from central banks or other governmental agencies through its network of connections.

Preparing the Fund Flows Budget

The next step in foreign exchange risk management is specifying all the financing requirements and fund flows in each currency which cannot (or should not) be altered. Examples are changes in working capital and debt repayments. In other words, this process determines the fund flows which will be necessary to keep operations operational in the normal business context. Pro forma income and balance sheets should also be prepared for the planning period, or at least for those accounts which will be exposed to changes in the foreign currency values.

Determining the Accounting Exposure

Being reasonably certain that a major change in exchange rates is forthcoming, a wise company will next seek to ascertain what would be the effect of the expected change on its financial position—that is, will it cause a gain or loss? To ascertain this, the company must first calculate its accounting exposure, of which there are two kinds. As described in Chapter 5, the first is *transaction* exposure and the second is *translation* exposure. And while the exact definition and method of calculating translation exposure varies from one country to another, the method to be used in the United States is clearly spelled out in FASB 8: the temporal method. As we saw, the temporal method defines exposure as any asset or liability carried at current value (as opposed to historical value) and defines *net* accounting exposure as the differences between assets and liabilities carried at current values. Thus for most companies, exposure would include cash, plus accounts and notes receivable (and inventory only if its market value is lower than cost), minus accounts and notes payable, and long-term debt.

The net exposure must be further divided and analyzed by specific currency. That is, a note payable in the local currency must be treated differently from a note payable in a foreign currency whose value is expected to change relative to the local currency. For example, if a Mexican subsidiary has a 10,000 peso note payable to a Mexican bank and the value of the Mexican peso relative to the U.S. dollar declines 5 percent, the net result is a 5 percent gain for the U.S. parent because the Mexican subsidiary will use 5 percent less (in dollar equivalents) to repay the Mexican bank. However, if the Mexican subsidiary has a dollar-denominated note payable to a *U.S.* bank of similar amount and the Mexican peso declines 5 percent, the U.S. company would record a loss because the Mexican subsidiary will use 5 percent more pesos to repay the dollar debt. Thus to calculate its *overall* net accounting exposure, a firm must determine its net exposure in each currency in which it has assets or liabilities carried at current value. For a large multinational company with operations and transactions in more than a hundred countries and currencies, this procedure is not exactly an easy task.

Once the overall net exposure has been calculated, a firm is then in a position to estimate the effect on its financial position of the expected change in currency values. This is done by multiplying the net exposure times the expected change in exchange rates. In the example of the U.S. company with a Mexican subsidiary, if the subsidiary has a net *negative* exposure of a million pesos (that is, its liabilities are greater than its assets carried at current value) and the peso is expected to decline 5 percent against the U.S. dollar, then the expected impact would be a 5 percent foreign exchange *gain* for the U.S. parent to the tune of 50,000 pesos (or, more specifically, the U.S. dollar equivalent of 50,000 pesos). If the subsidiary had a *positive* net exposure of one million pesos, then the U.S. parent could anticipate a 5 percent (50,000 peso) *loss*.

Acting on the Accounting Exposure

Once a firm has calculated the potential financial impact from an exchange rate change, it is then faced with several options:

1. It can choose to do nothing.
2. It can choose to alter its net accounting exposure.
3. It can cover its existing accounting exposure.
4. It can do some combination of the three alternatives.

Doing nothing is a strategy most often selected when conditions are expected to result in a *gain*. These conditions would prevail when (a) the net exposure is positive in a currency which is expected to rise in value, (b) the net exposure is negative in a currency whose value is expected to decline, (c) the sum of the expected gains from exposed positions in some currencies is greater than the sum of the expected losses from exposed positions in other currencies, or (d) the overall net exposure is zero.

The first two conditions require no elaboration. The third condition applies when a company may have positive exposures (net asset exposures) in some currencies which are expected to increase in value and others which are expected to decrease in value. For example, suppose a company has positive exposure in both deutsche marks and pesos. If the expected foreign exchange gain in deutsche marks exceeds the expected loss in pesos, the company overall will show a gain. The fourth condition applies when a company has both a positive and a negative exposure in the same currency. This can result from having a negative exposure of 10,000 pesos in one subsidiary but a positive 10,000 peso exposure in another subsidiary. It can also occur in a situation similar to the third condition except that the expected global gains from exposed positions in all currencies equal the expected global losses.

The key point is that the company must ascertain its *global* exposure in currencies, and not just the exposure in each subsidiary. The reason is that the company may not need to take any corrective action even if it has potential foreign exchange losses in several subsidiaries, so long as its global exposure will not result in a loss. This consideration may enable the company to avoid considerable headaches and expenses related to reducing or covering its exposure at the subsidiary level. In other words, the subsidiaries may not have to take any action at all.

Rearranging the Accounting Exposure

Rearranging the accounting exposure is an appropriate strategy when the conditions listed above do not exist, and the firm expects a foreign exchange loss. If accounting exposure is the difference between assets and liabilities whose values are subject to change when exchange rates change, it follows that the exposure itself can be changed. This can be done by adjusting the amounts of assets and liabilities included in the exposure. For example, local currency held by the U.S. company's Mexican subsidiary is subject to a decline in its translated value if the Mexican peso declines relative to the U.S. dollar. So too would the subsidiary's peso-denominated accounts receivable and peso-denominated debts. To minimize the negative effects of a peso depreciation on these exposed accounts, the subsidiary could speed up collection of its peso-denominated accounts receivables and get rid of its pesos on hand—perhaps investing them in land or some other asset whose value would not be affected by a shift in the exchange rate. Since the U.S. dollar value of its peso debts would decline with the depreciation of the Mexican peso, the company could keep its present level of peso debt or increase the debt to help offset any peso monetary assets it could not decrease.

On the other hand, the Mexican subsidiary's dollar-denominated payables and loans would increase in amount if the peso declined. To avoid these potential losses, the subsidiary could speed up its repayment of dollar-denominated payables and loans. At the same time, any dollar receivables or dollars on hand in the Mexican subsidiary would be worth more *after* the peso declined, resulting in a translation gain. The Mexican subsidiary could increase its dollar-denominated accounts receivable or delay the collection of existing ones, and try to increase its holdings of dollars or other currencies that are expected to rise in value against the peso. By carefully juggling the composition and amounts of its peso-denominated and foreign-currency-denominated assets and liabilities that comprise its accounting exposure, the firm can reduce, eliminate (balance), or even reverse its net accounting exposure.

However, before getting too excited about rearranging the exposure as a cheap and riskless way of protecting against exchange losses or avoiding the use of covering or hedging techniques, a few sobering words of caution are in order. Rearranging the *accounting* exposure can also affect the firm's *economic* exposure. More important, changing the firm's *economic* exposure may be far more risky and costly than losses from changes in exchange rates. How and why this may come about is the subject of the next section.

Accounting Exposure versus Economic Exposure

Of the several possible definitions of economic exposure, one which is suitable here is "the loss of future business, or opportunity cost." *Opportunity cost* in this sense means the cost of the profitable business opportunities a firm passes up when it takes certain actions which prevent it from taking advantage of other alternatives. To be more specific, the opportunity cost of doing business on a cash only, no-credit basis is the loss of additional sales which might be made if the company were willing to provide credit to buyers. Similarly, the opportunity cost of having a company's investable funds all tied up in long-term nonliquid assets is the loss from having to forgo potentially more profitable short-term investments. Very interesting, you say, but what does this have to do with foreign exchange risk management? A great deal.

As an example, suppose a company has a net asset exposure in a currency whose value is expected to decline. Ignoring temporarily the concept of economic exposure, the firm could rearrange its exposed assets and liabilities to bring the accounting exposure to zero: reduce the appropriate assets and increase the appropriate liabilities until the sums of the two are equal. To accomplish this, it could discontinue local currency sales on credit, speed up collection of local currency receivables, delay payment of its own local currency payables, increase its local debt, and get rid of all its local currency by investing in land. However, these actions make the firm extremely illiquid, more heavily in debt, on worse terms with its customers and creditors, and in danger of losing customers who need to buy on credit. Any one of these results alone, and certainly several of them in combination, will increase the firm's economic exposure, which means the firm is not in as sound a business position as it was previously. Angering its existing customers by speeding up the collection of accounts receivable and angering its potential customers by not extending credit could affect the company's future revenue streams. Increasing its debt puts the firm under a future cash outflow squeeze to repay the debt when it comes due, while investing funds in long-term illiquid assets further decreases working capital and liquidity. In sum, by attempting to decrease its accounting exposure the company increases its economic exposure. Any gains from doing the former may be more than offset by losses from the latter. The real trick, as Aristotle pointed out centuries ago (although probably not with reference to foreign exchange risk management), is to find the golden mean.

Applied to foreign exchange risk management, the *golden mean approach* entails carefully analyzing the accounting exposure to make sure that nothing can be done to change it further without significantly increasing the firm's economic exposure. If some things still can be done in this regard, they should be done in order to minimize the cost of covering the remaining accounting exposure by means of contractual devices.

Once this golden mean has been achieved, if there remains an accounting exposure which is expected to result in a foreign exchange loss, then the firm has two options left. It can do nothing, or it can cover the accounting exposure by utilizing one or a number of techniques which are discussed below. Again, the choice largely hinges on the availability and cost of the covering techniques and the firm's policies toward risk.

Determining the Operational Constraints Which Cannot Be Violated

This step involves examining corporate policies and government restrictions with respect to hedging strategies. Corporate policies may preclude swap arrangements because of bad experiences with them, or may preclude costly hedging policies owing to a shortage of corporate funds. Government restrictions may preclude or limit forward foreign exchange contracts or local bank loans in periods of tight money. Clearly there is little point in considering hedging methods that would be unacceptable to the company or the country.

Identifying the Acceptable Alternatives

When a company has minimized its exposed position and still wants to protect itself from the losses attendant upon an anticipated change in exchange rates, it has several options. Among them are (1) the forward exchange market, (2) loans from a foreign bank, (3) foreign currency swaps, (4) arbiloans, and (5) credit swaps (using covered interest arbitrage).

Using the forward exchange market can reduce the risk of a loss from an unfavorable change in exchange rates when foreign funds will be paid or received at some future date. For example, assume that a U.S. company has signed a contract to purchase equipment from a German manufacturer for a price of DM18,630, the bill to be paid in thirty days. If the current spot rate is $1 = DM1.863, the cost in dollars would be $10,000. If the value of the mark was expected to rise over the thirty-day period, however, the U.S. dollar purchase price would also rise, as more dollars would be needed to purchase the marks. This would represent an additional cost (loss) to the U.S. purchaser. To protect against this potential loss, the U.S. company could enter into a thirty-day forward contract to buy deutsche marks at the going rate for thirty-days forward. If this forward rate were $1 = DM1.857, the U.S. company would have to pay $10,032 in thirty days to buy the marks from the forward seller, which would in turn, be paid to the German supplier. The direct cost to the U.S. purchaser of using the forward market would be $32. Whether this action would prove to be wise would obviously depend on what the spot rate turned out to be on the thirtieth day. If it turned out to be higher than the forward rate, $1 = DM1.857, the U.S. company would have saved money by *not* using the forward market. For example, if the spot rate remained the same, using the forward market cost the company $32 more than it would have had to pay otherwise. But if the spot rate ended up lower than the forward rate, then the company actually saved money by incurring the forward coverage cost of $32. For example, if the spot rate ended being $1 = DM1.850, the company would have had to pay $10,070 to buy the needed 18,630 marks, an additional $70. By using the forward market, the company saved $38 ($70 − $32). Nonetheless, the final purchase price would be higher than the $10,000 initial price on day one, so the net result, even with forward market coverage, was an additional cost (loss). However, using the forward market eliminated the risk of an even higher cost (loss). In this sense, the coverage could be construed as an insurance premium—protecting against a greater loss.

Borrowing from a foreign bank can also reduce potential foreign exchange losses. Suppose a U.S. truck manufacturer has a contract to sell a truck to a British company for $20,292 but the buyer insists on paying in pounds sterling rather than dollars. Further assume that the spot rate is $1 = £.49281 and the terms of sale call for payment in thirty days. If the spot rate in thirty days is the same as on day one, the U.S. seller receives £10,000, which could be converted to $20,292. However, if the spot rate increases (the pound depreciates against the dollar), the U.S. dollar value of the £10,000 will be less than $20,292, and the U.S. manufacturer will incur a loss.

To protect against such a loss, the U.S. supplier could borrow £10,000 from a British bank for thirty days, convert the £10,000 at the spot rate on day one to $20,292, and invest the dollars in an interest-bearing account in the United States. At the end of thirty days, the U.S. seller receives £10,000 from the British buyer and uses this to repay the British bank. The cost of this method of coverage is the difference between the interest received in the United States and the interest which must be paid to the British bank, or the difference between U.S. and British interest rates. If the U.S. interest rate is 6 percent and the U.K. rate 8 percent, the total cost would be approximately $34.

$$\left[\frac{(.08)\ £10,000}{12} \times 2.0292\right] - \left[\frac{(.06)(\$20,292)}{12}\right] = \$34$$

Thus $34 represents the cost of covering the potential loss on the sale of the truck.

The same £10,000 loan procedure could be used by a U.S. company to cover a £10,000 net asset position for itself or for its foreign subsidiaries. For example, if one of its subsidiaries has a net asset position of £10,000 and the pound is expected to decline in value, the subsidiary faces a potential foreign exchange *translation* loss. Borrowing £10,000 and converting the money to another currency which is expected to increase in value relative to the pound would have two beneficial effects in terms of foreign exchange risk management. First, it would increase the net asset position of the company in a currency expected to increase in value, resulting in a foreign exchange gain. Second, the £10,000 loan would increase the net liability position in a currency that is expected to decline in value and, in this specific example, eliminate the potential loss if the £10,000 net asset position of the company were left uncovered.

A *foreign currency swap* can similarly reduce potential losses from a change in exchange rates. A foreign currency swap is a simultaneous spot and forward transaction in the forward market, with the forward purchase reversing the spot transaction. Suppose a British subsidiary borrows £10,000 for thirty days from its U.S. parent to increase its working capital. This £10,000 loan is subject to an exchange rate loss for the parent if the pound depreciates against the dollar (that is, if the dollar value of the £10,000 will be less in thirty days when the subsidiary repays the loan). To avoid this risk, the U.S. parent could arrange a currency swap. If the spot rate is £1 = $2.0292, the parent company could convert $20,292 to £10,000 and send the pounds to the subsidiary. At the same time, the parent could enter into a thirty-day forward contract to sell pounds for dollars at the going forward rate (£1 = $2.0259) in order to cover its loan. If the parent wants to charge its subsidiary the going U.S. rate of interest (the opportunity cost of lending to its subsidiary rather than investing the dollars in the United States for thirty days), it would need to purchase forward $20,394:

$$\$20,292 + \frac{(.06)(\$20,292)}{12} = \$20,394$$

This procedure would cost £10,067 at the forward rate of £1 = $2.0259: (20,394 × .4936). The net cost to the company is the difference between the pounds lent and the pounds needed to fulfill the forward contract: £67 (roughly 8 percent on an annual basis).

An *arbiloan*, another variety of the currency swap, is a technique of financing by interest arbitrage. This method is used primarily when a subsidiary or parent in a high-interest-rate, tight-money market needs funds, but can obtain them only from a foreign money market. In an arbiloan, the company has one of its affiliates in a surplus, cheap-funds market borrow money in its behalf. These funds are converted at the spot rate into the currency of the initiating company (the real borrower rather than the intermediate borrower). Simultaneously, the real borrowing company enters into a forward contract with the same maturity date as the loan to repurchase the foreign currency needed to repay the loan. The cost to the real borrower is the foreign interest rate *plus* the cost of the forward exchange protection, if the foreign currency forward sells at a premium, or *minus* the cost of the protection, if the foreign currency forward sells at a discount. In the previous example of the British subsidiary and the U.S. parent, the subsidiary asks the parent to borrow $20,292 from a U.S. bank in order to lend the subsidiary £10,000. If the U.S. interest rate is 6 percent and the forward rate is £1 = $2.0259, the subsidiary buys forward $20,394 (principal plus interest) at a cost of £10,067—again, a total cost to the subsidiary of £67. The only difference between the foreign currency swap and the arbiloan was that a foreign bank was used as the source of funds rather than the parent company (which was presumably short of funds itself).

Credit swaps are still another variety of swap, although rarely used compared to the other forms because their costs are higher. They are used primarily in lending funds to affiliates in weak currency countries where there is no forward market or where there are legal restrictions on the use of forward exchange contracts. For example, suppose a Brazilian subsidiary of an American company needs to borrow money, but the Brazilian banks have no loanable funds. In this situation, the parent company can deposit dollars in the U.S. account of a Brazilian bank; and, because this deposit creates additional funds, the Brazilian bank can lend money to the Brazilian subsidiary of the U.S. parent. When the Brazilian loan matures, the Brazilian subsidiary repays the Brazilian bank, which in turn has its U.S. branch return the dollar deposit to the U.S. parent. In this manner, neither the parent nor the foreign bank nor the subsidiary is exposed to any gain or loss from exchange rate fluctuations.

However, there are several catches to this seemingly great technique. First, the U.S. dollar loan to the foreign bank is generally interest-free, whereas the local currency loan to the subsidiary is usually interest-bearing. Second, the local currency loan to the subsidiary is usually significantly *less* than the spot rate equivalent of the dollar deposit. In other words, if the spot rate between the dollar and the local currency (LC) is $1 = LC20, the swap rate might be $1 = LC10. Thus depositing $10,000 in the U.S. account of a foreign bank results in only LC100,000 being lent by the foreign bank to the foreign subsidiary, rather than LC200,000. Stated another way, if the foreign subsidiary needs a loan of LC200,000 the parent company would have to deposit $20,000 rather than $10,000, and it would incur an opportunity cost from having to tie up that much more money in a non-interest-bearing loan. Finally, the credit swap arrangement typically covers only the principal amount of the loan and not the interest on the principal. The latter could serve as a return on the parent's investment or could pay U.S. interest if the parent company itself had to borrow the dollar funds. Thus the credit swap too has certain associated costs which are generally higher than those of other methods of coverage. For all these reasons, the credit swap is used sparingly, usually when other coverage is not available.

In sum, these are the principal direct means of covering the exposure to changes in foreign exchange rates. Each alternative has a certain direct, identifiable cost associated with it, and often opportunity costs as well. In the more sophisticated models of foreign exchange risk management, the cost of each strategy should be estimated in terms of maximum use, minimum use, and most likely use. In addition, each alternative strategy has an uncertain risk attached: the risk that exchange rates will not change as anticipated. It should also be reiterated that not all these covering alternatives are always available to the multinational firm. Sometimes, government laws or company policies preclude or limit the use of some alternatives. Sometimes, alternatives exist in theory but not in reality, such as when there is no forward market for a particular currency. Thus the process of covering exposure is often more difficult in reality than these pages make it seem.

Plugging the Information into the Computer

This step is reasonably straightforward, assuming a computer and a good model. For a good discussion and analysis of the use of computer-based models, see Eugene Carter and Rita Rodriguez, "Foreign Exchange

Exposure: Models for Management."[2] Although the computer is not essential, it obviously speeds up the generation of the spectrum of solutions.

Choosing the Right Strategy

This procedure pertains to the company's aggressiveness or defensiveness with regard to foreign exchange risk management. The company now has a spectrum of solutions, each with a specific cost and risk. Which course of action it ultimately chooses depends on whether the company is a risk-taker or risk-averter, whether it can afford the risks and costs, and how much confidence it places in the accountants and financial officers who developed the foreign exchange risk management plan.

FOREIGN EXCHANGE RISK MANAGEMENT IN PRACTICE

An example of a sophisticated foreign exchange risk management model in use should help clarify the whole process. The example, taken from an article by Bernard Litaer, is based on a well-known billion-dollar company—referred to as Ace—headquartered in New York. Its treasurer is determining the financing and hedging policy for a wholly owned subsidiary in Argentina.[3]

The planning horizon is six months, and the data are expressed in monthly time units. The corporate economist who follows the Latin American currencies came up with estimates for the devaluation probabilities and amounts for the peso over the next six months. The curve in Figure 8 presents these estimates. The probability of a devaluation in month 1 is zero, but it increases to 40 percent in month 3. Thereafter, it decreases steadily until it reaches 5 percent in month 6. The minimum probable devaluation varies between 9 percent and 15 percent during this period, while the maximum probable devaluation increases from 15 to 24 percent. The increasing spread of the devaluation amounts shows that the economist grows more uncertain about the data the farther into the future he looks. The fins represent the likely devaluations and their variabilities.

The cash and exposure budgets for the subsidiary set forth the future

---

[2]Eugene Carter and Rita Rodriguez, "Foreign Exchange Exposure: Models for Management," *Euromoney*, March 1978, pp. 95–111.
[3]Litaer, "Managing Risks."

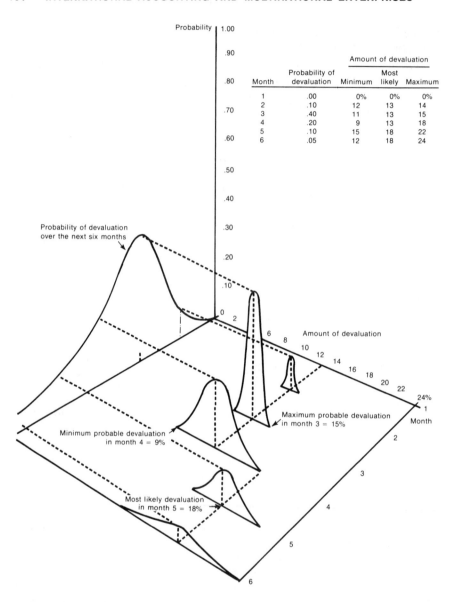

| | | Amount of devaluation | | |
Month	Probability of devaluation	Minimum	Most likely	Maximum
1	.00	0%	0%	0%
2	.10	12	13	14
3	.40	11	13	15
4	.20	9	13	18
5	.10	15	18	22
6	.05	12	18	24

Figure 8. Probabilities and amounts of devaluation of the Argentinian peso, month 1 through month 6. (Source: Bernard Litaer, "Managing Risks in Foreign Exchange," *Harvard Business Review*, March–April 1970, p. 135.)

financing requirements and the net exposure before any new financing and hedging are done. New cash requirements fluctuate between $1.0 million and $4.5 million per month, and the highest amount is expected for month 4. The bulk of these requirements relate to operating expenses and repayments of old debts. The exposure budget rises steadily from $1.5 million in the first month to $6 million during month 6. Ace has a policy of not speculating on foreign exchange, and the net exposure therefore will never be allowed to be negative.

The treasurer has five financing and hedging transactions from which to choose:

1. *Straight dollar financing.* The effective annual cost of a loan in the United States is assumed to be 11.1 percent, with a comparatively low variation in this cost.
2. *Foreign (local Argentinian) bank loans.* Four interest ranges are considered for three-month lines of credit:
   a. Between 20 and 24 percent annual effective interest. Only small amounts are available at this cost: between $200,000 and $400,000 per month.
   b. Between 24 and 31 percent annual effective interest. Available amounts fluctuate between $600,000 and $800,000 per month.
   c. Between 31 and 41 percent annual effective interest. About $2 million can be borrowed per month at this cost.
   d. Between 41 and 50 percent annual interest. Practically any amount can be borrowed at this cost.
3. *Forward exchange contracts.* Argentina controls the rights to purchase forward peso contracts. Ace International qualifies for only two forward contracts—a contract of $300,000 in month 4 and another contract of $600,000 in month 5. The annual cost is 25.5 percent.
4. *Swap transactions.* Three-month swaps are available to cover Ace exports from Argentina. The annual expense is 15.3 percent, and the maximum monthly ceiling is $500,000.
5. *Bond transactions.* Excess cash can be invested in prime-rate commercial paper or treasury bonds, which the treasurer will divest when Ace needs additional cash. In Argentina, the yield on these bonds is 12 percent.

No other transactions are considered.

The problem for the treasurer is to decide which transactions should be performed to meet the subsidiary's cash needs while taking into account the present net exposure and the outlook for Argentina's peso.

The Solution

Of the whole set of optimal policies the computer generated only two are described here: a very conservative policy and a rather aggressive one. The transactions in the policies for each of these solutions are listed in Table 7–2. As the table shows, the model gives exact instructions

TABLE 7–2. Conservative and Aggressive Solution to Ace International's Financing and Hedging Problem (dollar figures in millions)

	CONSERVATIVE SOLUTION	AGGRESSIVE SOLUTION
Dollar financing		
Month 1	Use $1.0	Use $2.0
Month 4	Use $1.5	Use $1.5
All other months	Do not use	Do not use
Foreign bank loans with these effective annual interest rates:		
20% to 24%	Use in all months at maximum	Do not use in month 1; use in all other months at maximum
24% to 31%	Use in all months at maximum	Use at maximum in months 3, 4, 5
31% to 41%	Do not use in month 1; use in all other months at maximum	Do not use
41% to 51%	Do not use in month 1; use in small amounts in all other months	Do not use
Forward exchange contracts	Use in all months at maximum	Do not use
Financial swaps	Use in all months at maximum	Use in all months at maximum
Bond transactions		
Month 1	Buy $0.5	Buy $1.1
Month 2	Sell $0.5	Sell $0.5
Month 3	Buy $1.1	Buy $0.8
Month 4	Sell $1.1	Sell $1.4
Total expected costs	$0.75	$0.5
Total risk (measured by maximum possible cost with 5% probability)	$0.8	$1.0
Net exposure		
Month 1	$1.6	$2.0
Month 2	0	$1.0
Month 6	0	$3.5
All other months	0	0

Source: Bernard Litaer, "Managing Risks in Foreign Exchange," *Harvard Business Review*, March–April 1970, p. 137.

about how the treasurer ought to use the available foreign bank loans, forward exchange contracts, financial swaps, and bonds.

The conservative solution has a low risk but a high expected cost—$750,000—for all financing and hedging during six months. The risk is low: there is a .05 probability that an additional $50,000 will be needed, bringing the total potential cost to $800,000. The aggressive solution has a lower expected cost: only $500,000. However, the risk is high: there is a .05 probability that as much as an additional $500,000 in costs will be incurred, bringing the potential total to $1 million.

Under the conservative policy, net exposure amounts to $1.6 million in the first month, but is reduced to zero in all subsequent months. Because the probability of devaluation in month 1 is zero, little effort is made to reduce the net exposure. In all later months, however, this policy guarantees a perfect hedge. The aggressive solution also has a very high exposure in the first month, some $2 million. This amount, which is even higher than the net exposure before any hedging is performed, is the result of the heavy dollar financing allocated for purchasing Argentine treasury bonds in month 1. (Treasury bonds are an exposed asset and therefore increase the net exposure.) In months 2 and 6, some of the net exposure remains—$1.0 million and $3.5 million respectively—because the aggressive treasurer judges additional hedging to be more expensive than the risk of devaluation loss justifies.

A closer look at how each policy treats the five alternatives for financing and hedging reveals the following.

Dollar financing possibilities are used in two months only—months 1 and 4. The financial requirements of month 1 are met by this source of funds, as are the bulk of the bond purchases. The more aggressive solution uses this transaction more extensively than the conservative one during month 1. For both policies, another $1.5 million is imported to help meet the heavy cash requirements during month 4.

Foreign bank loans are used simultaneously as a source of cash and as a hedge. The conservative policy tends to hedge even at a high cost, a tendency borne out by the extensive use of local credit. The cheapest loans are used at capacity during all six months, including those with a low probability of devaluation, and even the more expensive ones are used during all months except month 1. The aggressive solution is more discriminating: no hedging at all is done during month 1, and loans with an effective cost of 24 to 31 percent are used only when there is the highest probability of devaluation; namely in months 3, 4, and 5. It completely disregards the more expensive hedges, which explains why the net exposure is not reduced to zero during all months.

Forward exchange contracts are pure hedges and consequently do not make new cash available. The conservative solution accordingly recommends the purchase of the two forward exchange contracts available, and the aggressive solution neglects them entirely.

Financial swaps are a comparatively cheap source of cash and hedging, and therefore both policies recommend their maximum use.

Bond transactions perform the task of leveling cash requirements. Under the conservative policy, the treasurer buys bonds in month 1 and sells them during month 2. Since sources of cash are cheap during month 1, and heavy cash requirements have drained all cheap sources of financing in month 2, it is best to borrow greater amounts of cheap money early and invest it until it is needed. The same kinds of transactions occur on a larger scale during months 3 and 4, for similar reasons. The cash requirements of month 4 are the heaviest of all, and therefore it is logical to channel funds from month 3 to month 4 so as to even out the cash needs.

The more aggressive solution involves essentially the same bond transactions, but on a larger scale. In the first month, $1.1 million of bonds are purchased with the imported dollars, and a part of the bonds are sold in month 2. Another $0.8 million are acquired during month 3. Finally, in month 4, the heavy cash requirements are partially met by selling all $1.4 million accumulated in bonds.

To summarize, the conservative solution has a high cost but a low risk. The exposure is reduced to zero in all months except the first one by extensive use of local bank loans, financial swaps, and forward exchange contracts. Bonds are used to level out cash requirements during the first four months. The more aggressive solution carries more risk, but it offers a lower expected cost. It relies more heavily on dollar financing and disregards all the more expensive hedges. The resulting exposure is therefore considerable during the months in which the probability of devaluation is low. Bond transactions are used more extensively in the aggressive than in the conservative solution.

These solutions are only two of the many on the entire efficient frontier. The conservative solution would correspond to policy B shown earlier in Figure 7, while the aggressive solution would be policy A. The treasurer ultimately bases the choice of solution on company policies and preferences. After choosing, all the relevant recommendations are implemented for month 1. Then, if the treasurer is still confident of the estimates at the beginning of month 2, the model's recommendation for that time unit of the planning period is implemented. If there is reason to doubt some of the key estimates, the problem is run through the computer once again.

CONCLUSIONS

Managing foreign exchange risk constitutes one of the most complicated functions performed by multinational enterprises. The sophistication and costs required are considerable, which also suggests that a company should weigh these costs against the benefits expected from adopting an extensive system of foreign exchange risk management. For many a company, the personnel, time, and related costs may exceed the benefits: lower foreign exchange losses. Such a company may be better off in managing only its *transaction* exposure, for example, but only if the potential losses are substantial. Unfortunately, no one can precisely predict the losses, and only after the fact can one assess whether the foreign exchange risk management undertaken was wise.

If there is any consolation for accountants in foreign exchange risk management, it is that they are not likely to be directly involved in making most of these decisions. But they do play an important supportive role, supplying the accounting information on which the ultimate decisions are based. The funds flow and the accounting exposure determinations must be prepared accurately and suitably and must be transmitted to the appropriate persons in a timely fashion. This may require the design and implementation of new information collection and reporting procedures. Close coordination of activities is necessary not only within the accounting staff but also between it and the treasurer's staff. Accountants are more heavily involved in the treatment and reporting of gains and losses from foreign exchange rate changes, but an understanding of the entire process of foreign exchange management will clarify the accountant's role in that process.

A final comment on foreign exchange risk management concerns the potential change in FASB 8. As discussed in Chapter 6, the 1980 FASB exposure draft on the treatment of foreign exchange gains and losses specifies the use of the all-current method for measuring exposure. One effect of this proposed change would be that virtually all companies would have positive (asset) exposures. Because the bulk of U.S. investment abroad is in strong currency countries, this implies that most U.S. multinationals will experience more translation *gains* as long as the dollar remains weak against strong currencies such as the yen, the franc, and the deutschemark. This in itself may lessen the need and pressures for foreign exchange risk management. In addition, the 1980 exposure draft proposes that exchange gains and losses be removed from the income statement and be carried instead directly to the balance sheet. Removing the effect of exchange rate changes from the income statement would also lessen the current importance given foreign exchange risk management. However, even if the exposure draft becomes the new standard, foreign exchange risk management will continue to be important, albeit of somewhat less so than it was during the latter half of the 1970s.

STUDY QUESTIONS

7–1. What are the major risks associated with foreign exchange risk management?

7–2. What are the major costs?

7–3.   Explain the difference between accounting exposure and economic exposure.

7–4.   Give some examples of changes in the accounting exposure which would
    a.   adversely affect economic exposure;
    b.   favorably affect economic exposure.

7–5.   Explain what is meant by the statement: There is no single best solution to foreign exchange risk management.

7–6.   In deciding whether to cover an exposed position, what factors should be considered?

7–7.   In deciding how to cover an exposed position, what factors should be considered?

7–8.   Other than financial restrictions, what factors constrain the foreign exchange risk management decision?

7–9.   Why is it important for an accountant to understand foreign exchange risk management?

7–10. Discuss the implications of FASB's 1980 exposure draft on foreign exchange gains and losses on the relative importance given foreign exchange risk management. Why, even if the changes are adopted, will foreign exchange risk management still be important?

CASE

INTERNATIONAL DISTRIBUTORS, INC.

It had been a rough week for Dana Curtis. Two weeks ago the executive committee of International Distributors, Inc. had called on her to explain the company's foreign exchange risk management system. Prior to 1977, the company had experienced no significant gains or losses from changes in foreign exchange rates, but the final figures for 1977 had shown a loss in excess of $36 million, the result of changes in exchange rates. Needless to say, the executive committee had not been pleased with this result, particularly of its adverse effect on the company's earnings per share. As the person on the corporate staff most knowledgeable about foreign exchange risk management, Dana was questioned about why the losses had occurred, then was asked to prepare a review paper on the company's operational environment and policies with regard to foreign exchange.

Existing Policies and Strategies

International Distributors' main policy on foreign exchange—considered by many people to be risky—called only for hedging foreign exchange transactions and commitments. Its accounting translation exposure was *not* covered or altered in order to minimize foreign exchange losses. The committee that had established this policy had recognized the risk that neglecting its translation exposure could result in significant losses if exchange rates moved in certain ways. However, all foreign currency debts were paid (or expected to be paid) by affiliates out of earnings in the local currencies and were not guaranteed by the U.S. parent. In addition, the committee had been concerned that altering the translation exposure might worsen the company's underlying business prospects. And finally, during the five years that the policy had been in effect, the company had experienced exchange gains.

The Changing Environment

Prior to 1977, the company had utilized the current-noncurrent method of defining translation exposure, which, given the nature of the business, had almost always resulted in a net asset position for each subsidiary as well as for the company as a whole. Because 70 percent of the company's operations were in Europe, largely in strong currency countries, the net asset position had resulted in translation gains. After 1976, the company was required to comply with FASB 8 and use the temporal method. Since then the company's inventory has been removed from the list of exposed accounts and translated at historic rates, which caused the company's exposed position to shift from net asset to net liability.

As the major European currencies continued to increase in value relative to the dollar, the net liability position caused major translation losses. In addition, the countries with weak currencies (relative to the dollar) where International Distributors had operations had experienced a temporary strengthening of their currencies. Thus no exchange gains materialized from having exposed liability positions in weak currency countries, which were expected to partially offset the losses in hard currency countries. Finally, competition in all the company's markets had increased significantly. The marketing staff had recommended that credit sales and terms be expanded in order to gain an advantage over competitors, but the corporate staff wanted to analyze this proposal in terms of its implications for cash flows and foreign exchange exposure.

Questions

1. What are the strengths and weaknesses of the company's policy with respect to foreign exchange risk management?
2. Should its policy be changed because of the changing conditions?
3. What might be the impact of the marketing department's recommendation on the company's exchange gains and losses? What other factors should be considered before the recommendation is adopted?
4. If the company's policy is not to be changed, how would you write the paragraph in the company's annual report that explains the policy in light of the exchange losses?
5. If FASB 8 is replaced with the 1980 exposure draft, what would the impact be on International Distributors' foreign exchange risk management procedures and policies?

8

Accounting for Inflation Worldwide

At the mere mention of inflation, people conjure up images of the collapse of the world monetary system and the end of civilization, gold bugs declaim about the presses that work overtime printing paper currencies in Latin America, and Europeans recall with horror how the German mark shriveled in value from 4 per dollar to 4.2 billion per dollar in the 1920s. Inflation is a focus of interest around the world among economists and government fiscal and monetary policy makers, and even accountants are getting into the act. This chapter discusses what inflation is and what it does to business; looks at alternative ways to account for inflation; examines specific guidelines for inflation accounting in the United States, United Kingdom, the Netherlands, and Brazil; and highlights the difficulties facing a multinational enterprise that operates in a variety of inflationary environments and is subjected to myriad reporting regulations.

WHAT IS INFLATION?

Inflation is a sustained increase in the price index from one period to the next. Because attitudes toward inflation vary from country to country, it might be more accurate to say that inflation occurs when the price index rises above a tolerable level. In 1978, for example, Germans were troubled when the rate of inflation crept up to nearly 4 percent in the first quarter. In Italy, which ended 1977 with inflation at an annual rate of 17 percent, there would have been dancing in the streets if the inflation rate could have been kept down to that of Germany. And then there was Argentina, one of the acknowledged world leaders in inflation, with a rate of 175.5 percent in 1978, down sharply from its 443.2 percent in 1976. Most countries express inflation as the quarterly or annual change in the consumer price index, which is based on a broad basket of consumer goods. The wholesale price index and the gross national product price deflator, and other indexes, are also used in some countries.

Table 8–1 compares rates of inflation worldwide using the consumer price index, the most widely used index for comparative purposes. As noted, inflation was at fairly low levels in the early 1970s, but it took off in 1974, largely as a result of the oil price increases instituted by OPEC (the Organization of Petroleum Exporting Countries). Hardest hit were the developing countries where inflation increased by 28.3 percent in 1974. In Latin America, the increase was even higher at 34.5 percent. By 1978, the rate of inflation had begun dropping worldwide to a level of only 9.6 percent, compared with the higher level of 15.3 percent in 1974. However, the table shows that inflation began heating up again in 1979.

By the end of the first quarter of 1980 the rate of inflation in the United States had risen to 14.7 percent, which was higher than the industrial world average of 12.4 percent. However, inflation in the developing countries, in general, was over 35 percent and in Latin America it was over 55 percent. With few exceptions, inflation appears to be moving to higher levels, creating problems for everyone.

 ✗ What are the major reasons for inflation? The classical explanation is that there is too much money chasing too few goods. In other words, the demand for products exceeds the supply. Sometimes the money supply expands too rapidly, putting plenty of money in people's hands when there are not enough goods for them to buy. This pushes up prices on available goods. Thus government monetary policy is critical. Fiscal policy can also be important—if the government expands its service programs, for example, putting more purchasing power in people's hands without an expansion in the production of goods.

Argentina is a good example of fiscal and monetary policy leading to inflation. Because of a strong export sector and a control on imports, Argentina enjoyed a trade surplus in 1978 of $2 billion. Those dollars were converted into newly issued pesos for local consumption, leading one key government leader to estimate that 80 percent of 1978's inflation was due to the trade surplus. As imports are encouraged, the trade surplus should shrink to a less inflationary level.[1]

Sometimes, supply bottlenecks in one sector of the economy can create shortages in other sectors, leading to price increases as demand outstrips supply. This could occur in primary products such as raw

[1]*Wall Street Journal*, 16 July 1979, p. 18.

TABLE 8–1. Annual Increase in the Consumer Price Index for Selected Years

	1972	1974	1978	1979
United States	3.3	11.0	7.7	11.3
Japan	4.4	24.3	3.8	3.6
West Germany	5.5	7.0	2.6	4.1
Britain	7.3	16.0	8.3	13.4
Switzerland	6.7	9.7	1.1	3.6
Canada	4.8	10.9	9.0	9.2
World	5.8	15.3	9.6	12.0
Industrial countries	4.5	13.1	6.8	9.1
Developing countries	12.7	28.3	24.7	28.9

SOURCE: *International Financial Statistics,* published by the International Monetary Fund.

materials as well as in manufactured components. Or the unilateral price increase of an essential good, such as oil, may have a rippling effect. The quadrupling of oil prices in 1973 touched off an increase in inflation in 1974 that the world may never recover from. Although it would be unfair to blame worldwide inflation solely on oil prices, the effect is obvious.

It was mentioned that a trade surplus can contribute to inflation; the same is true of a deficit. In a world of floating exchange rates, the currency of a deficit country is bound to weaken over time through a gradual depreciation or a formal devaluation. As was explained in Chapter 4, it takes more of a country's currency to purchase one unit of foreign currency after a devaluation than it did before. Therefore, the local price of imported goods tends to rise over time, as does the price of locally competitive products. How much of this increase fuels inflation depends on how important are imports in the nation's consumption patterns.

Some of these examples relate to *cost-push inflation,* in which an increase in the costs of production factors such as oil or labor tends to push up the price of products using those factors. Other examples relate to *demand-pull inflation,* in which excessive demand and purchasing power pull up the price of products that consumers want. As we look at ways to account for inflation, we will consider the distinction between a general rise in the price level and price increases in specific sectors of the economy or even for specific products.

Impact of Inflation on the Firm

Inflation affects both the balance sheet and the income statement, which results in some strange operating decisions both by managers who understand inflation and by those who don't. In terms of the balance sheet, financial assets such as cash lose value during inflation since their purchasing power diminishes. For example, if a business holds cash during a period when inflation rises by 10 percent, that cash buys 10 percent less goods at the end of the period than it could at the beginning. Conversely, holding financial liabilities such as trade payables is wise because the business would be paying its obligations in the future with cheaper cash. The one caveat here is that financial liabilities, such as short- and long-term bank notes, often carry very high interest rates in inflationary economies. In 1979, for example, interest rates at banks in Argentina were about 6.9 percent per month.

The effect of inflation on nonmonetary assets is reflected in the income statement as well as the balance sheet. During a period of rising prices, replacing inventory and fixed assets becomes increasingly expensive. This could lead to higher profits since current sales dollars are being matched against inventory that may have been purchased several months earlier and against depreciation that is computed on property, plant, and equipment that may have been purchased several years ago.

Those balance sheet and income statement effects could lead the firm into a liquidity crunch as the cash generated from revenues is consumed by the ever increasing replacement cost of assets. In addition, depreciation on old assets is not building a cash fund large enough to purchase the newer, more expensive replacement assets. The overstatement of profits that results from matching old costs with new revenues could lead to demands from shareholders for more dividends, even though the firm is watching its cash dwindle.

The tax consequences of inflation are also obvious. As profits rise, so does a firm's tax liability, causing a further outflow of cash. Much has been said in recent years about how inflated financial statements misrepresent a firm's real operating position. The concern is that analysts and investors cannot make wise financial decisions without understanding the impact of inflation. And what happens if the government decides to slow down inflation by raising interest rates, reducing the money supply, or imposing wage and price controls? The liquidity crisis becomes more severe and the operating problems are compounded as the firm complies with government regulations.

WAYS TO ACCOUNT FOR INFLATION

There are two philosophies on accounting for inflation: adjustment for general price-level changes and adjustment for specific price changes. General price-level or constant dollar accounting is concerned that the value of money has gone down, whereas specific price or current cost accounting is concerned that the cost of specific assets has gone up. It is possible to apply these approaches to all items in the financial statements that can be adjusted or to only some of the items. Also, the approaches can be used separately or in conjunction with each other. Whatever the approach, it is necessary to identify which accounts are to be adjusted, what is to be the basis for the adjustment (such as an index), and where the adjustment is to be reflected in the financial statements.

Constant Dollar Accounting

The general philosophy supporting *constant dollar accounting* is to report assets, liabilities, revenues, and expenses in units of the same purchasing power. The attitude is that the unit of measure—referred to here as the dollar, although it would be pounds sterling for British statements, cruzeiros for Brazilian statements, and so on—should be uniform but that the basis for measuring the financial statements (for example, historical cost) should not change.

In most countries of the world, financial statements are prepared on a historical cost/nominal dollar basis. This means that the statements are not adjusted for changes in the general price level. Under historical cost/constant dollar accounting the nonfinancial items in the financial statements (inventory, plant and equipment), are restated to reflect a common purchasing power of the dollar, usually at the ending balance sheet date. For example, assume that a firm purchased a machine on January 1, 1979 for $10,000 and that the general price level, as measured by the consumer price index, increased by 15 percent during the year. On December 31 the machine would appear on the balance sheet at $11,500 [10,000 + (10,000 × .15)] less accumulated depreciation. The amount implies that it would take $11,500 of end-of-year purchasing power to buy what $10,000 bought on January 1. For the year-end financial statements, the financial assets and liabilities (cash, receivables, payables) would not be adjusted since they are already stated in terms of December 31 purchasing power, but all other assets, liabilities, revenues, and expenses would be adjusted. When the 1978 and 1979 financial statements are compared, however, all of 1978's accounts—including the financial assets and liabilities—would be restated to December 31, 1979 purchasing power in order to compare with 1979's financial statements.

There is some feeling that constant dollar accounting should be applied to financial assets and liabilities as well. Cash, for example, loses purchasing power during an inflationary period since it cannot purchase as much at the end of the period as it did at the beginning. Debtors benefit during inflation, however, because they can pay their debts at the end of the period with cash whose purchasing power has fallen. Therefore, a firm that has increased its net financial asset position during an inflationary period suffers a loss in purchasing power, whereas a firm that has increased its net financial liability position enjoys a gain in purchasing power.

Under constant dollar accounting, a firm can realize a gain from holding an asset during an inflationary period, such as the $1,500 gain in our example ($11,500 − $10,000). Where should that holding gain, as well as holding losses, be recognized? They could be reflected in the income statement as a holding gain or loss, or they could be reflected on the balance sheet as an adjustment to invested capital. Both approaches are used worldwide, as we shall see.

The last issue deals with the *index* to be used. As noted earlier, the consumer price index is the one most widely used to measure inflation around the world. It measures the change in prices for a broad range of consumer goods and services that are purchased for final consumption. The index is very broad and may not reflect the direction and magnitude of the change in prices that directly affect a given firm; however, it does reflect the general change in prices and therefore in a currency's purchasing power.

Current Cost Accounting

As we have seen, *current cost accounting* is concerned with the rise in the cost of specific assets, not with the overall loss of purchasing power of a currency. Under this concept, income is not considered to be earned until the firm has maintained the replacement cost of its productive capacity. Under current cost accounting, a new basis for valuing assets replaces the traditional historical cost.

There are two major approaches to current cost accounting: current entry price (or replacement cost), and current exit price (or net realizable value). *Replacement cost accounting*, the most widely accepted method, is used for most classes of nonfinancial assets. Under this approach, assets are valued at what it would cost to replace them. Whether the value should reflect the same asset being replaced or a similar asset performing the same function but with higher technology has been the subject of considerable discussion. The *current exit price approach* values assets, especially finished goods inventory, at what they could be sold for, less costs to complete and sell the items. In Dutch *exit value theory*, a further distinction is made between liquidation value and the going concern concept. Under *liquidation value*, the asset is valued at its estimated sales price on a forced sale assumption. Under the *going concern concept*, the asset is valued at the estimated sales price upon normal completion of production.

As is the case under constant dollar accounting, current cost accounting results in holding gains and losses when nonfinancial assets are revalued. The gains and losses in these holdings can either be taken into the income statement or be reflected on the balance sheet as a capital adjustment account. The final issue is the determination of current values. For inventory, suppliers' lists are most commonly used since they reflect the most current prices for the items. Fixed assets are more complex. Property and plant are usually revalued according to a specific index, such as a construction cost index. Equipment could be revalued on the basis of a supplier list or engineering estimates—especially for machinery that is custom designed and built. Appraisal values are also a possibility for fixed assets. It is obvious that current cost accounting is more complex to administer since it requires a mixture of actual prices, estimates, appraisal values, and indexes for homogeneous groups of assets.

Current Cost–Constant Dollar

Although constant dollar and current cost accounting have been discussed separately, many theorists believe the two should be combined. For example, assume that a firm purchased an asset at the beginning of the period for $100 and that the asset's replacement value is computed to be $105 at the end of the period while overall inflation was 10 percent. The holding value of $5 is offset by the fact that the asset cost $110 in end-of-period purchasing power. In addition, it is possible to mix current cost and constant dollar accounting by computing the gain or loss in purchasing power on monetary assets and liabilities while computing the current cost on nonmonetary assets.

Other Possibilities

In discussing constant dollar and current cost accounting, the assumption was made that total adjustments of the financial statements would take place. The adjusted statements could replace the historical cost statements or be supplementary. However, numerous partial adjustments have been tried in various countries. In countries such as Peru, adjustments are made to certain assets, such as fixed assets. Peru's government publishes an index that firms must use, and the index doesn't really correlate with either a specific asset cost or the consumer price index. The offset to the value increase goes to a capital adjustment account entitled *revaluation surplus.*

For many years the United States has allowed firms to use *last-in, first-out* (LIFO) inventory valuation, so the cost of goods sold tends to reflect replacement cost. Inventory is carried on the balance sheet at old values, however. The practices of four countries—United States, United Kingdom, the Netherlands, and Brazil—are explained later in more detail.

Problems

In spite of the high rates of inflation worldwide and the general agreement that inflation distorts financial statements and can create operating problems, there is no consensus as to how or even whether financial statements should be adjusted. Firms complain that extra financial statements are difficult to prepare and create confusion in the minds of statement users. The preparation of current cost statements requires substantial subjective evaluations with little consistency from firm to firm, which could create problems when comparisons are made. Many people argue that current values are irrelevant because no firm is going to replace all its assets at once. Opponents of constant dollar accounting argue that the only relevant impact of inflation on a business relates to the current replacement cost of its assets. Clearly, one could argue for and against every position—historical cost, current cost, constant dollar. The literature is replete with the pros and cons of each approach. As the debate continues, let's look at the experience of a few key countries.

THE UNITED STATES

As shown in Figure 9, inflation gradually crept up in the United States during the 1970s, with the exception of 1978. The major sources of influence on the development of inflation accounting proposals have been the Securities and Exchange Commission (SEC) and the Financial Accounting Standards Board (FASB).

The Securities and Exchange Commission

Inflation accounting has taken numerous twists and turns over the years, but the SEC dropped a bombshell on the corporate world in 1976 with Accounting Series Release 190 on replacement cost accounting. ASR 190 required disclosure of the following information in the 10-K report (an annual report that must be filed with the SEC):

1. The current replacement cost of inventories.
2. The cost of goods sold, using replacement costs of goods and services sold.
3. The current cost of replacing productive capacity (both gross and net of depreciation).
4. The amount of depreciation, depletion, and amortization of productive capacity carried at replacement cost.
5. The basis for determining the above values.
6. Other information of a qualitative nature (difficulties in generating data, usefulness of information, and so on).

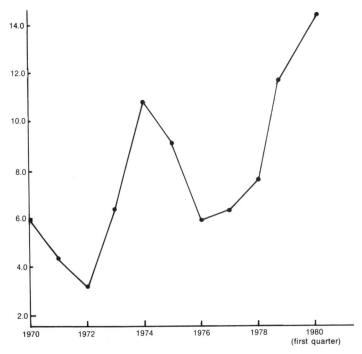

Figure 9. Annual increase in the consumer price index, United States, 1970–1979. (Source: *International Financial Statistics.*)

This information was supplemental to the primary historical cost financial statements and needed to be disclosed only in the 10-K report, although reference to the effect that the information was in the 10-K had to be included in the annual report to shareholders.

Although ASR 190 was superseded by FASB 33, which is discussed later, it provided an interesting insight into corporate reactions to inflation reporting and into the impact of specific price changes to financial statements. Table 8–2 summarizes the experience of 257 U.S. companies from a variety of industries in applying ASR 190 for 1976 reporting, the first year in which it had to be used. Note that only 17 percent of the firms disclosed in the annual report to shareholders the same information contained in the 10-K. Normally, the firms would explain that more complete replacement cost information could be found in the 10-K and would then proceed to lecture on the evils of relying on the information for anything meaningful.

The costing techniques in Table 8–2 relate to the four methods of determining replacement cost for productive capacity. *Direct pricing* applies current prices to assets or homogeneous groups of assets. Direct pricing could come from actual invoices of items purchased recently, price lists of suppliers, or standard costs that reflect current prices.

TABLE 8-2. Summary of Statistical Tabulation of Replacement Cost Disclosure Practices

	NUMBER	PERCENTAGE
Total companies surveyed	257	100%
Practice regarding extent of annual report disclosures		
Complete (i.e., identical to Form 10-K disclosure)	44	17%
Condensed	213	83
	257	100%
Replacement costing technique employed for *major portion* of productive capacity		
Direct pricing	72	28%
Unit pricing	28	11
Functional pricing	64	25
Indexing	93	36
	257	100%
Manner of handling "other cost savings" that would result from replacement		
Cost of sales adjusted	14	5%
Cost savings quantified but cost of sales not adjusted	2	1
Cost savings discussed but not quantified	198	77
Cost savings not mentioned	43	17
	257	100%
Types of caveats included		
Does not necessarily represent current value	195	76%
Does not consider all effects of inflation and/or represent "true" net income	206	80
Imprecise and subjective	226	88
Not actual replacement plans	237	92
Other types of information or comments included		
Relationship of cost to selling prices discussed	129	50%
Environmental impact discussed	66	26
Impact on rate making discussed	26	10
Additional supplemental inflation disclosures included (e.g., current values or GPP adjustments)	4	2
Significant facilities (over 10% of total) not to be replaced	18	7
Impact of fully depreciated assets discussed	30	12
Industry organization assistance noted	16	6
Regulations quoted	52	20
Replacement with used equipment discussed	7	3

SOURCE: Arthur Andersen & Co., *Disclosure of Replacement Cost Data—Illustrations and Analysis,* May 1977.
NOTE: In some cases totals are not shown above since one registrant can be included in several categories, thus making totals irrelevant.

Unit pricing is a variation of direct pricing where a current cost per unit (such as the cost per foot of building construction) is applied to the number of units being revalued. *Functional pricing* applies a current cost per unit of a processing function (such as in a food processing plant) times the number of units being processed. An index, adjusted for technological change, can also be applied to a homogeneous group of assets.[2]

The application of ASR 190 has generated a flurry of studies attempting to measure the impact of inflation on financial statistics. In one study involving the companies that comprise the Dow Jones Industrial Average, it was found that for 1976 the earnings per share went from $4.81 on an historical cost basis to $1.85 on a replacement cost basis, the dividend payout ratio went from 42.9 percent to an astounding 90.4 percent, the return on common equity dropped from 12.2 percent to 3.0 percent, and the effective tax rate increased from 42.3 percent to 57.9 percent.[3]

ASR 190 has had an important impact because firms have been forced to experiment with collecting and reporting the data, and analysts have had the use of the data. As noted in a study on ASR 190 by the Financial Executives Research Foundation, however, "management is almost unanimously opposed to present replacement cost disclosure," and "sophisticated investors and professional analysts do not believe that present disclosure of replacement costs is useful in making investment and credit decisions."[4]

The Financial Accounting Standards Board

The accounting profession has not been successful over the years at resolving accounting for inflation—an issue many feel has no solution. FASB's initial attempt was an exposure draft that was issued in 1974 and then "deferred to future periods." However, the implementation of ASR 190 and the progress by FASB on the conceptual framework of accounting resulted in renewed actions. Finally in September 1979 FASB issued Statement 33, *Financial Reporting and Changing Prices*, more familiarly known as FASB 33. In the statement the board expressed concern for management, creditors, current and prospective investors, and the general public. It then identified four ways that the statement should help users: (1) in assessing future cash flows, (2) in assessing

---

[2]For a more detailed discussion of the computation of replacement costs under ASR 190, see Ernst & Ernst, "SEC Replacement Cost-Requirement and Implementation Guidance," *Financial Reporting Developments*, Retrieval No. 38555, January 1977.
[3]David K. Eiteman, "S.E.C. Replacement Accounting and the Dow Jones Industrials," presented at the annual meeting of the Academy of International Business, 1977.
[4]Haskins & Sells, "The Week in Review," 22 December 1978, pp. 4–5.

enterprise performance, (3) in assessing the erosion of operating capability, and (4) in assessing the erosion of general purchasing power.[5]

FASB 33 applies to all public enterprises that have inventories and property or plant and equipment (before deducting accumulated depreciation) amounting to more than $125 million, or total assets amounting to more than $1 billion (after deducting accumulated depreciation). The inflation-adjusted information is to be published as supplementary financial information since the traditional historical cost statements are to remain as the primary financial statements. FASB 33 requires a combination of constant dollar and current cost information in order to encourage experimentation and help assess the impact of different kinds of information. FASB noted that in response to its exposure draft issued in 1978, "many preparers and public accounting firms emphasized the need to deal with the effects of general inflation; users generally preferred information dealing with the effects of specific price changes."

In order to comply with FASB 33, the following supplementary information needs to be disclosed:

1. Information on income from continuing operations on historical cost/constant dollar basis.
2. The purchasing power gain or loss on net monetary items (not to be included in income from continuing operations).
3. Information on income from continuing operations on a current cost basis: (a) cost of goods sold at current cost and (b) depreciation and amortization expense of property, plant, and equipment.
4. The current cost amounts of inventory and property, plant, and equipment.
5. Increases or decreases in the current cost amounts of inventory and property, plant, and equipment, net of inflation.
6. Summary information for the five most recent fiscal years:
   a. Net sales and other operating revenues.
   b. Historical cost/constant dollar information.
      (1) Income from continuing operations.
      (2) Income per common share from continuing operations.
      (3) Net assets at fiscal year-end.
   c. Current cost information.
      (1) Income from continuing operations.
      (2) Income per common share from continuing operations.
      (3) Net assets at fiscal year-end.

[5]All quotes and references to the statement can be found in Financial Accounting Standards Board, *Statement of Financial Accounting Standards No. 33—Financial Reporting and Changing Prices*, Stamford, Conn.: FASB, September 1979.

(4)   Increases or decreases in the current cost amounts of inventory and property, plant, and equipment, net of inflation.
d.   Other information.
(1)   Purchasing power gain or loss on net items.
(2)   Cash dividends declared per common share.
(3)   Market price per common share at fiscal year-end.

The preferred way to determine current cost is by the direct pricing method referred to earlier, rather than by indexing. The increases and decreases in current costs are not to be included in income from continuing operations, and current costs don't even need to be reported if there is no material difference between current cost and constant dollar information. Current cost information didn't need to be disclosed until the 1980 annual reports, but constant dollar information had to be presented in the 1979 reports.

Although it is left up to each firm to select a proper way of presenting constant dollar and current cost information, Exxon's 1979 Annual Report contains a good example of how the information can be reported. Tables 8–3 and 8–4 provide balance sheet and income statement adjustments for 1979, and Table 8–5 provides the five-year supplementary financial data adjusted for inflation. Exxon's lengthy explanation of the supplementary data is well written and helps explain the data in the tables. Note that crude oil and product purchases under costs and other deductions were not adjusted for specific or general price changes. This is because Exxon carries its inventory at LIFO and therefore does not have to make any income statement adjustments. This may not occur in annual reports of other firms.

Supplemental Information on Inflation Accounting*

Inflation during 1979 continued at a high rate in the United States, further eroding the purchasing power of the dollar. This trend continues to distort the conventional measures of financial performance. Historical dollar accounting (as reflected in the financial statements) during times of significant and continued inflation does not reflect the cumulative effects of increasing costs and changes in the purchasing power of the dollar.

Investments in plant and equipment, for example, made over an extended period of time are treated as though the dollars from these periods were stated in common units of measurement. Since the purchasing power of the dollar has declined significantly from the time these investments were made (the 1979 dollar, for example, is worth $.53 compared with the 1970 dollar), this decline should be considered for a proper assessment of economic results.

Inflation also effects monetary assets, such as cash and receivables, which lose a part of their purchasing power during periods of

*Exxon Annual Report, 1979. Reprinted with permission.

TABLE 8–3. Income from Continuing Operations and Other Changes in Shareholders' Equity Adjusted for Changing Prices, for the Year Ended December 31, 1979

	AS REPORTED AT HISTORICAL COST (millions of dollars)	ADJUSTED FOR	
		GENERAL INFLATION	SPECIFIC COSTS
		(millions of average 1979 dollars)	
Income from continuing operations			
Total revenue	$84,809	$84,809	$84,809
Costs and other deductions			
Crude oil and product purchases	40,831	40,831	40,831
Depreciation and depletion	2,027	3,270	3,932
Other	14,070	14,070	14,070
Interest expense	494	494	494
Income, excise and other taxes	23,092	23,092	23,092
Total costs and other deductions	$80,514	$81,757	$82,419
Income from continuing operations	$ 4,295	$ 3,052	$ 2,390
Gain from decline in the purchasing power of net amounts owed		998	998
Increase in current cost of inventories and property, plant and equipment during 1979			9,333
Less effect of increase in general price level during 1979			6,634
Excess of increase in specific prices over increase in the general price level			2,699
Net Income	$ 4,295		
Adjusted net income		$ 4,050	
Net change in shareholders' equity from above	$ 4,295	$ 4,050	$ 6,087

SOURCE: Exxon Annual Report, 1979. Reprinted with permission.

inflation since they will purchase fewer goods or services in the future. Conversely, holders of liabilities benefit during periods of inflation because less purchasing power will be required to satisfy these obligations in the future. This benefit is illustrated when a 1970 debt of one dollar can be satisfied with a payment of a 1979 dollar which has the equivalent purchasing power of $.53.

TABLE 8-4. Summarized Balance Sheet Adjusted for Changing Prices at December 31, 1979

	AS REPORTED AT HISTORICAL COST (millions of dollars)	ADJUSTED FOR	
		GENERAL INFLATION	SPECIFIC COSTS
		(millions of average 1979 dollars)	
Assets			
Inventories	$ 5,481	$ 7,585	$11,558
Property, plant and equipment	26,293	35,796	45,418
All other assets	17,716	16,892	16,892
Total assets	49,490	60,273	73,868
Total liabilities	26,938	25,599	25,599
Shareholders' equity	$22,552	$34,674	$48,269

SOURCE: Exxon Annual Report, 1979. Reprinted with permission.

The following information is presented in an experimental fashion to help overcome these shortcomings of historical accounting. The adjustments made to the historical dollar results are made in accordance with the principles of inflation accounting as enumerated in Financial Accounting Standards Board Statement No. 33—Financial Reporting and Changing Prices, which forms the basis for these supplemental statements.

The first approach (see Table 8-3) is to adjust the historical dollars to dollars of the same general purchasing power. For example, if the inflation rate is 5 percent from one year to the next year, then 5 percent more dollars are needed in the second year just to maintain the same general purchasing power. This adjustment to common units of measurement—constant dollars—is accomplished by using an index which measures inflation. Statement No. 33 prescribes the use of the Consumer Price Index for All Urban Consumers (CPI). Therefore, the constant dollar method starts with historical dollars as recorded using generally accepted accounting principles and adjusts these dollars to reflect changes in purchasing power (inflation) using the CPI.

A second approach is also used in the accompanying statements (see Table 8-4) to adjust for the current costs of inventory and plant and equipment, which for Exxon have generally increased over time at a rate higher than that of the CPI. Current replacement costs have been used for these items. That is, specific prices that would have to be paid currently have been used as replacement costs for inventory of crude oil and products and property, plant and equipment. Prices for these items have increased at a different but generally much higher rate than general inflation as a result of, for example, the increased cost of crude oil and the escalation in the costs to build and equip petroleum refineries.

For the most part, the replacement data represent replacement in-place and in-kind. No consideration has been given to the replacement of assets with a different type, to improved operating cost efficiencies of replacement assets, and similar situations. The replacement costs used, while believed reasonable, are necessarily subjective. They do not necessarily represent amounts for which the assets could be sold or costs which will be incurred, or the manner in which actual replacement of assets will occur. Land has been valued based on appraisal or on estimated current market prices. Development costs of oil and gas producing facilities have been updated by use of appropriate indices.

In Table 8–3, the first column shows the results of operations as shown in the Consolidated Statement of Income on page 25. The middle column reflects restatements for the effects of general inflation. Since in 1979, the cost of goods sold was already stated in 1979 dollars only one adjustment is necessary. The adjustment of $1,243 million to depreciation is to restate this cost in terms of 1979 dollars based upon the restatement of property, plant and equipment as shown in the second table. In the third column, the further adjustment of depreciation to reflect the increases of the specific costs of the facilities over the effect of general inflation adds $662 million to the current charge for this item. The two depreciation adjustments maintain the same methods, useful lives and salvage values as used in computing historical depreciation.

After these adjustments, the income from continuing operations of $4,295 million has been lowered to $3,052 million in terms of constant purchasing power (general inflation) and to $2,390 million on the basis of specific prices. Dividends paid in 1979 represent 40 percent, 56 percent and 72 percent, respectively, of these income amounts.

Statement No. 33 requires that income taxes paid not be modified for the effects of either constant dollar or specific price adjustments. Therefore, the 68 percent effective tax rate for historical earnings becomes an effective 75 percent for constant dollar results and 79 percent for specific price earnings.

Table 8–3 also shows other changes in shareholders' equity, which occurred during the year as a result of inflation. The first is the gain, applicable to both methods, resulting from the decline in purchasing power of the dollar in the net monetary amounts owed by the company. Most of the company's current assets, except inventories, and the current liabilities and long-term debt are considered to be monetary items. Since the monetary liabilities at year-end 1979 were larger than the monetary assets, a gain is shown. This gain represents the change in the amount of purchasing power required at the end of 1979 to pay these net liabilities versus the higher amount of purchasing power that would have been required to pay them at the end of 1978. With inflation at 10 percent, for example, a gain of $100 thousand would occur for each million dollars of net liabilities held throughout the year.

The second adjustment is applicable only to the specific price method and represents the added increase in costs during the year due to increases in the specific costs for inventory and property, plant and equipment over that which is attributed to the increase due to the effects of general inflation as measured by the CPI. This increase is written off by means of the increased depreciation charge previously mentioned.

These changes in shareholders' equity when added to income from continuing operations resulted in adjusted net income of $4,050 million using the general inflation or constant dollar method and in net changes in shareholders' equity of $6,087 million using the specific

TABLE 8–5. Supplementary Financial Data (millions of dollars except per share amounts)

	YEARS ENDED DECEMBER 31				
	1975	1976	1977	1978	1979
Unadjusted for inflation					
Income from continuing operations	$ 2,456	$ 2,615	$ 2,443	$ 2,763	$ 4,295
Per share	5.49	5.84	5.45	6.20	9.74
Return of income from continuing operations on average shareholders' equity, percent	15.4	15.1	13.1	14.0	20.1
Historical cost information adjusted for general inflation (average 1979 dollars)					
Income from continuing operations	1,961	2,355	1,983	2,052	3,052
Per share	4.38	5.26	4.43	4.60	6.92
Gain from decline in purchasing power of net amounts owed	337	277	441	617	998
Adjusted net income	2,298	2,632	2,424	2,669	4,050
Per share	5.14	5.88	5.41	5.99	9.19
Total revenue	65,765	67,059	70,023	72,191	84,809
Dividends, per share	3.37	3.47	3.59	3.67	3.90
Market price at year-end, per share	58	69⅜	56¼	52⅝	52⅝
Net assets at year-end	30,114	31,146	31,847	32,599	34,674
Return of adjusted net income on average shareholders' equity, percent	7.7	8.6	7.7	8.3	12.0
Historical cost information adjusted for specific costs (average 1979 dollars)					
Income from continuing operations		1,944	1,336	1,245	2,390
Per share		4.34	2.98	2.79	5.42
Gain from decline in purchasing power of net amounts owed		277	441	617	998
Excess of increase in specific prices over increase due to general inflation		2,999	1,807	(377)	2,699
Net change in shareholders' equity		5,220	3,584	1,485	6,087
Per share		11.66	8.00	3.33	13.81
Net assets at year-end		42,781	44,642	44,211	48,269
Return of net change in shareholders' equity on average shareholders' equity, percent		12.8	8.2	3.3	13.2
Average consumer price index	161.2	170.5	181.5	195.4	217.4

SOURCE: Exxon Annual Report, 1979. Reprinted with permission.

cost method. This compares with the $4,295 million of historical net income.

Table 8–4 presents the balance sheet at year-end 1979. The first column is a summary of the historical dollar balance sheet shown on page 24. The middle column restates the inventory and property, plant and equipment for the effects of general inflation. The categories "All other assets" and "Total liabilities" are merely restated in average 1979 dollars using the CPI. Both the LIFO inventory and property, plant and equipment have been built up over the years as inventory quantities have increased and as plant capacities have been added or replaced. The adjustments shown on the table restate these prior year additions in terms of average 1979 dollars. That is, an inventory or plant addition made in 1970 is increased in amount to reflect the increased number of 1979 dollars required to equal the general purchasing power originally invested. For example, it takes almost twice as many 1979 dollars to equal the same purchasing power as that used for an investment in 1970.

The last column shows the adjustments for specific prices paid by Exxon which have increased faster than the CPI. The inventory has been restated based upon the cost of replacing the entire inventory at current costs. Since the purchase prices of crude oil and petroleum products have increased faster than general inflation, particularly in 1979, and since the inventory has been carried on the LIFO basis, the inventory using specific prices is about $3,973 million greater than the results after adjustment for general inflation. The adjustment to property, plant and equipment made in a similar fashion results in a $10 billion adjustment indicating the magnitude of the higher costs being incurred by Exxon over and above the level of general inflation. The specific replacement cost data were mainly based on internally developed plant construction and equipment purchase indices.

The sum of all of these adjustments results in the restatement of shareholders' equity—the investment base. The adjustment for general inflation increases the historical shareholders' equity, as shown on the second table, of about $23 billion to a constant dollar basis of $35 billion. In other words, it would take $35 billion of 1979 dollars to provide the same purchasing power as the $23 billion represented in the financial statements. Additional adjustments for specific prices raise the shareholders' equity to $48 billion. This means that an additional $13 billion investment of 1979 dollars would be required to provide for the replacement costs of specific inventories and plant, over the adjustment for the effects of general inflation.

Table 8–5 is a five-year summary of results. The historical cost information for the years 1975 through 1978 have been adjusted for the effects of general inflation and for specific prices (from 1976) in the same manner as has been discussed for the year 1979. Income from continuing operations is composed of the same factors as shown on Table 8–3. As shown on this table and in the discussion in the Financial Highlights section, the return on average shareholders' equity is considerably lower when both the results and the investment base are adjusted for the effects of general inflation. The return is also lower when adjusted to a specific price basis. These decreases reflect the erosion taking place in the capital base of the company from the continuing high levels of inflation now being faced by the general public, the oil and gas industry, and Exxon.

It will be instructive to monitor the impact of FASB 33 on corporate reporting in the United States. The fact that FASB is requiring the information to be supplementary and is not permitting controversial items such as the purchasing power gain or loss and value adjustments from current costs to affect operating income shows that there is still substantial uncertainty as to what the information means and how it will be used.

The Dilemma of the Multinational Enterprise

The multinational enterprise that operates in multiple environments is subject to a variety of record-keeping requirements and must develop expertise in each of the countries. In addition, it needs to see whether home-country reporting requirements are applicable solely for domestic operations or for worldwide operations as well. Consolidated financial statements become laborious as firms need to keep multiple sets of books with multiple adjustments. A U.S. firm with a subsidiary in the United Kingdom is required to keep sufficient data to yield four sets of financial statements: (1) historical cost according to U.K. generally accepted accounting principles, (2) current cost and constant dollar supplementary financial statements for U.K. purposes, (3) historical cost according to U.S. generally accepted accounting principles for consolidation purposes, and (4) current cost information for consolidated supplementary disclosure to satisfy FASB 33.

FASB 33 requires current cost and constant dollar adjustments. For current cost adjustments of assets held in foreign operations, the assets need to be restated to current cost in the foreign currency and translated into dollars at the balance sheet exchange rate (the current rate). This is known as the *restate-translate* method. The board allows an exception when current costs in the foreign currency are difficult to determine. The firm may elect to translate the assets into dollars at the historical exchange rate and apply a specific index to the asset to reflect current costs. This is known as the *translate-restate* approach. For constant dollar adjustments, the board recommends that firms translate into dollars at appropriate exchange rates all accounts subject to the adjustments. Then the accounts are adjusted for U.S. rather than foreign price-level changes. This is obviously the translate-restate approach. For assets that are carried at current cost/constant dollars, they are first restated to current cost in the foreign currency, translated into dollars at the current exchange rate, and restated for purchasing power changes with the consumer price index in the United States. This is consistent with the philosophy that U.S. shareholders are concerned with gains or losses on the purchasing power of the U.S. dollar.

As can be seen, the situation for the multinational is complicated by the numerous financial statements and inflation adjustments that have to be made in home and host countries. Managers can become confused when they are faced with historical cost statements prepared in local currency, those same statements translated into dollars, the local currency statements adjusted for inflation according to local requirements, and additional inflation-adjusted information required for U.S. reporting. It remains to be seen what FASB 33 will yield. Managers will want to know which statements to pay attention to while planning the management of corporate assets. As can be seen, the decision is a difficult one in the international context.

THE UNITED KINGDOM

As shown in Figure 10, the United Kingdom has experienced a great deal of double-digit inflation over the past few years. The profession and the government have been active in generating proposals, beginning with a provisional standard issued in 1974 by the Accounting Standards Committee of the English Institute of Chartered Accountants which recommended supplemental price-level-adjusted financial statements. However, the Sandilands Committee on Inflation Accounting, a government-sponsored committee, issued a recommendation in 1975 that favored eliminating historical cost statements completely and substituting current value accounting in their place. Revaluations were to be based on a set of government-published indexes for 52 classes of capital assets and inventory.

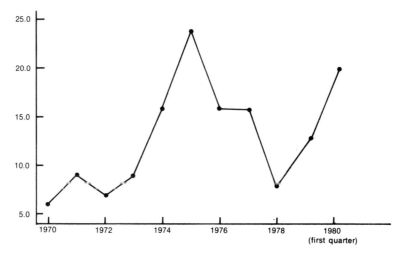

Figure 10.   Annual increase in the consumer price index, United Kingdom, 1970–1979. (Source: *International Financial Statistics.*)

In 1976 the Accounting Standards Committee of the Institute responded with Exposure Draft 18 (ED 18)—better known as Son of Sandilands—which also recommended the adoption of current value accounting but with additional disclosure on the impact of inflation on monetary assets and liabilities. ED 18 was defeated by the members of the institute in 1977, because they were not ready for the mandatory retirement of historical cost accounting. The ASC released the *Hyde Guidelines* in 1977 which recommended three supplementary adjustments: a depreciation adjustment, a cost of sales adjustment, and a "gearing" adjustment.

SSAP 16

In May 1979, the ASC issued ED 24, "Current Cost Accounting," which reflects a transition from constant dollar accounting (1974) to current cost accounting (1975) to a mixture of the two (1976 and 1977). ED 24 became the foundation for Statement of Standard Accounting Practice 16, "Current Cost Accounting" (SSAP 16) issued by the ASC on March 31, 1980. It was to be adopted by firms whose accounting period started on or after January 1, 1980.

SSAP 16 will be followed by some 5,000 to 6,000 firms, representing all listed companies, all nationalized companies, and private companies above a certain size. FASB 33, on the other hand, relates to 1,300 or so of the largest public companies.[6]

SSAP 16 requires that the following current cost information be presented in the annual report:

1. A current cost profit and loss account with
    a. Current cost operating profit derived after making depreciation, cost of sales, and monetary working capital adjustments and
    b. Current cost profit (after operations) attributable to shareholders derived after making a gearing adjustment.
2. A current cost balance sheet with
    a. Fixed assets and inventory at net current replacement cost and
    b. A capital maintenance reserve to reflect revaluation surplus and deficits, the monetary working capital adjustment and the gearing adjustment.
3. Current cost earnings per share.[7]

---

[6]"Accounting for Inflation in Britain," *World Business Weekly*, 21 April 1980, p. 41.
[7]For a complete discussion, see "Statement of Standard Accounting Practice No. 16: Current Cost Accounting," *Accountancy*, April 1980, pp. 99–110.

The *monetary working capital adjustment* (MWCA) reflects the impact of inflation primarily on trade payables less trade receivables rather than all monetary working capital items. The index used to adjust those items is the one applied to inventory rather than the more general consumer price index. Note that the MWCA is considered an adjustment to operating income, unlike the purchasing power gain or loss on net monetary items in FASB 33, which is simply a separately disclosed item. A gearing adjustment is made to show the benefit to shareholders from inflation when the business is financed by net borrowings. A relatively complex adjustment is made to the difference between total liabilities and monetary assets, except for the trade receivables and payables adjusted in the MWCA. A general consumer price index is not used to make the adjustment, so the adjustment is not analogous to the one made in FASB 33. The gearing adjustment is included in the final profit figure.

Examples of what the British supplementary reports might look like are shown in Tables 8–6 and 8–7.

TABLE 8–6. Income Statement (in thousands of pounds)

Turnover (sales)		£20,000
Profit before interest and taxation at historical cost		2,900
Less: current operating profit adjustment (see note)		1,510
Current cost operating profit		1,390
Gearing adjustment	370	
Interest	200	170
Current cost profit before taxation		1,560
Taxation		730
Current cost profit attributable to shareholders		830
Dividends		430
Retained current cost profit		400
Current cost earnings per share		27.7 pence

NOTE: Current adjustments		
Cost of sales	£	460
Monetary working capital		100
		560
Additional depreciation		950
	£1,510	

SOURCE: *Accountancy*, May 1979, p. 43. Reprinted with permission.

TABLE 8–7. Balance Sheet (in thousands of pounds)

Assets employed		
Fixed assets		£ 8,530
Net current assets		
Inventory	£4,000	
Trade debtors less trade creditors	800	
Other current liabilities	(1,000)	3,800
		£12,330
Financed by		
Capital and reserves		
Issued share capital	£3,000	
Capital maintenance reserve (see note)	3,030	
Retained profit	4,300	£10,330
Loan capital		2,000
		£12,330

NOTE: Capital maintenance reserve		
Balance at January 1		£1,180
Surplus on revaluations		
Land and buildings	£ 200	
Plant and machinery	1,430	
Inventory	490	£2,120
Monetary working capital adjustment		100
		2,220
Gearing adjustment		370
		1,850
Balance at December 31		£3,030

SOURCE: *Accountancy,* May 1979, p. 43. Reprinted with permission.

SSAP 16 differs from FASB 33 in a number of ways. First, it separates the inflationary impact on monetary items into the MWCA and the gearing adjustments. Second, these adjustments become a part of profit rather than a separate figure. Third, the adjustments are comprehensive, involving both a balance sheet and an income statement. Fourth, more firms are involved, as mentioned earlier. Fifth, the current cost adjustments can be complied with in the following ways: "(a) presenting historical cost accounts as the main accounts with supplementary current cost accounts which are prominently displayed; (b) presenting current cost accounts as the main accounts with supplementary historical cost accounts; or (c) presenting current cost accounts as the only accounts accompanied by adequate historical cost information."[8] Finally, SSAP 16 is concerned with current cost adjustments

[8]Ibid., p. 102.

only, as opposed to general price level adjustments. The MWCA and gearing adjustments are not exactly general price level adjustments as explained above. The ASC is considering general price level adjustments as part of future refinements of SSAP 16.

THE NETHERLANDS

Figure 11 shows that The Netherlands has not had quite as much trouble as the United Kingdom with inflation. Although inflation soared to 10.5 percent in 1975, it has been consistently under the double digit range and more closely at par with that of the United States. However, the Dutch have been aware of current cost accounting for a long time. The extensive training of Dutch accountants in business economics has resulted in an accounting philosophy that is concerned with values and costs and with sound business-economic principles and practices. There are no set requirements for the use of current cost accounting, as either primary or supplementary information, but there is a clear preference for it. In a series of studies issued by the Tripartite Study Group beginning in 1974, the preference for current cost accounting was reemphasized with the comment that current cost information on profit and equity should be contained in the footnotes to financial statements based on historical cost.[9] Although a number of large firms use current cost statements as their primary statements, it is more common to see partial current cost statements or historical cost statements with supplementary disclosures.

If there are no requirements for current cost or constant dollar accounting, why be concerned about The Netherlands? First of all, Professor Theodore Limperg is often called the father of replacement value theory because of his pioneering works in The Netherlands in the early 1900s. He focused on the strong relationship between economics and accounting and felt that income should not be earned without maintaining the source of income of the business from a going-concern standpoint. Therefore, income is a function of revenues and replacement costs rather than historical costs. In addition, he felt that current cost information should be used by all decision makers—management as well as shareholders. The second reason for looking at The Netherlands

---

[9]"A Response from the Netherlands," *The Journal of Accountancy*, March 1978, pp. 44–45.

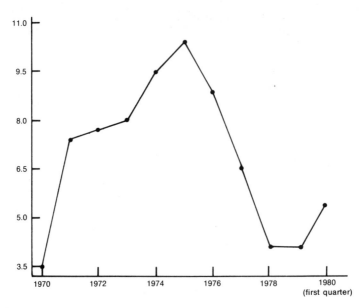

Figure 11. Annual increase in the consumer price index, Netherlands, 1970–1979. (Source: *International Financial Statistics*.)

is a large Dutch multinational, called N. V. Philips, which uses current cost rather than historical cost financial statements.

N. V. Philips

Philips uses current cost with some constant dollar adjustments to monetary items. Under its current cost accounting system both balance sheet and income statement accounts are adjusted. For inventory, standard costs are determined at the start of each year. As prices change during the year, an index is developed by the purchasing department for homogeneous groups of assets and is applied to the standard cost to yield the current cost. The indices are prepared quarterly or bimonthly in situations where inflation is moderate and are prepared monthly for situations where inflation is more extreme. Current costs are determined by the purchasing department for fixed assets (either individually or in homogeneous groups), by the engineering department for specially designed pieces of equipment, and by the building design and plant engineering department for buildings. As is the case with inventory, indexes are often used to update current values of homogeneous groups of assets. The increase (or decrease) in value to inventory and fixed assets due to specific price changes is credited to a *revaluation surplus* account in equity rather than to the income statement. The effect of inflation shows up in the income statement as a higher cost of goods sold (due to increases in inventory prices) and higher depreciation expense.

In addition to the current cost adjustments, Philips makes allowances for changes in the general price level. Where monetary assets exceed monetary liabilities, a charge is made to profit and loss to reflect the loss in purchasing power. This is different from the U.S. case where the purchasing power loss is reported but not included in income.[10]

In order to assist the U.S. readers of its annual report, Philips includes separate information in the report which reconciles net profit to what it would be under U.S. generally accepted accounting principles. There is also a short discussion of the major differences between U.S. and Dutch accounting principles as followed by Philips. The case is notable because Philips was not forced to adopt current cost accounting, and yet it has successfully done so for internal and external purposes for its operations worldwide.

BRAZIL

Figure 12 illustrates the difficult problem Brazil has had with inflation in the 1970s. In March 1964 a military government came into power as the result of a bloodless revolution with the intent of transforming Brazil into an economic power. Two problems were rampant inflation and a weak currency. In an effort to resolve these problems without pushing the economy into a depression, the government came up with several policy decisions that have been modified and refined over time. One policy involves relatively small, frequent devaluations (every four to eight weeks) rather than a huge devaluation every year or so. In a given year these mini-devaluations are supposed to approximate the difference between the Brazilian and world rates of inflation.

Living with Inflation

Inflation is complex, and controlling it involves both monetary and fiscal policies. At the same time, firms need to realize that they may have to learn to live with more inflation than they would like to. As noted in Figure 12, government policies were able to bring inflation down to a tolerable level (for Latin American countries) by 1974 while enjoying relatively rapid economic growth. But the quadrupling of oil prices really stung Brazil, which imports all its oil, and sent prices skyward again. As part of the process of learning to live with inflation, Brazilians

---

[10]More detail can be found in "The 1973 Annual Report of N. V. Philips—The Netherlands," in the Report of the AAA Committee on International Accounting, *Accounting Review*, Supplement 1976.

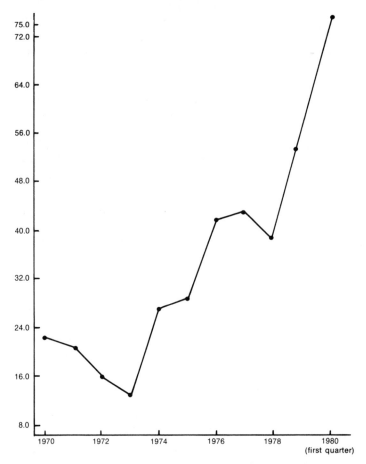

Figure 12.   Annual increase in the consumer price index, Brazil, 1970–1979.
(Source: *International Financial Statistics.*)

developed a complex system of indexing which involves maintaining purchasing power of certain monetary assets and liabilities as well as adjusting certain financial statement items for the effects of inflation. The system is very dynamic and subject to numerous changes annually.

In 1978 the monetary correction concept was changed so that currently an index, called the readjustable government treasury bond (ORTN) index, is applied to certain balance sheet accounts (permanent assets and shareholders' equity). *Permanent assets* are assumed to be property, plant and equipment, accumulated depreciation, investments in equity securities, deferred charges, and related amortization. This is essentially the application of a general price-level index to write up certain balance sheet accounts. Inventory, which is carried at the lower of FIFO or average cost or market, is not adjusted for general price-level changes.

As the asset and equity accounts are adjusted, what happens to the balancing items? In the British case, as you will recall, the monetary working capital and gearing adjustments are treated as adjustments to profit in the supplementary statements, but the current cost adjustments are not, except as higher cost of sales and depreciation expense. In Brazil, the net monetary correction is charged to income for book and tax purposes if the equity position exceeds the permanent asset position. If it is the other way around, however, the net monetary correction is not charged to income for book and tax purposes unless the equity position exceeds the permanent asset position.[11]

Certain long-term liabilities are also adjusted to reflect the change in purchasing power, and these adjustments are considered charges to operating income in contrast with the net monetary correction, which is the last item reported before tax. The Brazilian experience, in a total business and economic context, is being carefully watched by many developing countries with problems and aspirations similar to Brazil. The accounting experience is different from the others we have looked at because the adjusted statements are the primary statements, and yet not all accounts affected by inflation (such as inventory and certain monetary working capital items) are dealt with.

CONCLUSIONS

The problem of inflation is worldwide, although the rate of increase in prices varies from country to country. Responses to accounting for inflation have developed unevenly over the past two decades. In general Latin American countries responded to inflation accounting issues earlier than have the industrial nations because they have had a longer history (at least in modern times) of high rates of inflation. The notable exception to this rule is The Netherlands, which has allowed inflation accounting as a result of the strong influence of economic theory.

In the decade of the 1970s the rapid increase in the rate of inflation led to several important responses from the industrial countries, notably FASB 33 in the United States and SSAP 16 in the United Kingdom. The responses of these two countries are interesting. The differences in the two approaches to current cost versus general price level accounting and the role of inflation adjustments on the earnings statements are as

---

[11]Ernst & Whinney, *E & W International Series—Brazil*, 1979, p. 5. A more detailed discussion on how to determine the amount of the restatement to include in income and the amount to be deferred.

significant as the similarities. One suspects that this issue is going to be difficult to resolve in terms of international harmonization because of the substantial difference of opinion on what inflation adjustments should accomplish.

STUDY QUESTIONS

8–1. What are some of the reasons why inflation occurs?

8–2. How does inflation affect the financial statements of the firm? What operational problems does inflation create?

8–3. Compare the philosophies behind
a. constant dollar accounting
b. current cost accounting
c. current cost/constant dollar accounting

8–4. Compare and contrast the requirements of ASR 190 and FASB 33. Which provides better information? Explain your answer.

8–5. Compare FASB 33 and SSAP 16. Be sure to identify the major similarities and differences between the two standards.

8–6. How has the development of replacement cost accounting differed in The Netherlands and in the United States?

8–7. How have the economic circumstances of Brazil affected the accounting practices there as related to inflation, and so on?

8–8. How do national differences in inflation rates affect the operations of multinational enterprises?

8–9. Obtain copies of annual reports from U.S. multinationals for fiscal years ending on or after December 25, 1979. What information do they provide about changing prices? Compare this to their annual reports of 1978.

8–10. The diverse inflation accounting reporting requirements are one more source of confusion to the manager and the accountant in a multinational environment. What are the benefits and problems in adopting an international standard for reporting information about changing prices? Do these apply to all international standards too?

8–11. Note how Brazil's high inflation rate has been accompanied by frequent devaluations of the cruzeiro. Does this mean that translated accounts automatically reflect the changing price levels? Using the International Monetary Fund's *International Financial Statistics*, compare exchange rate and price-level changes of several countries over the long run and the short run.

CASE

ROYAL DUTCH PETROLEUM COMPANY

The Royal Dutch Petroleum Company (RDPC), a Netherlands holding company, owns a 60 percent interest in the Royal Dutch/Shell Group of Companies and derives nearly all its income from the Group. The Group is one of the largest oil and refined gas companies in the world and is owned by RDPC (60 percent) and the "Shell" Transport and Trading Company, Limited (40 percent), an English company. The two holding companies are owned by a broad base of private investors around the world. The following chart from RDPC's 1978 annual report explains the composition of shareholders:

Parent Companies' Shareholding

Royal Dutch has about 600,000 shareholders and Shell Transport about 400,000. Shares of one or both companies are listed and traded on stock exchanges in eight European countries and in the United States.

The estimated geographical distribution of shareholding interest in each parent and in the two combined at the end of 1978 was:

	Royal Dutch	Shell Transport	Combined
United Kingdom	2.0%	96.1%	39.6%
Netherlands	36.7	0.1	22.1
Switzerland	25.9	0.3	15.7
United States	17.4	0.9	10.8
France	9.1	2.1	6.3
West Germany	4.7	—	2.8
Luxembourg	2.4	—	1.4
Belgium	1.4	0.1	0.9
Others	0.4	0.4	0.4
	100.0%	100.0%	100.0%

Royal Dutch/Shell is a diversified energy company with operating companies in exploration, refining, and marketing of oil and natural gas, as well as chemicals, metals, coal, and nuclear energy in over 100 countries. Oil and natural gas is the most important industrial segment, claiming 91 percent of Royal Dutch/Shell's total operating revenues and 98 percent of its earnings from operations. The geographical distribution of revenues and earnings is fairly well dispersed. The most important areas in terms of nonaffiliated sales and other revenues are Europe (41.9 percent), United States (23.7 percent), Far East and Australasia (15.5 percent), and other Western Hemisphere (15.2 percent). Earnings from operations come from the United States (32.9 percent), Europe (30.3 percent), and Far East and Australasia (23.6 percent).

Financial statements are kept in the accounting principles and currency of each separate company. The Shell Oil Company is a U.S. corporation owned by Royal Dutch/Shell. Shell Oil's financial statements are generated in U.S. dollars according to U.S. generally accepted accounting principles and are translated into pounds sterling for consolidation with the Royal Dutch/Shell Group, whose financial statements are prepared in pounds sterling according to British generally accepted accounting principles. RDPC then picks up its 60 percent interest in the net assets of Royal Dutch/Shell in pounds sterling and translates them into Dutch guilders at the year-end rate.

The effects of inflation on Royal/Dutch Shell's financial statements are extensive and complex, extensive because of the relatively high levels of world inflation in recent years and complex because Royal Dutch/Shell operates in so many countries with different rates of inflation and different ways of accounting for inflation. In the 1978 Annual Report of RDPC, the following information is disclosed on accounting for inflation in the financial statements of Royal Dutch/Shell:

> In the absence of an accounting standard which not only has international acceptance but can also be satisfactorily applied to assets and operations specific to the oil extractive industry, supplementary financial statements are again provided restating the historical sterling amounts in pounds of current purchasing power. These figures go some way towards eliminating the distorting effects of inflation on the historical figures. . .
>
> In the United States, the Securities and Exchange Commission requires certain replacement cost data to be filed. This requirement is being followed, but it is not believed that the information is sufficiently objective and comprehensive to merit inclusion in this Report.

Elsewhere in the report, a more detailed discussion of the reason for and basis of restating the financial statements, as well as a summarized statement of income, summarized statement of assets and liabilities, change in net assets, financial ratios, and changes in the purchasing power of the pound sterling are given. It is noted that "since historical rates of exchange are used to translate certain assets and liabilities so as to portray the historical cost of those assets in sterling terms, restatement has been made by applying the United Kingdom Retail Price Index."

Adjustments for inflation are also made by the RDPC. However, since RDPC is not an operating company, its inflation adjustments do not reflect inflation in The Netherlands. Instead, it provides supplemental information on its 60 percent share of dividends from Group companies, earnings retained by Group companies, and Group net assets in pounds sterling adjusted for inflation using the United Kingdom Retail Price Index. This information is not translated into Dutch guilders.

In the notes to the financial statements of the Royal Dutch/Shell Group as contained in the Annual Report of RDPC, the following statement was made on the setting of accounting standards:

Accounting Standards

During 1978 there were a number of major external developments affecting the future of financial reporting. The Group took full advantage of the consultation processes which the various national and international accounting bodies provide by participating in discussions and presenting submissions on the major issues involved.

In formulating the approach to these new developments, attention has primarily to be paid to the need to provide Group financial information in a manner acceptable to its users throughout the world. It has always been the aim to use a synthesis of accepted practices in at least the Netherlands, the United Kingdom, and the United States to this end. It is paradoxical that the adoption of new accounting standards, designed to narrow differences in accounting treatment within national boundaries, should actually increase differences internationally. This is now happening and may grow worse. Investigation seems essential into the fundamentals of financial reporting such as its objectives and qualities, the definitions of the elements of financial statements and methods of measurement. At present, inadequate search for international accord is being undertaken in these areas. More detailed agreement on accounting standards is likely to be achieved if these basic questions can be settled. This is a field in which the International Accounting Standards Committee could perhaps be expected to take a lead.

If financial reporting is to be preserved as an impartial and therefore reliable form of communication, it seems essential that the professional bodies, in consultation with the parties involved, should continue to have responsibility for formulating accounting standards; it is to be hoped that these bodies will move with some urgency to achieve much closer international co-operation than exists at present. Anything less than true harmonization of accounting standards, where the underlying circumstances are similar world-wide, will not be in the best interests of the very many users of the financial statements of the Group, nor indeed of multinational groups generally.

Questions

1. Which of the ways discussed in the chapter does Royal Dutch/Shell use to account for inflation?
2. Do you agree with their statement on the requirements of the SEC?
3. How would you compare the method of accounting for inflation that Royal Dutch/Shell used with what is now required in the United States and United Kingdom?
4. Do you agree with the way Royal Dutch/Shell accounts for inflation of operations in countries outside of Britain? Explain.
5. Is RDPC's approach to accounting for inflation consistent with that which is used by Philips, another Dutch company?
6. How would you evaluate the statement on international accounting standards by Royal Dutch/Shell in terms of the inflation issue?

9

Disclosure of Information

The *Economist*, in an article citing a *Financial Times* survey of disclosure habits of a hundred European companies, had this to say about disclosure:

> The Italians generate much hot air but little hard fact: 1 175-page annual report from Fiat is described as "the most useless in the whole survey." The British provide best financial information, but the least data about employees. The Swiss, whose natural reticence provides much of their national income, score predictably low marks. . . . Socially-conscious Swedes . . . produce the best profit forecasts.[1]

The article does point out that the quality of disclosure is improving worldwide because of capital market pressures and the regulation of the U.S. capital market by the Securities and Exchange Commission. The SEC has such a pervasive influence on disclosure because it regulates the disclosure practices of the U.S. multinational enterprises, which aggressively seek capital from around the world. Since the disclosure requirements are among the highest found anywhere, they tend to lift the quality of disclosure of firms from other countries that are in competition with U.S. firms for the same capital. As pointed out by Choi, "competition in the capital markets is emerging as the primary motivating force" behind fuller disclosure of financial information.[2]

---

[1]"Behind the Figures," *The Economist*, 24 March 1979, p. 106.
[2]Frederick D. S. Choi, "European Disclosure: The Competitive Disclosure Hypothesis," *Journal*

This chapter discusses the purpose of disclosure and how disclosure regulations are set, compares practices worldwide, and looks at specific issues relative to international business activities.

As pointed out by the International Accounting Standards Committee (IASC),

> Financial statements must be clear and understandable. They are based on accounting policies which vary from enterprise to enterprise, both within a single country and among countries. Disclosure of the significant accounting policies on which the financial statements are based is therefore necessary so that they may be properly understood.[3]

In recent years, especially in the United States, the amount of disclosure in and related to financial statements has increased in order to give statement users more information of higher quality on which to base decisions. While there is often an attempt to separate accounting standards from disclosure standards, the two areas are closely related, and both require an understanding of the needs of the users of financial statements. Accounting standards are designed to record economic events with the needs of the users in mind, whereas disclosure is designed to present these recorded economic events to the users.

Who Are the Users?

The determination of users is critical in investigating disclosure similarities and differences worldwide. The Financial Accounting Standards Board (FASB) has defined the principal users as "present and potential investors and creditors and other users [interested] in making rational investment, credit and similar decisions."[4] According to the IASC, the users are "especially shareholders and creditors (present and potential) and employees. Other important categories of users include suppliers, customers, trade unions, financial analysts, statisticians, economists, and taxing and regulatory authorities."[5] In many of the developing countries and the controlled economies of Eastern Europe, the primary user is the government. In Britain the *Corporate Report*, a report which discusses the objectives of financing reporting, lists seven kinds of users:

---

of International Business Studies, Fall 1974, p. 23. See also Jeffrey Arpan, "International Differences in Disclosure Practices," *Business Horizons*, October 1971, p. 70.
[3]International Accounting Standards Committee, "Disclosure of Accounting Policies," *International Accounting Standard No. 1* (London: IASC, January 1975), p. 5.
[4]Financial Accounting Standards Board, "Statement of Financial Accounting Concepts No. 1—Objectives of Financial Reporting by Business Enterprises," *The Journal of Accounting*, February 1979, p. 91.
[5]IASC, IAS 1.

the equity investor, the loan creditor, the employee, the analyst-adviser, the business contact (customers, trade creditors, suppliers), the government, and the public (taxpayers, consumers).[6]

Given this diversity of users, does a firm need to issue reports with multiple levels of disclosure? Even though the British Corporate Report is concerned with identifying different needs for different classes of users, its final comment is, "The reporting responsibility we identify is an all-purpose one, intended for the general information of all users outside those charged with the control and management of the organization. In short, we are concerned with general purpose reports designed for general purpose use."[7]

In the United States, firms required to file with the SEC give more extensive investor-oriented information in their filings than is commonly contained in the annual report to shareholders. Often government agencies such as the Internal Revenue Service require certain disclosures that may not be relevant to everyone. Finally, as financial reporting transcends national boundaries, new disclosure decisions must be made with respect to language, currency, and accounting principles. These issues are treated at length later.

Who Influences Disclosure Standards?

There are many forces influencing the improvement of disclosure standards worldwide. As mentioned earlier, in the United States the SEC remains very influential. A government organization, the SEC was set up in 1934 to establish and regulate financial disclosure practices as identified by the Securities Act of 1933 and the Securities Exchange Act of 1934. The agency's major influence can be found in its Regulation S-X, identifying the form and content of required filings, and in its Accounting Series Releases, which modify and amplify the basic requirements.

Also influencial in disclosure in the United States is the Financial Accounting Standards Board. FASB has focused on setting standards for financial statements and believes that accounting standards and disclosure are inexorably intertwined and therefore must be treated together. In its Objective to Financial Statements, FASB intimated that it was expanding its sphere of influence beyond the financial statements to include the whole area of financial reporting. FASB is a private rather than public sector source of influence and has an impact on decisions made by the SEC, as well as being influenced by the SEC.

Most countries have private sector influence to varying degrees on

[6]Tom Climo, "What's Happening in Britain?" *The Journal of Accounting,* February 1976, p. 56.
[7]Ibid, p. 57.

setting disclosure requirements but rely heavily on government regulation, usually in the form of companies acts. One major exception to this is the United Kingdom. Its Companies Act does include specific items with regard to disclosure, but the Stock Exchange provides the major source of influence. The Stock Exchange, a private institution, has the authority to set disclosure rules that affect all British companies whose shares are traded publicly. This authority is not available to the Department of Trade of the British government.[8]

In the case of both the SEC in the United States and the Stock Exchange in the United Kingdom, the obvious influence on disclosure is the capital market. As competition for scarce capital increases, firms must enter the major capital markets of the world in order to attract new investors, which means they must upgrade their level of disclosure.

Four other institutions with varying degrees of international influence are referred to periodically here and were discussed more extensively in Chapter 3: the International Accounting Standards Committee (IASC), the European Economic Community (EEC), the United Nations (UN), and the Organization for Economic Cooperation and Development (OECD).

The EEC is in the process of issuing a series of directives that relate to financial disclosure. The directives do not constitute laws in the member states but are orders to the member states to bring their laws into line with the requirements within a certain period.[9] The Fourth Directive, adopted in 1978, deals with the content, object, and format of accounts, including specific disclosure provisions. Other directives will be released on group accounts, auditing, and so on.

The UN has become involved through the Commission on Transnational Corporations operating under the aegis of the United Nations Economic and Social Council. The commission appointed a Group of Experts on International Standards of Accounting and Reporting, whose report was released in 1977 and is currently being revised.

The OECD, an organization that includes most of the free European countries plus the United States, Canada, Japan, Australia, and New Zealand, has also become involved in disclosure of financial information. The OECD Committee on Financial Markets issued recommendations on minimum disclosure rules in 1976 that were accepted by the Council of Ministers of the OECD.

The IASC, as pointed out in Chapter 3, has issued a number of standards and exposure drafts. Most of them deal with disclosure standards designed to help international readers of financial statements

---

[8]George J. Benston, "Public (U.S.) Compared to Private (U.K.) Regulation of Corporate Financial Disclosure," *The Accounting Review*, July 1976, pp. 483–498.
[9]For further discussion of the Directives, see Deloitte Haskins and Sells, *The Fourth Directive* (London: 1978).

understand the basis on which the statements are prepared. Although most significant countries of the world have representation on the IASC, the committee has no power to enforce its standards. Thus, the onus of responsibility falls on each country's representatives. To date, the IASC has proven to be a good forum for the discussion of disclosure issues but has not caused a great deal of movement toward the harmonization of disclosure standards.

COMPARATIVE DISCLOSURE WORLDWIDE

As noted earlier, a good accounting system needs to have good accounting standards that reflect economic events, and these events need to be communicated to users. In the absence of uniform standards, many people feel that increased disclosure of the basis of the financial statements would be useful. However, good disclosure is not a substitute for good accounting; the two should work hand in hand. Even with good accounting standards, certain information needs to be communicated to users, and the extent of this disclosure varies dramatically worldwide. Issuers of statements prefer to limit disclosure in order to avoid preparation costs and to preserve secrecy but must adhere to externally mandated requirements and, to a lesser extent, competition.

Local versus Transnational Disclosure

As described in Chapter 2, local disclosure rules evolve from the complex educational, sociocultural, legal-political, and economic forces of each country. Sometimes nationalism becomes so strong that it is virtually impossible to change local requirements to fit international standards. This occurs in countries where disclosure principles are minimal (such as Switzerland) or tailored to government needs (such as Peru and Egypt) as well as in advanced countries (such as the United States) where the level of disclosure is considered high enough without conforming to international rules.

Transnational disclosure occurs when a firm needs to issue financial statements for foreign investors and other foreign users. For transnational reporting, many firms simply translate the narrative of the report into the language of the foreign users—often English. However, there may be no attempt to change the underlying standards on which the financial statements were prepared. In this case, extensive disclosure may be necessary to help the reader understand how the statements were prepared in order to facilitate decision making. Firms such as N. V. Philips' Gloeilampenfabrieken of The Netherlands include a section in their English language version which delineates the major differences in Dutch and U.S. accounting principles and quantifies the impact on earnings.

Other firms change their entire financial statements to conform with a foreign or international reporting standard. In a recent study on the financial statements of Japanese firms it was found that 10 of 92 firms prepared their statements according to generally accepted accounting principles (GAAP) in the United States.[10] In addition, all foreign firms seeking to list their shares on the New York Stock Exchange must file financial statements with the SEC prepared according to U.S. GAAP or at least reconciling to U.S. GAAP, as is done by Philips.

Impact of IASC

In order to improve the quality of disclosure worldwide, the IASC has issued a number of standards. Among the recommendations in its first standard are the following points:

- Financial statements should include clear and concise disclosures of all significant accounting policies which have been used.
- The disclosure of the significant accounting policies used should be an integral part of the financial statements. The policies should normally be disclosed in one place.
- Wrong or inappropriate treatment of items in balance sheets, income statements or profit and loss accounts, or other statements is not rectified either by disclosure of accounting policies used or by notes or explanatory material."[11]

The IASC subsequently issued IAS 5, which deals with information to be disclosed in the financial statements. The standard sets minimum levels of disclosure for specific categories in the balance sheet and income statement. It also points out that the disclosures may be modified by subsequent standards that deal with specific accounting subjects.

Although the pronouncements of the IASC have not had much effect on accounting standards and reporting practices in the United States, their impact has been felt in the United Kingdom. It was pointed out in Chapter 6 that the United Kingdom was concerned that its proposed standard on foreign currency translation be in harmony with IASC's International Exposure Draft 11 (IED 11). In U.K. literature there is constant reference to IASC standards and their relationship to U.K. standards. There is a conscious effort to work with IASC guidelines,

---

[10]Hiroshi Yoshida, Kenji Shiba, and Lilia Teresa Sagara, "A Survey of Accounting Reports on Foreign Exchange Gains and Losses in Japan," *Working Paper No. 49* (Kobe, Japan: Institute of Economic Research, Kobe University of Commerce, February 1979).
[11]IASC, IAS 1, p. 8.

even though that attitude is not necessarily prevalent elsewhere. Sometimes IASC standards are so flexible as to allow any practice—such as is the case with inflation accounting and translation and financial statements.

Group Accounts

One of the major differences in financial reporting worldwide concerns the presentation of group accounts. A group is defined as a parent company and all its subsidiaries. To qualify as a subsidiary, a company must be controlled by another company (the parent). In addition, a parent may have an interest in an associated company, defined by the IASC as a company that is not a subsidiary but whose parent holds at least a 20 percent voting interest.

There are three options in presenting the accounts of the group to outsiders: (1) present parent company financial statements only, (2) present parent company financial statements but also include consolidated financial statements, or (3) present consolidated financial statements only. The consolidated statements normally include domestic and foreign operations, but separate domestic and foreign consolidated statements could be presented. As discussed briefly in Chapter 6, consolidated financial statements are statements in which like items of assets, liabilities, revenues, and expenses are combined on a line-by-line basis to present the parent and its subsidiaries as one single entity or enterprise. Table 9–1 compares the policies of several countries in presenting group accounts. Note that the United States is out of step with the rest of the industrial world where parent as well as consolidated reports are presented.

When consolidation takes place, transactions between the parent and its subsidiaries or among related subsidiaries are eliminated from the statements. Thus the consolidated statements reflect transactions of the group with outsiders. When parent company statements only are presented, there are many ways to distort the financial statements. Prior to 1977, when it became mandatory to publish consolidated financial statements in Japan, the following practices were common:

> During periods of slack turnover, some parent companies have been known to ship merchandise to their subsidiaries and list the goods as sold, even though the subsidiaries didn't have any customers on hand. Workers also could be transferred from a parent to a subsidiary to lower unit costs. And managers skipped over for promotions in the head office could be transferred to subsidiaries, where their performances couldn't be as easily seen.[12]

---

[12]*Wall Street Journal*, 6 February 1977, p. 6.

TABLE 9–1. Practices Followed by a Majority of the Companies in Presenting Group Accounts

PARENT COMPANY STATEMENTS ONLY	PARENT COMPANY STATEMENTS SUPPLEMENTED BY CONSOLIDATED STATEMENTS		CONSOLIDATED STATEMENTS ONLY
Brazil	Australia	Malaysia*	Bahamas
Costa Rica	Botswana*	Mexico*	Bermuda
El Salvador	Denmark*	Netherlands*	Canada
Guatemala	Dominican Republic	New Zealand*	Panama
Honduras	Fiji*	Nigeria*	Philippines
Ivory Coast	France*	Norway*	United States
Island of	Germany*	Singapore*	
Jersey	Hong Kong*	South Africa*	
Nicaragua	Ireland*	Sweden*	
Senegal	Jamaica*	Trinidad	
Spain	Japan*	United Kingdom*	
	Kenya*	Venezuela*	
	Korea*	Zambia	
	Malawi*	Zimbabwe Rhodesia*	

SOURCE: Price Waterhouse, *International Survey of Accounting Principles and Reporting Practices* (Canada: PWI, 1979).
*Required practice

As an example of the difference between consolidated and unconsolidated earnings, Toshiba, a large Japanese multinational, showed an unconsolidated net income of $30 million in 1976 which would have been a $13 million net loss on a consolidated basis.[13] Consolidated financial statements help eliminate or at least minimize some of these problems so that users can get a pretty good idea of the results of operations and the financial position of the entire group.

There are situations where consolidation of certain subsidiaries may not take place. According to International Accounting Standard 3 (IAS 3) of the IASC, the three major reasons for avoiding consolidation are (1) that control is likely to be temporary, (2) that the ability of the parent to control assets is impaired, or (3) that business activities are dissimilar.[14] In a survey by the American Institute of Certified Public Accountants it was found that 364 of 600 firms surveyed consolidated all subsidiaries Of those that did not, 119 chose not to consolidate foreign subsidiaries

[13]"Japan's Accounting Shake-up," *Business Week*, 25 April 1977, p. 114.
[14]"International Accounting Standard No. 3: 'Consolidated Financial Statements,' " *Accountancy*, September 1976, p. 102.

primarily because the local government or economic environment impaired the parent's ability to control the subsidiaries.[15]

According to the rules of consolidation, an *associated company* (one which the parent does not control) is not consolidated with parent statements. In some cases, companies have tried to avoid consolidation by divesting ownership in a subsidiary. For example, in Japan, where since 1977 consolidation is required for subsidiaries owned 50 percent or more by the parent,

> Mitsubishi Chemical Industries Ltd., Japan's largest chemical concern, reduced its equity interest in deficit-plagued Asia Oil Company to 48.7% from 74.7%, apparently to avoid wrapping the petroleum venture into consolidated results. Showa Denko K.K., another chemical concern, sold half its money-losing aluminum subsidiary late last year to just squeak under the definition of a unit that needn't be consolidated.[16]

Minority Interests

It is appropriate and desirable for a company with minority interests in several companies to report the results of those operations. There are two ways to do this: the cost and equity methods. According to the more conservative *cost method*—which is favored in much of continental Europe—the income of a minority interest is not reflected in parent or consolidated income until a dividend is declared to the parent. In some countries the dividend is not even recorded until the treasurer has the money stashed away in the corporate vault. Alternatively the *equity method* is less conservative and reflects the investor orientation of the United States, focusing on earnings potential. Under the equity method, income is recognized on parent and consolidated financial statements as soon as it is earned—whether or not a dividend is declared.

Two major pronouncements may shape the future use of the equity method—IAS 3 by the IASC and the proposed Seventh Directive by the European Economic Community (EEC). The Seventh Directive has yet to be issued officially, but the betting is that it will have a dramatic effect on the ultraconservative members who do not care to consolidate foreign with domestic operations or use the equity method of accounting for earnings. IAS 3, which deals with all aspects of consolidation, is crucial because it requires that the equity method be used for reporting profits of associated companies and subsidiaries not consolidated. The

---

[15]American Institute of Certified Public Accountants, *Accounting Trends and Techniques* (New York: AICPA, 1975), p. 48.
[16]"Japan's Accounting Shake-up," op. cit.

United Kingdom, in its SSAP 1 (Accounting for the Results of Associated Companies) recommended the equity method, which is in harmony with IAS 3. It is hoped that more countries will follow the United Kingdom's lead. Given the United Kingdom's influence in setting EEC directives and its desire to follow IASC standards, more progress may yet be made.

General Disclosure

Precisely how bad disclosure is worldwide is fairly difficult to assess because one must define the needs of the users in order to measure and compare disclosure. Most studies of disclosure have been conducted by U.S. researchers who were biased toward the investor orientation. However, even foreign analysts are aware of the general lack of disclosure. According to one Swiss analyst, "We [The Swiss] have no uniformity in financial reporting. Only a few legal requirements, like having to publish an annual report and a balance sheet. But it can be just three lines."[17] The article goes on to point out that the Swiss hesitation over disclosure covers up some of the world's most conservative accounting. And a study by the French stock exchange revealed that 34.8 percent of the annual reports published in 1978 for listed firms carried "markedly insufficient" information and only 12 percent provided "excellent" reports to shareholders.

In an empirical study by Barrett, the disclosure practices of the 15 largest publicly held firms in the United States, United Kingdom, Japan, France, West Germany, The Netherlands, and Sweden were compared over the period 1963–1972. Given that firms might issue different financial statements for local investors, international investors, and so on, Barrett selected the most consolidated sets of financial statements and therefore the ones most relevant to international investors. He drew the following conclusions:

> The results of this study (1) . . . support the theme that the extent of financial disclosure in the annual reports of major, publicly held U.S. corporations *was* greater, on average, than that found in the annual reports of major publicly held corporations in Japan, Sweden, the Netherlands, Germany, and France during the 1963 to 1972 period; (2) indicate . . . that the U.S. annual reports were not uniformly better than those of these other five countries in terms of specific categories of disclosure; (3) imply that the extent of financial disclosure in the annual reports of major, publicly held U.S. corporations was no greater, on average, than that found in the annual reports of similar British corpo-

[17]"The New Chic—Swiss Stocks," *Forbes*, 5 March 1979, p. 34.

rations; and (4) provide evidence . . . that there is a relationship between the extent and quality of financial disclosure and the degree of efficiency of national equity markets.[18]

It should be noted that the time frame covered ended in 1972, and a review of recent annual reports of companies worldwide demonstrates a marked improvement in disclosure.

DISCLOSURE OF SEGMENTED RESULTS

Usually consolidated financial statements tell a shareholder or creditor little about a firm's business by product group and geographical area. Without segmented data, the outside user would have to rely on the unaudited narrative for information. Segmented data is discussed here from the perspectives of U.S. requirements, those of the EEC, and those of the OECD.

The U.S. Perspective

In 1977, FASB issued Statement 14, "Financial Reporting for Segments of a Business Enterprise." The statement focused on disclosure of information on four segments: industry, foreign operations, export sales, and major customers. For industry segments, firms are called on to group products or services worldwide and then select for reporting purposes segments whose revenue, profits or losses, or assets are 10 percent of the combined revenue, profits or losses, or assets of the identifiable segments of the firm. Industry segments are normally determined by the nature of the product so that similar products are grouped together. For example, IBM groups its segments into data processing, office products, federal systems, and other business. Armstrong Cork Company's segments are floor coverings, ceilings, furniture, and industry products and other. Du Pont divides its segments into chemicals, plastics, specialty products, and fibers. Once the industry segments are identified, the following information is to be disclosed: revenue, operating profit or loss, and identifiable assets. This information is to be provided as a supplement to the main financial statements in interim as well as annual statements.

FASB 14 also requires that sales be disclosed to major customers. If 10 percent or more of total corporate revenue is derived from sales to a single customer, that amount of sales must be disclosed. The classes of major customers specifically identified are any single customer, domes-

[18]M. Edgar Barrett, "The Extent of Disclosure in Annual Reports of Large Companies in Seven Countries," *The International Journal of Accounting,* Spring 1977, p. 19.

tic government agencies in the aggregate, and foreign governments in the aggregate.

The international aspect of FASB 14 deals with foreign operations and export sales. Firms are to disclose information about domestic and foreign operations. Foreign segments can be disclosed in the aggregate, by groups of countries or by individual country. Most disclosure involves one form of aggregation or another; few firms disclose information by separate country. In order to qualify, a segment must meet one of two conditions: either its revenue from sales must be at least 10 percent of consolidated revenues or its identifiable assets must be at least 10 percent of consolidated assets. Once this test has been met and the segments identified, each segment's revenue from sales to unaffiliated customers, revenue from intracompany sales, operating profit (or loss), and identifiable assets must be disclosed.

The determination of international segments varies considerably from firm to firm, as does the volume of information per segment. IBM uses three geographical segments—United States, Europe/Middle East/Africa, and Americas/Far East—which corresponds with its organizational structure. Du Pont uses only three segments also: United States, Europe, and other foreign. The third segment provides only 10.4 percent of consolidated sales, which explains its aggregation. Many companies, in trying to disclose as little foreign information as possible, simply aggregate the data into "total foreign."

In general, as mentioned earlier, the amount of information disclosed varies considerably from firm to firm. Table 9–2 illustrates the information provided by Textron for business segments and geographic operations. Under geographic operations, Textron discloses the loss on currency translation. In addition, Textron discloses the U.S. exports to each geographic segment. FASB 14 requires that a firm disclose its exports sales if they are at least 10 percent of consolidated revenues. The firm can decide whether to disclose the export sales in the aggregate or by area. Textron obviously preferred the latter approach. Export sales are sales from the U.S. parent—not sales of a Brazilian subsidiary to Mexico, for example.

There are two other sources of standards for segmented disclosure in the United States: the Securities and Exchange Commission and the Federal Trade Commission. The differences among the three approaches are too numerous to identify here.[19] However, FASB 14 is the only approach requiring information on a geographical basis and on export sales. The SEC and FTC concentrate on industry segments. The SEC is committed to bringing its reporting requirements into line with FASB, which will eliminate separate reports for shareholders and the 10-K report.

---

[19]For a detailed discussion of the three approaches, see Ernst & Ernst, *Financial Reporting of Business Segments*, Retrieval No. 38619 (Cleveland: Ernst & Ernst, July 1977), pp. 24–28.

TABLE 9–2. Textron Business Segments and Geographic Operations (in $ millions)

	BUSINESS SEGMENTS							
	AEROSPACE							
YEAR 1977	HELI-COPTERS	OTHER AERO-SPACE PRODUCTS	CON-SUMER	INDUS-TRIAL	METAL PRODUCT	CREATIVE CAPITAL	ADJUST. AND ELIM.	CONSOLI-DATED
Sales—trade	$817.2	$150.0	$782.9	$567.7	$484.4	$ -0-	$ -0-	$2,802.2
Sales—intersegment	.3	18.7	.1	3.9	5.5	-0-	(28.5)	-0-
Total sales	$817.5	$168.7	$783.0	$571.6	$489.9	$ -0-	$(28.5)	$2,802.2*
Operating profit	$ 67.9	$ 11.1	$ 87.3	$ 54.2	$ 61.8	$ 10.3	$ -0-	$ 292.6
General corporate expenses								21.6
Interest expense—net								9.8
Income before income taxes								$ 261.2
Depreciation	$ 8.7	$ 3.0	$ 16.8	$ 14.1	$ 9.5	$ -0-	$ 1.2	$ 53.3
Capital expenditures	$ 9.0	$ 4.8	$ 21.2	$ 15.7	$ 14.2	$ -0-	$ 4.7	$ 69.6
December 31, 1977 Operations' assets	$264.4	$ 62.7	$469.0	$242.1	$311.2	$132.5	$ (3.4)	$1,478.5
Corporate assets								259.8
Total assets								$1,738.3

	GEOGRAPHIC OPERATIONS					
YEAR 1977	U.S.	WESTERN EUROPE	CANADA	AUS-TRALIA	OTHER	ADJUST. AND ELIM.	CONSOLI-DATED
Sales—trade	$2,393.2	$154.3	$ 58.7	$ 52.4	$143.6	$ -0-	$2,802.2
Sales among geographic areas	47.7	5.5	6.9	-0-	.2	(60.3)	-0-
Total sales	$2,440.9	$159.8	$ 65.6	$ 52.4	$143.8	$ (60.3)	$2,802.2*
Operating profit before effects of currency translation	$ 253.3	$ 10.0	$ 4.2	$ 7.4	$ 25.9	$ (4.7)	$ 296.1
Gain (loss) on currency translation	(.1)	.1	(1.9)	(1.0)	(.6)	-0-	(3.5)
Operating profit after effects of currency translation	$ 253.2	$ 10.1	$ 2.3	$ 6.4	$ 25.3	$ (4.7)	292.6
General corporate expenses							21.6
Interest expense—net							9.8
Income before income taxes							$ 261.2
U.S. exports		$ 83.9	$ 61.4	$ 9.0	$387.7	$ -0-	$ 542.0
December 31, 1977 Operations' assets	$1,240.0	$169.9	$ 33.9	$ 45.2	$ 92.7	$(103.2)	$1,478.5
Corporate assets							259.8
Total assets							$1,738.3

SOURCE: Textron *Annual Report*, 1977.
*Except for sales (principally from the aerospace business segments) to the U.S. Government and sales to a foreign government (13 percent), Textron does not sell more than 10 percent of its annual volume to any single customer.

From a theoretical and practical standpoint, geographical segments should be determined to help the investor make some kind of risk analysis. However, typical groupings currently don't provide that for most companies. Although Nicaragua and Mexico are geographically proximate, from an economic or political-risk standpoint they are not very similar. Likewise, the Americas/Far East segment of IBM is not useful for the investor, even though it makes sense from IBM's organizational standpoint. It would be more sensible to the investor to aggregate countries according to weak or strong currencies (vis-à-vis the parent currency), industrial or developing country, politically and economically stable or unstable, than to use simple geographical proximity or organizational lines. The only suggestions given for geographical segments in FASB 14—with no strong preference—are proximity; economic affinity; similarities of business environments; and the nature, scale, and degree of interrelationship of the operations in various countries.[20]

The OECD Perspective

The OECD issued a Code of Conduct which, among other things, called for improved disclosure of information about operations. In terms of segmented information, the OECD recommended the disclosure of the geographical areas and principal activities in each area; operating results and sales by geographical and industry segments; capital investment by geographical and, where practicable, industry segments; and the average number of employees by geographical segment. The only guidelines given for geographical segments are these:

> While no single method of grouping is appropriate for all enterprises, or for all purposes, the factors to be considered by an enterprise would include the significance of operations carried out in individual countries or areas as well as the effects on its competitiveness, geographic proximity, economic affinity, similarities in business environments and the nature, scale and degree of interrelationship of the enterprise's operations in the various countries.[21]

The Code of Conduct is a guide, but the OECD has no power to force companies to adhere to its disclosure principles. However, it is a pattern for national accounting bodies to follow in setting up their requirements. There are obvious major differences between FASB 14 and the OECD guidelines.

The EEC Perspective

Before the EEC Fourth Directive was issued there was no common standard for segmented disclosure in Europe, and wide differences existed from country to country. A survey was conducted on the segment-reporting practices of the hundred largest industrial multinational companies based in the EEC and listed on stock exchanges in 1973. Of the firms surveyed, 92 percent provided sales data by segment, 49 percent provided profits, 28 percent production, 26 percent assets and 7 percent capital expenditure.[22] Differences in disclosure between

---

[20]Ibid., p. 17.
[21]*The OECD Observer* No. 82, July/August 1976, p. 14.
[22]S. J. Gray, "Segment Reporting and the EEC Multinationals," *Journal of Accounting Research*, Autumn 1978, p. 244.

the British and Continental European firms are summarized in Table 9–3. In general, the level of disclosure was higher for the British firms. Sales data are more frequently disclosed for both sets of companies, but the British were stronger on disclosure in all areas except production by volume and assets analyses. The study concluded that the major reason for the differences in disclosure was differential stimulus to disclosure provided by the regulatory environment of legal, professional, and stock market requirements.

The EEC Fourth Directive is adding a new dimension to segmented disclosure in Europe. Adopted in 1978, the directive requires that sales be analyzed by industrial (or product) and geographical segments. Admittedly, this is a far cry from U.S. requirements and not much different from what the hundred largest European firms were already disclosing. However, all firms will now be required to disclose sales by segment.

Textron's segmented disclosures which are illustrated in Table 9–2 are more extensive than those of a typical U.S. company. Table 9–4 illustrates the comprehensive segmented disclosures of sales and export data of the Swedish Match Company. Note that group sales are presented in matrix form by country and product group. As is typical in Europe, only sales data are presented, however. The export data are more comprehensive than required in FASB 14 in that exports from each country are given rather than just exports from the parent country.

Table 9–5 presents a territorial analysis from the 1979 annual report of Imperial Chemical Industries Limited, a British multinational enterprise. Notice that ICI's sales and profit data are more like those of a U.S. than a Continental firm. The company provides more breakdowns on export sales than would be found in the report of a U.S. company. Although ICI does not provide a geographic or product segment breakdown of assets, elsewhere in the report it does provide capital expenditures sanctioned and made by geographical area for the year.

A noteworthy disclosure provided by ICI is its breakdown of employees worldwide, as illustrated in Table 9–6. This type of disclo-

TABLE 9–3. Segmented Disclosures

	PERCENT OF U.K. COMPANIES	PERCENT OF CONTINENTAL COMPANIES	PERCENT OF TOTAL COMPANIES
Sales—Industry Segment	86.7	76.4	81
Sales—Geographical Segment	93.3	70.9	81
Profits—Industry	77.8	12.7	42
Profits—Geographical	75.6	3.6	36
Production (by volume)	6.7	45.5	28
Assets	24.4	27.3	26

SOURCE: Adapted from S. J. Gray, "Segment Reporting and the EEC Multinationals," *Journal of Accounting Research*, Autumn 1978, p. 246.

TABLE 9–4. Group Sales of the Swedish Match Company, 1978 (in millions of Swedish kroner)

SALES PER MARKET	TARKETT	KATRINE-FORS	MATCHES	PACKAG-ING	ARENCO	CARD-BOARD	OTHER ACTIV-ITIES	TOTAL	TOTAL GROUP EXPORTS FROM RESP. COUNTRY
Sweden	322	630	36	376	130	2	191	1,687	921
EEC									
Belgium	5	53	35	1	14	23	5	136	43
Denmark	24	49	29	62	8	1		173	3
France	20	170	285	10	34	4	61	584	121
Italy	2	6	20	2	6		1	37	
Netherlands	16	32	57	18	19	9	4	155	35
Great Britain	9	103	49	33	32	40	4	270	18
West Germany	31	523	90	133	136	229	13	1,155	366
Other EEC countries		4	2	2	3			11	
Total, EEC	107	940	567	261	252	306	88	2,521	586
Rest of Europe									
Finland	33	8	4	7	3		4	59	21
Norway	39	207	20	39	6		5	316	1
Portugal	1	22	12		1		1	37	3
Switzerland	2	6	34	39	8	2	3	94	15
Spain				1	5			6	
East Germany		29	2		2			33	
Austria	18	3	9	7	5		4	46	3
Other countries	1	3	1	3	33		2	43	
Total, rest of Europe	94	278	82	96	63	2	19	634	43
Other countries									
Morocco			19		8			27	
Rest of Africa		5	44	2	49		5	105	
Dominican Republic			8	35				43	
United States	8	17	24	1	56		13	119	16
Rest of Americas	3	4	67		35		3	112	
Philippines			47	18	1		2	68	2
India					2			2	
Pakistan			7	3				10	
Rest of Asia	4	15	46	2	34	3	3	107	
Australia, Oceania	6		2		6		1	15	
Total, other countries	21	41	264	61	191	3	27	608	18
Total	544	1,889	949	794	636	313	325	5,450*	1,568†
Deduct: Internal sales	−8		−1	−14	−12	−17	−44	−96	−443
Total, Skr m.	536	1,889	948	780	624	296	281	5,354	1,125

SOURCE: 1977 Annual Report, Swedish Match. Reprinted by permission.
*Includes sales between divisions, but not within them.
†Covers export of products manufactured in the respective countries, including total internal export sales.

sure is found more commonly in the United Kingdom and Continental Europe because of the interest in providing employee-related information. U.S. firms might separate employees into U.S. and "other" categories but rarely with such extensive geographic breakdowns. ICI's disclosures are more in line with the recommendations of the UN and OECD.

SOCIAL RESPONSIBILITY AND SOCIAL ACCOUNTING

Social accounting is inexorably intertwined with social responsibility. On a global scale, social responsibility and social accounting encompasses three main areas:

TABLE 9–5. Territorial Analysis/Imperial Chemical Industries Limited

This part of the review analyzes the results in each of the main geographical areas of the Group's operations. The sales and trading profit made by companies located in each area are shown in the following table. Export sales and their related profits are included against the territories from which those sales were made; the sales figures differ, therefore, from those in the chart where sales are shown according to the territory in which the customer is located.

	SALES		TRADING PROFIT	
	1979 (£MILLION)	1978 (£MILLION)	1979 (£MILLION)	1978 (£MILLION)
United Kingdom				
Home sales	2,229	1,798		
Exports (at invoice value)	1,254	970		
	3,483	2,768	470	370
Continental Western Europe	921	744	31	(2)
The Americas	799	743	37	30
Australasia and the Far East	720	659	77	65
Indian sub-continent	97	116	13	12
Other countries	81	69	5	4
	6,101	5,099	633	479
Inter-territory eliminations	(733)	(566)	—	—
Royalty income	—	—	22	25
Totals as in profit and loss account	5,368	4,533	655	504

SOURCE: Imperial Chemical Industries Limited, 1979 Annual Report.

1. Environmental quality (for example, pollution).
2. The impact of the firm on its employees and community (in ways other than pollution).
3. National income accounting.

Particularly since the 1960s, there has been renewed public awareness of the negative aspects and effects of industrialization and new technology. It is clear that a new social consciousness is emerging globally, although to different degrees in different countries. Intelligent and prudent managers in today's world should realize that their organization's success rests not only on profit performance but also on social achievement. Social responsibility accounting as discussed in this chapter focuses primarily on the disclosure of such information. Chapter 14 contains a more extended discussion on the nature of social responsibility accounting and how that is likely to develop in the future.

TABLE 9-6. Personnel/Imperial Chemical Industries Limited

The Group. The average number of people employed by the Group in 1979 was 148,200 (1978, 151,200) and they were located in the following areas

	1979	1978
United Kingdom	89,400	92,500
Continental Western Europe	10,700	10,700
The Americas	20,200	19,500
Australasia and the Far East	15,500	15,700
Indian subcontinent	10,500	11,000
Other countries	1,900	1,800
	148,200	151,200

The Group's policy is to staff its operations with nationals of the country involved. At the end of 1979 the number of UK nationals working abroad was 415 and a further 200 non-British personnel were serving away from their own countries. The object of international staff movement is to fill positions until suitable local nationals can be developed, to pass on experience, and to develop staff of high potential likely to occupy senior positions in the Group. Decisions about the content of personnel policies are made locally. The aim of the Group is to be a good and progressive employer and to earn a reputation as such in each territory in which it operates.

SOURCE: Imperial Chemical Industries Limited, 1979 Annual Report.

The Content of a Social Report

The breadth and depth of information disclosed in a social report varies considerably from country to country, as does the medium selected for disclosing the information. For example, a firm may choose to report social responsibility information in its annual report (either in the narrative sections, the financial data sections, or in notes to the financial data section) or in a special separate publication not part of the annual report. Regardless of the communication vehicle utilized, the most common topics having to do with social accounting are the following: environment, equal opportunity, personnel, community involvement, products, disclosure of codes of conduct, and business ethics. In a given country social accounting may focus on only a few of the above categories. While several efforts are underway in the UN, OECD, and EEC to improve social disclosures, these efforts are still in the developmental stage.

There is wide variation from company to company and from country to country on the qualitative versus quantitative presentation of inputs and outputs. *Inputs* refer to specific social programs put into effect, such as the installation of air pollution control equipment. *Outputs* refer to the impact of the programs, such as the reduction of specific pollutants in the atmosphere. The following possibilities are those most likely to be found in company disclosures.

1. Inputs and outputs are expressed in literal (nonquantitative) form.
2. Inputs are stated in quantitative terms, generally in monetary form (expenses, investments) and outputs are in quantitative but nonmonetary form (physical measures, social indexes).
3. Inputs and outputs are expressed in quantitative, monetary terms.

Following are examples illustrating how the same information would be presented in these three kinds of reports.

1. The company spent considerable funds on a plan to reduce accidents in the plant and is happy to report that its efforts have been eminently successful.
2. The company spent $500,000 on a plan to reduce accidents in the plant, and it has achieved a 50 percent reduction in the accident rate.
3. The company spent $500,000 on a plan to reduce accidents in the plant, and it has saved $1 million in injury-related claims and expenses as a result.

Variations Worldwide

The quantitative nonmonetary approach is the basis of the law in France called the *Bilan Social* (which, roughly translated, means social balance sheet), and is used primarily by business. This is similar to the *Social Jaarrerslag,* prescribed in The Netherlands. French nationalized companies use some highly sophisticated methods in certain accounts, such as the *comptes de Surplus* (surplus accounts), to measure periodically how marginal productivity gains contributed to each constituency and in what proportion.

The Swedish social reports use monetary measures for social input and value added distribution among shareholders, in combination with physical measures for outputs. One recent report by the Fortia Group included the results of a survey using social indicators as a measure of social achievement. In Germany's *Sozial Bilanz,* inputs are in monetary terms accompanied by comments on their achievement of social objectives.

Generally, only short statements about social responsiveness are found in the annual reports of large U.S. companies. However, one quite sophisticated approach is utilized by ABT, a Boston-based consulting group. In its American Social Audit it presents a balance sheet and income statement where net social income is calculated for several constituencies: the company and its stockholders, its employees, its clients, the general public, and the community. In fact, ABT utilizes a double-entry system to arrive at its net social income, or net contribution to society for the year.

As these examples show, there are really only two approaches to social reporting: one utilizing the terminology, procedures, and formats of accounting and the other employing methods that are not accounting-based. The real advantage of the accounting approach is that it permits the distinction between social investment and social expenses and ultimately produces a balance sheet and income statement. As such, it facilitates *managerial* social accounting within traditional guidelines: setting objectives, plans, and budgets; allowing variance analysis; and facilitating corrective actions. In fact, some European companies have published their forecasts or plans in terms of social objectives and responses, and they follow up during the next year with a comparison of actual versus planned. Yet despite the natural appeal to accountants of this approach, the other approach remains closer to real life. The well-being of people both inside and outside the firm can rarely be expressed in quantitative terms. Thus caution should be exercised in extending this monetary approach to the social area.

The French Law

On July 12, 1977, France adopted a law requiring all French firms with 300 or more employees to prepare annual *social balance sheets*. These are submitted to company *works councils*, made up of representatives from both labor and management in all French undertakings with more than 50 employees. The new law covers all of the private sector (above the employment size minimum) and most of the public sector (including state-owned railways, utilities, and companies such as Air France and Renault). Compliance with the new laws varies somewhat according to the size of the company or subsidiary plants. However, the rule is that employers have to submit their first social balance sheets according to the following timetable:

1. By 1979, all undertakings with at least 750 workers and their constituent plants with at least 300 workers.
2. By 1082, all undertakings and plants with at least 300 workers.

In addition, by 1984 all social balance sheets must encompass three years (the current year plus the two previous years). And enterprises that have more than one plant of more than 300 workers must prepare and submit one social balance sheet for the enterprise as a whole *and* one for each plant.

Every social balance sheet must provide information in seven areas:

1. Employment.
2. Wage-related costs (benefit packages).
3. Health and safety protection.
4. Other conditions of work.
5. Employee training.
6. Industrial relations.
7. Other conditions of life relating to the undertaking, including housing and transportation provided to employees by the company.

Each of these categories is further divided into subcategories. For example, other conditions of work is subdivided into (a) length and arrangement of the workweek, (b) organization and content of work, (c) physical working conditions, (d) changes in the organization of work, (e) expenditures on improving working conditions, (f) works doctors, and (g) unfit workers. Each of these subcategories is, in turn, comprised of several quantifiable indicators. For example, under the physical working conditions subcategory are such numerical indicators as "the number of employees normally and regularly exposed to more than 85 decibels of sound on the job," "the number of employees . . . exposed to heat above the level specified in the Decree of May 10, 1976 . . ." and "number of samples, analyses of toxic substances and measurements thereof. . . ."

The French law is quite detailed and specific. It is also highly employee-oriented and hence quite narrow in scope. Yet it is also consistent with the environment: like other laws and accounting rules, it is legislated, codified, and standardized. It reflects the growing discontent of French workers, who wield considerable political clout (enough, at least, to get such a law passed), and the growing socialist orientation of the French society.[23]

It is evident from this discussion that social responsibility accounting is perceived as an increasingly important area of disclosure worldwide. The nature of the information being disclosed depends upon what each country feels is most important, but the consensus seems to be that corporate accountability extends beyond the traditional profitability measures of enterprise performance.

[23]We are particularly indebted to Professor Edmond Marques of CESA (France) for much of the material in this section on social responsibility. For more details see Edmond Marques, "The Firm: Its impact on Society; Introducing Societal Accounting," a paper presented at the Georgia World Congress Institute conference on Exploring the Brave New Worlds of Accounting, Atlanta, Georgia, 8 September 1978.

Value Added Statements

One interesting aspect of social accounting is the value added statement. Value added, which is becoming very popular in Europe, is primarily a two-step process. First, the firm identifies the value it adds in the production and sales process by subtracting from sales the materials and services purchased by the firm. Then, the firm separates the value added into various constituencies, such as employees, government, providers of capital, and the business itself. Table 9–7 shows the value added statement of Tate & Lyle, Limited, a prominent British commodity trading and agricultural company.

TABLE 9-7. Group Statement of Value Added (for the year ended 30 September 1979)

TATE & LYLE, LIMITED				
	1979 (£ MILLION)		1978 (£ MILLION)	
Turnover		1,190.4		1,146.8
Less bought-in materials and services		1,043.0		992.5
		147.4		154.3
Add share of associated companies' results	3.6		1.9	
Investment revenue and miscellaneous income and exceptional items	7.4	11.0	(1.6)	0.3
Value added		158.4		154.6
Applied in the following way:	%		%	
To pay employees Wages, pensions, etc.	63	100.3	64	99.1
To pay providers of capital				
Interest on loans	8 13.4		8 11.9	
Dividends to stockholders	4 5.8		4 5.8	
Share of minority interests	1 0.8	20.0	2 2.8	20.5
To pay governments Taxes on profits	7	11.6	8	12.8
To provide investment for growth				
Depreciation	12 18.5		12 19.0	
Retained profits	5 8.0	26.5	2 3.2	22.2
	100	158.4	100	154.6

SOURCE: Tate & Lyle, Limited, 1979 annual report.

A study of annual reports published in 1979 by 200 major companies from 18 countries revealed that European companies were most likely to provide value added statements. Table 9–8 summarizes the results of the study. Note that no U.S. firms provide such information. The European firms provide the information because of the strength of employee groups. Also, the British Corporate Report referred to earlier in the chapter strongly recommended the value added statement. It is obvious from Table 9–8, however, that the practice is still not uniformly widespread throughout Europe.

TABLE 9–8. Publication of Value Added Statements

	SAMPLE SIZE	COMPANIES PUBLISHING VALUE ADDED STATEMENTS
EUROPE		
France	15	2
Germany	15	8
United Kingdom	15	9
Netherlands	10	2
UK and NL*	2	2
Italy	10	1
Belgium	10	1
Switzerland	10	—
Sweden	7	1
Spain	5	—
Denmark	3	1
REST OF THE WORLD		
United States	30	—
Japan	15	—
Canada	15	1
Australia	15	3
South Africa	10	1
Singapore	5	—
Brazil	5	—
Hong Kong	3	—
	200	32

SOURCE: Stuart McLeay, "Value Added Statements: A Comparative Study," presented at the Third Congress of the European Accounting Association, Amsterdam, March 24–26, 1980.
*Shell and Unilever are operating companies jointly owned by British and Dutch interests. Hence they are better classified under a joint United Kingdom–Netherlands grouping rather than in one country or the other.

FORECASTS

The issue of publishing forecasts has been around for years and seems to have no solution. Obviously, managers use forecast information when they decide on future directions of the business. This information would be valuable for investors, creditors, government, and other users as well. However, forecasting is extremely difficult and imprecise, especially in the international arena. A multinational must forecast changing conditions in many countries for many product lines. In addition, it must forecast changes in exchange rates and the ways in which changes in one of its markets affect its operations in other markets. Thus preparing a forecast is a lot more difficult and hazardous for a multinational than for a domestic company. Once again, however, the inherent risks and difficulties do not make the firms turn away from preparing such forecasts for internal management purposes.

Management is also concerned lest it be held liable by external users for imprecise forecasts. The key is to have assumptions properly identified so that users can evaluate forecasts based on those assumptions. Auditing forecasts is a difficult but not insurmountable problem.

A company's external auditors are certainly well versed and knowledgeable about the company and its industry. This knowledge places them in a reasonable position to assess the forecast and its underlying assumptions. Admittedly, there may have to be a separate auditor's opinion stressing the cautionary nature of the forecast and perhaps attesting to its reasonableness and comprehensiveness. This second opinion would not be inordinately difficult to initiate, nor would it be too complicated to understand. Furthermore, auditors in many countries including the United States are already coping with price-level-adjusted statements (which also have a degree of imprecision inherent in them) and with some corporate reports which already *do* include management forecasts.

U.S. Practice

Most of the studies of corporate forecasts in the United States have focused on accuracy rather than extent or content.[24] Taken as a group,

---

[24]See for example, Barefield and Comiskey, "The Accuracy of Forecasts of Earnings Per Share," *Journal of Business Research*, July 1965, pp. 241–251; B. Basi, K. Carey, and R. Twark, "A Comparison of the Accuracy of Corporate and Securities Analysts Forecasts of Earnings," *The Accounting Review*, April 1976, pp. 244–254; R. M. Copeland and R. J. Marioni, "Executives' Forecasts of EPS Versus Forecasts of Naive Models," *Journal of Business*, October 1972, pp. 497–512; Financial Executives Institute, "How Accurate Are Forecasts?" *Financial Executive*, March 1973; B. L. Jaggi, "Further Evidence of the Accuracy of Management Forecasts *vis-à-vis* Analyst's Forecasts," *The Accounting Review*, January 1980, pp. 96–101.

these studies generally concluded: (1) Company forecasts tended to overestimate earnings. (2) While companies did slightly more accurate forecasting than analysts, not a great deal of difference was found in the accuracy of management and financial analysts (although for certain industries or time periods, analysts made slightly better forecasts). (3) Earnings can be forecast more accurately in some industries than in others. (4) The range of accuracy in company forecasts was considerable. What was also evident from these studies is that only a small percentage of U.S. companies publicly release their forecasts. For example, McDonald's study of corporate earnings forecasts published in the *Wall Street Journal* from 1966 to 1970 showed that there were only 201 corporate predictions during the entire period.[25] Furthermore, 152 of the companies released a forecast for just *one* of the four years.

One of the better studies of the *content* of published corporate forecasts was done by Bikki Jaggi in 1978.[26] He concluded that the informational content of forecasts published by companies *did* provide new and useful information to investors because stock prices of these companies changed significantly after the publication of these forecasts.

European Practices

Looking at practices in Europe, there are difficulties both in finding studies and in comparing them to those done in the United States. Two good recent studies are those by Barrett and Gray. Barrett's study focused on the broader issue of disclosure and whether American reports were superior (in terms of disclosure) to European and Japanese reports.

The only aspect of Barrett's study relating to forecasts concerned information on future capital expenditures. He concluded that the British and Japanese were well ahead of the U.S. firms with respect to planned capital expenditures.[27]

Gray's study is perhaps the most recent and comprehensive one on forecast disclosure in Europe.[28] His study examined the hundred largest industrial multinational companies based in the EEC in 1973 (45 British, 23 German, 20 French, 4 Italian, 4 Dutch, 3 Belgian, and 1 Luxembourg). His results showed that overall the extent of disclosure was somewhat low and largely qualitative: 58 percent included a state-

[25]Charles McDonald, "An Empirical Examination of the Reliability of Published Predictions of Future Earnings," *Accounting Review*, July 1973, pp. 502–510.
[26]Bikki Jaggi, "A Note on the Information Content of Corporate Annual Earnings Forecasts," *Accounting Review*, October 1978.
[27]M. Edgar Barrett, "Annual Report Disclosure: Are American Reports Superior?" *Journal of International Business Studies*, Fall 1975, pp. 15–20.
[28]S. J. Gray, "Managerial Forecasts and European MNC Reporting," *Journal of International Business Studies*, Fall 1978, pp. 21–32.

ment of business prospects, 56 percent included research and development data, 91 percent included actual expenditure data, and 51 percent included planned capital expenditure data. He also concluded that overall there was no statistically significant difference between British and Continental EEC companies, although German firms exhibited significantly greater disclosure than did French firms, and British firms made the greatest disclosure of capital expenditure data.

In assessing the environmental forces which might have influenced forecast disclosure, Gray examined the stock exchange regulations, the professional accounting standards, and the statutory legal requirements in each of the countries included in the study. In terms of legal requirements, he found little stimulus to disclose forecast and related data, except for the item of capital expenditure. In this specific area, quantitative data relating to capital expenditure actually contracted for were required in Ireland, The Netherlands, and the United Kingdom. However, only in the United Kingdom was the requirement extended to include amounts authorized by directors. In no country were there disclosure requirements of forecasts related to profits, sales, or cash flows. At the EEC level, there were a number of requirements concerning forecasts, but only of a very general and vague nature that information must be given in the management/directors report about the company's future development.[29] No guidance was provided as to the form this report should take.

Professional Requirements

Gray also found that there were no professional requirements at the national level relating to the disclosure of forecasts in annual reports. However, there has been some discussion of this topic by Britain's Accounting Standards (Steering) Committee. In its discussion paper "The Corporate Report," a major recommendation was that annual reports include a "statement of future prospects" indicating "profit levels, employment levels and prospects, and investment levels," and also include the major assumptions on which such forecasts were based. At the wider EEC level, however, there was little support from the profession for developments of this nature. At an even wider international level, the Accountants International Study Group (AISG), prior to its demise, called for an orderly progression toward the publication of profit forecasts.

---

[29]Commission of the European Communities, "Amended Proposal for a Fourth Directive for Coordination of National Legislation Regarding the Annual Reports of Limited Liability Companies, Brussels, 21 February 1974, Article 43.

Stock Exchange Requirements

Finally, in examining the rules of stock exchanges, it appeared that only in the United Kingdom and Ireland were there any specific rules concerning forecasts. The Federation of Stock Exchanges permits them but does not require them. The only requirement is that a company report explain why actual results "shown by the accounts for the period under review differ materially from any published forecast made by the company (previously)."[30]

The only other EEC country whose stock exchange says something about forecast disclosure is France. The Commission des Operations de Bourse has made suggestions that are contained in its recommendations on information to be included in company reports.[31] The Bourse recommends that a section of the report be headed Future Outlook and that information be provided on such subjects as corporate objectives, capital expenditure plans and expected returns, and anticipated financing arrangements. However, no mention is made of quantitative profit forecasts. And as Gray's and Barrett's studies showed, French companies were among the worst in Europe about disclosing forecasts.

What can be concluded from all these studies and observations about publishing company forecasts? A prudent conclusion would be that the outlook for disclosing forecasts is more cloudy than clear. While more and more groups are warming up to the idea, the majority remain cold to the prospect. And as is the case for most changes in accounting practice, until sufficient pressure is brought to bear, the likelihood of change is slight. In this sense, the barometer reading would show some pressure for change, but not much. However, as forecasting becomes less an art and more a science, and as pressures for external financing become greater, one can predict that there will be more disclosure of corporate forecasts in the future. It is clearly an area where accounting has considerable room and opportunity to grow.

CONCLUSIONS

Disclosure of more and higher-quality information in financial statements helps users make better decisions. Most disclosures are currently being set at the national level. However, the International Accounting Standards Committee, the United Nations, and the Organization for Economic Cooperation and Development are encouraging higher levels of standardized disclosure. The EEC is likely to be the only regional

[30]Federation of Stock Exchanges in Great Britain and Ireland, "Admission of Securities to Listing," note 27.
[31]Commission des Operations de Bourse, "L'information a l'occasion des Assemblées Générales Ordinaires," December 1971.

grouping of countries that is successful. However, the levels of disclosure so far discussed are not high.

As investors continue to cross national boundaries looking for projects to invest in, and as companies cross boundaries looking for additional sources of capital, the level of disclosure will continue to improve. One area of improvement is group accounting. Investors are no longer willing to settle for the parent company's results; they want information about all firms in the group. As consolidated reports become more widespread and the use of the equity method more accepted in the conservative continental countries, investors will have a clearer picture of the group.

Several issues of disclosure are particularly relevant for the multinational enterprise. One is the disclosure of foreign exchange gains and losses, as discussed in Chapter 6. Another is disclosure about geographical segments. In this area, international standards seem to lag behind FASB 14 in some ways but stand out in others, such as in employee-related information.

The two areas to keep an eye on in the future are social accounting and forecasts. In the former area, U.S. firms tend to focus on environmental and regulatory responsibilities, whereas the European firms seem to be more concerned with areas affecting the worker. Both social accounting and forecasts are subjective and imprecise, but they should take on increasing importance worldwide.

STUDY QUESTIONS

9–1. What are some of the factors that need to be considered in determining the nature and extent of disclosure in financial statements?

9–2. How similar do you think financial statement disclosure would be in Egypt (a socialist economy where most enterprises are state owned), the United States, and Switzerland? Why?

9–3. How useful would it be for an investor to read the financial statements of a foreign corporation translated into the language of the investor? What other possibilities are there?

9–4. What are the limitations of having access only to parent company rather than consolidated financial statements?

9–5. Compare the cost method and the equity method of disclosing the results of subsidiary and affiliate information. Why do differences exist worldwide in the use of these methods?

9–6. How would you compare the general level of disclosure of U.S. and foreign corporations?

9–7. Compare segmented results of operations as required in the United States, the EEC, the United Nations, and the OECD.

9–8.   What are some ways of defining social accounting? How would you characterize social accounting in the United States as compared to Europe?

9–9.   What is a value added statement? Why is it useful?

9–10.   Select the annual reports of several companies in the same industry and compare their disclosures along the following lines:

    a.   How much qualitative and quantitative information is devoted to the international dimension of the business in the president's letter to the shareholders and in the general business narrative?

    b.   What are the geographical breakdowns given in the segmented disclosures and what information is given?

    c.   How relevant are the geographical breakdowns in terms of assigning business risk?

    d.   Pick three firms in different industries and compare the same disclosures listed above across the industries.

9–11.   Send for the annual report of a foreign corporation and compare its disclosures with those of a U.S. corporation. Look at the kinds of information that are disclosed and at the ways that similar information is disclosed (such as segmented data and group information). One possibility might be to compare the annual reports of Imperial Chemical Industries Limited (British), Dow (U.S.), and Du Pont (U.S.). The address for the annual report of ICI is Imperial Chemical Industries Limited, Imperial Chemical House, Millbank, London SWIP 3JF, England.

CASE

MATTERHORN AG

Jack Stone is in a real quandry. He has only two weeks in which to make a final recommendation on the acquisition of Matterhorn AG, a company that manufactures high-quality mountain climbing equipment. Jack is on the international acquisitions staff of Leisure, Inc., a large U.S. company that specializes in recreational consumer goods for an increasingly fitness-conscious U.S. population. Leisure, Inc. has little experience in the international market but feels that Western Europe is a possibility. Jock Hansen, president and founder of Leisure, Inc., heard about Matterhorn AG from a mutual friend while skiing in Switzerland and asked his acquisitions staff to look into the matter.

Matterhorn AG is a Swiss corporation with a large percentage of the stock owned by Hans Groberg and his family. Hans started the business 30 years ago and is anxious to sell so that he can retire. He has two sons and one daughter who manage various subsidiaries of Matterhorn, but none of them are anxious to take over the business. Since beginning the business, some of the stock has been offered publicly, so Hans' personal holdings are less than 15 percent. However, his control over Matterhorn has never been questioned by other shareholders. The banks have provided substantial financing for Matterhorn and control most of the proxy votes of other shareholders at the annual meetings.

Part of Jack's dilemma is that he has no idea what to offer Matterhorn shareholders for their stock, which is currently selling for the equivalent of $1,900 on the Swiss stock exchanges. The Swiss Code of Obligations requires that financial statements be prepared, but they are very sketchy and don't have to be disclosed to the public. Jack computed a price/earnings ratio for Matterhorn and discovered that it was four times that of a similar company in the United States, and he suspects that Matterhorn's earnings were understated in comparison with U.S. generally accepted accounting principles. On the balance sheet, he noticed that certain fixed assets were carried at a value of one Swiss franc, even though their insured value was several million Swiss francs. In talking with a CPA who had experience in Switzerland, Jack found out that hidden reserves, which tend to understate the value of assets and overstate expenses, were allowed. Jack tried to get Matterhorn's accountant to show him how the hidden reserves really affected the books, but the accountant was hesitant to do so.

Another problem is trying to get a picture of the whole corporation. Matterhorn's financial statements—such as they are—contain the results of only the parent. Jack knows that at least ten subsidiaries controlled by Hans' children were not consolidated with Matterhorn's operations. Jack has tried to get copies of the financial statements of the subsidiaries and a summary of intercompany transactions but has still not received a response.

One thing that really irks Jack is that he can't get much financial data, but he can get all kinds of information from the company's social balance sheet about the quality of life of the workers. "Why would they go to such trouble for all that garbage?" muses Jack. He decides that it must be a public relations gimmick.

Jack knows he has to have an answer soon. He assumes that Jock wants the acquisition in order to write off his ski trip, but he doesn't want to recommend a lemon.

Questions

1. What are the major problems that Jack faces in trying to evaluate this investment opportunity?
2. Why is the consolidation issue so tricky here?
3. What are some major differences in disclosure between Switzerland and the United States as brought out in the case?
4. Why are the Swiss so conservative in their accounting? What role do the banks play in this conservatism? (For greater insight into this question, read The 1973 Annual Report of CIBA-GEIGY A.G.—Switzerland, in "Report of the AAA Committee on International Accounting," *Accounting Review*, supplement 1976.)

10

Transfer Pricing

Compared to strictly domestic business, pricing considerations in international business are more numerous, more complicated, and more risky. A firm must consider at least two sets of laws, two competitive markets, the reactions of two sets of competitors, and two governments. In turn, each of these considerations varies in importance and interaction over time. Thus the firm selling internationally is confronted with two different and constantly changing market collages. It should not be surprising that determining prices for international sales is difficult, even for the occasional exporter. Yet despite the problems, pricing is critical to the profitability of any business operation, domestic or international. As a result, pricing policies and procedures are highly secretive areas for virtually all firms. The cloud of secrecy enshrouding pricing also covers quasi-illegal or even outright illegal practices, making it even more difficult for outsiders to obtain pricing information.

This chapter focuses on some of the major considerations that influence pricing strategies, then moves to a more detailed analysis of setting prices for intercorporate transfers. The main reason for this approach is that while all prices are based to some extent on accounting costs and considerations, the determination of prices for sales to unaffiliated buyers is largely the responsibility of the marketing staff. On the other hand, pricing intracorporate transactions more directly involves the corporate accounting and financial staff. In fact, intracorporate prices are so important that they are almost always set at the highest level of corporate organizations, with the major input coming from the financial and accounting staff.

THE CLASSICAL THEORY OF
INTERNATIONAL PRICES AND PRICING

In classical economist David Ricardo's world of free competition and perfect knowledge, each country specialized in the production and sale of goods in which it had a comparative advantage. Allowing free mobility of goods, labor, and capital, the net result of free trade was the equalization of factor prices, goods prices, and standard of living, along with the maximization of total world utility. Even without factor mobility, the results were the same so long as goods were allowed to move freely. In Ricardo's theoretical world, uniform prices and pricing practices were both a theoretical and socially desirable result.

Although admittedly an oversimplified version of the classical theory of comparative advantage and free trade, this description provides a starting point for analyzing present pricing practices in international markets.

THE REALITY OF INTERNATIONAL
PRICES AND PRICING

Whether purely competitive markets ever existed is at best a theoretical, highly conjectural debate. Certainly no knowledgeable person would argue that today's world of international business is an example of such a situation. The governments of classical theory were without influence; today they are omnipresent; and today's trade and investment activity is highly managed and controlled by governments, firms, and banks. Governments use a host of trade and investment policies to restrict or encourage the extent, nature, and timing of international transactions.[1]

The large corporations which dominate today's commerce can exploit their monopoly advantages in both domestic and international markets by such practices as dumping, price discrimination, and intracorporate pricing. Similarly, the international banking community affects trade and investment by altering credit policies, interest rates, and the amount and types of international services available. In sum, in contrast to Ricardo's world, today's world of imperfect competition and knowledge gives ample opportunity and incentive for multinational firms *not* to price uniformly.[2] Following are some of the more realistic aspects of pricing in international markets, including several noneconomic considerations.

[1]Examples of these policies are tariffs, quotas, international agreements, currency controls, licensing rules, subsidies, and tax policies.
[2]See P. Kressler, "Is Uniform Pricing Desirable in Multinational Markets?" *Akron Business and Economic Review*, Winter 1971.

Factors Influencing Price Determination

For a truly multinational firm, its overall international competitive position is its major consideration in determining prices.

In analyzing its global competitive position, a multinational firm must consider not only the profitability of its sales and investments in both domestic and foreign markets, but also the ways in which they affect each other. Figure 13 depicts this pattern of interaction. An example is the use of intracorporate pricing to maneuver profits out of high-tax-rate countries into lower ones. A parent company can sell goods at prices *below* cost to its foreign subsidiaries in lower-tax-rate countries and buy from them at higher-than-market prices. The resultant loss in the parent's high-tax country adds significantly to the profits of the subsidiaries in low-tax countries, and in the process the multinational achieves a considerable reduction in its global taxes (see Figure 14). Viewed in this light, two separate types of international sales must be considered in terms of their effect on the firm's competitive position.

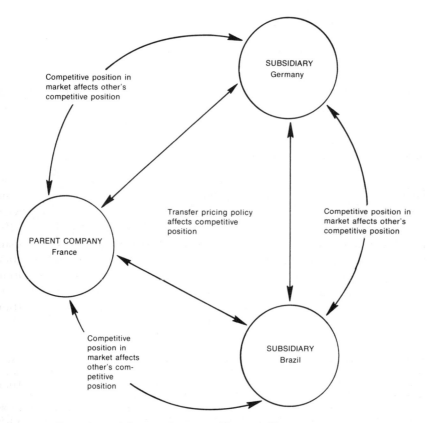

Figure 13. Transfer pricing and competitive position

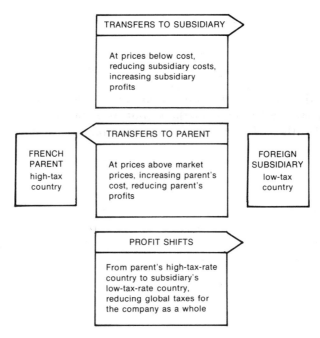

Figure 14. Transfer prices, taxes, and profits

The first is sales to unaffiliated buyers: entities not part of the corporate family. The second is sales to members of the corporate family: intracorporate sales.

Sales to Unaffiliated Buyers

In sales to unaffiliated buyers, important pricing considerations are such factors as buyer needs, tastes, purchasing power and preferences, and income and demand price elasticities.[3] The prices of goods and services largely determine the market share and profitability of the firm in that particular market and serve as the starting point for overall company strategy. Local income and turnover taxes, inflation rates, and practices of competitors are also of major importance in setting prices. Additionally, divisional performance and evaluation techniques become significant when the firm operates strictly on a profit center basis, particularly when intracorporate or interdivisional sales are substantial.[4] Once

---

[3]See *Solving International Pricing Problems* (New York: Business International, 1966); M. I. McCalley, "Pricing in the International Market," in Reed Moyer, ed., *Changing Marketing Systems* (Chicago: American Marketing Association, 1967); and David Rutenburg, "Three Pricing Policies for a Multi-Product Multinational Company," *Management Science*, April 1971.

[4]See R. Boyd, "Transfer Prices and Profitability Measurement," *The Controller*, February 1961; J. Boyer, "Intracompany Pricing's Effect on R.O.I. Analysis," *Financial Executive*, December 1964; J. J. Mauriel and R. N. Anthony, "Misevaluation of Investment Center Performance," *Harvard*

again, however, the local profitability and competitive position of the subsidiaries as they sell to unaffiliated buyers are usually less important than the subsidiaries' contribution to the profitability and competitive position of the *overall* corporation. This contribution is not always synonymous with the increased profit and improved position of an individual subsidiary or even the parent. As already mentioned, and as will be explained in greater detail later, the parent company may at times want to show losses in high-tax countries and have profits accumulate in lower-tax-rate countries. The pricing considerations related to this contribution-to-the-whole concept, which primarily involves intracorporate pricing, is an area about which significantly less is known.

Intracorporate Sales and Pricing

In its simplest yet broadest sense, intracorporate pricing is the determination of value for a good or service transferred among business units that share common ownership.[5] It encompasses the determination of interest rates for loans, charges for rentals, fees for services, prices for goods, and the methods of payment. It *excludes* the determination of prices quoted to unaffiliated buyers, although these prices can be both directly and indirectly affected by intracorporate prices. Furthermore, intracorporate prices are not necessarily equivalent to internal costs. They may be considerably below or above accounting costs, and in some instances they bear no direct relation to actual cost.

Historically, intracorporate pricing practices have caused considerable controversy. The controversy over transfer pricing has not pertained to its definition, however, but to its resultant effects. It has been identified as a powerfully manipulative tool used to avoid or substantially defer taxation of corporate income; to minimize ad valorem tariffs; to keep out, damage, or in some cases eliminate competition; to circumvent foreign exchange controls; to allow the corporate family to thwart the monetary and fiscal policies of governments.[6] Few specific multinational operations have caused such a clamor, and these allegations suggest that the considerations in setting transfer prices are more wide-ranging than those for determining prices to unaffiliated buyers. Before getting into more specifics of the uses and abuses of transfer pricing,

---

Business Review, March-April 1966; and J. Fremgen, "Measuring Profit of Part of a Firm," *Management Accounting*, January 1966.

[5]One can make a fine distinction between *intra*corporate prices and *inter*corporate prices by using the former to refer to sales among divisions of a single incorporated entity and the latter to refer to sales among different corporate entities of one large company. However, in this chapter *intracorporate* refers to any transfer made within the global corporate family. It is also used synonymously with internal transfers and transfer pricing.

[6]See James Shulman, "Transfer Pricing in Multinational Business," doctoral dissertation, Harvard University, 1966; *Solving International Pricing Problems* (New York: Business International Corp., 1965); and Jeffrey S. Arpan, *International Intracorporate Pricing: Non-American Systems and Views* (New York: Praeger, 1972).

some clarification of the nature and need for internal transfers is in order.

THE NATURE OF INTRACORPORATE TRANSFERS

Internal transfers among units of a multinational firm perform an integral and legitimate function in multinational companies, just as transfers between divisions of domestic companies do. For example, in a vertically integrated aluminum company, bauxite may be mined in Jamaica, processed into aluminum ingots in the United States, rolled into sheets in France, and sold in fabricated form to a German affiliate for further finishing and direct sale in Europe. Each stage involves an intracompany sale, requiring an actual transfer of materials and ownership (title), as well as compensating transfers of funds. Whether market prices are used in all cases—prices equivalent to those which would be competitively determined by interactions of independent buyers and sellers—or whether the buying and selling companies were independently owned would make no difference.

Even the discounts allowed to affiliates for bulk purchases or for special services would not be significantly different from or more uncommon than discounts offered to unaffiliated buyers for similar reasons. Furthermore, components or other semiprocessed materials are not necessarily sold in similar form to unaffiliated buyers, and therefore the selling unit should allow a discount to the purchasing affiliate to permit it to finish the goods for final sale at competitive market prices.

In this last case, there may not be any true market price for the goods being transferred, because the product is never sold in comparable form in the open market. However, this in itself would not mean the transfer price is somehow unfair or unjust. The real questions are (1) whether the transfer actually took place and (2) whether the costs included in the price transfer are fairly associated with the real cost of the goods.

Certain costs that may be included but would *not* be in this category are charges that really constitute hidden royalty or dividend payments, payments for unassociated research and development expenses, inordinately high allocations of overhead or administrative and selling expenses, and unassociated management service charges. The inclusion of any or all of these unrelated costs in the price of the goods sold internally can make the transfer price actually exceed the market price (if one exists). At first glance this result might appear to penalize the buying unit, yet it would not necessarily be disconcerting to either the buying or selling unit. This is because there are instances when such artificially higher-than-market prices would be desirable in order to achieve certain other company objectives. These instances are described in greater detail later.

Transfer Pricing in International Business

For the time being the total impact and importance of multinational firms' transfer pricing cannot be assessed precisely. Some statistics are useful and suggestive, but unfortunately none are very comprehensive. For example, the best single source of published statistics on transfer pricing pertains only to U.S. multinational firms, and these statistics were based on data from only 60 percent of the U.S. multinational population.[7] Nonetheless, some qualitative assessments can be made about the importance of transfer pricing.

1. In terms of world exports for all types of merchandise, the value of those being sold on an intracompany basis is significant: probably 30 percent of the total. World exports of all merchandise in 1970 totaled $309.2 billion; U.S. multinationals' exports entering world commerce that could be identified as intracompany amounted to $35.6 billion.[8] This figure includes exports from U.S. parents to their majority-owned foreign affiliates (MOFAs) and the exports of the MOFAs to the parents and affiliates in other countries (see Table 10–1). However, it excludes imports to and exports from *minority*-owned affiliates of U.S. multinational firms. Because U.S.-based multinationals accounted for roughly 60 percent of the value of all foreign investments in 1970,[9] the combined value of the intracompany transfers of *all* multinationals may approach twice the value of U.S. multinationals. Hence the 30 percent total figure.

In addition to these intracompany transfers, one should add the amount of transfers between multinational firms and their captive, although technically unaffiliated, suppliers. These would include transfers from companies whose output is for the most part purchased by a multinational firm. In these cases, the multinational exercises considerable monopsony power and largely dictates the prices of the goods it purchases. Unfortunately, there are no figures for the volume or value of such transfers.

2. Transfer pricing is increasing in importance as multinational firms loom larger in world trade, particularly in the export of manufactured

---

[7]U.S. Tariff Commission, *Implications of Multinational Firms for World Trade and Investment and for U.S. Trade and Labor: Report to Committee on Finance of the United States Senate and Its Subcommittee on International Trade* (Washington: Government Printing Office, 1973), particularly Chapters III and IV.
[8]Ibid., p. 278.
[9]EEC Commission Report 1048/III/73-E, Appendix I to Annex II, p. 2.

TABLE 10–1. Amounts of U.S. Multinational Firm Exports Entering World Commerce in 1970 That Can Be Identified as Intracompany

Exports by parents to majority-owned affiliates	$11.4 billion
Exports of majority-owned affiliates	$24.2 billion
(to U.S. parents, $8.1 billion)	
(to affiliates not in U.S., $16.1 billion)	
Total intracompany trade	$35.6 billion

SOURCE: U.S. Tariff Commission, *Implications of Multinational Firms for World Trade and Investment and for U.S. Trade and Labor: Report to Committee on Finance of the United States Senate and Its Subcommittee on International Trade* (Washington: Government Printing Office, 1973), particularly Chapters III and IV.

goods. Between 1966 and 1970, world trade rose by more than half its 1966 level (53 percent) while U.S. multinationals increased their global exports by 69 percent over the same period.[10] From 1966 to 1970 world exports of manufactured goods grew even faster, increasing by 65 percent. Yet this was not as fast as U.S. multinational-related exports of manufactured goods, which grew by 73 percent.[11] (See Table 10–2 for more detail.) Furthermore, intracorporate transfers' share of the total U.S.-based multinational trade in manufactured goods increased from 44 percent in 1966 to 49 percent in 1970, accounting for over 53 percent of the expansion in value during this period.[12]

3. Only a few industries accounted for the bulk of international intracorporate sales of manufactured goods. Again, looking at U.S.-based multinational statistics, three basic industries accounted for some 70 percent of the total in 1971: transportation machinery and equipment (41 percent), nonelectrical machines and equipment (18 percent), and chemicals (10 percent).[13] Electrical machinery (8 percent) and instruments (5 percent) accounted for half the remainder. These five industries do relatively more foreign sourcing and assembling than the other nine basic industries, which explains their extremely high share of intracorporate transfers.

4. In far more industries, intracorporate sales were the major source of multinational firms' sales expansion in manufactured goods from 1966 to 1970.[14] By industry, transportation increased 66 percent, nonelectrical machinery 57 percent, electrical machinery 64 percent, instruments

[10]Tariff Commission study, p. 278.
[11]Ibid., p. 280.
[12]Ibid., p. 317.
[13]Ibid., p. 315.
[14]Ibid.

TABLE 10-2. Comparison of Levels and Changes in Certain Multinational and Other Trade Aggregates, 1966-1970 (in billions of dollars)

	VALUE IN 1970	CHANGE, 1966-1970	
		AMOUNT	PERCENT
Exports of all merchandise			
World exports	$309.2	$107.4	53
Multinational-related exports	72.8	29.8	69
Other exports	231.9	78.9	52
Exports of manufactured goods			
World exports	201.4	79.4	65
OECD exports	176.2	68.5	63
Multinational-related exports	38.8	16.2	73
Breakdown of multinational-related exports of manufactured goods			
Exports from U.S.	21.7	8.0	59
to MOFAs	8.8	3.5	62
to others	12.9	4.5	53
Exports by MOFAs	17.0	8.2	93
to parents in U.S.	4.8	2.6	120
to affiliates in third countries	6.0	2.7	81
to unaffiliated buyers in third countries and U.S.	6.2	2.9	86

SOURCE: "Implications of Multinational Firms for World Trade and Investment and for U.S. Trade and Labor," *Report to the Committee on Finance of the United States Senate,* Washington: Government Printing Office, February 1973, p. 279.

70 percent, paper and allied products 57 percent, miscellaneous manufacturing 60 percent, rubber products 62 percent, textiles and apparels 69 percent, and printing and publishing 59 percent (see Table 10–3). In only three basic industries did the relative importance of intracorporate sales decrease, and only one of these—primary and fabricated metals—is quantitatively important in international trade, ranking fifth in both 1966 and 1970. The other two industries, lumber, wood, and furniture constituting one and stone, clay, and glass products constituting the other, accounted for only around 3 percent of total U.S. multinationals related trade.

5. It is not possible to say whether developed or developing countries have been affected more by international transfer pricing. The greatest volume of intracorporate transfers occurs among developed countries, but the impact on a developing country may be greater if its smaller economic base is dominated by multinational firms with substantial intercorporate transfers. Thus the size of the country's economic base, its concentration of multinational firms, their degree of international production integration, and the particular industries involved are

TABLE 10–3. Intracompany Trade and Its Relation to Multinational-generated Exports Worldwide, 1966 and 1970 (in millions of dollars)

| | TOTAL MULTINATIONAL-RELATED EXPORTS | | TOTAL INTRACOMPANY EXPORTS | | INTRACOMPANY EXPORTS AS PERCENT OF TOTAL MULTINATIONAL-RELATED EXPORTS | | GROWTH OF MULTINATIONAL-RELATED EXPORTS 1966–1970 | |
| | | | | | | | AMOUNT | SHARE OF INTRACOMPANY EXPORTS (PERCENT) |
	1966	1970	1966	1970	1966	1970		
All manufacturing	$22,541	$38,753	$9,842	$18,489	$44	$49	$16,212	53
Transportation equipment	6,500	12,398	3,640	7,509	56	61	5,898	66
Nonelectrical machinery	4,446	6,796	2,203	3,534	50	52	2,350	57
Industrial machinery and equipment	1,725	2,903	404	908	23	31	1,178	43
Computers and miscellaneous	1,566	2,283	1,036	1,457	66	64	722	59
Office machines	404	868	283	668	70	77	459	84
Farm machinery and equipment	751	742	480	501	64	68	– 9	– 234
Chemicals and allied products	2,973	4,512	1,113	1,817	37	40	1,539	46
Industrial chemicals	1,038	1,749	211	349	19	20	661	21
Plastics materials	515	859	296	598	57	70	344	88
Drugs	412	822	195	340	47	41	410	36
Electrical machinery and apparatus	2,074	3,343	699	1,511	34	45	1,269	64
Electronic components, radio, TV	710	1,309	225	647	32	49	599	71
Electrical equipment and apparatus	824	1,267	197	355	24	28	443	36
Primary and fabricated metals	1,534	3,130	329	475	21	15	1,596	10
Primary metals (except aluminum)	605	1,224	116	103	19	8	619	– 3
Fabricated metals (except aluminum, copper, and brass)	548	1,055	108	247	20	23	507	28
All other	381	851	105	125	28	15	470	5
Food products	1,406	1,790	441	608	31	34	384	44
Instruments	771	1,615	421	1,008	55	62	844	70
Paper and allied products	946	1,404	422	651	45	46	458	50
Miscellaneous manufacturing	503	931	82	338	16	36	428	60
Lumber, wood, and furniture	204	724	44	142	22	20	520	19
Rubber products	472	694	213	350	45	50	222	62
Stone, clay, and glass products	355	576	145	143	41	25	221	– 1
Textiles and apparel	200	523	52	272	26	52	323	69
Printing and publishing	157	317	38	131	24	41	160	59

SOURCE: U.S. Tariff Commission, *Implications of Multinational Firms for World Trade and Investment and for U.S. Trade and Labor: Report to Committee on Finance of the United States Senate and Its Subcommittee on International Trade,* Washington: Government Printing Office, 1973, particularly Chapters III and IV.

factors in assessing the impact of intracorporate sales. However, these factors must be considered in light of the overall corporate objectives of the firms and the particular environmental characteristics of the country, as is discussed in subsequent sections of this chapter.

TRANSFER PRICING SYSTEMS

Although individual company variations number in the hundreds, basically there are two types of transfer pricing systems in use: those based on internal costs and those based on external market prices. The former begin with some internally calculated cost—full cost, variable cost, marginal cost—and usually have added to this amount a fixed percentage markup, such as 10 percent, which allows a margin of profit to accrue to the seller. Although some companies use different cost bases and percentage markups for different products sold to different affiliates at different times, the cost-plus approach is the same. Transfer prices that are *not* based on cost usually begin with an established market price, such as the posted price for crude oil, but are subsequently sold at that price minus a fixed percentage discount such as 10 percent to allow a margin of profit to the buying unit. The customary justification for such discounts is that the purchaser is doing some product modification or adaptation not usually performed by unaffiliated buyers. Therefore, the affiliate should pay less for the product than those who buy the product in finished form.

Obviously, the derived prices of the two methods converge at some percentage markup and markdown: cost plus 50 percent equals a market price minus 25 percent for a good that costs $50 but has a market price of $100. Yet governments and competitors show a marked preference for market-based prices because they are reputedly less arbitrary and therefore fairer. It should be pointed out, however, that market-based prices are not necessarily less arbitrary or fairer than cost-based prices. The fact is that *both* prices can be highly arbitrary. On the one hand, all costs are arbitrarily determined, regardless of the accounting system a company uses. If a certain percentage of overhead is allocated to a product, the method of allocation, the percentage allocated, and the very decision to allocate are arbitrary.

The only true measure of cost is one that accountants do not as yet know how to measure: the full cost to the society of having the good produced and consumed, including all externalities and all opportunity costs.

On the other hand, transfer prices based on market prices can be just as arbitrary. Market prices reflect true value only when they are determined in a freely competitive market such as that envisioned by Ricardo. But in markets where either buyers or sellers influence the market price by changing the quantity supplied or demanded, a degree of arbitrariness is always present. By restricting supply, monopolists can maintain an artificially high price for the products they sell. On the other hand, by refusing to buy at high prices, monopsonists can maintain artificially low prices, and so on.

Thus what remains in reality is arbitrary costs and arbitrary market prices. Since both are arbitrary, what matters is their *degree* of arbitrariness—their distance from real value. In this respect, it is often argued that market-based transfer prices are relatively less arbitrary than those based on cost. But at times, and for certain products, even this is not always true. Where there is no true free market for a product, its internally computed cost can conceivably be the best approximation of its real value.

Which System to Use?

The point is that one intracorporate pricing orientation should not be rejected summarily by governments on the ground that it is arbitrary. All systems are arbitrary. The question should be: Does the system result in prices most reflective of true value? In some cases the question is, Does the system result in the most reasonable division of income between buying and selling units?[15]

From a company standpoint, cost-based prices have one distinct advantage over market-based prices: flexibility. Because any cost element that enters into the computation of the base price can be changed as well as the percentage markup, it is much easier to change a transfer price based on cost than one based on market price. For example, at year-end, a firm wishing to lessen the profit and income taxes of its foreign subsidiary may discover an unfavorable cost variance for the year. In reallocating the cost overrun to the prices of the goods already sold to the subsidiary, the parent charges the subsidiary for the adjusted difference, increasing the subsidiary's costs and lowering its profits and taxes.

How Fair Is a Transfer Price?

Before closing this section, one final problem deserves mention: how does one determine how fair a transfer price really is? When a freely competitive market price exists, the onus is clearly on the company to justify any departure from it.[16] This usually entails a defense of product differentiation: the firm does not sell an identical product, or one in form identical to the one in the free market. It is then up to the government agency to decide (a) whether such is the case, and (b) if it is, what degree of departure in price is commensurate with the difference in product. Where no readily identifiable market price exists, however, it is considerably more difficult for a government to determine a transfer price's fairness. This is particularly true when the selling firm has a monopoly of some kind on the product or does not sell it in comparable form to anyone outside the corporate family. In these instances, there is considerably less support for a price other than the internally calculated one. As anyone with the makings of a shrewd international accountant will recognize, it is to the advantage of firms that plan to deviate from market prices in their internal transfers to differentiate their products sufficiently.

---

[15]*Reasonable division of income* is of particular value when there is difficulty in assessing the validity or fairness of transfer prices.
[16]Subsequent amendments to and interpretations of § 482 of the U.S. Internal Revenue Act of 1954 identify three methods for determining an arm's-length price (which is used synonymously with competitive market price).

Now let's consider *why* firms find it desirable to manipulate intracorporate prices.

TRANSFER PRICE DETERMINANTS

As mentioned previously, a multinational company must consider how its pricing affects its own position and that of its affiliates as well as how its intracorporate transfers, their prices, and the competitive positions of its members affect each other. In turn, these factors must be considered in light of the company's myriad objectives.

Advantages of Low Transfer Prices

The goal most commonly mentioned, maximization of global after-tax profits, deserves first scrutiny. It is frequently alleged that a multinational company operates as a single monolithic structure, holding tight control over its markets, and astutely using its transfer pricing system to maximize profits in low-tax countries and minimizing them in high-tax countries. Theoretically and actually, this goal can be achieved by using intracorporate pricing, as was depicted in Figure 14.

If penetrating a foreign market is the company goal, part of the transfer pricing system described in Figure 14 can also be utilized effectively. Companies can underprice goods sold to foreign affiliates, and the affiliates can then sell them at prices which their local competitors cannot match. And if tough anti-dumping laws exist on final products, a company could underprice components and semifinished products to its affiliates. The affiliates could then assemble or finish the final product at prices that would have been classified as dumping prices had they been imported directly into the country rather than produced inside.

Transfer prices can be used in a similar manner to reduce the impact of tariffs. Tariffs increase import prices and apply to intracorporate transfers as well as to sales to unaffiliated buyers. Although no company can do much to change a tariff, the effect of tariffs can be lessened if the selling company underprices the goods it exports to the buying company. For example, a product that normally sells for $100 has an import price of $120 because of a 20 percent tariff. Yet if the invoice price were listed as $80 rather than $100, it could be imported for $96. Underpricing intracorporate transfers can also be used to get more products into a country that is rationing its currency or otherwise limiting the value of goods that can be imported. A subsidiary can import twice as many products if they can be bought at half price.

Advantages of High Transfer Prices

In other situations, artificially *high* transfer prices can be used to circumvent or significantly lessen the impact of national controls. A government prohibition on dividend remittances can restrict the ability of a firm to maneuver income out of a country. However, overpricing the goods shipped to a subsidiary in such a country makes it possible for funds to be taken out. High transfer prices can also be of considerable value to a firm when it is paid a subsidy or earns a tax credit on the value of goods it exports. The higher the transfer prices on exported goods, the greater the subsidy earned or tax credit received.

High transfer prices on goods shipped to subsidiaries can be desirable when a parent wishes to lower the apparent profitability of its subsidiary. This may be desirable because of the demands of the subsidiary's workers for higher wages or greater participation in company profits, because of political pressures to expropriate high-profit foreign-owned operations, or because of the possibility that new competitors will be lured into the industry by high profits. There are also inducements for having high-priced transfers go to the subsidiary when a local partner is involved, the inducement being that the increase in the parent company profits will not have to be split with the local partner. High transfer prices may also be desired when increases from existing price controls in the subsidiary's country are based on production costs (including high transfer prices for purchases).

Transfer pricing can also be used to minimize losses from foreign currency fluctuations, or shift the losses to particular affiliates. By dictating the specific currency used for payment, the parent determines whether the buying or selling firm has the exchange risk. Altering the terms and timing of payments and the volume of shipments causes transfer pricing to affect the net exposure of the firm.

Matching Price to Market Conditions

Table 10–4 summarizes the particular conditions that make it advantageous for firms to utilize a particular level of transfer price. The maximum advantage can be gained when all these conditions line up on a country basis. For example, the parent operates from a country with the characteristics calling for high transfer prices coming in and low transfer prices going out, while the subsidiary's country conditions call for the opposite.

Consider the left side of Table 10–4. If the parent sells at low prices to the subsidiary and buys from it at high prices, income is shifted to the subsidiary, lessening the overall tax burden. At the same time the impact of the high ad valorem tariffs in the other country is lessened and the financial appearance of the subsidiary is enhanced for local borrow-

TABLE 10–4. Conditions in Subsidiary's Country Inducing High and Low Transfer Prices on Flows Between Affiliates and Parent

CONDITIONS IN SUBSIDIARY'S COUNTRY INDUCING *LOW TRANSFER PRICES* ON FLOWS FROM PARENT AND *HIGH TRANSFER PRICES* ON FLOWS TO PARENT	CONDITIONS IN SUBSIDIARY'S COUNTRY INDUCING *HIGH TRANSFER PRICES* ON FLOWS FROM PARENT AND *LOW TRANSFER PRICES* ON FLOWS TO PARENT
High ad valorem tariffs	Local partners
Corporate income tax rate lower than in parent's country	Pressure from workers to obtain greater share of company profit
Significant competition	Political pressure to nationalize or expropriate high-profit foreign firms
Local loans based on financial appearance of subsidiary	
Export subsidiary or tax credit on value of exports	Restrictions on profit or dividend remittances
Lower inflation rate than in parent's country	Political instability
	Substantial tie-in sales agreements
Restrictions (ceilings) in subsidiary's country on the *value* of products that can be imported.	Price of final product controlled by government but based on production cost
	Desire to mask profitability of subsidiary operations to keep competitors out

SOURCE: Jeffrey S. Arpan, *Intracorporate Pricing: Non-American Systems and Views,* New York: Praeger, 1972.

ing purposes. In addition, the impact of foreign exchange rationing on imports from the parent and dividend payments to the parent are lessened, the subsidiary's ability to penetrate its local market is enhanced, the parent is less affected by its government's restrictions on capital outflows, and so on.

Under this set of conditions, the subsidiary's country gains somewhat more than the parent's: more funds, more taxable income, greater economic growth of the subsidiary, and more export revenues. It loses somewhat in other areas, however: local competitors may suffer adversely, have lower profits, pay less taxes, and lay off workers if the foreign subsidiary actively pursues a market penetration strategy. The government pays greater subsidies or gives more tax credits because of the subsidiary's artificially high value of exports and, like the government of the other country, has its national control lessened.

Unfortunately for firms, seldom do the conditions line up as nicely from their standpoint as depicted on either side of Table 10–4. It is far more likely that a country simultaneously will have conditions taken from both sides of the table. For example, a country experiencing balance of payments difficulties typically would be restricting dividend outflows *and* the amount or value of imports. A company using high transfer prices on sales to its subsidiary in such a country would gain in terms of taking out more money than it might otherwise have been able to get out, but would lose by having to decrease the quantity of imported materials its affiliate needs in order to compete. Alternatively, a country may have high ad valorem tariffs and high income tax rates. Underpricing goods shipped to an affiliate in such a country lessens the tariff duties and increases subsidiary profits due to lower input costs, resulting in higher taxes for the subsidiary. Therefore, in situations where a country has conditions taken from both sides of Table 10–4, the company must weigh the gains and losses from utilizing a particular level of transfer prices.

Discussed this far are the problems related to a two-country model. As additional countries are added arithmetically, the problems and headaches of transfer pricing grow geometrically. To begin to appreciate the complexity of a multicountry model, refer back to Figure 13 and assume that each of the three countries has a set of conditions taken from each side of Table 10–4. Theoretically and realistically, the multinational's management should weigh the overall gains and losses from each shipment and transfer price for each member. When we recognize that the specific combination of environmental conditions changes in each country over time, we begin to understand why the effort of constantly reevaluating and changing intracorporate pricing strategies becomes truly gargantuan.

Internal Matters Affecting Pricing

If these complexities are not enough, there are several other internal problems to consider. One problem concerns the evaluation of management performance. How are we to evaluate the profit performance of a subsidiary manager whose operations show a loss when it was parent executives who decided that the manager buy at artificially high transfer prices and sell at artificially low prices in order to shift profit to another subsidiary in a lower-tax country? And how do we compare the performance of two managers, who operate under exactly opposite conditions and instructions? One solution is to evaluate what a manager's performance would have been if the company had operated as an autonomous profit center—that is, had all its internal transfers been at market prices or their equivalents. However, this method requires separate records for performance evaluation and considerable estimation, clerical effort, and time.

The same sort of evaluation problems arise when parent executives want to know the real financial strength and position of individual companies within the corporate family. Obviously, the classic profit center analysis has its shortcomings when internal transfers are substantial and not at arm's-length prices.

An alternative to the profit center concept is the concept of a *contribution to the whole,* in which subsidiaries and managers are evaluated in terms of their contribution to the corporation's overall global position. This calls for evaluating managers in terms of their effectiveness in achieving the specific objectives assigned to them, with additional consideration for their efficiency. A more detailed discussion of these and other issues related to performance evaluation is contained in Chapter 12.

The other major internal problem concerns the sheer complexity of internal pricing decisions and their myriad results. For a large multinational firm an enormous amount of time and effort is required to determine and evaluate its transfer pricing strategies in terms of prices, flows, methods, and timings of payments. With dozens of subsidiaries handling hundreds of product lines in an assortment of constantly changing environments, there is an incentive to keep things simple. An additional incentive is the considerable number and stature of personnel involved in developing and evaluating transfer price strategy and in the attendant bookkeeping. The sheer cost of designing, organizing, and operating a complex transfer pricing system may make the undertaking not worth the effort. Some proof of this hypothesis can be found in the transfer pricing systems actually in use. Most of the world's multinational companies utilize relatively unsophisticated systems, and many do not consciously use them in any manner other than they would with unaffiliated buyers or sellers.[17] And as is discussed in the next section, the ability of multinational firms to utilize complex, manipulative transfer pricing systems is increasingly constrained by the governments of the countries in which they operate.

The Critical Nature of Government Concern

Governments are not all alike, nor are they all equally concerned about intracorporate prices and their effects. The Japanese, French, and Italian governments appear to rank among the least concerned, the United States, Canada, and a majority of developing countries rank among the most concerned.[18] The government attitude is important to a multinational in terms of its business–government relations. In the current world atmosphere of nationalistic fever and fervor, the position of multinationals is increasingly perilous. As a consequence, they are increasingly on the defensive in terms of justifying their presence and demonstrating their benefits to the countries concerned. Because most gov-

[17]Arpan, *International Intracorporate Pricing,* Chapter 4.
[18]Ibid.

ernments rightly or wrongly view market-based transfer prices as less manipulative, less suspicious, fairer, and hence more desirable than cost-based transfer prices, companies utilizing arm's-length prices have one less area of contention and possible conflict with governments.

In an increasing number of countries, national governments are stressing and even requiring market-price equivalents for international intracorporate transfers. In some cases, government officials have the authority to recompute non-market-based transfer prices to determine the proper tariff to be assessed. In others, they have the power to reallocate income in order to determine the income to be taxed. In the United States, §402 and 402(A) of the Tariff Act of 1930, as amended, and §482 of the Internal Revenue Service Code (including the appended regulations that went into effect in April 1968) clearly specify arm's-length, market-price-based prices for intracorporate transfers, both domestic and international. Under §482, the burden of proof is on companies to justify their use of other than arm's-length prices, and the tax commissioner is empowered to reallocate income in order to arrive at a reasonable division of income even if market prices were ostensibly used.[19]

Nor are other governments standing idly by. Whereas once they confined themselves to verbal criticisms, now they act. As examples:

1. Members of the Tokyo High Prosecutor's Office confiscated some 1,500 sets of files from the headquarters of Shell Oil's subsidiary to begin an investigation of its oil pricing process there.
2. In West Germany, members of the Berlin Cartel Office have investigated paper and drug prices that multinationals currently were charging their German subsidiaries.
3. The British government, as part of the 1975 Finance Act, has issued new tax regulations regarding transfer prices being set in connection with the sale of North Sea oil.
4. In the United States, the Federal Energy Administration started administrative action against Gulf Oil Corporation. Gulf was alleged to have overcharged itself for oil purchased from certain of its foreign subsidiaries to keep profits out of the United States and thus reduce its U.S. tax bill.
5. The developing countries are also getting into the act. IBM's transfer pricing practices are under investigation in a number of such nations.[20]

The increased government concern and action are making it not only difficult but dangerous to manipulate transfer prices. In addition, gov-

---

[19]See §482, Internal Revenue Code of 1954, as amended.
[20]William M. Carley, "Profit Probes: Investigations Beset Multinational Firms with Stress on Pricing," *Wall Street Journal*, 19 December 1974.

ernment officials are more sophisticated than they were about transfer pricing. So, while the incentives for manipulation still remain, the opportunities have decreased and the penalties have increased. This is not to say that there are no longer benefits to be derived from transfer price manipulation or no longer firms that are doing it. The heyday of transfer price manipulation is probably over, but transfer pricing will remain highly significant for multinationals and their financial and accounting staff.

NATIONAL DIFFERENCES IN TRANSFER PRICING SYSTEMS

There is some evidence that the nationality of the parent company affects the transfer pricing system utilized by multinationals and the relative importance given to the various factors considered in setting transfer prices. An early study of the intracorporate pricing systems of 60 foreign-based multinationals drew these conclusions:[21]

1. American, French, British, and Japanese managements seemed to prefer cost-oriented transfer prices, while Canadians, Italians, and Scandinavians preferred market prices. No particular orientation or preference along either line was discernible for German, Belgian, Swiss, or Dutch multinationals. Overall, however, the transfer pricing systems of foreign-based multinationals were generally less complex and more market-oriented than American systems.

2. Although foreign-based companies generally considered the same environmental variables when formulating guidelines for transfer prices, especially among the larger companies, there were distinguishable national differences in the relative importance attached to each of these considerations. These differences are summarized in Table 10–5.

As can be seen from the table, American, Canadian, French, and Italian companies considered income taxes to be the most important variable affecting transfer pricing policy, while British companies considered the improvement of the financial appearance of their U.S. subsidiaries as most important. With the exception of Scandinavian companies, inflation was also identified as an important variable in transfer pricing policy deliberations.

3. In contrast to the external influences just mentioned, foreign-based multinationals considered only about half as many internal param-

[21]Arpan, *International Intracorporate Pricing.*

TABLE 10–5. National Differences in Relative Importance Given to Variables in Transfer Price Determination

VARIABLES	PARENT'S NATIONALITY						
	U.S.	CANADA	FRANCE	GERMANY	ITALY	SCANDI-NAVIA	U.K.
Income tax	1	1	1	3	1	3	3
Customs duties	2	2	2	3	3	3	3
Inflation	1	2	2	2	2	3	2
Changes in currency exchange rates	3	3	2	2	3	3	2
Exchange controls	2	3	5	5	5	5	5
Improving financial appearance of subsidiary	3	3	3	4	4	4	1
Expropriation	3	3	5	5	5	5	5
Export subsidies and tax credits	4	2	2	4	2	4	2
Level of competition	4	2	2	3	2	3	3

SOURCE: Jeffrey S. Arpan, *Intracorporate Pricing: Non-American Systems and View*, New York: Praeger, 1972.
Weighting scale: 1 = high importance, 2 = medium importance, 3 = low importance, 4 = not mentioned, 5 = mentioned only with respect to operations outside the United States.

eters as their American counterparts did. With the exception of the British, most firms in the study viewed transfer pricing more as a means of controlling subsidiary operations than as a technique for motivating and evaluating subsidiary performance. This is largely explained by the fact that the use of the profit center concept was not widespread among foreign-based companies. Aside from control, one consideration deemed important by all firms was the acceptability of transfer prices to both host and parent country governments.

CONCLUSIONS

International transfer pricing has grown in importance with international expansion. It remains a powerful tool with which multinational companies can achieve a wide variety of corporate objectives. At the same time, international transfer pricing can cause relations to deteriorate between multinationals and governments because some of the objectives achievable through transfer price manipulation are at odds with government objectives and desires. Complex manipulated transfer pricing systems can also make the evaluation of subsidiary performance difficult and can take up substantial amounts of costly, high-level management time.

Yet despite these problems and an inherent desire to keep things simple, the advantages of transfer price manipulation remain considerable, given the market imperfections of today's international business environment. These advantages keep international transfer pricing high on the list of important decision areas for multinational firms. Accountants will therefore need to know about transfer pricing, be they employed by multinational firms, national tax authorities, other involved governmental agencies, or public accounting firms.

STUDY QUESTIONS

10–1.   Why are pricing decisions more numerous, complex, and risky in international business than in strictly domestic business?

10–2.   What are the realities of international business that make it possible and desirable for firms *not* to price uniformly?

10–3.   What is the essential difference between intracorporate sales and all other sales?

10–4.   What legitimate functions do intracorporate transfers and prices perform?

10–5.   What illegitimate, unethical, or otherwise questionable functions do intracorporate transfers and prices perform?

10–6.   Given that both cost-based and market-based transfer prices are arbitrary, what are the major advantages and disadvantages of each orientation?

10–7.   Why are tax considerations such an important factor in determining intracompany flows and prices?

10–8.   What are the advantages to a multinational of having a uniform pricing policy regardless of whether it is cost-based or market-based?

10–9.   Why do you suppose there are different nationality patterns and preferences in using one type of transfer pricing system over another?

10–10. It has been argued that the golden age of transfer pricing is over. That is, firms are no longer as able or willing to depart radically from the fair value of internal transfers. Why might this be the case?

CASES

EUROELECTRONICS S.A.

Randal Brooks, treasurer of Euroelectronics S.A., had just received a memo from W. R. Manifold, the treasurer of Euroelectronics' Irish subsidiary. The subject of the memo concerned the transfer pricing of Euroelectronics products and the forthcoming termination of the five-year tax holiday which had been granted to the Irish subsidiary by the government of Ireland. The arrival of the memo coincided with still another memo from the Brazilian affiliate of Euroelectronics, which pointed out a forthcoming increase in Brazilian tariffs on imported electronic goods. While Euroelectronics had not altered its basic transfer pricing system in five years, Brooks felt the time was appropriate to review the system to see whether any changes were necessary, desirable, or feasible.

The Pattern of Shipments and Transfer Prices

Euroelectronics S.A. was based in Paris and manufactured most of the components which were assembled at its subsidiary in Ireland. The finished product was sold throughout the world, but the company's biggest market was in Brazil, where its wholly owned sales subsidiary handled the importing and subsequent sales. For the past five years Euroelectronics had utilized a transfer pricing system which, in essence, had sought to minimize global taxes and risks. This was accomplished by underinvoicing (pricing below cost) components shipped from France to Ireland and overinvoicing finished goods shipped from Ireland to Brazil. The first procedure resulted in shifting profits from France to Ireland, where the company paid no taxes, thanks to the tax holiday. Furthermore, the income of the Irish subsidiary was not taxable in France because the French government taxed only income earned in France. The overinvoicing of finished goods to Brazil also shifted profits to Ireland and away from Brazil. It furthermore left less money in Brazil exposed to the high inflation rate, strict profit remittance controls, and generally higher economic and political risks.

Impact of Changes

The termination of the Irish tax holiday would mean that the Irish subsidiary's profits would thenceforth be taxed at 45 percent (compared to 50 percent in France and 30 percent in Brazil). The new tariff rate in Brazil was expected to increase from 20 percent of the import price to 80 percent—significantly increasing the purchasing expenses of the Brazilian subsidiary. The managers of Euroelectronics' Brazilian subsidiary had suggested that the transfer pricing procedure be changed to one of underinvoicing shipments from Ireland to Brazil (at 80 percent of fair market value). This, they argued, would lower Brazilian duties and expenses and shift profit to Brazil, where it would be taxed at a lower rate than in Ireland or France.

Questions

1. Based on the information in the exhibit on page 256, do you think the transfer pricing system should be changed? If so, in what ways?
2. What other factors should Brooks consider in deciding whether to change the existing transfer pricing system? How might consideration of these factors change your answer to question 1?
3. Would your answers be any different if Euroelectronics were headquartered in the United States? If so, why?

AT WHAT COST?

Uplift International, Ltd., which manufactures forklifts, is a multinational based in the United Kingdom. The forklift engines are designed and manufactured in its Manchester plant, then shipped to subsidiaries in Brazil and Canada where the forklift bodies are made. These subsidiaries, in turn, sell the finished forklifts worldwide. In 1980 Uplift introduced a line of forklifts featuring a new engine, on which it had spent several years and millions of dollars develop-

EUROELECTRONICS

CURRENT SITUATION

Irish Exports to Brazil +	Brazilian Duty	=	Brazilian Expense	Brazilian Net Revenues*	Brazilian Profit	Brazilian Tax
Transfer price $1,200,000 FMV** 1,000,000 Cost 500,000 (no taxes on $700,000 profit)	$240,000		$1,440,000	$2,000,000	$560,000	$168,000

FUTURE SITUATION IF NO CHANGE IN TRANSFER PRICES

Transfer price $1,200,000 (Irish taxes $315,000)	$960,000		$2,160,000	$2,000,000	($160,000)	0

FUTURE SITUATION IF TRANSFER PRICES CHANGED

Transfer price $800,000 (Irish taxes $135,000)	$640,000		$1,440,000	$2,000,000	$560,000	$168,000

*Revenues minus all other expenses
**Fair market value (arms-length)

ing. In an attempt to spread out and recapture the research and development costs of the new engine, Uplift had increased the transfer price of the engines sold to its Brazilian and Canadian subsidiaries. In both cases, however, it had encountered problems with government agencies.

First of all, the Brazilian government had stated that the new transfer price included, in effect, a hidden royalty payment from the subsidiary to the parent. Such payments were illegal by Brazilian law and hence the new transfer price was unacceptable. The Canadian Inland Revenue department also was unhappy with the new transfer price because it would result in higher expenses and lower taxes for the Canadian affiliate. This effect had also not gone unnoticed by the Brazilian government. Both governments were also concerned about the headquarters overhead allocation component in the transfer price. In their eyes, the parent had little justification for charging the subsidiaries for overhead which they did not really benefit from.

In 1981 Uplift lowered its transfer prices on engines shipped to Brazil (eliminating the R & D allocation) in order to comply with the Brazilian government's ruling. At that point, the Canadian, British, and Brazilian governments all became upset. The Canadians felt that if the Brazilian subsidiary wasn't going to be charged for research and development, then the Canadian subsidiary shouldn't be charged either. The British government was upset because it felt that Uplift should have been collecting R & D fees from its subsidiaries (which were obviously benefiting from it) Furthermore, by not collecting R & D fees, Uplift was shifting taxable income out of the United Kingdom and into Brazil. Meanwhile, the Brazilian customs authority had become upset because, as a result of the lower transfer prices, it was receiving less duty (tariffs) than before.

In sum, Uplift seemed to be in a position where it couldn't please anyone.

Questions

1. Was Uplift justified in attempting to allocate to its subsidiaries, via increased transfer prices, the development costs of the new engines? Would it be justified in allocating to its subsidiaries research and development costs of projects which ultimately did not result in any commercial application by the company?
2. If a company is justified in allocating overhead, R & D, and other similar expenses to its affiliates, what would be the most equitable method of doing so?
3. In situations where some countries will not allow subsidiaries to pay the parents for such allocations, how should a parent handle these "debts"? How should it handle the complaints of the other governments, such as those of Canada in this specific case, which do allow the allocation but object to the nonuniform pricing policies?
4. In the case of Uplift International Ltd., what can it do to resolve the intra-Brazilian government conflict between the tax and customs authorities?

11

Domestic and Foreign Taxation of International Operations

The game between tax authority and corporation or individual is an ancient one that is played with all the gusto of any natural rivalry. As the tax authority sets up a new defense to plug the gaps, the corporation adjusts its strategy and tries to open up a new hole or take advantage of existing ones. For the multinational corporation, every taxing authority around the world has its own set of defenses that must be adjusted to. The challenge is exhilarating and worthy of far more resources than the corporate tax director can be expected to have personally. Specialists in parent country tax law must be combined with specialists in tax law from each country where the firm operates as well as with technical advisers in exchange controls and cash flow possibilities. This chapter considers the philosophy of taxation, especially as it relates to foreign source income, and taxes related to revenues and earnings from international operations. The major focus is on U.S.-based corporations.

TAX SYSTEM PHILOSOPHY

Although tax systems vary around the world, it is commonly accepted that each country has the right to tax income earned inside its borders. That is where the similarity stops. Opinions diverge as to the classes of revenue considered taxable, how expenses are determined, and what kinds of taxes should be used (such as direct or indirect). In addition, there are differences in adherence to tax laws, as those who pay taxes—and those who don't—in countries such as Spain and Italy can attest.

Sources of Income

Source of income is a complex issue that has domestic as well as international dimensions. The domestic side involves deciding when income has really been earned and is therefore subject to tax. In addition, business practices and tax laws differ from country to country. For example, an important tax that affects business is the capital gains tax. Table 11–1 highlights the differences in taxing capital gains.

Our major concern here is with domestic versus foreign source income. *Foreign source income* is derived from the sale of goods and services abroad by a domestic company as well as from a foreign branch and from a foreign corporation in which the domestic company has an equity interest. Foreign source income from the export of goods and services is taxable when earned; that concept is applied worldwide. Tax incentives may be used to encourage exports, however, and these incentives have the effect of placing the foreign source income in a category different from other sources of income. Examples of using taxes as incentives to export are the Domestic International Sales Corporation (DISC) in the United States and the refund of the value added tax on exports in many European countries.

Taxing the earnings from foreign branches and foreign corporations is more complex. The *territorial approach* used by France and many other countries asserts that foreign source income should be taxed where earned and not mixed with domestic source income. The opposite *worldwide philosophy* treats all income as taxable to the parent. This leads to *double taxation* since usually that income is also taxed where it is earned. The two major ways to minimize double taxation where the worldwide philosophy exists is through the *tax credit* (where the firm is allowed a direct credit against domestic taxes for the foreign

TABLE 11-1. Tax Treatment on Capital Gains

COUNTRY	TAX RATE	HOLDING PERIOD
United States	just over 49%*	one year
Australia	exempt	one year
Belgium	exempt	none
Canada	22%*	none
Germany	exempt	six months
Italy	exempt	none
Japan	exempt	none
Netherlands	exempt	none
Sweden	23%*	two years
United Kingdom	30%	none

SOURCE: "Footnotes to the Above," *Wall Street Journal*, May 8, 1978, p. 20. Reprinted by permission. © Dow Jones & Company, Inc. All rights reserved.
*Excluding state and local taxes.

income taxes already paid) and *tax treaties.* In addition, countries that use the *worldwide approach,* such as the United Kingdom and West Germany, do not tax earnings of foreign subsidiaries until the parent receives a dividend. This approach, known as the *deferral concept,* is widespread except in the United States, where the deferral principle is applied to most but not all classes of foreign source income.

Within a given country, the tax authorities normally tax income on earnings of all corporations, even when they are owned by foreign sources. For example, the German subsidiary of General Motors is taxed like all German corporations. The domestic branch of a foreign corporation is normally taxed at the same rate as domestic corporations. In West Germany, however, the taxable income of the branch of a foreign corporation is subject to a 50 percent tax rate, whereas the profits of a domestic corporation are taxed at 56 percent for undistributed profits and 36 percent for distributed profits.

Tax Havens

A phenomenon that has emerged from the philosophy that foreign source income should not be taxed at all or should be taxed only when declared as a dividend is the tax haven. A *tax haven* is defined as "a place where foreigners may receive income or own assets without paying high rates of tax upon them."[1] Tax havens offer a variety of benefits, including low taxes or no taxes on certain classes of income. Because of these benefits, thousands of so-called *mailbox companies* have sprung up in such exotic places as Liechtenstein, Norfolk Island, and the Bahamas.

The major advantage of tax havens is tax reduction. There are four broad categories of tax havens:

1. Countries with no income taxes, such as the Bahamas, Bermuda, and the Cayman Islands.
2. Countries with taxes at low rates, such as the British Virgin Islands and Jersey.
3. Countries that tax income from domestic sources but exempt income from foreign sources, such as Hong Kong, Liberia, and Panama.
4. Countries that allow special privileges; generally their suitability as tax havens is limited.[2] An example is Brazil, which provides tax incentives for industrial development in underdeveloped regions of the country.

---

[1]Milka Casanegra de Jantscher, "Tax Havens Explained," *Finance and Development,* March 1976, p. 31.
[2]Jean Doucet and Kenneth J. Good, "What Makes a Good Tax Haven?" *Banker,* May 1973, p. 493.

These categories refer primarily to income taxes. Many tax havens have no estate, inheritance, or gift taxes, making them especially relevant for individuals. Some are characterized by banking secrecy, lack of close government supervision and interference, low cost of doing business, liberal banking regulations, and the lack of foreign exchange controls.[3]

It is possible that companies could operate in tax havens as legitimate operations and reap the tax benefits without the stigma of being called a tax haven or fictitious business. To take advantage of a tax haven, a corporation would ordinarily set up a subsidiary in the tax haven country through which different forms of income would pass. The goal is to shift income from high-tax to tax haven countries. This is normally accomplished by using the tax haven subsidiary as an intermediary. For example, a U.S. manufacturer could sell goods directly to a dealer in Germany and concentrate the profits in the United States, or it could sell the goods to a tax haven subsidiary at cost and then sell the goods to the German dealer, thus concentrating the profits in the tax haven corporation.

Obviously, the tax haven has effected substantial savings for the corporation. For the government that would like to collect the tax, the only solutions are to make sure that transactions between related firms are conducted at arm's-length prices and to prevent the tax-free accumulation of fictitious earnings in tax haven countries, as the United States has done. Until then, the principles of territoriality and deferral of foreign source income will continue to help firms derive the benefits of tax havens.

Determination of Expenses

Another factor that causes differences in the amount of taxes paid is the way countries treat certain expenses for tax purposes. Expenses are usually a matter of timing. If research and development expenses are capitalized, for example, their impact on taxable income will be spread over the period in which they are written off. If they are treated as expenses in the period in which they are incurred, the impact will be immediate. Opinions also differ from country to country as to the useful life of an asset. If one government allows a firm to write off an asset in five years whereas in another country the same asset has a taxable useful life of ten years, the tax burdens in the two countries will be quite different.

In the United States a firm is allowed to value inventory in cost of goods sold at LIFO (last in, first out), which tends to increase the cost of goods sold and decrease taxable income. This practice is prohibited in a

[3]de Jantscher, "Tax Havens Explained," p. 32.

number of other industrial countries. In Sweden, companies are allowed to write down inventories for tax purposes, which tends to reduce taxable income and therefore the tax liability.

What is noteworthy here is that there may be a big difference between the statutory and effective tax rate in a country. A high statutory tax rate with a liberal determination of expenses may result in a relatively low effective tax rate, and this is the rate that is of concern to the investor.

Another dimension of determining taxable income and deductible expenses involves the status of *perquisites*, or *perks*, a type of fringe benefits. Opinions differ worldwide on how perks should be treated for tax purposes. When President Carter spoke out against the three-martini lunch, he was attempting to eliminate a managerial perk—the free business lunch.

In Britain, perks are a national institution. Because of the high marginal personal income tax rate, corporations have found other ways to compensate employees—they provide automobiles, free parking, stereos, antiques, and even pay for spouses' expenses on business trips. The key, of course, is that the perks are not treated as income to the recipients. For less than $600 in income tax, for example, a top manager can receive a new car with a value of up to $19,000. This kind of substantial perk helps explain why the chairman of British Steel Corporation receives a salary of only $53,000 a year.[4]

Types of Taxes

The impact of taxation on a multinational depends in large part on whether the tax is considered an income tax. The reason for this will be clearer as we discuss the tax credit. Three taxes are the focus here: corporate income; withholding on dividends, royalties, and interest payments; and certain indirect taxes such as the value added tax.

Corporate Income Tax

The two approaches to taxing corporate income are the classical and integrated systems. The *classical system*, used in the United States, taxes income when it is received by each taxable entity. Thus the earnings of a corporation could be taxed twice—when they are earned by the corporation and when they are received as dividends by shareholders. The *integrated system* tries to take into consideration the corporation and the shareholder in order to eliminate double taxation. One way to do this is through a *split rate system* like Germany's,

---

[4]Richard F. Janssen, "In Britain, High Taxes Yield High Perks," *Wall Street Journal*, 19 April 1978, p. 24.

whereby taxable income is taxed on undistributed profits at 56 percent and on distributed profits at 36 percent. Another way is to tax all entities at the same rate but allow a credit to shareholders for taxes paid by the corporation.[5]

The European Economic Community has been considering a proposal initiated in 1975 to harmonize systems of corporate taxation. This would be a *partial imputation tax system*, taxing corporations at one rate and allowing a partial credit to shareholders for taxes already paid by the company on its profits. Six of the nine EEC members would be able to adjust to the new system easily since they already use some form of imputation. The three that would have had biggest adjustments are Luxembourg, The Netherlands, and West Germany. The first two use the classical system and would have to change their philosophy dramatically. Germany uses the aforementioned split rate system, but in addition, it allows shareholders a tax credit equal to their total dividend tax liability.

The relative taxability of a corporation and its shareholders is critical for a multinational, because in many cases the only shareholder of a foreign corporation is the parent corporation. Therefore, as IBM considers what to do with the cash from its German operations, it needs to determine whether it would be better off leaving the profits in the German company at the high statutory rate or remitting a dividend to the parent. In the latter case, the German subsidiary would be taxed at a lower rate than if the profits were retained, but IBM—as a shareholder—would have to pay tax on its dividends, since foreign shareholders are not allowed the tax credit described above. Which option would leave it with more cash to work with?

In addition to the direct corporate tax assessed at the federal level, many countries also have local taxes assessed directly on income. In Pennsylvania, for example, both foreign and domestic corporations are subject to a corporate net income tax at a rate of 10.5 percent. In Switzerland, where the federal rate is quite low (ranging from 3.63 to 9.8 percent), each canton imposes an income tax, which ranges from 5 to 40 percent.[6] As noted in the Swiss case, a preoccupation with federal rates could leave a firm open to a relatively large local tax.

Withholding Tax

The income earned by the foreign subsidiary or affiliate of a U.S.-based multinational is taxable in the foreign country, and the tax is levied

---

[5]M. A. Akhtar, "Taxation of Corporate Income: Some European Approaches," Federal Reserve Bank of New York, *Quarterly Review*, Summer 1977, pp. 27–32.
[6]See Ernst & Whinney, "Foreign and U.S. Corporate Income and Withholding Tax Rates," *E&W International Series* for data on other countries.

against the foreign corporation, *not* against the U.S. parent. However, the actual cash returns to the parent in the form of dividends, royalties (payments made by the foreign corporation to the parent for the use of patents, trademarks, processes, and so on), and interest on intracompany debt are taxable to the parent.

Normally a country levies a withholding tax on payments to the nonresident investor. This tax varies in size from country to country and depends on whether the country has a tax treaty with other countries. In Mexico, for example, the income of a domestic corporation (organized in Mexico but having shareholders who may or may not be Mexicans) and the branch of a foreign corporation are taxed at a rate of 42 percent, the same rate that is applied to royalty payments and most interest payments. In addition, a 4 percent gross receipts tax is levied against royalty payments.

Dividends are taxed at a rate of 21% for domestic and foreign shareholders.[7] Table 11–2 compares the withholding rates in several countries.

Indirect Taxes

In countries such as the United States the direct income tax is the most important source of revenue for the federal government. In other countries, indirect taxes are very important. In Europe the valued added tax (VAT), also called the tax on value added, is a source of considerable national income. In France, for example, VAT accounts for 24 percent of all national taxes. In Denmark VAT accounts for 19 percent of tax revenues compared with 53 percent from personal taxes, a common experience in the Scandinavian countries.[8] The VAT is a percentage tax applied to the value added at each stage in the production and distribution of goods and services. For example, if a miner mines ore and sells it for $100, he would apply the VAT (assume a rate of 10 percent) and charge the buyer $110, remitting the $10 VAT to the government. The buyer then processes the ore and sells it to a wholesaler for $300 plus 10 percent VAT, collecting $330, keeping $10 of the VAT as a refund for the amount he paid the miner, and remitting $20 to the government. The final consumer is the only one who does not get a VAT rebate.[9]

All the EEC member states are required to use the subtractive form of the VAT. This means that firms subtract from the selling price of their products the invoiced purchases from firms that include the VAT in *their* selling price and apply the VAT against the difference. This method is simple and easy to document. Although the method is uni-

---

[7]Ibid., p. 16.
[8]Felix Kessler, "Experience with VAT in Europe . . ." *Wall Street Journal,* 2 February 1979, p. 1.
[9]Matthew P. Landers, "Motivations Behind VAT Proposals," *Tax Executive,* October 1979, p. 25.

TABLE 11-2. Withholding Tax Rates Applicable to Foreign Investors

	DIVIDENDS	INTEREST	ROYALTIES
Australia	30%	10%	46%*
Brazil	25	25*	25
Canada	25	25	25
France	25	33⅓*	33⅓
West Germany	25	0*	25
Italy	10–30*	20	0–14*
Japan	20	20	20
Mexico	21	42*	*
Netherlands	25	0	0
Switzerland	35	0*	0*
United Kingdom	0	33	33
United States	30	30	30

SOURCE: Ernst & Whinney, "Foreign and U.S. Corporate Income and Withholding Tax Rates," 1979.

*Special rates apply for different situations. Most of the above rates vary with tax treaties.

form throughout the EEC, the VAT rates are not. In France, for example, there are four categories of goods and services, with exceptions for each category, and VAT rates per category ranging from 7 percent to 33 percent. In Britain the standard VAT rate is 8 percent; but luxury goods are taxed at 12.5 percent, and essentials such as groceries are exempted to minimize the impact on the poor.[10] At least 16 countries have adopted the VAT: Austria, Norway, Sweden, Argentina, Brazil, Chile, Mexico, and the nine members of the EEC.[11]

The VAT is important in international business because it is *not* considered a tax against income and therefore cannot be used in computing the tax credit. From a trade standpoint, exporters in VAT countries are allowed a rebate on the VAT paid to their suppliers, but they do not have to levy the VAT on the exports. Importers, however, are assessed a VAT on imports, which is considered a border tax.[12]

Tax Treaties

The last major item before considering the taxing of foreign source income is tax treaties. With the spread of business worldwide, income earned in one country may be subject to taxation in other countries. Differences in philosophy on how income should be taxed have given

[10]Kessler, "VAT in Europe."
[11]Ibid., p. 29.
[12]Richard W. Lindholm, "VAT Designed for the United States," *Tax Executive*, October 1979, p. 14.

rise to treaties between countries to minimize the effect of double taxation on the taxpayer, protect each country's right to collect taxes, and provide ways to resolve jurisdictional issues.

A pattern for tax treaties was developed by the Organization for Economic Cooperation and Development (OECD) in 1963 and later amended and reissued in 1977. That pattern, initially resisted by the United States, was accepted in principle in the model tax treaty approved by the United States in 1977. The treaty contains 29 articles dealing with such issues as the taxes covered, the persons and organizations covered, relief from double taxation, the exchange of information between competent authorities of contracting nations, and the conditions under which a treaty may be terminated. The model treaty also deals with issues such as who is allowed to tax income, how income is to be characterized, how expenses are to be allocated, what rights exist to certain types of deductions, and how rates of tax on foreign investors can be reduced.[13]

The United States has 26 tax treaties with 38 countries, which is low compared with other developed countries. Britain has treaties with 72 countries and restricted agreements with several others. Among other things, tax treaties have an impact on dividend, interest, and royalty payments. In West Germany, for example, the withholding rate not only on dividends and royalties but on the interest on certain loans is 25 percent, whereas the interest on loans secured by real property and interest from a permanent establishment such as an operating subsidiary in Germany are subject to a 50 percent rate. In the tax treaty with the United States, however, the withholding rate on dividends is reduced to 15 percent, and interest and royalty payments are totally exempt from withholding tax. The dividend rate rises to 25 percent under certain circumstances, but the benefits to a U.S. corporation are obvious in the case of royalties and interest. Canadian dividends, interest, and royalties are normally subject to a 25 percent withholding tax rate, but are subject to only 15 percent for U.S. firms as a result of the tax treaty.[14]

Although tax treaties are formal agreements between countries over certain tax principles, other forms of cooperation on tax issues exist. In 1979, for example, the tax authorities of Canada, France, Germany, the United Kingdom, and the United States entered into an agreement to coordinate the examination of the tax returns of multinational enterprises. The explicit objectives of the agreement are:

- Determination of correct tax liabilities and avoidance of double

---

[13]Robert J. Patrick Jr., "Leading Treaty Issues," *Tax Executive*, July 1977, p. 367.
[14]See Ernst & Whinney, "Foreign and U.S. Corporate Income," for other examples.

taxation where costs are shared or profits are allocated between taxpayers.

- Study of transfer pricing practices.
- Improvement of information exchange.
- Sharing of intelligence on tax avoidance techniques.
- Efficient use of government and company personnel.[15]

TAXES RELATED TO REVENUES AND EARNINGS
FROM INTERNATIONAL BUSINESS

There are profits to be made from international business, but what are the relevant tax effects? First it is important to separate earnings into two groups: (1) those generated in the parent country from the import and export of goods and services, and (2) those generated in a foreign country through a branch of the parent or a foreign corporation in which the parent has ownership. Our focus here is on U.S. tax law unless explicitly stated otherwise, so the United States will serve as the parent country.

A few key principles, among many that relate to taxation of foreign source income, are elaborated on here. The *deferral principle* implies that income is not taxed until received by the U.S. shareholder. Thus if the shareholder is entitled to income from a foreign source but has not yet received it, he may defer the recognition of the income until it is received. According to the *tax credit principle*, a firm gets credit for income taxes that have already been paid to a foreign government on income earned in that foreign country. This principle is important because the income is taxable to the U.S. firm (unless it is deferred), which means that in the absence of the tax credit the income would be taxed twice.

The equity and neutrality principles are sources of endless conflict in the taxation of foreign source income. The *equity principle* says that, under similar circumstances, taxpayers should pay the same tax. One side feels that foreign as well as domestic source income should be taxed at the same U.S. rate. The other side says that income earned in a foreign country should be taxed at the same rate as all income in that country and not at that rate plus the U.S. rate. The *neutrality principle* states that the tax effect should not have an impact on business decisions. One side feels that the foreign tax credit encourages firms to invest abroad because firms don't get a credit for income taxes paid to state governments in the United States. The other side feels that when

---

[15]Haskins and Sells, "The Week in Review," 26 October 1979, pp. 6–7; and Ernst & Ernst, "Tax Notes," April 1979, p. 1.

firms are taxed on foreign source income, they must forgo some investment opportunities because their competitors in foreign countries are not taxed twice on income.

Import and Export of Goods and Services

Few U.S. laws relate to taxing income earned from imports and exports. Prior to 1980 a U.S. firm was allowed to organize a Western Hemisphere Trading Corporation (WHTC), which was a U.S. corporation doing business in the Western Hemisphere outside the United States. The WHTC was taxed on its earnings at an effective rate lower than the one applied to other U.S. corporations. This was accomplished by allowing firms to reduce their taxable income by 14/48, thereby lowering the effective tax rate. However, this practice was gradually phased out by the Tax Reform Act of 1976.

Firms have also been able to minimize U.S. tax when importing from or exporting to foreign branches, subsidiaries, or affiliates through creative *transfer pricing*. A transfer price, as explained in Chapter 10, is a price on transactions between related firms, such as a parent and subsidiary. For example, in order to minimize the U.S. tax on earnings from exports, a parent company could sell to a parent-owned corporation in a foreign tax haven country at cost and then sell the goods to the final user at market, concentrating the profits in the tax haven country. However, § 482 of the Internal Revenue Code discourages this practice by requiring firms to treat all intercorporate transactions as if they occurred at arm's length. More on this later.

Domestic International Sales Corporation (DISC)

A DISC is a U.S. corporation organized to export goods and services. In order to stimulate exports, Congress created the DISC in 1971 with certain tax advantages. The DISC itself is not subject to corporate income tax, but a portion of the income is taxable to the shareholders. Although there are many kinds of DISC, the most common is formed by a U.S. manufacturer that remains as the only shareholder and uses the DISC to export merchandise. The DISC may be organized on paper only, or it may have an elaborate organization that does everything but manufacture the products. In most cases, it is considered a legal rather than an operating organization.

Although some of the DISC income is taxable to the shareholder when earned, the rest of it can be deferred until it is distributed as a dividend. In addition to deferring income, a DISC enjoys more liberal transfer pricing rules. A DISC is allowed to purchase export inventory from its parent at a lower price than is normally allowed under the arm's-length rules in order to concentrate profits in the DISC. Finally, a

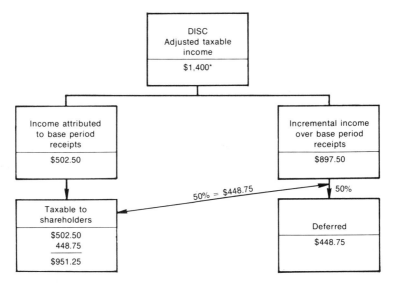

*The figures refer to the example that follows in Table 11–3.

Figure 15. Taxation of DISC income.

DISC may lend some of the deferred profits to its shareholder (the producer company) for a variety of export-related activities without the loan being considered a dividend. Such loans are called *producer loans.*

In addition to the requirement that the DISC be a U.S. corporation, the par value of its capital stock must be at least $2,500, at least 95 percent of its assets must be qualified export assets, and at least 95 percent of its gross revenues must be qualified export receipts. Examples of *qualified export assets* are inventory to be exported, cash and receivables, and facilities used for the storage of inventory. The *qualified export receipts* test is used to keep the parent company from sheltering other income in the DISC.

Since DISC is not a taxable entity, the parent is allowed to shelter some of the DISC income. However, some of the income must be declared by the parent when earned by the DISC, and any dividends declared by the DISC to the parent are immediately taxable. Figure 15 illustrates how income is split between the amount deferred and the amount deemed as a distribution to the shareholder. The latter amount must be included as income by the parent.

The deferral benefits apply to only 50 percent of the adjusted taxable income that exceeds the income attributed to the average export gross receipts for a four-year base period. The base period for 1980 income covers 1973–1976, and the period rolls forward one year for each succeeding year. The base period for 1981 income, for example, is 1974–1977. Table 11–3 illustrates how the deferral principle works.

TABLE 11–3. Deferral Principle, DISC

YEAR	ADJUSTED EXPORT GROSS RECEIPTS (AEGR)	ADJUSTED TAXABLE INCOME (ATI)
1973	$3,000	
1974	$3,500	
1975	$4,000	
1976	$4,500	
1980	$7,000	$1,400

Income attributed to base-period receipts

$$= \left[\left(\frac{\Sigma \text{ base period AEGR}}{4} \times 67\%^* \right) \div \frac{\text{AEGR of}}{\text{taxable year}} \right] \times \text{ATI}$$

$$= \left[\left(\frac{3,000 + 3,500 + 4,000 + 4,500}{4} \times 67\% \right) \div 7,000 \right] \times 1,400$$

$$= \$502.50$$

$1,400.00	ATI for 1980
502.50	income attributed to base period receipts
$ 897.50	incremental income
$ 502.50	portion of income attributed to base period receipts
448.75	50% of incremental income
$ 951.25	total taxable to shareholders
448.75	deferred (50% of incremental income)
$1,400.00	total adjusted taxable income

*The 67% is a percentage mandated by the Internal Revenue Service.

As noted in the example, the DISC provisions allow some of the income to be sheltered from tax, which would hopefully encourage or enable more firms to export on a competitive footing with foreign firms. There is no evidence to suggest that exports have increased as a result of the DISC legislation. In fact, there is evidence to suggest that the DISC has merely widened profit margins on exports and that the increase in export volume has been due to factors other than the DISC.[16]

Earnings from Foreign Branches and Corporations

In addition to exporting goods and services directly to the foreign buyer from production in the U.S., a MNE may choose to produce and sell in

---

[16]See Jane Offutt Burns, *The Domestic International Sales Corporation: An Empirical Investigation*, Ph.D. dissertation, Pennsylvania State University, 1976; and U.S. Treasury Department, Sixth Annual DISC Report.

the foreign country through a branch of the parent or through a foreign corporation in which the parent has an equity interest. The tax implications of these situations are interesting. The income or loss of a foreign branch must be combined with parent income for tax as well as book purposes. In most cases, however, a U.S. corporation does not declare income for tax purposes from a foreign corporation until it actually receives a dividend. This is the principle of deferral—the income is deferred from U.S. taxation until it is received as a dividend. As mentioned earlier in the chapter, the deferral principle is a basic tenet of the taxation of foreign source income.

The Controlled Foreign Corporation (CFC)

The deferral principle works most of the time, but an exception is made for a certain class of income (Subpart F income) of a certain type of corporation (a controlled foreign corporation). That income is not deferred but must be declared by the U.S. corporation as soon as it is earned by the foreign corporation. However, the place to start is to define a controlled foreign corporation (CFC). A CFC is a foreign corporation in which "U.S. Shareholders" hold more than 50% of the voting stock. A "U.S. Shareholder" for tax purposes is a person or enterprise that holds at least 10 percent of the voting stock of the foreign corporation. Table 11–4 illustrates how to determine whether or not a foreign corporation is a CFC. The first corporation is a CFC because shareholder A qualifies as a U.S. shareholder and holds more than 50 percent of the voting stock. The second corporation is also a CFC because shareholders A, B, and C all qualify as U.S. shareholders, and the total voting stock they control exceeds 50 percent. The third corpo-

TABLE 11–4. Determination of Controlled Foreign Corporations

SHAREHOLDERS AND THEIR PERCENTAGES OF THE VOTING STOCK	FOREIGN CORPORATION 1	FOREIGN CORPORATION 2	FOREIGN CORPORATION 3
U.S. Shareholder A	100%	35%	35%
U.S. Shareholder B		10	10
U.S. Shareholder C		10	5
U.S. Shareholder D			5
Foreign Shareholder E		45	45
	100%	100%	100%

ration is not a CFC since only shareholders A and B qualify as U.S. shareholders, and their combined total of the voting stock is only 45 percent.

Subpart F Income

Why does it make a difference for tax purposes whether a foreign corporation is a CFC? If it is not a CFC, its income is automatically deferred until remitted as a dividend to the shareholders. If a foreign corporation *is* a CFC, the deferral principle may not apply to certain kinds of income. In order to understand that, it is necessary to go back in history a few years. As was said earlier, sometimes U.S. corporations do business in tax haven countries and therefore benefit from low or nonexistent income taxes. If a tax haven corporation was actively involved in the production and sale of goods and services, there was no problem. However, the U.S. government noticed that many firms were setting up tax haven corporations just to avoid paying U.S. tax. Therefore, the Revenue Act of 1962 minimized the tax avoidance practices of multinationals. The act allowed a U.S. corporation to apply the deferral principle to its portion of income from the active conduct of a trade or business of a CFC, but it could not defer its portion of passive income, referred to as Subpart F income in the Internal Revenue Code.

Subpart F income is divided into seven groups: (1) insurance of U.S. risks, (2) foreign base company personal holding company income, (3) foreign base company sales income, (4) foreign base company services income, (5) foreign base company shipping income, (6) boycott-related income, and (7) foreign bribes.

The first category of Subpart F income, *insurance of U.S. risks,* arose because many U.S. corporations were setting up a foreign insurance subsidiary in a tax haven country and paying insurance premiums to the subsidiary on U.S. and foreign risks. The parent could deduct the premiums as expenses, and the subsidiary was paying little or no tax on the premium income. Now the income from the premiums is taxable to the parent when earned by the CFC.

Foreign base company personal holding company income is dividends, interest, royalties, and similar income that arises from holding rights rather than actually producing or selling goods and services. However, the income must be derived from sources outside the country where the CFC is organized. For example, if Multicorp established a holding company in Switzerland that owned Multicorp's subsidiaries in France and Spain, the dividends received by the holding company would be considered Subpart F income to Multicorp.

Foreign base company sales income arises from the sale or purchase of goods produced and consumed outside the country where the CFC is incorporated. For example, a U.S. firm could sell merchandise to an unaffiliated buyer in France but have the paperwork go through a tax haven CFC in Switzerland. On paper, the U.S. firm would sell to the Swiss firm (probably a wholly owned subsidiary), which would sell to the French firm. Prices would be set to concentrate profits in the Swiss firm. However, that income would be considered Subpart F income in the new law and would have to be declared by the U.S. firm. It should also be noted that the income is considered Subpart F income as long as the CFC in Switzerland is not actively involved in selling and servicing the product with its own staff. If that were to happen, the income would be active rather than passive.

Foreign base company services income arises from contracts utilizing technical, managerial, engineering, or other skills. For example, a U.S. hotel management firm could enter into a contract to manage a hotel for a sheikdom in the Middle East and have the management fee billed to a tax haven subsidiary in Switzerland. That fee would be considered Subpart F income to the U.S. firm.

Foreign base company shipping income arises from using aircraft or ships for transportation outside the country where the CFC is incorporated.

The inclusion of *bribes* and *boycotts* as Subpart F income is a phenomenon that came with the compliments of the Tax Reform Act of 1976. In order to penalize companies that supported the Arab boycott of Israel, Congress decided to classify income from these boycott operations as Subpart F income. Also, bribes paid to foreign government officials as explained in the Foreign Corrupt Practices Act of 1976 are considered a new class of Subpart F income, even though the bribes aren't really a form of income to the parent. These two twists of the law have nothing to do with tax avoidance, like the other dimensions of Subpart F income; they were included simply to punish offenders of other laws.

Now that we have divided foreign corporations into groups and income into types, let's summarize the tax implications. For foreign corporations that are not controlled foreign corporations, income is not taxable to the U.S. shareholder (the parent corporation) until a dividend is declared. For controlled foreign corporations, active income is also deferred, but passive or Subpart F income must be recognized by the parent when earned, regardless of when a dividend is declared. The only major exception to the rule is that if foreign base company income of a CFC is less than 30 percent of gross income, none of it is treated as Subpart F income. If the foreign base company income exceeds 30 percent of gross income, all the company's income is treated as Subpart F income.

The Tax Credit

It was pointed out that a key principle in the taxation of foreign source income is deferral. Another key principle is the *tax credit*. If a U.S. corporation has a wholly owned subsidiary in Canada, the Canadian corporation must pay corporate income tax of 46 percent of taxable income and withhold another 15 percent on dividends paid to the U.S. parent. If the parent is taxed again on the income in the United States at 48 percent, there wouldn't be very much left over. That's why the tax credit was adopted in 1918. That allows a U.S. corporation to reduce its U.S. tax liability by the amount of income taxes paid to the foreign government. It should be noted that the credit is available only for taxes on income paid directly by the U.S. corporation (such as the withholding tax on dividends) or deemed to have been paid by it. The *deemed direct tax* is the corporate income tax actually paid by the foreign corporation to the foreign government and deemed to have been paid by the U.S. parent. The Value Added Tax described earlier in the chapter is an example of a tax that would not qualify for the tax credit since it is on sales rather than income. The VAT could be considered a deduction to arrive at taxable income but not a credit to the U.S. tax liability.

The tax credit applies to all income that must be recognized by the parent—active as well as Subpart F income. The only exception to this is for income that arises from boycott-related activities. Foreign income taxes paid on that income are not eligible for the credit. The credit is available for income of foreign branches of U.S. corporations as well as for income of foreign corporations in which the U.S. parent has an equity interest. The following example in Table 11–5 illustrates how the tax credit can be computed. Even though the total credit as computed is $122,500, the parent may not be able to apply all the credit against the current year's tax liability because of the overall limitation set by the Internal Revenue Service. In order to illustrate how the limitation works, assume that a U.S. corporation's total worldwide income is $1 million, that its U.S. tax liability before credits is $480,000, and that its only foreign source income is what is computed in Table 11–5. The amount of income from the foreign operation included in the total worldwide income is figured as follows:

Dividend paid	$150,000
Deemed direct credit	100,000
Included in income	$250,000

TABLE 11–5. Computing the Tax Credit

Earnings before foreign tax (EBFT)	$500,000
Foreign income tax paid	200,000
Earnings after foreign tax (EAFT)	$300,000
Dividend paid to U.S. corporation	$150,000
Foreign withholding tax at 15%	22,500
Net dividend received by parent	$127,500
Computation of tax credit:	
Direct credit for withholding tax	$ 22,500
Deemed direct credit	
$\dfrac{\text{dividend}}{\text{EAFT}} \times \text{foreign tax}$	
$\dfrac{150}{300} \times 200,000$	100,000
Total credit	$122,500

The addition of the deemed direct credit to the dividend is known as *grossing up the dividend.* The overall limitation is computed as follows:

$$\text{Overall limitation} = \frac{\text{foreign source income}}{\text{total worldwide income}} \times \text{U.S. tax liability}$$

$$= \frac{250,000}{1,000,000} \times 480,000$$

$$= \$120,000$$

This means that the parent can take no more than $120,000 in credits. Since the credit as computed was $122,500, the total credit allowed is $120,000 and the final tax liability is $360,000 ($480,000 − $120,000). The excess credit of $2,500 ($122,500 − $120,000) can be carried back two years and forward five years and applied against income taxes of those years. If the computed credit had been $115,000 instead of $122,500, the parent would have been allowed to take the whole amount since it was less than the overall limitation.

In the example it was assumed that there was only one source of foreign income. If there had been several sources, the income would have been added together to get the foreign source income in the formula. A branch income or loss, Subpart F income, and dividends from foreign corporations would be included. Losses of foreign corporations or income retained by a foreign corporation rather than declared as a dividend would not be included. The credits from each of the foreign sources would have been added together, then compared with the upper limit, to determine the actual credit that could be applied against the U.S. tax liability.

The tax credit in the previous examples assumed a foreign corporation, but credits are allowed on any foreign source income. For example, a movie company may pay withholding taxes on royalties received from showing movies abroad, and the withholding tax would qualify for the tax credit. The same concept applies for an oil company that pays a withholding tax on royalties it receives for oil production abroad.

The firms could end up with large excess credits that can never be applied against the U.S. tax—even if they are carried back and carried forward. This is because many countries have higher tax rates than the United States. As pointed out in one article on high corporate tax rates abroad, "Britain . . . has a general corporate income tax rate of 52% and taxes North Sea oil production at about 70%. Norway's regular corporate rate is 33%, but its oil rate is 67%. . . . Nigeria's oil rate is 85% and Oman's is 70%."[17] This is why some multinationals could pay an effective tax rate for worldwide operations that exceeds the U.S. rate.

The distinction between different kinds of taxes, such as corporate income taxes and indirect taxes, is important since only corporate income taxes can be taken as a credit; all other taxes are treated as deductions to arrive at taxable income. The Internal Revenue Service is attempting to define very narrowly what is a creditable foreign income tax, which could cost multinationals billions of dollars in added U.S. income tax. Hardest hit would be petroleum and mineral extraction companies since they are often taxed by foreign governments on production of the resource rather than on income from sales. The IRS maintains that this royalty tax is a cost of doing business rather than a tax on income and therefore should not be a creditable tax. The resolution of this problem will have far-reaching effects on industry.

The Tax Effect of Foreign Exchange Gains and Losses

As mentioned in Chapter 5, foreign exchange gains and losses can occur from transactions which result in the conversion of foreign currency for domestic currency or vice versa and from the translation of foreign currency financial statements. The treatment of these gains and losses for tax purposes is not consistent with the requirements of FASB 8, and specific rulings on the tax effects have often been misleading, incom-

[17]*Business Week*, 28 January 1980, p. 122.

plete, and contradictory. However, a few general principles can be mentioned. According to FASB 8, foreign currency transactions must be accounted for by the two-transactions approach, which separates the sale or purchase from the financial receivable or payable. This distinction is usually made for tax purposes as well. Therefore, if an inventory item is purchased for DM1 million at an exchange rate of 58¢/DM, the entry would be:

Purchases	580,000	
Accounts payable		580,000

If the rate were to deteriorate to 59¢ during the accounting period, a loss would be reflected on the books as follows:

Loss on foreign exchange	10,000	
Accounts payable		10,000

However, the tax effect of the loss would not be recognized until the payable was closed out. Thus if at the time of settlement the exchange rate were to move to 58.5¢, the book entry would be

Accounts payable	590,000	
Gain on foreign exchange		5,000
Cash		585,000

For tax purposes, however, there would simply be a foreign exchange loss of $5,000 at the settlement of the foreign currency obligation, the difference between the opening and closing rates. There would also have to be an interperiod tax allocation on the books since exchange gains and losses do not correspond for tax and book purposes.

Effect on Long-Term Debt

The situation involving long-term debt is not as clear-cut. FASB 8 still requires a two-transactions perspective for long-term debt, with foreign exchange gains and losses being taken to income in the period in which they occur. The tax law is not consistent with FASB 8, however. In certain cases the IRS may allow a firm to treat the gain or loss arising from loans payable as an adjustment to the base of the asset which was purchased by it. Alternatively, the IRS may allow the firm to treat the gain or loss as a short-term capital adjustment, which has little tax effect. This is in contrast with the export-import situation described above where foreign exchange gains and losses are treated as ordinary gains and losses.

Effect on Branch Earnings

The tax effect of foreign currency changes on branch earnings is also confusing. Under the *profit and loss approach,* remitted branch earnings are translated at the rate in effect when remitted, and unremitted earnings are translated at the rate in effect at the end of the year. Under this approach, it is difficult to determine which portion of income is from operations and which is from exchange rate changes. The second approach allowed by the IRS is the *net worth method.* This translates the balance sheet under the current-noncurrent method described in Chapter 5, which is clearly different from FASB 8. Net income included for tax purposes is the difference between beginning and ending net worth adjusted for capital changes. It is a little easier under this approach to determine the foreign exchange gain or loss component.

Subsidiaries

Translation gains and losses from subsidiaries are not really recognized as such since only the dividend is included in net income, with the exception of Subpart F income. As you recall from the section on the tax credit, however, the deemed direct credit is determined by the formula:

$$\frac{\text{Dividend}}{\text{EAFT}} \times \text{Foreign tax}$$

The earnings after foreign tax in the formula can be computed under either the profit and loss or the net worth method.

Forward Contracts

Forward contracts are an added complexity because they are often entered into to minimize a book exposure. However, the contracts also have a tax effect since they are considered transactions. The gains on a contract may offset the loss on balance sheet exposure, so no gain or loss is recognized on the books. However, since the balance sheet loss may not be recognized for tax purposes the forward contract gain may result in a substantial tax cash flow. Obviously this has important ramifications on the size of a contract. Many firms enter into a larger contract than necessary in order to generate the cash for the impending tax payment.[18]

Recently the U.S. Tax Court ruled that exchange gains and losses on translation hedges should be treated as capital rather than ordinary gains

[18]David K. Eiteman and Arthur I. Stonehill, *Multinational Business Finance,* 2nd ed. (Reading, Mass.: Addison-Wesley, 1979), pp. 132–135.

and losses for two reasons: "(1) Subsidiaries are separately incorporated entities and, therefore, their earnings are not an integral part of the parent's business. (2) Exposures calculated according to accounting rules do not constitute real economic risks to be 'hedged' in the narrow Tax Court definitions of the word."[19] This is a real blow to the corporations since capital losses are not as favorably treated as ordinary losses.

Intercorporate Transfer Pricing—§482

As was discussed extensively in Chapter 7, a transfer price in international terms is one charged on the sale or purchase of goods and services between a U.S. corporation and a foreign corporation in which it has an equity interest and between related foreign corporations such as two subsidiaries of the same U.S. parent. Since the corporations are related, it is possible for the price to be creative and artificial for the purpose of shifting taxable income from high- to low-tax countries, for example. One of the biggest criticisms of the multinational is this alleged shifting of profits through transfer prices. What is there to keep multinationals from doing this at will? Tax authorities are the major deterrents. As a result of the Internal Revenue Code's §482 and subsequent revenue rulings, the ability of firms to artificially set prices has been reduced substantially, and cooperation with similar agencies worldwide has improved the ability of the IRS to monitor transfer prices.

Section 482 allows the Treasury Department to allocate income among related units if it feels that such allocation is necessary to prevent tax evasion. In order to determine whether a fair profit has been earned by each unit, the firm must show that it has charged an arm's-length or independent price. If there is no way to prove this, it must show that it has charged cost plus a reasonable profit. The IRS is a lot sharper than it used to be in detecting irregularities in transfer pricing policies. In the oil industry, for example, each major company has IRS transfer pricing experts who devote their entire time to determining the validity of transfer prices—with total access to corporate records. These agents discuss policies of the different firms worldwide as a cross-check of each firm's stated policies.

Allocation of Expenses—§861

In 1977 Regulation 1.861-8, known as §861, became a new thorn in the side of the multinational and a new IRS tool for reducing tax credits. This section allocates and apportions all of a firm's expenses, losses, and

---

[19]*Business International Money Report,* 4 May 1979, p. 153.

other deductions to specific sources of income (sales, royalties, dividends) and then apportions the expenses between domestic and foreign source income. Although all expenses must be allocated and apportioned, there are three major groupings of expenses: interest expenses, research and development expenses, and general and administrative expenses. The regulations give specific guidelines on the allocations, in some cases stating what classes of income certain expenses are to be allocated to. The guidelines range from very specific for some types of expenses (such as R & D) to very general for others.

If the income to which the expenses have been allocated is strictly foreign source, then the expenses are charged solely to foreign source income. If the expenses are attached to composite sources of income, then the firm must allocate the expenses between domestic and foreign source income based on guidelines set by the regulations.

The following example illustrates the impact these allocations could have on the tax credit. In the example, the U.S. company's only foreign source income is royalty income from country Z.[20]

	Worldwide	U.S.	Foreign
Gross profit and royalties	$3,100	$2,100	$1,000
U.S. expenses (before allocation)	1,600	1,600	
Taxable income by sources	$1,500	$ 500	$1,000

Tax liabilities:

U.S. tax—48% of $1,500	$720
Foreign income tax—30% of 1,000	300

$$\text{Tax credit limitation—} \frac{1,000}{1,500} \times 720 = \$480$$

Since the upper limit ($480) exceeds the actual foreign tax ($300), the U.S. company can take the full $300 credit. The U.S. tax liability would be $420 ($720–$300), and the total taxes paid worldwide would be $720 ($420 in the United States and $300 in country Z).

If a portion of the expenses were to be allocated to the foreign source income, the tax situation might appear as follows:

	Worldwide	U.S.	Foreign
Gross profit and royalties	$3,100	$2,100	$1,000
Expenses after allocation	1,600	975	625
Worldwide gross income	$1,500	$1,125	$ 375

[20]The example is taken from James W. Schenold, "A Tool for Maximizing Foreign Tax Credits," *Price Waterhouse Review* 2, 1978, pp. 38–51.

The U.S. and foreign tax liabilities would stay the same ($720 and $300), but the tax credit would change as follows:

$$\frac{375}{1500} \times 720 = \$180, \text{ the upper limit}$$

Since the upper limit is less than the taxes paid ($300), the U.S. company is constrained by the upper limit and the worldwide tax liability would be as follows:

$720	U.S. tax on $1,500
180	tax credit
$540	U.S. tax liability
300	foreign tax liability
$840	total taxes paid worldwide

As can be seen, this exceeds what the company would have paid in the absence of any allocation of expenses.

Given the complexities of the regulation and the high stakes involved in terms of tax credits, the firms are very concerned over tax planning. The major public accounting firms have devised computer programs to assist their clients. Two such programs are SEC861 by Price Waterhouse and INTERTAX II by Arthur Andersen.

What is the difference between §§ 482 and 861? Both of them refer to allocation, but §482 refers to allocations that have already been made. For example, if a parent loans money to a subsidiary, §482 is concerned that the parent has charged the subsidiary an arms-length interest rate. In the case of §861, the IRS is concerned that the parent has allocated to foreign source income the correct amount of interest expense on corporate indebtedness. In essence, §482 is concerned with allocating the proper taxable income to the parent at arm's length, while §861 is concerned with allocating corporate expenses to the foreign source income. The result in both cases is to have higher taxable income in the United States and lower taxable income abroad—and therefore lower tax credits.

Taxation of U.S. Citizens Abroad

It is the right of every country to tax the earnings of its citizens. However, the United States goes farther than most industrial countries by taxing the worldwide income of its residents. A survey by Business International revealed that of eight major Western countries, the United States is the only one that taxes its expatriates on worldwide income.[21]

[21]*Wall Street Journal*, 8 February 1979, p. 2.

This forces U.S. companies abroad to equalize the tax burden by paying their expatriates more or to replace their expatriates with locals.

Some relief for taxpayers is provided by the Foreign Earned Income Act of 1978. To understand the act, let's look at how expatriates used to be taxed. Prior to 1976, a U.S. citizen abroad was allowed an earned income exclusion of $20,000 or $25,000 (depending on the situation) and was taxed at the reduced bracket. In addition, the taxpayer was allowed a credit for all foreign income taxes paid. For example, if an expatriate earned $50,000 abroad and was allowed the foreign earned income exclusion of $20,000, he would declare taxable income to the United States of $30,000, would be taxed in the $30,000 bracket, and would receive a credit for foreign income taxes on the entire $50,000.

The Tax Reform Act of 1976 changed that by reducing the exclusion to $15,000 and requiring that the person be taxed at the rate *before* the exclusion. Using our previous example, the taxpayer would declare taxable income of $35,000, would be taxed at the rate in effect in the $50,000 bracket, and would be allowed tax credits only for foreign income taxes paid on the $35,000 rather than $50,000.

Predictably, the business community, especially expatriates living in high-cost areas, was incensed over the new ruling and began lobbying for change. The result was the Foreign Earned Income Act of 1978. The new act eliminates the exclusion that existed in the two previous ones, but it allows a deduction from income of allowances for excess living costs, such as cost of living, housing, schooling, home leave travel, and hardship area.[22] An extensive analysis by Ernst & Whinney leads to the following generalization:

> Expatriates who reside in countries whose effective foreign tax rate exceeds the U.S. tax rate (after taking into consideration either the $20,000 exclusion or the deductions for excess foreign living costs) will generally not be affected since the foreign tax credit will eliminate their U.S. tax liability. This will generally be the case in Belgium, Canada, and West Germany.
>
> Expatriates who reside in countries whose effective tax rate is less than the U.S. rate and whose deductions for excess foreign living costs are less than $20,000 will have to pay more U.S. tax under the 1978 Act. This would be the case, for example, in Brazil, France (in some cases), and the United Kingdom.
>
> Expatriates who reside in countries whose effective rate is less than the U.S. rate and whose deductions for excess foreign living cost are more than $20,000 will pay less U.S. tax under the 1978 Act. This

---

[22]For a complete discussion of these deductions, see Ernst & Whinney, "1979 Guide to U.S. Taxes for Citizens Abroad," Retrieval No. 48471.

would be the case for expatriates in Hong Kong, Iran, Japan, the Netherlands, and Saudi Arabia.[23]

CONCLUSIONS

This chapter has focused on general issues of tax philosophy worldwide as well as specific issues of U.S. taxation of foreign source income. It is obviously not easy for the corporate tax planner who must minimize tax payments worldwide to be thoroughly familiar with tax principles at home and abroad. Gradually and systematically over the years the IRS has added more and more provisions to the law to discourage firms from generating foreign source income. In spite of the restrictions, there are a number of degrees of freedom under which the firms can operate. Thus it behooves the tax planner to take advantage of tax treaties and to concentrate income where possible in a low-tax country and maximize tax credits when income must be recognized in the United States.

The example of a U.S. company using the Netherlands Antilles as the home of its offshore finance subsidiary illustrates this point. Because of tax treaties and tax laws, the finance subsidiary is able to issue a bond to foreign bond holders who are not required to pay a withholding tax on interest received. The U.S. parent is able to pay the interest expense to the subsidiary, claiming the interest as a taxable expense, and the subsidiary does not have to pay a withholding tax to the U.S. government. Because corporate tax rates are so low in the Netherlands Antilles, the parent is able to claim a full tax credit when income is earned.[24]

STUDY QUESTIONS

11–1. A company has subsidiaries in host countries A and B. Country A has a statutory corporate tax rate of 48 percent, while Country B's is 52 percent. What are some specific reasons why country B's effective tax rate might actually be more favorable to the firm?

11–2. Assume a VAT of 8 percent. What would be the selling price and taxes at each stage if the following were the values added?

---

[23]Ernst & Whinney, "The New Tax Law for Americans Overseas," January 1979, p. 3.
[24]Alan S. Lederman, "Offshore Finance Subsidiary," *Journal of Taxation*, August 1979, pp. 86–90.

Seller	Value Added by Seller
Extractor	$200
Processor	300
Wholesaler	50
Retailer	50

What would be the difference in the effect of the VAT on a U.S. wholesaling subsidiary in the VAT country if (1) it exported the good to the U.S. market or (2) it sold the good to local retailers?

11–3. What amount of income would be deferred and what amount would be deemed a distribution to the shareholder for a DISC with the following gross receipts and income:

Year	AEGR	ATI
1974	$2,000	
1975	4,000	
1976	4,500	
1977	5,500	
1978	6,000	
1981	10,000	$2,500

How, specifically, could this treatment of income meet the objectives of the DISC legislation?

11–4. Which of the following are CFCs and which are not? Why?

Shareholders and Their Percentage of the Voting Stock	Foreign Corporation 1	Foreign Corporation 2	Foreign Corporation 3
U.S. shareholder A	10%	5%	19%
Foreign shareholder B	25	20	21
U.S. shareholder C	15	20	14
U.S. shareholder D	15	5	18
Foreign shareholder E	25	15	13
U.S. shareholder F	10	35	15
	100%	100%	100%

Why is this distinction important?

11–5. ABC Company has income from the following countries:

Country	Type of Operation	EBFT	Income Tax Rate
USA	parent	$400,000	50%
X	branch	(2,000)	40
Y	CFC	30,000	0
Z	100% owned	100,000	60

The subsidiary in Z declares a 50 percent dividend; Z's withholding tax on dividends is 10 percent. Both the branch and the CFC retain all earnings. What is ABC Company's overall U.S. limitation and what is the tax liability in each country? If the foreign taxes paid exceed the overall limitation, how would the excess be treated?

11–6. Two separate court cases in the 1960s which dealt with §482 of the U.S. Internal Revenue Code involved Eli Lilly and Company and PPG Industries. The courts ruled in favor of PPG Industries and against Eli Lilly. Refer to the cases to determine the basis for these decisions.

11–7. Several articles have suggested ways to minimize the adverse effects of §861 of the Internal Revenue Code. Recommend ways that these suggestions can be used by multinational enterprises.

11–8. Assume that Bermuda is used by a U.S. multinational to shelter its foreign source income from U.S. taxes. Discuss the positive and negative aspects of the use of tax havens from each of these points of views:
   a. Bermuda
   b. the United States
   c. the multinational corporation.

11–9. How does the existence of classical and integrated corporate tax systems affect the financing decisions of multinational corporations?

11–10. One tax concern of multinationals is whether the foreign taxes they pay are creditable in their home country. VAT, for example, could be deducted to determine taxable income, but cannot be taken as a credit to U.S. tax liability. When would this treatment actually be advantageous to a firm?

11–11. On June 1, 19X1, ABC Company, a U.S. firm, sells £10,000 worth of merchandise on account to an importer in the United Kingdom with payment due on September 30. During that time, the exchange rates were:

June 1	$2.2767/£
July 31	$2.2870/£
August 31	$2.2848/£
September 30	$2.2730/£

Show journal entries (a) according to FASB 8 and (b) according to tax law. Assume no hedging. If ABC's tax year ends on August 31, what will be the tax effect, if any, of the foreign exchange gain/loss in 19X1? in 19X2? Compare these with the financial reporting of foreign exchange gain or loss for the same periods.

11–12.   How might a firm's actions to offset the controversial effects of FASB 8 be detrimental from a tax standpoint?

11–13.   Taxation is a macropolicy tool available to governments to influence economic behavior. Compare recent tax legislation in several countries. What might the governments be trying to accomplish with respect to international business operations?

11–14.   Discuss some of the factors which influence tax planning in multinational enterprises.

11–15.   One of the most hotly debated tax treaties passed recently was the U.S.–U.K. treaty. Find out what you can about the treaty and why it was so controversial.

CASES

ELI LILLY AND COMPANY*

Eli Lilly and Company, whose corporate headquarters are in Indianapolis, Indiana, is engaged "in the discovery, development, manufacture, and sale of products in three principal industries: human health, agriculture, and cosmetics." (1979 Annual Report) For sales of $2.2 billion in 1979, 53.7 percent were in human health, 36 percent in agriculture, and 10.3 percent in cosmetics. Eli Lilly's success extends worldwide with 40 percent of sales and 27 percent of earnings coming from outside of the United States.

Prior to 1940, Eli Lilly was not too interested in the foreign market, concentrating most of its sales in the domestic market. J. K. Lilly, Jr., who was head of domestic marketing, assumed responsibility for export sales in 1940 and decided to improve the firm's market position in foreign markets. Initially, Mr. Lilly tried to promote foreign sales through domestic divisions, but without much success. He therefore decided to set up two wholly owned domestic subsidiaries to promote export sales: Eli Lilly International Corporation (International) to service business in the Eastern Hemisphere, and Eli Lilly Pan-American Corporation (Pan-American) to service the Western Hemisphere.

*The information for this case is found in *U.S. Tax Cases* 67-1, 1967, Commerce Clearing House Inc., 83,535 — 83,544.

In order to encourage sales, management decided to sell goods to International and Pan-American at a substantial discount that increased with volume. This incentive contributed to strong growth in export sales over the next few years.

In 1946, Eli Lilly instituted another organizational change by making International the sole distributor of Lilly products worldwide. International sold to unrelated wholesalers in the Eastern Hemisphere and to Pan-American in the Western Hemisphere. Pan-American qualified as a Western Hemisphere Trade Corporation, which was allowed a special deduction in computing taxable income. The deduction was determined by multiplying taxable income by a fraction, the numerator of which was 14 and the denominator the tax rate for the year. Assuming a 48 percent tax rate, a Western Hemisphere Trade Corporation would have an effective tax rate of 34 rather than 48 percent. This provided a distinct advantage for Lilly to sell products to wholesale distributors in the Western Hemisphere through Pan-American instead of directly from International. The same advantage did not exist for sales to wholesale distributors in the Eastern Hemisphere.

Initially, sales to International from Eli Lilly were made at a discount of 60 percent from domestic prices on finished and packaged merchandise, and at Lilly's cost plus 15 percent on bulk merchandise. In 1952, however, this policy was changed. Because International and Pan-American were having trouble making a profit, Eli Lilly decided to forego its own profit by selling to International at a price that recovered manufacturing cost of goods sold, plus royalties payable by Eli Lilly to third parties, plus all operating expenses incurred by Eli Lilly incident to the servicing of the export business. International sold the products to Eastern Hemisphere distributors at suggested domestic retail price less 15 percent. International sales to Pan-American, however, were at its cost of goods sold plus administrative and selling expenses allocated to International's business with Pan-American. There was no provision for specific profit to International on its sales to Pan-American.

Questions

1. What is the effect on Eli Lilly's overall corporate tax liability of the pricing policy described above?
2. According to the chapter, how do you think that the Internal Revenue Service might have responded to Eli Lilly's pricing strategy?
3. What could Eli Lilly have done to avoid problems with the Internal Revenue Service?
4. What changes have occurred in the tax laws recently that would change the situation described in the Eli Lilly case?

COMPAGNIE FISCHBEIN, S.A.*

David Fischbein, who migrated from Russia at the turn of the century, operated a partnership with his son during the 1930s and early 1940s specializing in repairing industrial sewing machines and selling rebuilt industrial sewing machines. David and his son Harold were fairly successful, but David wasn't content to repair and sell someone else's products for the rest of his life. In the early 1940s David decided to try his hand at inventing, and he came up with an idea for making a small bag-closing machine. After four years of design changes and modifications, the Fischbein machine was ready for the market, which enthusiastically received it. The machine was the first as well as the only one of its kind.

Business was so good that David decided to set up two separate companies: David Fischbein Manufacturing Company (DFMC) and the David Fischbein Company (DFC). The DFMC handled the manufacturing of the machine, which was sold exclusively to DFC, the sole shareholder of DFMC. DFC was a closely-held family corporation involving David's immediate family.

In the early 1950s DFC decided to expand sales into Latin America through David Fischbein Western Sales Corporation (DFWSC) a wholly owned subsidiary of DFC. DFWSC did not manufacture any of its own bag-closing machines, but purchased them from DFMC and sold them abroad. In spite of DFWSC's early success, it was obvious that the market in Europe had considerably greater potential than that of Latin America. Therefore, in 1956 DFC organized a wholly owned subsidiary in Belgium by the name of Compagnie Fischbein, S.A. (CFSA). CFSA became the international selling arm of DFC.

At the time CFSA was organized, DFC had to decide whether to manufacture the machines in the United States and ship them to CFSA, or allow CFSA to assemble as well as sell the products. DFC soon found the following advantages to assembly in Belgium: (1) local assembly qualified the machines for a Belgian certificate of origin, which gave CFSA access to the European Economic Community countries without tariff and quota restrictions; (2) it was cheaper to assemble products in Belgium due to lower labor and overhead expenses; (3) many components could be purchased more cheaply from suppliers in Belgium than from DFMC; and (4) it was easier to comply with European standards (such as the types of plugs and voltage of motors) by producing in Europe.

CFSA assembled the bag-closing machines from parts supplied largely by DFMC, although some of the 283 parts were purchased locally as mentioned above. The assembly took six hours and involved 58 different steps, ranging from tailoring some of the more sophisticated parts, to assembly and final

*The background for this case and the quotes contained in the case are found in *United States Tax Court Reports*, Vol. 59, 1973, pp. 338–361.

testing. The mechanics were highly trained and most had worked for CFSA for many years. In spite of this, CFSA's operations accounted for less than 20 percent of the cost of the machines sold.

CFSA's selling efforts were fairly minimal. It maintained no sales force as such, preferring to operate through exclusive distributors around the world. Only 5 percent of its sales came in other ways. CFSA provided support for its distributorships via trade fairs and advertising, but it was not heavily involved in direct sales to consumers. In 1966, CFSA's total sales of $737,853 came from 47 different countries. Sales in Belgium were less than 10 percent of the total. Europe was the largest market with over 80 percent of the total sales. The top four countries in sales were Germany, France, England, and Spain.

Prior to the Revenue Act of 1962, DFC would not have had to declare CFSA's income in DFC's U.S. taxable income until a dividend was declared. The Revenue Act of 1962, however, changed that by requiring certain "U.S. shareholders" to report their portion of income earned by controlled foreign corporations if that income were considered Subpart F income. In looking at CFSA's operations, the Internal Revenue Service decided that DFC owed back taxes on CFSA's foreign source income for 1964–1967. The IRS maintained that "the components purchased by CFSA were so perfect that they only had to be simply put together in short periods of time by not too highly skilled mechanics, whose tasks in this operation were nothing more than ministerial functions." It contended that CFSA's income was foreign base company sales income because it qualified under the following two tests: "(1) the property which is purchased [from a related person] is manufactured . . . outside the country under the laws of which the controlled foreign corporation is created or organized, and (2) the property is sold for use, consumption, or disposition outside such foreign country."

CFSA maintained that its income was not foreign base company sales income because it manufactured the end product, thereby qualifying for a major assembly operation. The code specifies that packaging, repackaging, labeling, or minor assembly would not be enough to exclude a firm from foreign base company sales income provisions. However, operations are substantial if the product sold by the controlled foreign corporation is, in effect, not the product purchased from the related party.

Questions

1. Explain whether CFSA qualifies as a controlled foreign corporation and DFC qualifies as a "U.S. shareholder."
2. Why did the IRS think that CFSA was earning Subpart F income? Why did the rules for Subpart F income come into being?
3. According to the information given in the case and the chapter, do you think that CFSA's income was foreign base company sales income? Substantiate your answer.

4. Do you feel that CFSA was set up to avoid paying U.S. income tax?
5. Why didn't DFC take advantage of economies of scale by expanding the capacity of DFMC in the United States and exporting its products?
6. If you feel that CFSA's income is foreign base company sales income, what else could it do to become excluded from that category?

12

Information Systems, Organization, and Control

The complexity and risks of international business operations provide many opportunities for things to go wrong, or to vary from what was expected. Unexpected changes in currency values, in government policies, and in business conditions materially affect the success of any international operation. International businesses therefore have to plan and monitor operations with particular care.

In order to minimize surprises, and especially unfavorable results, a firm doing business internationally must thoroughly investigate the decision to be made *before* making it. This process is more difficult than the similar process for a domestic operation because the variables, alternatives, and unknowns are more numerous. In addition, the available information on which to make decisions is usually not as complete or as reliable as that for domestic decisions.

Second, the structure of the organization in which decisions are made and through which decisions are implemented and monitored is also different from the structure of a domestic company. If not properly adapted, the appropriate information may not be collected and disseminated to the person who has the authority and responsibility for making the decision. In addition, an inappropriate organization structure may preclude taking full advantage of profitable opportunities or may result in adverse performance.

Finally, the nature of international business operations makes control more difficult and more critical. Operating in many distant countries with diverse environments and degrees of instability and with people of many nationalities makes the need for control greater and simultaneously poses more problems in achieving control.

For international operations to be successful, particularly those of a multinational enterprise, considerable attention must be devoted to information systems, organizational structure, and control. Each must be carefully designed in itself and in terms of each other to make sure they are suitable and mutually supportive.

INFORMATION SYSTEMS

It is said that multinational firms owe their very existence to computers. And even though many multinationals existed *before* computers, both intuition and logic support the idea of a symbiotic relationship between computers and multinationals. The underlying reasons arise from three facts:

1. Any large organization, domestic or multinational, requires the collection, analysis, and storage of a tremendous amount of information for its own use and for reporting to others.
2. Any organization operating internationally has to have information not required by domestic companies. It also has an accompanying host of collection, analysis, and communication problems. More about these distinctly international problems later.
3. While computers cannot solve all problems of communication, analysis, and control, their capabilities in information transmittal, storage, and analysis are essential to the efficient operation of a multinational enterprise.

Because most multinationals are large and all of them operate internationally, one cannot underestimate their gargantuan information needs and the role of computers in the operation of an integrated information system. There is also a decided link between information systems and managerial decision making. Making good decisions in the complex environment of international business requires a great deal of timely information. Usually a premium is attached to response time— the time required to identify and adjust to changes in markets, laws, and competitors' moves. Thus the information system is critical to decision making and affects the firm's competitive position and its ultimate success.

There is also a necessary link between the information system and the control system. A control system must insure that there is goal congruence among all the elements of the organization and that operations are in harmony and consistent with goals. It also must be able to assess the results of operations, in terms of plans as well as of changes in the environment. Yet a control system is no better or worse than the information and decision making systems on which it relies. Hence the symbiotic relationship.

The information system has to be suited to the structure and philosophy of the firm. For example, if a firm operates through a highly decentralized structure, its information and control requirements will be different from those of a highly centralized firm. Put another way, largely autonomous subsidiaries do not require as much control *from* the parent and therefore need not transmit information as frequently *to* the parent. Thus the adequacy, suitability, and timeliness of the information are all key determinants of the success of decision making and control systems, particularly those of multinational enterprises.

Information Needs

In one sense, the information needs of a multinational are similar to those of a domestic corporation. Information has to be assembled and used in reports to—

1. *Government and government agencies,* such as details about taxes, prices, wages, pensions, and OSHA and EPA compliance.
2. *Shareholders and creditors,* such as consolidated financial reports, activity summaries, and future commitments.
3. *Management,* such as projections, budgets, expenditures, variances, and the effects of inflation.
4. *Labor,* such as wages and benefits, training and development, and expenditures.
5. *Other publics,* such as social responsibility activity and warranty information.

At the same time there are other information needs peculiar to a multinational.

1. Financial positions and operations in each country should be reported and analyzed separately, regionally, and ultimately globally, and often also by major product lines.
2. Information related to the economic risk of assets in each country should be collected and analyzed in terms not only of their potential local impact but also of their possible repercussions on global operations.
3. Separate yet integrated goals and strategies must be made for each operation. These must be based not only on global corporate objectives but also on the specific economic, legal, sociocultural, and political environments in each country of operation. They are often based on highly variable and not always comparable data for each country.

In themselves, these additional information needs are significant and require considerable time, effort, and expense over and above what a domestic enterprise requires. At the same time there is another set of problems caused by operating internationally which further complicates the collection, analysis, and communication of information. It is to these problems we now turn.

Information Problems

Many Users

First of all, reconsider our five basic categories of information users: government, shareholders and creditors, management, labor, and other publics. If a company is operating in at least two countries, it has at least two governments, two managements, two labor forces, and two publics requiring information. If it has owners and creditors in both countries, as most multinationals do, it has a double complement of users. Doubling the number of users doubles neither the pleasure nor the fun, however, because the same reports are seldom acceptable to the same types of users in different countries. In other words, the two governments require that certain information be prepared in certain ways, but seldom are their ways identical.

To give a more specific example, the Brazilian tax authority requires that tax records and reports be prepared according to Brazilian tax laws and accounting procedures, while the U.S. Internal Revenue Service requires that they be prepared in accordance with U.S. tax law and accounting procedures. As Chapter 2 showed, because tax and accounting procedures are significantly different from one country to another, the multinational cannot submit the same tax return to Brazil and the United States. Yet *both* governments require information regarding the profit of the Brazilian subsidiary in order to ascertain how much each can tax it. Similarly, what information the various publics in each country want to know also differs from country to country, as does their ability to understand whatever information is provided.

In most cases, the company must prepare local accounting reports using local language, currency, and accounting procedures. This in itself complicates the task. Furthermore, many global or regional aggregations of information require conversion or translation into one common language and currency, as well as the utilization of common accounting procedures. This is particularly true for tax and financial consolidations and top management reports.

Distance and Culture

Several additional problems are caused by distance and culture. Because of the great distances between operating units of a multinational, significant trade-offs are to be considered in terms of the speed of communication: the faster the speed required, the more expensive the communiqué. Because a multinational cannot usually afford to wait a considerable time to receive information by inexpensive channels such as the mail, it has to pay the higher costs of telephone, Telex, and so on.

As an added complication, it is difficult for someone sitting in a Paris headquarters office to fully or even adequately comprehend developments in Zaire. The perception of the causes or seriousness of a problem is likely to be different for someone who is actually on site and someone who is a great distance away. This perceptual problem is further exacerbated if the person in Zaire is of a different nationality and culture from the person in Paris. That is, the very *perceptions* of the significance and seriousness of a problem are influenced by the background of the observer, and the greater the differences in observer backgrounds, the greater the likelihood of differences in perception.

Cultural differences can also complicate the timely collection and reporting of information. In many countries, the concept of time is considerably different from that in the United States: theirs is not the same sense of urgency, and even though a U.S. parent may insist that a foreign subsidiary report desired information to headquarters by noon on the first working day of each month, the foreign manager may choose not to do so because other things come up which he feels are more important. After all, what difference will one day's delay make, or two, or three . . . . Thus distance and culture interact to affect not only the *nature* of the information exchanged, but *what* information is exchanged, *how* the information is perceived, and how *timely* the information transmittal.

Finally, complications arise because information that is readily available and reliable in one country may not be available at all in another country. What top management in Britain may regard as a routine information request could pose enormous difficulties for the manager in Tanzania in terms of the time, money, and effort required to obtain it. The British managers may not be aware that the information they request is not easily obtainable or perhaps is not available at all.

If all these rather general problems appear horrendous, consider the implementation and operation of a multinational information system, which is even more tortuous.

The Magnitude of Reporting

A study at Eastman Kodak revealed that some managers were annually receiving 200 regular financial reports consisting of 1,300 documents.[1]

---

[1]A. F. Brueningsen, "Kodak's Financial Information and Reporting System," *Management Accounting*, September 1975.

Table 12–1 summarizes the types and numbers of another multinational company's reports to headquarters. This summary *excludes* all basic financial statements and budgets and all reports prepared only at subsidiary levels. Table 12–2 provides an idea of the volume of financial reports passing through a multinational headquarters.

TABLE 12–1. Types of Reports to Headquarters

1. Corporate Controller	
a. Management reports, such as—	12
Accounts receivable aging	
Consolidated income and sales (a flash report)	
b. Consolidations—not tabulated	
c. Government reports, such as—	
Department of Treasury, such as	4
Foreign Currency Forms FC-3/3a and FC-4	
Foreign Exchange Form C-3	
Department of Commerce	8
Foreign units—data partly for Department of Commerce merchandise, Forms F-1 and F-2	
Domestic units—data partly for Department of Commerce merchandise, Forms D-1, 2, & 3	
Proxy questionnaire	2
2. Corporate Treasurer	
a. Corporate finance, such as—	12
Cash forecast for month	
Debt calendar	
Calculation of cash excess (deficit) for month (ahead)	
b. Tax	8
c. Pensions	10
d. Payroll	7
e. Risk management	8
f. Shareholders records	2
3. Industrial Relations, such as—	13
Pension plan history cards, for new entrants only	
Employee stock purchase plan	
4. Investor Relations, such as—	9
Dividend reinvestment plan	
Investor relations report	
5. Legal	3
6. Systems and Data Processing	3
Total (excludes reports at the subsidiary level only)	106

SOURCE: George C. Watt, Richard M. Hammer, and Marianne Burge, *Accounting for the Multinational Firm*, New York: Financial Executives Institute, 1977, p. 244.

TABLE 12–2. Frequency of Affiliate Reports to Headquarters

MONTHLY	QUARTERLY	SEMI-ANNUALLY	ANNUALLY	TOTAL
35	20	10	35	100
× 12	4	2	1	—
420	80	20	35	555

Number of reporting field locations, say	× 100

Total reports processed at headquarters	55,500

SOURCE: George C. Watt, Richard M. Hammer, and Marianne Burge, *Accounting for the Multinational Corporation,* New York: Financial Executives Institute, 1977, p. 244.

Thus the sheer volume of reports raises the question of information overload. Yet whatever the magnitude of the problems—volume, frequency, uniformity, reliability, suitability, and so on—the issue cannot be dismissed as insurmountable. As was mentioned earlier, the information and control system is the life-support system of the multinational and therefore cannot be ignored.

The Design of the Reporting System

One of the biggest problems related to the design and operation of a global reporting system is uniformity. Should the information reporting requirements be the same for all affiliates? *Requirements* in this sense refers to the format of reports, the underlying accounting methods used to prepare them, and the frequency of their preparation and transmittal. The advantages of a uniform system need little elaboration. If all reporting units utilize the same format, accounting principles, and reporting time periods, the managers of both parent and affiliates have an easier time understanding the information received, making comparisons among affiliates, and aggregating or disaggregating the information. A uniform system also facilitates the allocation of revenues and expenses among units which interact with each other.

However, the very nature of international business operations makes establishment of an integrated, uniform accounting and reporting system extraordinarily complicated. Each country has its own unique accounting and taxation system; the operations and objectives of a multinational or affiliate in one country may be quite different from those in other countries; the capabilities, motivations, and desires of personnel in each culture are different; and so on. Thus there is an inherent conflict between a multinational's *desire* to have a uniform system and its *ability* to develop and implement one. This is particularly true for highly centralized companies. Let's take a look at how one well-known multinational has approached this problem by examining the internal reporting system of the Coca-Cola Company.

The Coca-Cola Company

The Coca-Cola Company is one of the most widely recognized multinational firms, with operations in virtually every country in the world. Its beverage division continues to dominate the company's business, but in recent years it has diversified into other foods and water treatment products. Foods, Aqua Chem Inc., Consumer Technologies, and the Wine Spectrum constitute the remaining four divisions.

The company is organized along two separate but related lines: administrative units and legal entities. The legal entities are the accounting, taxation, and other legal units. The administrative units are the traditional organization chart units. Each operating group is headed by a president, who is also an executive vice president of the company.

Figure 16 shows the administrative units of Coca-Cola. The beverage business is subdivided into three geographic groups: the Americas, Europe and Africa, and the Pacific. Each geographic group is subdivided further. For example, the Americas group is divided into Latin America and the United States. The Europe and Africa group is subdivided into Central Europe, Northern Europe, Southwest Europe, the Balkans and Southwest Asia, the Soviet Union, Africa and the Middle East, and Southern Africa. In each of these geographic divisions there are functional specialists in planning, marketing, finance, law, public relations, and so on, and each is headed by a manager.

Within each geographic division there are many field operations or field offices. Thus the Central European division of the Europe and Africa group has field offices in Italy, Austria, Switzerland, and Germany. Each field office is staffed by functional specialists and headed by a manager. Particularly large field offices are subdivided even further. Thus the German field office of the Central European division of Coca-Cola's Europe and Africa Group is made up of a North Germany office, a South Germany office, a military sales office, and three bottling plants. See Figure 17 for a pictorial representation of these further subdivisions.

Moving down the administrative units—to the bottling plants, for example—brings us close to the legal entities, but they are not exactly the same in all cases. A specific concentrate plant in Ireland may be within the administrative jurisdiction of the Irish field office, but may

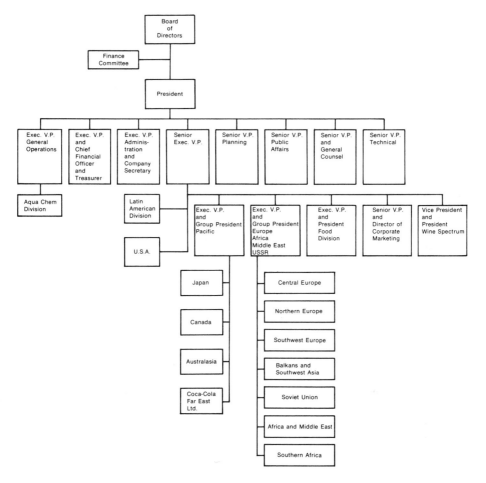

Figure 16. Organizational chart of the Coca Cola Company, 1981. (Reproduced with permission.)

itself not be an administrative unit. In addition, it may sell concentrate to another company legal entity in another administrative region, such as Greece. From an administrative responsibility standpoint, the manager of the Irish administrative field office is responsible only for sales in Ireland, not for the sales of the Irish concentrate plant—which may be greater or less than the sales in Ireland. The same is true throughout the rest of the organization.

If all this sounds a bit complicated and confusing, it's because it is. However, Coca-Cola has devised a comprehensive management information system which allows it to take the accounting data supplied by the legal entities and assign it to administrative units, aggregate it, consolidate it, and disaggregate it as needed.

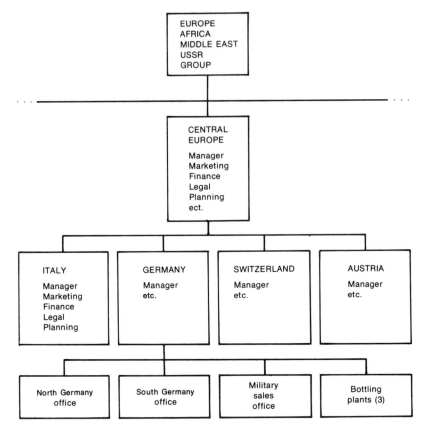

Figure 17. Suborganizational of the Coca Cola Company. (Reproduced with permission.)

Internal Reporting System

The legal entities of the worldwide Coca-Cola Company are the reporting units, the bulk of which report monthly. Their reports form the basis for calculating the profit and loss statements for all the administrative units. Each legal entity develops its own reports in both local currency (at year-end) and dollars (monthly). The profit and loss reports are Telexed to corporate headquarters in Atlanta in coded form and standardized format by the thirteenth day of each month, while sales volume reports are sent in by the sixth day of each month. The Telexed reports are printed out on three-part paper for preliminary analysis, then punched on paper tape, loaded back into a computer by way of a G.E. time-sharing system, and transferred to tape discs. Finally, computer programs analyze and balance the reports.

The three-part paper is used to prepare quick preliminary reports that are sent to top management: one copy goes to an internal review group within the Financial Reporting Department, which looks for anything unusual; one copy is sent to the reporting group, which prepares a set of short manual reports; and one copy is filed as a reference. The preparation of the consolidated profit and loss statement, from receipt of Telexes to consolidation, including elimination of all intracorporate transactions from gross profits on sales, ordinarily takes one to two days. If satisfactory, the information is taken off G.E. time sharing and put into the home office computer for storage. After one further in house consolidation of all operational data, consolidation entries (tax entries) are made. Then, individual final reports are issued, typically 2 inches thick, which are broken down by administrative units monthly and, for tax purposes, by legal entities at year-end.

The monthly reports include profit and loss and balance sheet data, both fully consolidated and by administrative regions, and also include special reports on volume, foreign exchange exposure position, cash positions, borrowings, and accounts receivables. The reports are sent to all the executive vice presidents, the chief financial officer, and the controller. Subsequently, divisional managers and divisional financial officers get consolidated financial reports for their divisions and certain key areas within their divisions. Before these final reports are received at the divisional level, most of the divisions received the same information that was earlier sent to headquarters from the legal entities in their jurisdiction. In some cases they request and receive certain information not sent to headquarters. Upon receipt of the final reports from headquarters, the divisional managers compare them with the preliminary reports they received from the legal entities. If any big discrepancies appear, telephone calls are enough to make the necessary reconciliations.

The Reporting Format

All reporting entities report by means of a standard format and code procedure, although the number of data units supplied by each entity depends on how many products and administrative units they supply, as well as which services they perform. The data transmitted allows the company to identify all transactions readily and make management decisions more easily. The reporting format is divided into location classifications, account classifications, and dollar amounts. Each location classification is divided into three four-digit codes. The first identifies the bookkeeping legal/accounting entity location, the second identifies the administrative unit, and the third identifies the legal/accounting entity in the event of an intracorporate transaction. The account classifications consist of four-digit codes followed by dollar amounts.

Once in house, each four-digit account code is converted to a twelve-digit account number followed by the location classification. If an accounting entity has no transaction in a specific account, zeros are entered into the amount column.

As an example, a legal entity in the beverage division would report monthly on its sales by volume, value, and customer of Coca-Cola (concentrate, bottles, and cans), other carbonated beverages, and non-carbonated beverages, consisting of up to 25 separate classifications. Operating expenses are broken down by marketing (direct media by product, other direct marketing expenses, administrative expenses, and so on), sales and distribution (by product and type), service, field administration, and general administration. In this manner every financial report received from the accounting entities worldwide is uniformly prepared and submitted.

The sophisticated uniform information system just described is not unique to Coca-Cola. Other large U.S. multinationals, such as IBM and G.E., have similar systems. The similarities of these global information systems suggest their importance and the significant benefits. As was mentioned previously, however, an information system must be consistent with the organizational structure of the company and the extent and diversity of its operations. For example, there is little need for a small, single-product company with only one foreign subsidiary to have as complex an information system as that of Coca-Cola. In addition, as the extent and diversity of a company's international operations increase, its organizational structure will change, requiring appropriate changes in the company's information system.

ORGANIZATION ISSUES

If a multinational is to function effectively and efficiently it must collect, process, analyze, and report an enormous variety of information in a timely and consistent manner. What is more, the flow of information should be consistent with areas of responsibility for decision making. In other words, those responsible for specific decisions should be receiving information needed for those decisions. For example, the corporate treasurer is usually responsible for allocating funds but not for subsidiary performance evaluation. Therefore, the treasurer should be provided with information on sources and uses of capital but not on subsidiary performance unless it pertains to sources and uses of funds. Stated in its simplest form, the information flow should parallel organizational responsibilities if the system is to function properly. This is easier said than done because the structure itself undergoes changes as the organization moves from domestic to multinational status.

Structures and Patterns

In Chapter 1, the typical evolution of a firm's international business activities was described along with some of the attendant implications for organization structure and control. Although no two multinational enterprises have *identical* structures or evolve in identical ways, several patterns are discernible. Beyond the stage where a firm has established an international division some decisions have to be made concerning the next organizational change. There are four choices:

1. To maintain the international division but reorganize it by product line or geographic area.
2. To eliminate the international division and go to a worldwide product division organization.
3. To eliminate the international division and go to a worldwide geographic division organization.
4. To eliminate the international division and go to a matrix organization.

Illustrative organization charts of these options are depicted in Figures 18 through 20.

There are numerous factors to be considered in deciding which form of organization should be selected. Among the more important factors are the following:

- The existing working relationship between the international division and the domestic product or functional divisions.
- The differences in the technological component of the products.
- The similarity of the customers for the products.
- The geographic location and concentration of the customers.
- The similarity of the national environments in which the products are being sold or manufactured, such as political and economic stability, methods of distribution, and laws.

The International Division

The primary advantage of maintaining the international division is that the expertise remains centralized, providing for better cooperation, coordination, and synergism with regard to international activities. However, communication and coordination with domestic product divisions are likely to be problems, particularly if product division managers are evaluated only on their domestic sales or profits. Disputes over

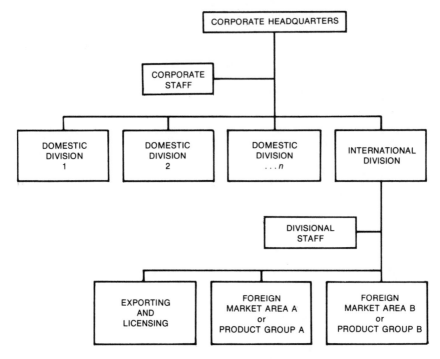

Figure 18. Complex international division organization

production scheduling, product modifications, and the pricing of goods sold from the product divisions to the international division are usually exacerbated as the international division grows in importance.

Organizing by Product Division

If these problems become significant, the company may opt for the worldwide product division organization. In this structure, each product division is given responsibility for all activities, domestic and international. Its main advantages are that many of the problems that characterized the international division arrangement are eliminated, and the growth in sales and profits more closely matches investments. At the same time, the advantages of the international division are lost as the international expertise is decentralized, and the company may end up with multiple offices in several countries. The worldwide product division organization appears to work best when (1) the product divisions are highly autonomous, (2) foreign expertise is of limited importance and the foreign environments are stable, (3) there is a high technological component to the product and rapid changes in technology, which

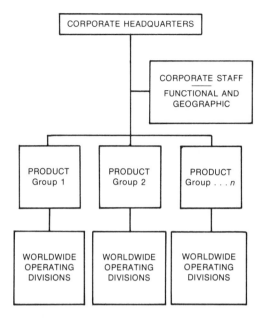

Figure 19. Global product-oriented organization

requires technologically sophisticated sales personnel, and (4) international operations are vertically integrated.[2]

Geographic Organization

If these four characteristics are not present, the company might benefit more from a worldwide *geographic* organization. Its main advantage is that it provides intimate and specialized knowledge of each geographic region—for example, there are experts on European countries, Latin American countries, African countries, and so on. This organizational form tends to be best suited for companies (1) with a small number of products whose use is complementary, (2) whose products are not particularly technology-intensive or sophisticated, (3) whose foreign environments are quite diverse and unstable, and (4) whose foreign governments are big customers or whose business is politically sensitive. Particularly in the last two cases, personnel with intimate knowledge of the countries and personal contacts with key people in the countries are likely to be critical for successful operations.

[2]An example of international vertical integration is an aluminum company that mines bauxite in Jamaica, processes the bauxite into aluminum ingots in the United States, rolls the ingots into sheets in France, makes aluminum tubes from the sheets in Germany, and sells the final product in England.

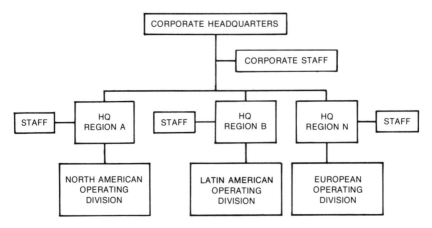

Figure 20. Global geographically oriented organization

Global Grid Structure

The most complicated organization structure for a multinational enterprise, and one which has not been implemented by many, is the *global grid*. As shown in Figure 21, the grid organization chart is three-dimensional. Along one axis are the product divisions, along the second axis are the geographic areas, and along the third axis are the functional divisions such as marketing and finance. In the grid organization a foreign subsidiary reports to a product manager, an area manager, and at least one functional manager. This structure is complex and cumbersome, yet for certain multinationals it makes sense—notably those whose products, operational environments, and internal expertise are such that none of the other three organizational forms is workable. Dow Chemical Company was one of the first to adopt a grid structure, and according to at least one report, the structure does work.[3] The grid organization has also been adopted by Japanese companies such as Canon. The grid seems most appropriate for a multinational that is highly diversified in both its products and markets and is truly global in its operations and perspective.

A Question of Perspective

In what has become a classic taxonomy in international management, Howard Perlmutter classified multinational organizational policies into three varieties: ethnocentric, polycentric, and geocentric.[4]

[3]William C. Goggin, "How the Multidimensional Structure Works at Dow Corning," *Harvard Business Review*, January–February 1974, pp. 54–65.
[4]Howard Perlmutter, "The Tortuous Evolution of the Multinational Corporation," *Columbia Journal of World Business*, January–February 1969, pp. 9–18.

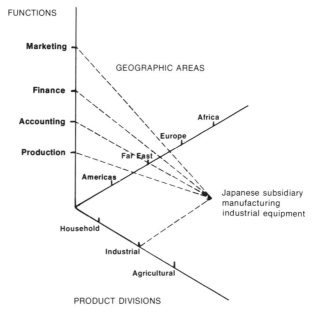

Figure 21. Global grid organization

Ethnocentric Orientation

In the *ethnocentric orientation*, the parent company's perspective is dominant: the attitudes and policies of the parent are viewed as the best and most appropriate for all foreign operations. From this perspective, management is concerned only with the subsidiaries' contribution to the parent's income and financial position. Decision making tends to be highly centralized and controlled from headquarters, and standardized policies are applied in all foreign locations. The parent's policies and procedures are transplanted, largely unchanged, to foreign soil. In addition, subsidiary performance is judged in the parent company's currency, using the measurement techniques of the parent company's accounting system. Standardized accounting procedures and centralized information and decision making systems are typical of companies with such a management perspective. This ethnocentric orientation usually stems from a belief that the parent company's policies, procedures, and perspectives are better than the foreign ones. It is typical of companies relatively new to international business operations.

Polycentric Orientation

At the other end of the continuum is the *polycentric orientation*. If ethnocentrism reflects a parent company perspective, polycentrism reflects a subsidiary perspective. When in Rome, do as the Romans do. The polycentric orientation recognizes the diversity of international business environments and the need for greater autonomy at subsidiary levels. As a result, both the organizational structure and the decision making are more decentralized, with fewer parent company controls. Subsidiary performance is usually judged in subsidiary country currency and terms, using foreign country yardsticks. Even with this approach, the parent company needs information from the subsidiaries for tax returns, management reports, and often corporate financial reports. This aggregation/consolidation requirement, regardless of perspective, usually calls for a standardized format. Thus the polycentric approach typically necessitates a dual accounting and reporting system—one with a foreign environment perspective and a second one with a parent country perspective. The polycentric approach is most common where the company's markets are quite diverse and where there is less need for coordinating activities, such as in a company that is not vertically integrated.

Geocentric Orientation

Between these two extremes is the *geocentric* or *global orientation*, reflecting a concern for the results of global operations rather than strictly those of the parent company or the local subsidiaries. As an example, a geocentric orientation would concern itself with minimizing the global tax on the company's worldwide income, as opposed to minimizing the parent company's taxes (ethnocentric) or each subsidiary's taxes (polycentric). Similarly, the corporate goal would be to minimize global losses from foreign exchange rate fluctuations, rather than parent company losses or individual subsidiary losses. A geocentric orientation further calls for obtaining factor inputs such as labor, capital, equipment, and materials at their lowest worldwide cost; manufacturing where the total production costs are lowest; and selling in countries where profit margins are highest. In short, the geocentric approach is highly systematic and coordinative, with all operating divisions and subsidiaries judged on their global impact, contributions, and results.

A highly complex information system is required by this approach, and one that is also typically standardized for all operating units. The main difference in information system design between the geocentric and ethnocentric perspective is that the latter would adopt a system based on the procedures of its parent company's country. Under the geocentric perspective, the system adopted would be more of a blend of the best aspects of several countries' systems. In reality, however, the geocentric approach is extremely difficult to achieve. Most host country governments are concerned with maximizing the favorable effects of the local subsidiaries of multinationals and frown on a global orientation which might result in closing a plant for reasons not related to economic conditions in the local country. An example would be moving a locally profitable plant from Brazil to Ireland because a change in tax law in Ireland would provide greater global tax and competitive benefits to the parent company if its subsidiary were there instead of in Brazil. Foreign stockholders who own stock in only a subsidiary company usually share this attitude, as do subsidiary managers, creditors, workers, and others who are involved with only a part of the enterprise. Not many headquarters managers themselves possess a geocentric attitude. This observation is particularly important because the attitude and orientation of top management usually determine the orientation and organization of the company as a whole.

Several inferences can be made from all this:

1. In an ethnocentric company there are likely to be tight controls, centralized decision making, and uniform procedures, all based on parent company perspective and procedures. Its organizational structure will tend to have an international division or global product division, with largely one-way communication from parent to subsidiaries.
2. A polycentric organization has fewer controls, less centralized decision making, and less uniformity in procedures. A geographic orientation is likely, and there tends to be less communication in general, but more *two-way* communication.
3. In a geocentric organization, certain critical operations and decisions tend to be centralized while other less essential ones do not. In general, however, there is considerably more control and centralization than in a polycentric organization. The main difference between ethnocentric and geocentric organizations lies in their perspective more than in their organization structure. However, the grid structure may be the best suited and most applicable for a geocentric orientation because it more easily incorporates and facilitates worldwide expertise, decision making, and information flows.

The Information and Organization Interface

Before discussing control systems and issues, a word about the relationship between the organization structure and the information system.

As a domestic company changes to a multinational company, there are attendant changes in both organizational structure and information system. The changes in information system are necessitated by both the changing structure and responsibilities and the increased amount and complexity of international activities. Even if the structure does not change substantially, the sheer volume and diversity of information required increases significantly as new customers, products, and environments are added. This calls for modifications in the information system. When a company's organizational structure changes, the entire information system has to be reevaluated and modified so that information keeps on flowing to the right people in the right places at the right time. To avoid information overload there is also a need to eliminate extraneous information. Thus the information and organizational structure interface must be examined periodically and modified as necessary. Finally, both the information system and the organizational structure must be consistent with the level and degree of control desired by the multinational. It is to these control issues that we now turn.

CONTROL ISSUES

There is an obviously strong relationship between the structure of a company, its information system, and its control system. In general, a highly centralized, ethnocentric company would exercise tight control; a decentralized, polycentric company would exercise much less control; and a geocentric company's control system would tend to approximate the ethnocentric's. Several factors need to be mentioned, however, which may alter these relationships. The two major ones are (1) the differences in control of specific functions as opposed to all functions, and (2) the waxing and waning of control in a multinational over time, within the organization structure.

Centralized versus Decentralized Control

In terms of activities such as marketing and finance, seldom is control uniform over all functions. One reason is that the diversity of foreign environments and particularly laws makes it impractical or even impossible to exercise uniform, tight control over all functions. For example, foreign labor laws may restrict the number of expatriate managers or may strictly regulate the hiring and firing practices of foreign subsidiaries. In such cases, subsidiary personnel practices have to be decentralized. Similarly, the channels of distribution and methods of advertising vary significantly from one country to another, usually requiring greater subsidiary autonomy and less parent control. The other major limitation on uniform control exercised by headquarters over all functions is the fact that not all functions are equally critical for corporate success, either in a particular country or globally. For example, marketing know-how may be the critical competitive advantage for certain companies or for certain industries. This is largely true for low technology, nondurable consumer product companies. On the other hand, for high-technology industrial equipment manufacturers, product or process technology is often the critical competitive advantage, whereas for other multinationals it may be their financial management know-how.

Each multinational tends to centralize decision making and exercise tight control over the functions it perceives as critical for its success—those that provide the major competitive advantage. Therefore it is not uncommon to find centralization and tight control of marketing activity in some multinationals while decentralization and loose control of marketing is the order of the day in others. However, certain functions are commonly decentralized in almost all multinationals, and others are almost always centralized. Representative of decentralized functions is personnel and industrial relations, whereas finance is generally centralized. Most studies of multinational control systems have shown that the most critical control area is the finance function.

Controlling the Finance Function

As was explained in Chapters 5 and 6, changes in exchange rates can have a significant effect on financial performance and position. And as was explained in Chapter 7, foreign exchange risk management becomes simultaneously more important and more difficult as the company's international activities expand. Because the subsidiaries' needs and holdings of foreign currencies are varied yet often interrelated, there is a compelling need for a headquarters perspective and control of foreign exchange risk management. For example, one subsidiary's attempt to reduce or cover its net asset exposure in pesos may be unnecessary and costly if another subsidiary has an offsetting net liability exposure in pesos. In addition, some covering options may not be available to one subsidiary owing to government restrictions on their use but may be available to the parent or an affiliate in another country. Finally, knowledge of worldwide interest rates, forward rates, and financial market conditions is likely to be more comprehensive at headquarters than at the subsidiary level. For all these reasons, the foreign exchange risk management function is typically centralized at parent headquarters.

For many of the same reasons, the other major financial decisions are also typically centralized. In raising capital, the headquarters treasurer is in a better position to know the cheapest sources of funds worldwide as well as to obtain these funds and negotiate for the lowest rates and best terms. At the same time, the headquarters treasurer is more likely to be aware of a profitable use for a subsidiary's surplus funds in some other country or in another subsidiary than local subsidiary managers would be. In addition, the intracorporate movement of funds such as loans, dividends, and royalties and the timing of their movement can have significant tax and consolidated financial reporting effects of which the subsidiary managers may not be aware. In sum, financial decisions can so significantly affect the company's bottom line and are so complex in a global setting that the financial function usually remains highly centralized at parent headquarters. This has been shown to be true almost regardless of a company's decentralization of other functions or its organization structure.

Changes over Time

The other factor that may affect general organizational and control relationships is the changing control exercised by the parent over time. Several classic studies of multinational control systems revealed a pattern of control which can be called *waxing and waning*.[5] In the beginning of international activities, relatively little control is exercised by headquarters management. This is primarily because early international activities are small compared to the domestic activities that dominate top management's time. As international activities take up more and more of the firm's time and attention in terms of sales, profits, and investments, headquarters recognizes the need for closer control over the international operations, as well as for better coordination and integration of international and domestic activities.

This recognition usually manifests itself in an organizational change, such as moving to a worldwide product division structure, but it may also entail tighter control within the existing structure. For example, the international division may remain intact, but its autonomy may be curtailed, and new policies may require more frequent reporting to, and consultation with, corporate headquarters.

However, as the international activities become larger and more diversified, the control exercised by headquarters usually begins to diminish. The sheer complexity of managing international activities in widely diverse and constantly changing environments makes tight control exceedingly difficult. In addition, over time the company develops considerable management expertise in the field, which allows headquarters to be more confident in decentralized decision making. And because there is a premium attached to responding quickly to changing environmental conditions, the lead and lag times for communication and decision making need to be shortened. This usually entails more decentralization and less control. It must be remembered, however, that control does not diminish uniformly for all functional areas. It diminishes first for the less critical functions, while the more critical ones are kept under tighter control for a much longer time.

[5]For an excellent treatment of waxing and waning, see S. Robbins and R. Stobaugh, *Money in the Multinational Enterprise: A Study in Financial Policy* (New York: Basic Books, 1973).

Planning and Control Functions

Control mechanisms and procedures can be classified broadly into two types: those that seek to have the right decisions made by the right people and those that assess whether the right decisions were made by the right people. To use a sports analogy, the former constitute the rules of the game and the book of plays; the latter constitute the after-game analysis. To use a management accountant's terminology, the former is the budget and the latter is the analysis of variance.

Plans and Budgets

The control mechanism critical to the pre-game phase of business activity is the plan. While the planning horizon varies from company to company, most multinationals utilize both a yearly plan and a longer plan covering two to ten years. To the extent feasible, the plan details the objectives for the firm and its operating divisions and subsidiaries—usually in terms of such criteria as market share, profitability, and levels of expenditures and investments. In most multinationals these plans are collectively determined by means of consultations with the top management of each subsidiary, the appropriate regional or product managers, and members of the executive committee. Consultation with the field officers is a way to obtain a realistic assessment of the subsidiaries' capabilities and opportunities under specific competitive and environmental conditions. Of course, the degree of involvement from the field will vary with the orientation of the headquarters management (ethnocentric, polycentric, or geocentric), as will the ultimate responsibility for the decisions on the final plan. By whatever process, what eventually evolves is a plan with specific objectives and budgets for each operating unit. In addition, the plan typically establishes the relative autonomy of each operating unit. One way to accomplish this is by specifying the borrowings or expenditures that can be made by each subsidiary without headquarters approval.

Other Control Mechanisms

In addition to the plan and budget, there are a host of other control devices including company policy statements and manuals covering such areas as political contributions and involvement, bribery, codes of conduct, compliance with various laws, disclosure of information, and reporting procedures. Operations manuals tend to enumerate who is to take what actions in specific situations; how reports are to be drawn up; when; and to whom, by what means, and how often they are to be submitted. Owing to their greater specificity, it is more difficult to have globally applicable operations manuals, yet there are obvious benefits to standardization of procedures. Standardization reduces confusion and corporate headaches and facilitates the transfer of personnel.

As was mentioned previously, standardizing the information collection and reporting function is almost imperative. Essentially the same analysis and conclusions apply to a standardized, globally applicable policy manual, although standardizing policies is probably less complicated than standardizing procedures. Particularly for U.S.-based multinationals, an even stronger reason for standardizing certain policies is the extraterritorial jurisdiction of U.S. laws. Many U.S. laws have an extraterritorial reach—that is, their applicability extends to the foreign operations of U.S. companies. Antitrust laws and the Trading with the Enemy Act are classic examples. More recent laws dealing with the conduct of international business by a parent and its affiliates, and ones which clearly necessitate a statement of worldwide company policy, are the Anti-Boycott Law and the Foreign Corrupt Practices Act. In all these cases, it is the responsibility of the U.S. parent to ensure that personnel in foreign operations are both aware of, and in compliance with, the U.S. laws—even if a local foreign law specifically permits a practice which is illegal in the United States. More about the Foreign Corrupt Practices Act in Chapter 13.

The other category of control procedures concerns analyzing whether multinational operations are consistent with the plans and objectives. This area of control, the classic *feedback system*, encompasses two questions. Were the company's procedures followed correctly? What was the company performance compared to the plan? The first question falls largely in the audit area, discussed in detail in Chapter 13. The second question concerns performance evaluation.

Performance Evaluation

As was mentioned earlier, one of the key determinants of a firm's success is its ability to know how well its operations are going and how they are affecting overall corporate performance. Unless the firm knows to what extent operations are in accordance with plans, and unless it can affix responsibility for what happens, the parent cannot be considered in control or able to take corrective action. There is also a need for the company to assess the performance of subsidiary managers and reward them appropriately. This is necessary in order to keep managers motivated and adhering to the plans, and gives importance to the system of performance evaluation. One problem, however, is deciding on what basis to evaluate performance. A more difficult issue is whether performance should be evaluated on a relative, comparative basis, or on an absolute basis.

Basic Considerations

It is doubtful that any single measure is adequate for judging performance, and therefore multiple measures are often used. Among them are profitability, market penetration, productivity, labor relations, personnel development, and public and government relations. Table 12–3 provides a fairly comprehensive checklist for evaluating affiliate performance.

While a checklist makes it possible to identify particular areas of performance concern, it is far from sufficient. First of all, not all performance areas are of equal importance. Each firm must decide the relative importance of each factor and weight it accordingly. Second, the objectives for individual subsidiaries often differ, which may necessitate different factor weights for each subsidiary. Third, time is an implicit comparison factor in performance evaluation. How did this year's performance compare to that of the previous year?

Other problems inevitably surface when attempting to evaluate performance. For example, it is difficult to compare the performance of subsidiaries when there are significant differences in product lines, operating environments, and objectives. In addition, there can be marked differences in financial evaluation if the analysis uses foreign currency amounts as opposed to the currency of the parent company. For example, a local currency profit may translate as a loss in the parent company's currency.

In this case, it is difficult to say whether the foreign subsidiary manager did a good job or bad job, unless the criteria are clearly specified. Yet despite these problems, multinationals must evaluate performance. To examine how they do it requires a look at some empirical research.

Three Recent Studies

Three major empirical studies of performance evaluation systems of multinationals done in the past ten years are those by Robbins and Stobaugh,[6] McInnes,[7] and Morsicato.[8]

Robbins and Stobaugh studied nearly 200 U.S.-based firms, representing almost all major U.S. industries with investments abroad, and ranging in size of total foreign sales from $20 million upward. With

[6]Ibid.

[7]J. M. McInnes, "Financial Control Systems for Multinational Operations: An Empirical Investigation," *Journal of International Business Studies*, Fall 1971, pp. 11–28.

[8]Helen Morsicato, *An Investigation of the Interaction of Financial Statement Translation and Multinational Enterprise Performance Evaluation*, Ph.D. dissertation, Pennsylvania State University, 1978, and *Currency Translation and Performance Evaluation in Multinationals* (Ann Arbor, Michigan: UMI Research Press, 1980).

TABLE 12–3. Evaluating Foreign Subsidiary Performance

A meaningful evaluation of the operations of foreign subsidiaries is a first step in improving present performance, implementing future planning, allocating corporate resources, and providing for the promotion and compensation of executives.

PROFITABILITY EVALUATION

1. Determine what shall constitute the investment figure; for example, total funds invested, net assets, or net fixed assets.
2. Determine the basis for computing profit. This may be actual dollar remittances, or total book profits.
3. Adjust for distortions due to the position of a sub in an international profit plan; tax factors may have pegged profits through artificial pricing, royalty, management, and interest arrangements.
4. Apply the standard financial ratios used in domestic evaluation: rate of return on investment, liquidity, sales and inventory turnover, return on sales, and sales margin analysis.
5. Check the disposition of funds available for acquisition and investment where the local manager is independent.
6. Watch the distribution of assets, especially in an inflationary economy. Has the local manager hedged properly?
7. Analyze performance against budgeted goals and determine why variances, if any, occurred.
8. Temper these considerations with the outlook for actual long-term dollar profits; be sure that immediate profitability does not hamper future performance.

MARKET PENETRATION AND PRODUCT PERFORMANCE EVALUATION

1. Check percentage of market in toto and by product.
2. Gauge the degree of competition, local and foreign.
3. Consider the impact of substitute products in the market.
4. Judge the treatment of export sales by the sub, both of its own products and of those of related companies.
5. Weigh the reliance of the sub on captive sales to related companies, to U.S. parent, and to dependent local buyers.
6. Review the level of the sales effort (wholesale, retail, ultimate consumer). Don't penalize the sub for an erroneous selection of distribution channels by the parent.
7. Analyze the sub's advertising and promotion program.
8. Note the frequency of suggestions for new-product development and improvements of existing items.
9. Check the quality of after-sales servicing.
10. Appraise the performance and attitudes of distributors under the sub's control.

PRODUCTIVITY EVALUATION

1. Determine production per hour, without regard to cost.
2. Relate output costs, using either value added, or sales billed.
3. Adjust for such variables as wage scales, volume of production, degree of automation, efficiency of equipment.
4. Express productivity in physical units where inflation and currency deterioration might distort a monetary figure.

TABLE 12–3 (*Continued*)

LABOR RELATIONS EVALUATION

1. Assess employee morale and attitudes.
2. Examine the general administration of personnel policies.
3. Consider the effectiveness of training programs.
4. Calculate work time lost through absenteeism, turnover.
5. Review union relations, especially for time lost owing to walkouts and strikes.

PERSONNEL DEVELOPMENT EVALUATION

1. Count the number of promotions within departments.
2. Note the transfers to higher posts in other units of the company group.
3. Determine the number of promotable personnel available.
4. Assess the worth of the sub's medium- and long-range personnel-need forecasts.

PUBLIC AND GOVERNMENT RELATIONS EVALUATION

1. Appraise degree of identification and national goals.
2. Assess the tenor of community relations.
3. Check relations with local and national business leaders.
4. Review relationships with government officials.

PLANNING EVALUATION

1. Search for clear statements on future targets.
2. Weigh the balance between long-range goals and short-term requirements.
3. Examine the coordination of functional and staff planning at all levels in the foreign sub.
   Finally, temper these quantitative and qualitative factors with the judgment of an experienced international executive and the priority a particular company may place on one or more of these evaluation categories.

SOURCE: *Business International,* February 28, 1964.

regard to measures of financial performance, the main conclusions from their research were as follows:

1. The many tangible and intangible items which entered into the original investment calculations are rarely taken into account in evaluating the foreign subsidiaries' performance—for example, the value or cost of a parent company's loan guarantee for a subsidiary, costs of safety stocks of inventory for foreign and U.S. operations, the potential cost of being excluded from a market by a competitor who moves first.

2. Foreign subsidiaries are judged on the same basis as domestic subsidiaries.

3. The most utilized measure of performance for all subsidiaries was return on investment (ROI).

4. Due to the inherent limitations and problems of calculating ROI

equitably for all subsidiaries, nearly all the multinationals used some supplementary device to gauge foreign subsidiaries' performance.

5. The most widely used supplementary measure was comparison to budget.
6. The budgets used were a yearly capital budget (including a list of individual projects with an indication of their profitability) and an operating budget containing pro forma income statements, balance sheets, and cash flow projections (prepared monthly or quarterly for the forthcoming year).
7. Even the firms that used budgets as supplementary measures selected ROI as the key item in the budgets.
8. Less than half (44 percent) judged subsidiary performance in terms of translated dollar amounts, and only 12 percent used both standards.

McInnes later studied thirty U.S. multinational manufacturing companies and also focused on financial control and performance measures. The companies in his sample were of moderate size ($100 million to $300 million in sales), had at least 20 percent of their assets and sales abroad, and had operating entities in six or more foreign countries. His major findings were quite similar to those of Robbins and Stobaugh:

1. Of the thirty firms, nineteen utilized identical techniques for evaluating the performance of foreign and domestic subsidiaries.
2. In virtually all cases where there were differences in technique, more techniques were used for *domestic* subsidiaries.
3. ROI was cited by a majority of the firms as the most important evaluation criterion.
4. Where differences occurred, firms tended to put more emphasis on purely financial techniques of analysis for foreign subsidiaries and more emphasis on operating control techniques for domestic subsidiaries.

The more recent study by Morsicato focused on the use of dollar and local currency information in evaluating subsidiary performance—that is, translated and not translated. Her study of seventy U.S. multinationals in the chemical industry revealed that profit, return on investment, budget compared to actual profit, and budget compared to sales were in order of frequency the measures most commonly employed *after translation* into dollars. Budget compared to actual profit, budget compared to actual sales, and profit were the most frequently utilized measures in local currency *before translation*. Also, how often these measures were used depended on whether the measures were translated into dollars or remained in local currency. This was particularly true for ROI and cash flow measures, as shown in Table 12–4. One of the major contributions of the Morsicato study is its excellent discussion and analysis of the differences in the budgeting and performance evaluation process resulting from using local versus parent country currency.

Taken as a group, these studies show that there is little significant difference between the performance evaluation systems utilized for domestic and foreign operations.

Implications of the Studies

One of the more curious aspects of these empirical studies was their finding that multinationals rely on ROI as the major or even the only measure of performance. Where intracorporate transfers are significant and are not at arm's-length prices, the ROI income numerator is highly arbitrary and, in one sense, fictitious. Also, a subsidiary manager whose evaluation is based on ROI may choose to borrow heavily in the local currency, affecting the borrowing capacity of the entire firm and potentially the price of its stock, as well as possibly subjecting the parent's

TABLE 12–4. Financial Measures Used as Indicators of Internal Performance Evaluation

AFTER TRANSLATION IN U.S. DOLLARS (PERCENT)	BEFORE TRANSLATION IN LOCAL CURRENCY (PERCENT)	FINANCIAL MEASURES
80.0	52.9	Return-on-investment (assets)
48.6	31.4	Return-on-equity
21.4	18.6	Residual income
81.4	70.0	Profit
65.7	35.7	Cash flow potential from foreign subsidiary to U.S. operations
45.7	38.6	Budget compared to actual return on investment
78.6	72.9	Budget compared to actual profits
72.9	72.9	Budget compared to actual sales
34.3	30.0	Ratios
12.9	11.4	Others

SOURCE: Helen Morsicato, *Currency Translation and Performance Evaluation in Multinationals,* Ann Arbor, Michigan: UMI Research Press, 1980.
NOTE: These figures represent the percentage of the total 70 firms which report using each particular measure.

consolidated financial statements to a significant translation loss if the borrowings are in hard currencies. Perhaps most important, ROI is *not* appropriate for some foreign operations, such as subsidiaries producing only for other subsidiaries, marketing subsidiaries buying all their products from other affiliates, or subsidiaries striving to break into highly competitive markets.

Relating Evaluation to Performance

The problems related to using ROI as a standard of performance apply to other measures as well. Virtually any financial ratio analysis or payback period method suffers from similar limitations if it is uniformly applied to all subsidiaries. The main reason is that a multinational's objectives for its affiliates are based on the reasons for their creation and their particular operating environment. Some subsidiaries serve as sources of products, funds, or services for others. Some try to maintain market share, others try to increase it. Some face strict profit remittance controls by foreign governments, others do not. These differences in objectives and operating environments call for different performance measures. This need *is* recognized by most multinationals, even if only slightly, as evidenced by their reported use of multiple measures of performance. At the same time, there is a need to have some uniformity in performance evaluation so as to simplify the procedures and to enable intersubsidiary comparisons.

The need for standardization brings us back to the one method of performance evaluation which can meet most criteria without undue limitations: the comparison of performance to plan. This method is probably the only globally applicable evaluation method. It permits each affiliate to be judged on its own, according to the plan it was given, and can be used to compare subsidiary performances. However, it is a reasonable basis of performance measurement only if the original plans were logical and reasonable. Therein lies one danger of the *comparison to plan* technique. The other danger is that subsidiary managers' input to the plan may be tempered by their desire to surpass the plan's expectations. For example, they might deliberately paint a bleak picture, such as stating that they will need a larger budget to achieve a 5 percent growth in sales when in fact they could achieve a 10 percent growth with a smaller budget. If given the larger budget, they can show a greater than 5 percent growth in sales and appear to have done a great job even though they could have achieved the same results with less money. However, if the planning and budgeting process is sufficiently deliberative, participative, iterative, and honest, both these dangers can be minimized.

Other Evaluation Issues

Several other performance evaluation issues need to be mentioned. First, it is neither realistic nor advisable for most firms to treat all subsidiaries as independent, autonomous operations, such as profit centers. Foreign affiliates are an integral and strategic part of the larger worldwide family. Their true value evolves from their contribution to this larger whole, rather than from their individual performance. It is precisely this characteristic that gives the multinational its strength and competitive advantage. Therefore, individual subsidiaries' performance in their respective countries should remain largely a secondary criterion for evaluation, regardless of the performance measures used.

A second issue concerns the effects of changes in exchange rates on measures of performance. If a significant change occurs in the exchange rate of either the subsidiary's or parent company's country, *translated* financial performance measures have two components. One component is the results that can be attributed to performance, and the other is the results that are attributable to changes in the exchange rate. Because managers have no control over exchange rates, it is neither fair nor desirable to judge them on results that are brought about by changes in exchange rates, unless they know they are to be evaluated on a translated basis and are given the responsibility for managing their foreign exchange risk. As was explained earlier, this is less desirable than having headquarters retain responsibility for this activity. Thus there is a need to separate out the results from exchange rate changes when assessing subsidiary management performance. In the *comparison to budget* method, this would entail using an unchanged exchange rate basis when comparing results with the original budget, or comparing results with a budget that is restated using the changed exchange rates, or simply comparing the budget expressed in the foreign currency with the foreign currency results.

A third issue concerns the impact of the evaluation system on the performance of subsidiary managers. Managers tend to act in ways which will make them look good when performance evaluation time comes around. Thus many management actions must be considered in this light. Unless the method of performance evaluation is consistent with the objectives of the firm, subsidiary managers may undertake actions that are in their best interest but not in the best interest of the firm. The example given earlier of the effect of heavy local borrowing by a subsidiary manager to make his ROI look good showed what could result.

Finally, the method of performance evaluation should be clearly understood by the managers and actually utilized by the company. If the managers do not understand the system, its intended results will not be achieved. And if the method used for performance evaluation is not the one that is supposed to be used, the firm will have a hard time keeping its managers.

CONCLUSIONS

The information system of a multinational enterprise is its life support system. Without the appropriate collection, transmittal, and analysis of necessary information, the firm could not survive. The complexities, uncertainties, and obstacles in international operations are simply too great to be overcome without a well-designed and functioning information system. Perhaps to a lesser extent, the same applies to its organization structure and to its control system. Furthermore, the three must support each other and be designed with the others in mind.

The internal and external demands on a multinational increase geometrically as it grows in size and complexity. These demands have also increased in general during recent decades, particularly the external demands emanating from governments and societal groups. While historically somewhat neglected, information systems, organizational structure, and control systems are certain to receive more attention in the coming decades. They thus represent areas where accountants can apply their skills in fostering future improvements.

STUDY QUESTIONS

12–1.   What are the basic objectives of management information and control systems? Are they any different for a multinational enterprise than for a domestic enterprise?

12–2.   What are the unique requirements and problems in terms of the design and operation of an information system for a multinational firm?

12–3.   What are the unique requirements and problems of a multinational firm's control system, particularly its system of performance evaluation?

12–4.   Discuss the advantages and disadvantages of various evaluation measures used by multinationals to assess foreign subsidiary performance.

12–5.   Discuss the relationships between a multinational firm's information system, organizational structure, and control system.

12–6.   Explain why there might be different information system and control system problems for a multinational firm operating only in developing countries compared to one operating only in developed countries.

12–7.   Discuss why a multinational enterprise must periodically alter its organizational structure, and what implications such changes may have for the firm's information and control systems.

12–8. Discuss why the importance of information systems, organizational structure, and control systems may vary in terms of specific functions such as marketing, finance, and industrial relations.

12–9. In domestic accounting literature, there are a number of behavioral considerations related to the design and operation of a control system. What behavioral considerations might be unique to the control system of a multinational enterprise?

12–10. Could it be argued that a large multinational, operating a variety of businesses in more than a hundred countries, is never really able to control itself? Why or why not?

CASES

AUTOPARTS INC.

Autoparts Inc. is a large U.S.-based multinational with production operations in some twenty countries. In April the company acquired a small Italian firm which had been family owned and operated for more than twenty years. The Italian management had reacted strongly and negatively to the new parent company's plan to revamp the Italian firm's accounting system in order to bring it in line with that of the other Autoparts affiliates.

The Two Systems

Six years before the Italian acquisition, Autoparts implemented a complex, standardized internal reporting system for all its subsidiaries. A major objective of the system was to provide headquarters with directly comparable accounting information in a precise and timely fashion. Headquarters believed that such a system was necessary to facilitate the aggregation and disaggregation of financial data for reporting to its many constituencies and for internal management decision making. Headquarters also believed that the sophisticated system forced managers to plan better, think in terms of the United States impact of their operations, and maintain better control over their operations. All reports were to be prepared by the affiliates in English, in dollars, and according to U.S. generally accepted accounting principles (GAAP). Thirty basic items related to the income statement were due at headquarters by noon on the first Monday of each month, and forty data items related to the balance sheet were due at headquarters on the following Wednesday. More extensive data were due quarterly, including trial balances with more than 1,000 lines of data and narrative comments. Complete data were due at year-end, along with extensive comments regarding performance in local currency, dollars, and comparisons to budgets and plans.

The Italian firm's existing accounting staff did not measure up to that of Autoparts, to put it mildly. The former owner had required only sporadic internal reports and had made even fewer external reports. The Italian accounting staff consisted of eight people, only two of whom had much formal accounting background, and none of whom spoke English or had any understanding of U.S. GAAP.

Resistance to the New System

The Italian staff believed that the proposed reporting requirements were burdensome, and neither necessary nor feasible. They had gotten along without them for years, and—more to the point—they were not capable of preparing the reports according to Autoparts' requirements. Furthermore, because they were not accustomed to such procedures, complying with the strict deadlines and rules would pose significant difficulties and hardships on them. They also argued that much of the data required by headquarters was of little value to the subsidiary and of no value to the accounting reports they were required to prepare by Italian law. They were also concerned that the Italian government, and particularly the tax authorities, might question them on why the reports submitted to Autoparts headquarters would show significantly different results than those submitted in Italy.

Questions

1. Is the Autoparts system of standardized reporting an intelligent one? What considerations support it and argue against it?
2. Is the Autoparts policy of no exceptions, no excuses a logical one? What factors argue for this policy and against it?
3. Based on your answers to questions 1 and 2, should the Italian subsidiary be forced to adopt the Autoparts system as is, with modifications, or not at all?

NIESSEN APPAREL, INC.

Juan Valencia was upset. As general manager of the Niessen Apparel Peruvian assembly plant, he believed that his performance over the past two years was not being fairly evaluated. He had recently sent a memo to parent company headquarters itemizing his complaints and asking for an immediate response. Charles Niessen, the present of the company, asked his son Chuck to review the matter and report back to him immediately because he didn't want to risk losing Valencia (who had threatened to quit).

Background

Niessen Apparel was a medium-size U.S. manufacturer of women's and children's clothing. Because of rising domestic production costs, Niessen had investigated the possibilities of sewing the garments outside the United States, after which they would be shipped back and sold in the United States. In this manner, they would lower overall production costs and be in a better position to compete with both domestic and imported products. This could be achieved by utilizing cheaper labor in a developing country for the most labor-intensive parts of the production process—assembly—and taking advantage of §807 of the U.S. Tariff Code. This section allowed U.S. companies to export components to a foreign operation, then import the finished products, paying duty only on the value added outside the United States rather than on the full value of the product. Thus, a product imported from a Peruvian §807 operation would have a smaller tariff than one imported from a strictly Peruvian company. This, of course, would give a U.S. company an advantage over a foreign company *not* owned by a U.S. corporation. For example, a product costing $100 imported from Peru might have a tariff of $20 levied against it (20 percent of its value). However, if the product had $50 worth of U.S. components in its value, then under §807 the U.S. tariff would be $10 (20 percent of the value added outside the United States). Thus the full §807 import price would be $110 compared to the $120 import price of the non-§807 import.

The Method of Performance Evaluation

In order to justify the Peruvian sewing plant, Niessen believed that it should be evaluated as a profit center. This would allow the operation's profitability to be compared to the next best alternative use of funds. Valencia was to be responsible for the profitability of the Peruvian operations and was to be evaluated and rewarded on that basis. In addition, Niessen believed that the subsidiary's performance should be evaluated in terms of U.S. dollars rather than local Peruvian currency, since its value to him and his company was its contribution to U.S. earning power.

Problems with the Operations and Systems

Initially, a transfer pricing system was established on an arm's-length basis for all intercompany shipments. This was consistent with the profit center concept in that any other method would result in artificial profits. However, over the past two years the transfer prices on components shipped to Peru had been increased and the transfer prices on finished goods shipped back to the United States had been decreased. These changes were made so as to take better advantage of §807 (pay less import duty) by increasing the U.S. content and decreasing the foreign value added of the finished product. This change in strategy was considered desirable by the U.S. marketing people, who wanted to sell more competitively in the United States, and by the treasurer, who wanted to save on import duties. In order to avoid problems with U.S. and Peruvian government agencies, the transfer prices had been adjusted gradually but steadily each month. Helping to conceal this procedure was the continued decline of the Peruvian currency relative to the U.S. dollar. This, in itself, increased Peruvian import (purchasing) costs while lowering U.S. import prices (costs).

While the effects of the new transfer prices and currency values worked out very well for the U.S. marketing manager (whose profits increased significantly), just the opposite occurred for Sr. Valencia. The performance evaluation of its subsidiary's operations deteriorated to the point where one member of the U.S. staff who was unaware of what had been going on suggested that Valencia be fired or the Peruvian operation be terminated. In addition, Valencia's annual salary bonus had virtually disappeared because it was based largely on his subsidiary's profit performance. To make matters worse, slower than anticipated U.S. sales growth had caused a cutback in shipments to and from Peru, idling much of the Peruvian capacity. And because the Peruvian subsidiary sold only to the U.S. parent, it could not use its surplus production capacity, causing its costs to rise further and its profits to decrease further.

Questions

1.   What were the strengths and weaknesses of Niessen Apparel's original method of performance evaluation?
2.   What factors should Niessen consider in deciding whether to change the company's method of performance evaluation?
3.   Should the old evaluation method be changed for the Peruvian operation? If so, why and how?

13

Internal and External Audits Worldwide

Published financial statements serve a variety of purposes for investors, creditors, regulators, and planners. How do we know whether these statements accurately reflect what is going on in the business? Remember, that financial statements are prepared by managers, and managers have a vested interest in the statements. Could managers massage the figures a little to make them look better than they are (or worse, if the reader is a tax authority)?

And what of the accountability for assets? Top managers want to be sure that the firm's assets are safeguarded at all levels and used properly in the generation of profits. At the same time, investors want to be sure that top managers practice what they preach by using assets properly as well. In the aftermath of Watergate, thousands of stories told how managers at all levels laundered cash and falsified books and records in order to bribe foreign government officials.

How do we solve these twin problems of internal controls and external reliability? The answer lies in an adequate system of internal controls, including internal auditors and independent, highly qualified external auditors. This chapter looks at internal control systems of multinational enterprises, compares and contrasts external auditing worldwide, and shows how the large public accounting firms are organized to perform the external audit of a multinational enterprise.

THE INTERNAL AUDIT

All large corporations are concerned that employees operate in a way that is consistent with corporate policy. Corporate policy and procedures in all areas of the business—personnel, marketing, and production as well as accounting—are normally communicated to personnel through codes of conduct and procedures manuals. A good control system starts with these codes of conduct and standard operating procedures, but the firm needs to determine whether these codes and procedures are being followed. The internal audit function is one of the cornerstones in determining compliance.

To demonstrate how the internal audit function works, let's look at the Alcoa Corporation. The internal audit department of Alcoa is headed by a general manager who is responsible for the actions of the chief internal auditor, the manager of international auditing, and the manager of EDP auditing. The general manager reports directly to executive management as well as to the Audit Committee of the Board of Directors. The major role of the Internal Audit Department is to evaluate internal control, which is set up by management to (1) safeguard corporate assets, (2) check the accuracy and reliability of data, (3) promote operational efficiency, and (4) encourage adherence to prescribed managerial policies and procedures. Obviously the internal audit is concerned with much more than just accounting controls; it also includes substantial operational controls. The Alcoa internal audit is divided into packages that are related to the basic systems required to administer the business (for example, sales), the need for review of specific policies (for example, equal employment opportunity), managerial need, profit improvement, and coordination with independent public accountants.[1]

Problems of the Internal Auditor in a Foreign Operating Environment

Although the role of internal auditor is the same for foreign as well as domestic operations, the foreign operating environment creates unique problems. Among the environmental considerations are local accounting practices, foreign currency, local legal and business practices, language and customs, and distance. Although most large companies attempt to standardize their accounting practice worldwide, it doesn't happen everywhere. Local records may be kept according to local accounting procedures, which makes it difficult to use a standardized audit package. Also, the infrequency of audits (because of distance) may mean that there are insufficient accounting data to provide a clear audit trail.[2]

---

[1] For more extensive information, see Alcoa's "Internal Audit Department."
[2] Marikay Lee, "The International Auditor," *Internal Auditor*, December 1978, p. 45.

Adapting to Local Business Practices and Customs

The local business practices and customs can also create problems. For example, expenses may be paid by cash rather than check, making cash control difficult. This is especially true in developing countries where checks are not widely used. The following example illustrates the problems of conducting a test of accounts receivable in a foreign location:

> Accounts receivable confirmations are one example of how an international auditor must adjust or revamp auditing procedures. In most cases, the confirmation letter itself must be translated into another language. Relying on the customer to return the confirmation is another problem because foreign customers lack experience with confirmations. It may not be the custom for local auditors to send confirmations for accounts receivable or even to confirm year-end bank balances. The mail service may also be inefficient and unreliable, and it may take weeks before the confirmation letter is received by the customer—if the customer receives it at all.
>
> If the international auditor doesn't plan to be in a country long enough for the confirmations to be sent and returned, alternate auditing procedures must be implemented or alternate means of receiving the confirmations must be applied. For example, the international auditor may arrange to have the confirmations mailed to a local public accounting firm or other independent source which will forward them to the international auditor. However, if the international auditor continually travels to other international audit locations, this procedure is unsatisfactory.[3]

Foreign Currency Restrictions

Foreign currency restrictions and transfer requirements should be known for each country in which the auditor works. Ignorance of local customs can be a handicap when the auditor deals with personnel who are not bilingual. Having to rely on a translator means the auditor may not be getting the full story. The inability or difficulty of adapting to the local environment could create personal problems that might render the internal auditor less than fully effective.

Distance

A final problem is distance. Farflung operations are not audited as frequently or as thoroughly as the domestic operations, which makes the foreign audit even tougher. It is often impossible to conduct preaudit and postaudit visits, so most communication has to be by telephone,

[3]Ibid.

Telex, or mail. The previous example of confirming accounts receivables illustrates the difficulty of distance. When postaudit problems arise, it may be impossible to get an answer quickly or to communicate adequately. If too many people are sent to conduct an audit far from headquarters, a great deal of money could be wasted. If too few people are sent, the scope of the audit may be too narrow because of time constraints. Furthermore, distances often hinder flexibility in personnel.[4]

Alternatives to the Traveling Auditor

These comments refer primarily to a traveling auditor. However, there are other possibilities: a resident auditor who is a local national; a resident auditor who is an expatriate from the headquarters country or is a third-country national (TCN)—that is, someone from a country other than the headquarters or local operation; or a traveling team of auditors. Local nationals obviously have an edge in knowledge of the language, culture, and business customs, but the expatriate is more familiar with headquarters procedures. The TCN can be a cross between the two but is still considered a foreigner in the host country.

Table 13–1 summarizes the pros and cons of using traveling, local resident, and expatriate resident auditors.

Although it is possible to use domestic auditors on temporary assignment to perform internal audits, they tend to be more specialized than regular international internal auditors. The latter need to be generalists, with skills in operational as well as financial audits. Also, the need for language skills and cultural adaptability make it advisable to identify a cadre of international internal auditors where possible. The smaller multinationals tend to use home office auditors for foreign duties, but some larger firms are using regionally based auditors with greater frequency. In Alcoa's organization, the work of foreign-based audit staffs is under the direction of the manager of international auditing, who works on the same level as the chief internal auditor and manager of EDP auditing and reports to the general manager of the Internal Audit Department.

This movement from central to regional audit staffs is characteristic of multinationals. One firm that uses a centralized audit structure has only fourteen staff auditors, with six of them responsible for international operations. About 25 percent of the firm's foreign operations have their own staffs, which are independent of local management. A large electronic data processing company, with 40 percent of its revenues generated abroad, has an internal audit staff of 77, 21 of them assigned to international operations on five continents. The firm has organized its

[4]Ibid.

TABLE 13-1.   Decision Variables for Selecting Internal Auditors

	HOME-BASED AUDITOR VISITING OTHER COUNTRIES	LOCAL NATIONAL RESIDENT AUDITOR	EXPATRIATE RESIDENT AUDITOR
Initial investment (per man)	Language training: $1,200–$1,500 Air travel per nonpeak season trip: $600–$800	Six months' investment in training Salary: $12,000–$15,000 Travel: $ 600–$ 800	Language training: $1,200–$1,500 Moving expenses: $6,000–$10,000
Single, small audit location	Generally, not economically sound in any case; it would be better to request a management letter from the outside auditors		
Several small audit locations within same country	Generally sound, provided return engagements are anticipated	Generally not sound unless growth expectations in the short run indicate that the investment is warranted	
Several small audit locations scattered over several countries	Generally not sound; too much investment in languages	Generally sound if growth expectations in medium-range future warrant it	Generally not sound; too much investment in languages
Single, medium-size audit location	Generally sound for one man on an extended trip, provided return engagements are planned	Generally not sound unless growth expectations in the short run indicate that the investment is warranted	
Several medium-size audit locations within same country	Generally not sound; too much travel between countries with attendant weariness from travel through time zones or excessive investment in languages	Generally ideally suited to this type of setup	Generally ideally suited to this type of setup
Several medium-size audit locations scattered over several countries	ditto	ditto	Could be sound if not too many languages are involved; could also work well jointly with a foreign national
Several large audit locations within same country or scattered over several countries	ditto	Ideal, provided not too many languages are involved	Ideal, provided not too many languages are involved

SOURCE: Lee D. Tooman, "Starting the Internal Audit of Foreign Operations," *Internal Auditor,* November-December 1975, p. 60. Copyright 1978 by the Institute of Internal Auditors, Inc. Reprinted by permission.

staff on a regional basis with its foreign auditors performing functions similar to the domestic auditors. Sometimes U.S. auditors assist in conducting the large foreign audits, but only on a temporary basis.[5]

FOREIGN CORRUPT PRACTICES ACT

Whether influence is bought with baksheesh (Middle East), mordida (Mexico), dash (West Africa), or bustarella (Italy), it can be very costly indeed because of the Foreign Corrupt Practices Act of 1977. The SEC, in investigating Watergate and its aftermath, was astounded at the extent to which corporate executives and employees falsified books and records and circumvented internal control systems (where they existed) in order to make foreign bribes. The SEC response—the Foreign Cor-

[5]"Two Different Approaches Toward Internal Controls Stress Foreign Operations," *Business International Money Report,* 9 February 1979, pp. 52–53.

rupt Practices Act (FCPA)—is affecting the way companies operate abroad and account for and control those operations.

Bribery itself has been termed everything from extortion to just another part of the marketing mix in international business. The problem of the multinational is that it operates in a variety of countries with different business practices and laws and competes with companies from other countries that also have different sets of business laws and customs. Let's look at each one of these problems. The SEC investigations have highlighted a number of points. Bribes are usually paid because the receiver of the bribe (normally in the foreign country) has a strong market position or has control over an aspect of the environment that can have a strong impact on the firm's operations.

Bribes to Place or Receive an Order

If the recipient is a purchasing agent, he is usually confronted with an array of salesmen competing for a substantial amount of business. The firms—one or all of them—may be so desperate for the contract that they offer the purchasing agent a fee for the sale. Conversely, the purchasing agent may smell an opportunity and base his choice from among equally good competitors on the highest fee he can extract. American Hospital Supply Corporation, for example, paid a 10 percent commission (totaling $4 million to $5 million from 1972 to 1975) to certain individuals before it could sell hospital equipment to the Royal Cabinet Office of Saudi Arabia for the new King Faisal Specialist Hospital.[6]

Bribes to Government Officials

Sometimes bribes are paid to government officials other than purchasing agents. In Mexico, for example, six tire companies paid $420,000 in bribes to an official so that they would be exempt from price controls.[7] Tax authorities are frequent recipients of bribes, especially in countries like Italy and Spain where taxes traditionally have been negotiable.

Political Contributions

There is a fine line between paying bribes to *influence* the political process and making contributions to *support* the political process. In the United States it is illegal for corporations to make political contributions, even though individuals can if they so desire. In many countries, it is not

---

[6]Lee H. Radebaugh, "International Corporate Bribery: A New Dimension in Accounting," *The Multinational Corporation: Accounting and Social Implications* (Urbana Ill.: Center for International Accounting, 1977), p. 22.
[7]Ibid., p. 23.

only legally permissible but expected that corporations will make contributions. Whose system should the multinational defer to?

Paving the Way

Another dimension of the political process involves what is euphemistically known as grease payments, those made to a government official to do something he should be doing anyway. Some examples are to "expedite shipments through customs, or to speed processing of certain documents; secure required permits or licenses; or obtain adequate police protection."[8]

Extortion

A final dimension of making payments to the political system involves extortion. In 1970, Gulf Oil Company paid $3 million to the reelection campaign of former President Park of South Korea, and Gulf officials assert that they were told by a representative of President Park that Gulf's continued prosperity depended on their making the payment.[9]

These illustrations show that payments are made to get an edge on competitors, to cause government officials to bend or ignore laws, to grease normal channels, to support the political process, and to try to ensure the ability to continue operating. Sometimes the payments are made in countries where such shenanigans are accepted business practice, and sometimes they are made in countries where the payments are illegal. Sometimes they are initiated by the company and sometimes by the recipient.

An added complication is that payments could be made without headquarters approval. It is virtually impossible to do business in many Middle Eastern countries except through a local agent. If a fee is paid to the agent to expedite business, who is to say what the fee is used for? Similarly, a local subsidiary, staffed by local nationals attuned to their environment, may play the payments game like everyone else.

Impact of FCPA on U.S. Firms

We mentioned earlier that another problem of bribery is the legal and customary practice of U.S. competitors from other countries. It has been argued that U.S. firms are losing business because their competitors continue to pay bribes. West German companies, for example, are allowed to pay bribes and can deduct the cost as a business expense

[8]Ernst & Whinney, "Foreign Corrupt Practices Act of 1977," Retrieval No. 38748, February 1978, p. 5.
[9]Radebaugh, "Bribery," p. 23.

for tax purposes.[10] A former chairman of the British Overseas Trade Board comments that there is little support for antibribery legislation because exports count for 30 percent of their GNP. After Japan's former prime minister was arrested and jailed on charges of receiving Lockheed payments, he was reelected to the lower house of parliament in a landslide.[11]

What has been the FCPA impact? It prohibits anyone from using interstate commerce to make an offer, payment, or promise to pay anything of value for corrupt reasons. The payment must be to a foreign government official or political party to use influence wrongfully to help the company obtain, retain, or direct the business. The law includes making payments to someone like an agent who will eventually work through a foreign government official or political party. It does exclude from the definition of foreign government official someone whose duties are essentially ministerial or clerical.[12]

The Justice Department will go after anyone suspected of violating the bribery provisions of the FCPA, and penalties include a fine of up to $1 million for a company and up to $10,000 and five years in prison for an individual. Recently, the Criminal Division of the Justice Department offered to provide guidance to companies contemplating making bribes. A ruling would be provided the company within thirty days of submitting the required documentation. The division indicated that it would "assign a low priority to prosecuting small payments made to compete with bribe-paying foreign companies in countries where extortion by local officials is routine." However, it would aggressively pursue payoffs to win sales from U.S. competitors and in countries that are trying to enforce their own antibribery laws.[13]

Accounting Implications

Clearly, bribery is illegal and could have an impact on the way some firms market their goods and services in certain countries. But what does that have to do with accounting and internal auditing? Remember that a good control system is designed to safeguard corporate assets and that the internal auditor is responsible for testing compliance with the system. During its investigation of foreign bribes, the SEC found out that firms were falsifying records in order to disguise improper transactions, were failing to disclose the true purpose of some transactions, and were simply not recording some transactions.[14] In the first case, firms

---

[10]*Wall Street Journal*, 2 August 1979, p. 1.
[11]Ibid., p. 22.
[12]Public Law 95-213, Foreign Corrupt Practices Act of 1977, §§ 103 and 104.
[13]*Wall Street Journal*, 9 November 1979, p. 10.
[14]Hurd Baruch, "The Foreign Corrupt Practices Act," *Harvard Business Review*, January-February 1979, p. 33.

would either overstate revenues or expenses to hide bribes or report fictitious transactions. In the case of American Hospital Supply, the sales price of the equipment was increased enough to cover the amount of the kickback to the Saudi government purchasing agent, and the agent was then paid a "consulting" fee. In the case of the tire companies in Mexico, one company disguised its bribe by paying an engineer for services that were never rendered. The engineer then gave the cash back to the company, and the company used the cash (which was never recorded on the books, obviously) for the bribe.[15]

The second case mentioned above—failing to disclose the purpose of transactions—usually refers to payments made to agents and distributors for unspecified purposes. This is often referred to as the quality of the disclosure. The entry has been made, but what does it mean? The final point mentioned above is the total failure to report transactions. For example, Braniff Airways sold 3,626 tickets in Latin America for $900,000, did not record the sales, and kept the cash proceeds in a bank account that was not part of the regular financial statements. In Braniff's case, the funds in the secret bank account were used to pay extra commissions to travel agents and tour promoters. Other firms keeping similar off-the-book bank accounts used the funds to bribe foreign government officials.[16]

There are two accounting implications of these cases. First, books and records were not being kept properly, so financial statements did not accurately reflect underlying transactions. Second, firms were encouraging the corrupt practices or had such a poor control system that the practices were going on in spite of corporate policy to the contrary. As a result, the FCPA added two other provisions to the one on bribery: one dealing with record keeping and the other with internal controls. The record keeping provisions are to "make and keep books, records, and accounts, which, in reasonable detail, accurately and fairly reflect the transactions and dispositions of the assets of the issuer." In other words, if you are going to bribe someone, be sure you record and disclose it accurately—debit bribery expense and credit cash. Of course, if you do that the Justice Department will throw you in jail for making the payoff in the first place. But, if it's any consolation, the SEC will give you high marks for disclosure.

The second accounting implication relates to internal accounting controls. According to this provision, each firm is to "devise and maintain a system of internal accounting controls sufficient to provide reasonable assurances that (i) transactions are executed in accordance with management's general or specific authorization; (ii) transactions are recorded as necessary (1) to permit preparation of financial statements in

---

[15]Radebaugh, "Bribery," pp. 24–25.
[16]Ibid.

conformity with generally accepted accounting principles or any other criteria applicable to such statements, and (2) to maintain accountability for assets; (iii) access to assets is permitted only in accordance with management's general or specific authorization; and (iv) the recorded accountability for assets is compared with the existing assets at reasonable intervals and appropriate action is taken with respect to any differences."[17]

It has always been assumed that management would require good records to be kept and would design and implement an adequate internal control system. However, this is the first time that violation of these principles could lead to civil liability and criminal prosecution. In addition, the accounting provisions of the FCPA may be violated even though no foreign bribes are paid. Most firms didn't realize this when the law went into effect, but the government has legislated accounting procedures in an area where they had never before ventured. As a result, firms are paying much closer attention to the design and implementation of their control systems.

In order to comply with the FCPA, a firm needs strong support from four levels: management, the internal auditors, the external auditors, and the board of directors.

Management

Top management needs to set the proper atmosphere for compliance with the FCPA by agreeing to abide by its provisions, formulating a written policy, communicating that policy to employees, and making sure the policy is understood and adhered to. IBM's code of conduct as it relates to political contributions and questionable payments is as follows:

> IBM will not make contributions or payments to political parties or candidates. Nor will IBM bribe or make payoffs to government officials, civil servants or anyone. This is a single worldwide policy. If you ever are approached for what you believe is a questionable payment, report the circumstances to your manager as soon as possible.
>
> In many countries political contributions by corporations are illegal. In other countries they are legal, but IBM will not make them in either case. Nor will IBM provide things other than direct cash payments which may be considered contributions. For example, if you want to campaign for a political candidate, the company will give you reasonable amounts of time off from work without pay, commensurate with your duties. IBM encourages people to be involved in politics,

---

[17]Public Law 95-213, § 102.

but on their own time and at their own expense. If IBM were to pay you while you were campaigning, your salary could be considered a contribution to the candidate or party you were supporting.

With respect to accurate reporting, IBM management requires that "all reporting of information—whether sales results, hours worked or equal opportunity efforts—should be accurate and timely and should be a fair representation of all the facts. It should not be organized in any way that is intended to mislead or misinform the reader."[18]

In emphasizing the importance of the role of management, former Secretary of the Treasury W. Michael Blumenthal, while chairman, president, and chief executive officer of the Bendix Corporation, said "the role of the chief executive is crucial in ensuring that his business operates in accordance with the standards set for it. . . . It is he who interprets the demands that society makes on his business and reconciles them with his business goals. He analyzes the problem, makes the decision, sets the tone." Blumenthal then outlines the strategy of the CEO, who

1. Formulates a policy to deal with the problem.
2. Exemplifies his policy by his own behavior.
3. Communicates his policy within the company and to the company's publics.
4. Directs his colleagues to apply the policy in concretely specified ways.
5. Institutes controls to ensure that these directives are followed.
6. Applies sanctions and awards.
7. Ensures that the policy will continue to govern the company's behavior through programs of recruitment, training and promotion.[19]

These actions are the critical starting point in developing the controls necessary to comply with the FCPA.

The actual controls put in place by management are designed to prevent (or deter) personnel from making errors as well as to detect errors in procedure—both financial and operational—that may have occurred. The system should take into account the specific considerations mentioned earlier in the chapter with respect to the FCPA: proper access to and use of corporate assets and accurate accounting for those assets.

---

[18]IBM Corp., *Business Conduct Guidelines*, pp. 10, 12.
[19]W. Michael Blumenthal, "Top Management's Role in Preventing Illegal Payments," *Conference Board Record*, August 1976, p. 15.

Internal Auditors

The internal audit staff worries about much more than the FCPA, and a cost/benefit analysis would preclude adding enough auditors to eliminate all risk of noncompliance. However, a number of things can be done by the auditor. In a recent study on what internal auditors are doing to evaluate their company's internal control system, it was found that the following standard methods were used in order of frequency: written audit programs, compliance testing, statistical sampling techniques, internal control questionnaires, and flow charts. As a result of the FCPA, more firms are beefing up their emphasis on flow charts, which are useful in documenting procedures and providing an overview of the entire control system.[20]

A number of firms are following the advice of the Minahan committee, the Special Advisory Committee on Internal Accounting Control of the AICPA, to audit transactions cycles rather than specific accounts, such as cash. One explanation of the *cycle concept* is that there are five business cycles: revenue, financial reporting, expenditure, conversion (production), and treasury. These cycles are all interrelated, obviously. For example, the revenue cycle interacts with the treasury cycle by providing cash receipts, it generates information for the financial reporting cycle, and it results from selling goods and services produced in the conversion cycle. According to one method of auditing transactions flows, objectives are identified from the FCPA as described earlier, more specific control objectives are then identified for each transactions cycle, and control techniques are developed to make sure that each control objective is met.[21]

It is the role of the internal auditor to make sure that these control techniques, which are normally translated into basic operating procedures, are adhered to. Obviously it would be difficult, if not impossible, to do this with every procedure the company has developed. Thus the internal audit department needs to assess the areas of greatest risk and determine the scope of work necessary to test compliance. Any deviations from procedure should be corrected and reported to top management. As a result of its problems with corporate bribery in the 1970s, Gulf Oil upgraded the internal audit function to a corporate vice presidential position reporting directly to the chairman with free access to the audit committee of the board of directors.[22] This move greatly strengthened the role of the internal audit function and its ability to deal with irregularities in the control system.

---

[20]Corine T. Norgaard and Robert W. Granow, "Internal Auditing's Response to the Foreign Corrupt Practices Act," *Internal Auditor*, December 1979, p. 60.
[21]Robert Mednick, "Transaction Flow Auditing," *Financial Executive*, July 1979, pp. 60–62.
[22]Radebaugh, "Bribery," p. 37.

External Auditors

The role of the external auditor is discussed in more detail later, but it is appropriate to look at this role in relation to the FCPA now. There is the feeling on the part of the general public that independent auditors should be able to detect fraud and noncompliance with the FCPA. However, generally accepted auditing standards as developed by the AICPA call for an examination of the books and records to determine problems that may have a material effect on the financial statements. While the auditor is always keeping an eye out for questionable or illegal acts, he is concerned with those having a material effect, whereas the FCPA is concerned with those leading to *any* effect. This creates some obvious problems.

As pointed out earlier, corporations often devised creative ways to hide corrupt practices. If a company records a $40,000 payment to an engineering consultant as a legitimate business expense, how is the auditor to know whether the money is funneled back to the company and used as bribe money? Will the engineer tip him off? In the words of one independent auditor:

> What we and other auditing firms found, when it came to the work of helping our clients uncover the skeletons in their closets, was that 90 percent of illegal payments had to be discovered through interrogation of the individuals involved or likely to know, once there was a hint that such payments might exist. Normal auditing techniques are not, and probably never will be, adequate to uncover this sort of thing. . . .[23]

Given this background, what is the auditor to do? The steps outlined for the internal auditor earlier are similar to those followed by the external auditor. Greater attention must be paid to types of transactions and geographical areas where there is a high probability of illegal acts. This is why a general and specific risk analysis is so critical. As pointed out by one auditor, "specific skepticism naturally focuses on companies that have large sales to foreign governments, significant operations or sales in countries with traditionally relaxed commercial standards, or companies that are subject to capricious governmental regulation, which can create a strong temptation to lubricate the wheels with a bit of grease."[24]

What happens if the external auditor believes that an illegal act may have occurred? Statement of Auditing Standards (SAS) 17 of the AICPA, "Illegal Acts by Clients," provides the answer. The auditor first talks to management and management's legal counsel to decide whether further

---

[23]Walter E. Hanson, "A Blueprint for Ethical Conduct," *Journal of Accountancy*, June 1978, p. 82.
[24]Ibid.

tests are necessary to determine if an illegal act has occurred. If the illegal act has occurred, the auditor reports the fact to top management in order that corrective action can be taken. If management corrects the problem and the effect of the illegal act is immaterial, there should be no problem. If the effect is material, it may have to be disclosed in the financial statements. If management refuses to cooperate or disclose the necessary information, the auditor may have to qualify his opinion, express an adverse opinion, or completely withdraw from the audit. An obvious part of the audit is to pay close attention to the internal control system of the firm and express an opinion on those controls to management.

Board of Directors

The final group directly concerned and able to affect the internal control system as it relates to the FCPA is the board of directors. It is up to management to design and implement an action plan relative to the FCPA, but it is up to the board to monitor the timeliness and execution of the plan. The board cannot bury its head in the sand, because it could suffer the consequences of noncompliance with the FCPA. The board is normally composed of insiders (current and past executives of the company) as well as outsiders. There has been a strong movement in the past few years to have each board form an audit committee which has substantial outside representation. The audit committee should be responsible for reviewing the scope of the audit before the audit is done and then for reviewing the results, especially comments related to the adequacy of the internal control system.

As mentioned earlier, the Criminal Division of the Justice Department decided to provide guidance to companies about the legality of payments the companies were contemplating making. Even though the SEC refused to go along with the Justice Department, it decided in early 1980 to investigate how the FCPA affects U.S. companies operating abroad and will decide later whether to take further action.[25]

THE EXTERNAL AUDIT

The growth of national and international capital markets has turned the spotlight on the auditor as an important credibility link between the corporation and the investor-creditor. Outsiders are interested in an objective, independent view on the financial statements of a firm. National corporations—especially in countries where the auditing pro-

---

[25]*Wall Street Journal*, 9 November 1979, p. 10.

fession has not achieved an international reputation—are turning increasingly to multinational public accounting firms to certify their financial statements in order to attract international investors. The use of international auditors emphasizes that auditing standards and practices, like accounting standards and practices, vary considerably from country to country. Let's consider some of the differences, especially in the requirements and standards for audits and qualifications of auditors, and to look at the process of harmonization.

Guideline Sources and Requirements

The development of auditing standards is a complex interrelationship of cultural, legal-political, and economic variables in a given country, so one would not expect total uniformity. Auditing standards come from either the public (government) or private sector. The former source of influence is prevalent in developing countries where the accounting profession is not well organized or of sufficiently high quality. The government often takes the lead by incorporating audit requirements and, to a lesser extent, standards into law. This thrust is also evident in industrial countries like France, which is legalistic and prescriptive and where the auditing profession has been established and regulated by law historically.

This approach can be contrasted to the United States, where the SEC requires that an audit be conducted but does not say how. This is left to the accounting profession through auditing standards developed by the AICPA. A similar approach is followed in the United Kingdom and Canada. The audit profession originated in Britain yet it has no generally accepted auditing standards issued and approved by the profession.

There are wide differences in requirements for audits. In the United States, annual independent audits are required of firms listed on national securities exchanges and firms with more than 500 shareholders and assets of more than $1 million whose securities are traded over the counter. However, most other large companies have audits, and many banks and regulatory agencies require them. In Brazil, a company whose shares are traded on one of the stock exchanges or over the counter must prepare audited financial statements, but such firms account for only a very small portion of the total number of firms. The same requirement exists in Mexico. The list goes on, but the common thread is that audit requirements are tied to securities exchanges in most countries.[26]

---

[26]See Ernst & Whinney, *Worldwide Statutory Audit and Reporting Requirements*, E&W No. 48468, 1979 for information on other countries.

This is no longer the case in Europe, however. The Fourth Directive of the European Economic Community requires all public and private corporations, with the possible exception of small companies, to have an annual audit. This rule applies to local subsidiaries of companies outside the EEC as well.[27] This directive won't have any effect on Ireland and Britain, which already comply, but other countries are going to face substantial changes. In Belgium, only quoted companies had to have an audit, and in Denmark, France, Germany, and The Netherlands few private companies had to be audited. However, all public companies had to be audited even before the Fourth Directive.[28]

Differences in Audit Standards

Just because a large number of countries require an audit doesn't mean that all audits are done the same way.

Financial statements come from the books and records of the firms, which reflect the underlying transactions that the firm engages in. The term *audit* could mean—as it does in Switzerland—that the financial statements accurately reflect the books and records of the firm. The audit would entail tracing the data from the books and records to the financial statements, a relatively simple process. The auditor would rely primarily on the honesty of management and would not be as concerned as his counterpart in the United States or Britain with confirming inventory taking or bank balances.

A more extensive audit would see whether the books and records accurately reflect the original transactions. This would involve a more extensive investigation of the internal control system to make sure that corporate procedures for recording transactions are clearly established, communicated, and followed. It would also involve more extensive tests of original transactions and how they eventually flow through the records to the financial statements. In Britain, for example, it is regarded as normal practice for the auditor to be present at inventory taking. Similarly, accounts receivable are normally confirmed as a test of internal controls over sales.[29] In many countries, the required standards for field work may be less than what is carried out in practice. In Sweden, for example, there are no provisions for confirming accounts receivable, but most auditors do so. The observation of inventory taking is common practice, even though it is not required.[30]

---

[27]Ibid., p. 28.
[28]E. G. Bartholomew, "Harmonization of Financial Reporting in the EEC," *Accountancy*, October 1979, pp. 50–51.
[29]American Institute of Certified Public Accountants, *Professional Accounting in 30 Countries*, New York: AICPA, 1975, p. 608.
[30]Ibid., p. 553.

There are many reasons why audit standards vary from country to country. In the United States and United Kingdom there are broadly based capital markets and highly qualified, highly thought of accounting professions. The capital markets require that financial statements be independently verified, and the profession has developed and refined audit standards over time. The air of skepticism has encouraged fairly rigid tests. Culture often plays a part as well. In Japan, it is said that bank deposits and loans payable are obtained from the company rather than by independent confirmation because independent confirmation would show too much distrust in company personnel, which could mean a loss in face.

In other cases, prevailing business practices also affect audit standards. Until recently, it was difficult for nonresident auditors to confirm bank balances in Germany. German bankers have said that the reason for the reluctance was that they provide information for customers daily, which makes year-end confirmations unnecessary. Also, until recently German audit practices did not require confirmations of bank balances, which gave weight to the banks' belief that such practice was unnecessary. In spite of this, German banks routinely provided bank confirmation to local auditors, even though they would not do so for foreign auditors.[31] Is the problem one of business practices or distrust of foreigners—a cultural problem?

Differences in audit standards and practices can often be reflected in the auditor's opinion in the annual report. At least the opinion expresses the major concern of the auditor. The following report by Arthur Young & Company to the board of directors and shareholders of Textron, Inc. is fairly typical of a U.S. audit report:

> We have examined the accompanying consolidated balance sheet of Textron Inc. at December 30, 1978 and December 31, 1977 and the related consolidated statements of income, retained earnings, capital surplus, changes in shares of capital stock and changes in financial position for the years then ended. Our examinations were made in accordance with generally accepted auditing standards and, accordingly, included such tests of the accounting records and such other auditing procedures as we considered necessary in the circumstances.
>
> In our opinion, the statements mentioned above present fairly the consolidated financial position of Textron Inc. at December 30, 1978 and December 31, 1977, and the consolidated results of operations and changes in financial position for the years then ended, in conformity

---

[31]Michael Harding, "Problems of Obtaining Bank Confirmations in Germany," *Accountancy*, August 1977, p. 88.

with generally accepted accounting principles applied on a consistent basis during the period.

Arthur Young & Company
February 13, 1979

The report makes reference to the financial statements examined, the consistent application of generally accepted accounting principles, the use of generally accepted auditing standards, and the judgment of auditors. The Auditing Standards Board of the AICPA is contemplating the following changes to the standard report.

- Clarify that the financial statements are management's representations.
- Modify the description of the audit process and refer to its inherent limitations.
- Delete the word "fairly" from "presents fairly . . . in conformity with generally accepted accounting principles."
- Delete any reference to "consistency" in the application of accounting principles.[32]

The following report is typical of the German short form audit report, which is usually shorter than the name of the auditing firm. The report is for Steag A.G., a German energy company similar to a utility.

According to our audit, made in conformity with our professional standards, the consolidated financial statements and the related report of the Board of Management comply with German law.

Düsseldorf, April 22, 1977

Treuarbeit
Aktiengesellschaft
Wirtschaftsprüfungsgesellschaft
Steuerberatungsgesellschaft

Dr. Jordan   ppa. Baumeister
Wirtschaftsprüfer   Wirtschaftsprüfer

Notice the reference here to German law rather than generally accepted accounting principles.

The next report is from a Swedish firm, the Swedish Match Com-

---

[32]Deloitte, Haskins & Sells, "The Week in Review," 7 March 1980, p. 3.

pany. The report refers to the Companies Act rather than generally accepted accounting principles and also makes other statements with reference to the appropriation of earnings and the responsibility of certain corporate officials.

> We have examined the annual report and the consolidated financial statements, the accounting records and the administration by the board of directors and the managing director for the year 1977 in accordance with generally accepted auditing standards.
>
> Certain of the subsidiaries' accounts have been examined by other auditors and we have relied on their reports in connection with our examination of the consolidated financial statements.
>
> **Parent Company**
> The annual report has been prepared in accordance with the requirements of the Swedish Companies Act.
>
> We recommend that the Company's statement of income and balance sheet be adopted,
>
> that the unappropriated earnings be dealt with in accordance with the proposal in the directors' report, and
>
> that the board of directors and the managing director be discharged from responsibility for their administration in respect of the year 1977.
>
> **Consolidated Financial Statements**
> The consolidated financial statements have been prepared in accordance with the requirements of the Swedish Companies Act and using the purchase method as mentioned in Note 1 to the accounts.
>
> We recommend that the consolidated statement of income and the consolidated balance sheet be adopted.
>
> Stockholm, March 21, 1978
>
> Göte Engfors   Jörgen Eskilson   K B Smith
>   Authorized   Chartered Accountant
>   Public Accountant
>   Partners in Price Waterhouse & Co.

The final report is from Nippon Electric Company, Ltd., a Japanese utility. This report is included not because it is typical of a Japanese report but because it was generated for capital markets outside of Japan. Therefore, the Japanese statements needed to be restated according to U.S. generally accepted accounting principles prior to certification. Notice the qualification of the report, since Nippon Electric did not follow FASB 14. However, this omission was apparently accepted by the SEC.

To the Board of Directors and Shareholders of Nippon Electric Co., Ltd.
(Nippon Denki Kabushiki Kaisha)

We have examined the consolidated balance sheets of Nippon Electric Co., Ltd. and its consolidated subsidiaries at March 31, 1979 and 1978, and the related consolidated statements of income and retained earnings and of changes in financial position for the years then ended, expressed in yen. Our examinations were made in accordance with generally accepted auditing standards and accordingly included such tests of the accounting records and such other auditing procedures as we considered necessary in the circumstances.

The company has not presented segment information for the years ended March 31, 1979 and 1978. In our opinion, the presentation of segment information concerning operations in different industries, export sales and major customers is required by accounting principles generally accepted in the United States of America for a complete presentation of consolidated financial statements. In our report dated June 20, 1978, our opinion on the 1978 financial statements was unqualified. However, in view of the fact that the 1978 financial statements have been restated to exclude the presentation of segment information referred to above, our present opinion on the 1978 financial statements is different from that expressed in our previous report.

In our opinion, except for the omission of segment information as discussed in the preceding paragraph, the consolidated financial statements examined by us present fairly the financial position of Nippon Electric Co., Ltd. and its consolidated subsidiaries at March 31, 1979 and 1978, and the results of their operations and the changes in their financial position for the years then ended, in conformity with accounting principles generally accepted in the United States of America consistently applied.

Price Waterhouse & Co.

All these reports refer to generally accepted auditing standards or professional standards. This is not true in all countries. Swiss auditors merely state that the accounts have been examined in accordance with the provisions of the law. Auditing standards vary so much from country to country that "in accordance with generally accepted auditing standards" is limited in its universal meaning. Only when worldwide auditing standards are developed and adhered to will that statement have universal significance.

The Auditors Themselves

High audit standards are worthless if there are no auditors to implement them. Certification varies from country to country, and there may be different levels of certification in the same country. In Peru, anyone who has graduated in accounting from an accredited university receives a government license to conduct an audit. There are no experience or other special certification requirements. In Indonesia, the situation is the same as in Peru except that an accountant must work with the government for three years before being allowed to practice publicly. In the United States, each state has its own requirements for certification which combine a mix of education and skill and a common examination administered by the state but prepared by the Board of Examiners of the AICPA. In Pennsylvania, for example, an applicant is required to have 24 accounting credits before taking the exam and can be certified upon successfully completing the exam, having two years' experience with a public accounting firm and a bachelor's degree, or having one year's experience and an MBA degree. The common examination contains questions on auditing (3½ hours), accounting theory (3½ hours), accounting practice (two exams, 4½ hours each), and business law (3½ hours). In order to perform an audit for a company that registers with the SEC, an accountant must be certified.

Although these requirements are more rigid than those of Peru, they are not as rigid as those of West Germany. A wirtschaftsprufer (WP) in Germany, similar to a CPA in the United States, must be a college graduate, must have a minimum of six years' experience, at least two of which must be with a WP, and must pass a series of exams and write a thesis discussing auditing theory and practice. It is difficult to become certified before age 30 and normal to expect certification at age 34 to 36.

In Switzerland nearly anyone, regardless of professional qualifications, can act as an auditor. A statutory audit, which certifies that financial statements come from the books and records according to the legal statements, does not have to be done by anyone specialized, like a CPA. The auditor cannot be a director or employee but may be a shareholder or have other financial interests in the company. An independent audit is required for firms above a certain size, and stricter auditing standards apply. However, even though more specialized knowledge and training are required of the auditor, certification is not.

In France, a statutory examiner is required to examine the financial statements of corporations annually. The statutory examiner has to have a diploma, certifying that a fairly simple exam has been passed, and two years' experience. The audit itself is not as extensive as one would find in Britain or the United States. The more prestigious member of the profession is the expert comptable (EC). The EC must meet fairly rigorous educational requirements, must pass a set of preliminary exams leading to a diploma of advanced accounting studies, must work under the supervision of an EC for three years, must be certified in a specialized area by written and oral exams during these three years, must then sit for a higher auditing exam, and finally must present and defend a thesis to the examining board. An expert comptable serves more as a business and tax adviser to management than as an auditor since the latter role is less specialized and less lucrative and since the law prohibits the same person from performing both roles.

Who determines certification? In the United States, the SEC requires that an audit be done by a CPA, but it allows the profession to determine certification. In the United Kingdom, government statute lists the professional organizations whose members can conduct audits, but the organizations themselves determine education, training, examination, and experience requirements. As was noted earlier, in Peru and Indonesia it is government legislation, not the profession, that determines qualifications for certification. This is also common in Continental Europe, where the profession tends to be established and regulated by law. A notable exception is The Netherlands, where the profession is fairly independent of the government.

There are efforts under way in the EEC to establish the requirements for auditors in the Eighth Directive. The British are skeptical of the directive, which is much like the prescriptive French approach, because it is so legalistic and deals only with audits, not with the full range of services provided by a British auditor. The British are afraid that this would destroy their existing auditing profession because it might cause people to narrowly specialize in auditing just to become certified. This is what has happened in France with the difference between statutory auditors and expert comptables.

MULTINATIONAL PUBLIC ACCOUNTING FIRMS AND EXTERNAL AUDITS

The world's largest public accounting firms are scrambling for an even larger share of the action in international business by expanding abroad through mergers, acquisitions, and new offices. Before taking a look at the international dimensions of their operations, however, let's see how the domestic operations of the big firms are organized. The revenues or fees of the public accounting firms are derived from three areas: accounting and auditing, tax, and management consulting. The percentage of total fees from each of the three product groups varies from company to company. To give you an idea of the differences from firm to firm, Arthur Andersen derives 58 percent of its fees from accounting and auditing, 19 percent from tax, and 23 percent from administrative services.[33] For Price Waterhouse, the relative percentages are 79, 11, and 5.5, with another 4.2 percent from other sources.[34] Most other firms fit somewhere in between. Although accounting and auditing services are bread and butter for the firms, tax usually outranks management consulting for the number two spot. Most firms usually have a national partner in charge of each product group to coordinate research and development and provide direction and assistance nationwide.

The real strength of the organization lies at the office level. Each office has several levels of professionals—partners, principals, managers, senior accountants, staff accountants. One of the partners is designated the managing partner of the office and is therefore responsible for its profitability. Partners and principals (at the organizational level of a partner, but not accountants) are responsible for generating revenues in their areas of expertise. In some firms, regional partners supervise the work of managing partners of a variety of offices and in turn report to the managing partner of the firm, who is in turn responsible to the partners of the firm—the equivalent of shareholders in a corporate setting. The partners of the firm share in the nationwide profits, much like the shareholders of a corporation.

Reasons for Expansion

Why have public accounting firms expanded abroad, and how have they expanded? The three major reasons for overseas expansion are client service, a defensive management strategy, and an offensive management strategy.[35] The first reason is obvious since accounting firms get their revenues by serving clients. Obviously, too, they expand abroad to give a broader range of service. Client service is also the main defensive strategy: to prevent erosion of service to an existing client. If a firm were not to expand abroad, it might find its clients going to a competitor that has a broader geographical service base.

Although the offensive strategy was listed as third, it has pushed into the forefront lately—especially in Europe. As the various directives come on line in the EEC, accounting principles are becoming more uniform, and the need for audits increases. The growing strength of many European economies is creating more European-based multinational enterprises that need the auditing services of a worldwide public accounting firm. Thus in the late 1970s a rash of mergers and acquisitions was announced as the U.S.- and U.K.-based public accounting firms sought to strengthen their presence in Europe. With the market wide open there, compared with the highly competitive, relatively

[33]Arthur Andersen & Co., *Annual Report*, 1979.
[34]*Wall Street Journal*, 16 October 1979, p. 16.
[35]Frederick H. Wu and Donald W. Hackett, "The Internationalization of U.S. Public Accounting Firms: An Empirical Study," *The International Journal of Accounting*, Spring 1977, p. 86.

sluggish growth potential in the United States, Europe appears to be the focus of expansion for a while.

Servicing Multinational Clients

Given the need for expansion, in what ways have the firms serviced their multinational clients? The simplest way is for a partner or staff member to travel from the home office to service a client abroad. This would be sufficient as long as the foreign sector was a small part of the client's overall operations. However, this approach is unsatisfactory in the long run owing to the complexity of the international audit and tax environment and the increasing internationalization of most of the firms' larger clients.

Beyond the traveling auditor approach are two philosophically different approaches: the branch or affiliate and the correspondent.

Branch Offices

Some U.S. firms have set up *branches* abroad. These branches may be separate legal entities that use the parent firm's name. Home office personnel fill the important positions until domestic personnel can be trained to take over. In some cases local firms are acquired; in others, new firms are established. The branch concept, coupled with a strong central management, provides for tighter control over services.

Correspondents

The *correspondent* relationship is multifaceted, in that it can be very weak or very strong. At one end of the scale, the local correspondent may be a representative that performs services for more than one accounting firm. A very loose operating relationship may exist. At the other end of the scale, a very strong correspondent relationship may exist where the local firm performs services exclusively for one foreign public accounting firm.

In some cases the correspondent relationship may involve a joint partnership between the U.S. and local firms. In the early 1900s, Arthur Young & Company set up a joint partnership in London and Paris with the British firm of Broads, Patterson, and Co. It also set up a joint partnership in Canada with the Canadian firm of Clarkson, Gordon, and Co. In other cases, the U.S. and local firms simply have a close working relationship. For example, the British correspondent might audit the records of the British subsidiary of a U.S. corporation that is the client of the U.S. public accounting firm.[36] Another strategy is to

---

[36]Lee H. Radebaugh, "A Multinational Partnership? The Public Accounting Firm," presented at the Annual Meeting of the Academy of International Business in Dallas, Texas, 30 December 1975.

use a licensing agreement where a local firm uses the name and technical advice of the large foreign firm in exchange for a royalty payment.[37]

Whether the U.S. firm expands abroad through strong or weak correspondent relationships, the fact remains that the partners in other countries are separate, autonomous organizations. Unlike a corporation, which retains equity control over its farflung operations, these partnerships are built on mutual benefit and service. There *are* situations where the U.S. firm owns the foreign operations, but those are the exception rather than the rule. Arthur Andersen & Company is fairly centralized; its chairman and vice-chairmen have worldwide responsibility, and there is profit sharing among its international partners; but it is the only public accounting firm so organized.

Many firms have organized a worldwide partnership to integrate operations. Each member partner (such as United States, Britain, Canada, Continental Europe) retains its separate identity, but a more cohesive cooperative effort exists among the firms through the international partnership. In 1979, for example, Ernst & Ernst announced the formation of a new international firm named Ernst & Whinney International with offices in 71 countries. The U.S. partner changed its name to Ernst & Whinney to be consistent with the international partnership. EWI now has partners in the United States, Canada, United Kingdom, Continental Europe, Middle East, Far East, Australia/New Zealand, Africa, and Central and South America. The partners range in size from 14 offices in Canada to 117 in the United States. The stated purpose of the move is "increased ability to maintain uniformly high quality standards around the world; better coordination of investment in research, communications, and professional development; and more effective management of human resources."[38] Part of the reason for its desire to strengthen the international organization is that foreign fees made up 25 percent of total fees in 1977 and are expected to reach 40 percent by 1985.

Other firms have done similar things for similar reasons. In 1978, Haskins & Sells changed its name to Deloitte, Haskins & Sells to bring the name into line with the name used outside the United States. Its major partner, Deloitte & Co. of the United Kingdom, made the same move. Price Waterhouse & Co. is the U.S. partnership of Price Waterhouse International, a worldwide partnership that individuals (rather than separate firms) belong to. Similar stories could be told about Coopers & Lybrand; Peat, Marwick, Mitchell & Co.; Touche Ross; and Arthur Young of the Big Eight in the United States.

Smaller firms are also involved in cooperative international efforts. Main Lafrentz belongs to a federation of 36 firms in 39 countries and is

[37]Hackett and Wu, "Internationalization of Accounting Firms," p. 87.
[38]From a pamphlet distributed by Ernst & Ernst in January 1979 announcing the change.

contemplating associating with a group of European firms that are interested in expanding their coverage worldwide.

Problems of Servicing Clients Internationally

What problems do the firms face in trying to service clients internationally? The major problems listed in one study are dealing with different accounting standards, monetary exchange and fluctuations, business ethics, recruitment and training of local staff, unfavorable government policies toward foreign firms, and language and cultural barriers.[39] Combined with the differences in accounting or auditing standards and in the qualifications of personnel is the issue of quality control. The firms are concerned that substandard work by foreign auditors could impair their ability to express an accurate opinion. As a result, the international partnerships concentrate on training and internship or foreign residency programs. The cultivation of a high-quality local staff is the only solution to nationalism and is the best solution for the problems in dealing in different business and accounting environments.

After all is said and done, public accounting firms exist to audit the financial statements of their clients, and this is no easy task. All the problems discussed in the section on internal audits of multinational enterprises come back again. IBM, which operates in more than 125 countries, has to comply with the regulatory standards of every country where it operates as well as the U.S. regulatory standards; and U.S. regulations apply to all operations, not just those in the United States. Its auditor, Price Waterhouse, has to be sure that it expands the scope of its work sufficiently to express an opinion. This means it must do the work itself or rely on someone else to do some of the work. The control of the audit rests in the engagement partner in charge of the audit. He, in consultation with corporate personnel, decides what work is to be done worldwide and by whom. He must develop, deliver, and monitor the results of the audit plan for every operation in every city where the corporation has a presence. He works through a specific partner in each foreign location attached to that segment of the audit.

HARMONIZATION OF AUDITING STANDARDS

Previous sections in this chapter pinpoint similarities and differences in auditing standards and auditors' qualifications and highlight efforts under way in the EEC to harmonize audit requirements and the certification of auditors. Given the differences in the background and training of accountants, the attitudes as to what an audit should accom-

---

[39]Hackett and Wu, "Internationalization of Accounting Firms," p. 90.

plish and how it should be conducted, and the business and cultural environment, can auditing standards ever be harmonized? The answer is probably no, given such complicating factors as nationalism and pride. But the chances of harmonization are better for auditing standards than for accounting principles.

The organization most actively involved in harmonizing auditing standards worldwide, as noted in Chapter 3, is the International Federation of Accountants (IFAC). IFAC was organized in October 1977 at the International Congress of Accountants in Munich as the successor of the International Coordination Committee of the Accounting Profession. Unlike the International Accounting Standards Committee, which is concerned with setting uniform accounting standards, IFAC is more concerned with auditing and accountants, and it initially approved seven standing committees: Auditing Practices, Education, Ethics, International Congress, Management Accounting, Planning, and Regional Organizations. IFAC started with a membership of 63 professional accountancy bodies from 49 countries. Both numbers have grown steadily, reaching 72 accountancy bodies in 55 countries by early 1980.

The auditing Practices Committee is scheduled to develop guidelines on auditing and reporting practices and seek to promote voluntary acceptance of such guidelines. The first International Auditing Guideline was the *Objective and Scope of the Audit of Financial Statements*. Exposure drafts have been issued on audit engagement letters, basic principles governing an audit, and planning. In addition, work is being done on interbank confirmation requests, internal control, using the work of another auditor, and controlling the quality of audit work.

The Education Committee is working on the prequalification education and training of accountants as well as continuing education requirements. The Ethics Committee is working on advertising and publicity of accountants; technical competence; integrity, objectivity, and independence of auditors; and statements on ethical behavior.[40] The other committees are working in areas that are not directly related to auditing but should help to improve accounting practices worldwide.

CONCLUSIONS

The Foreign Corrupt Practices Act has eliminated most of the bribing of foreign government officials by U.S. firms and has changed the way U.S. firms operate abroad. Whether the Justice Department will decide to loosen up the requirements remains to be seen. However, record keeping and internal controls will never be the same. The changes in

---

[40]International Federation of Accountants, *Newsletter*.

accounting, though costly, should improve the quality of records for material transactions.

As can be seen, the international dimension of auditing is challenging and exciting and covers issues that are extensions of their domestic counterparts as well as issues that are unique to the international environment. Only when internal and external auditors recognize the environmental elements that affect their work and adjust accordingly can they provide the service that is required.

STUDY QUESTIONS

13–1. Discuss the role of the internal auditor. Indicate similarities and differences between the internal auditor's role in domestic and in multinational operations.

13–2. What additional challenges exist for an auditor working in the international environment? Compare these for the external and internal auditor.

13–3. Discuss the forms of organization and types of personnel that a firm can use when conducting an international internal audit. What are the advantages and disadvantages of each?

13–4. What are the legal and accounting implications of the U.S. Foreign Corrupt Practices Act?

13–5. What are the roles of (a) management, (b) the internal auditors, (c) the external auditors, and (d) the board of directors in assuring compliance with the U.S. Foreign Corrupt Practices Act?

13–6. Compare and contrast the external audit function in various countries.

13–7. How do the selection and certification of auditors differ from country to country?

13–8. Compare the process of setting auditing standards in different countries. Suggest some environmental factors that might explain any differences.

13–9. Can auditing practices be standardized internationally? Support your opinion.

13–10. Why have public accounting firms expanded internationally? Compare the forms of organization they have used. What are the advantages and disadvantages of each?

13–11. Using journal and newspaper articles on bribery, generate some examples of the accounting dimensions of bribery other than those listed in the chapter.

13–12. Write to several companies and ask for their codes of conduct; see how they compare with the one used by IBM that is cited in the chapter.

13–13. Using monthly or quarterly publications of public accounting firms—such as *World* by Peat, Marwick, Mitchell or *Review* by Price

Waterhouse—report on stories written about foreign office activities of the firms.

13–14. Compare the audit reports of several foreign corporations to see how similar they are within their own countries as well as across countries. Include reports of U.S. companies as well. Try to find companies from different countries that may be audited by the same international public accounting firm.

CASE

STAR OIL COMPANY

"How did I ever get stuck in this rat's nest?" thought Herb Johnston as he sat in his office in Seoul, Korea.

It was 1970, just prior to a crucial national election, and Herb had come from a meeting with S. I. Kim, a high official in the Democratic Republican Independent Party (DRIP) of President Chung. Kim had just demanded a $5 million political contribution from Star Oil for the reelection of President Chung, who was facing a stiff challenge.

When Herb balked at paying such a large sum, Kim angrily replied, "Either put up the money I am asking for or you and Star Oil can pack up your bags. I'm here to get the money, not negotiate."

At that point, Herb walked out. What do I do now? he thought.

Star Oil had begun investing in oil refining facilities in Korea in the early 1960s because of a surplus of crude oil from its Middle East fields and the belief that Korea was going to be industrializing heavily and would therefore be a good place for investment. Herb was transferred there in 1969 as the general manager of the subsidiary, with instructions to do whatever was necessary to be successful. Marv Hansen, Herb's predecessor, was now Herb's boss.

As Herb reviewed the situation, he became more and more uneasy. In 1966, Marv Hansen had paid $900,000 to Chung's campaign, with approval from corporate headquarters. Although corporate political contributions are legal in Korea, Marv had recorded the contribution as a consulting expense, and neither Marv nor the CEO felt it necessary to inform the auditor or the board of directors about the contribution.

Herb was concerned about other aspects of the environment. Star Oil was required to make payments to different levels of government officials, ranging from low-level tipping to kickbacks. It was customary to give gifts to govern ment clerks and officials during three holiday seasons: Chusok (similar to Thanksgiving), Christmas, and the New Year. Higher officials got more expensive gifts, which were recorded as entertainment or miscellaneous expenses.

Marv had said that the wheels of progress do not turn without lubrication, and Herb soon found out how true this was. In order to keep permits or licenses from being lost or delayed, Herb had to pay $50 to $200, depending on the level of approval needed. Herb was told that these payments were needed to supplement the low salaries of government employees. Customs officials had to be paid off to get goods into the country, railroad switchmen had to be paid off to see that cargo was handled properly, planning boards had to be paid off to ensure approval of refinery expansions.

Even the military got into the act. Last year, Herb landed a lucrative contract to supply oil to the Ministry of Defense. Then the purchasing agent informed Herb that he would have to pay a kickback so that the Ministry of Defense could bolster its forces on the border of a neighboring hostile country. Herb offered to lower his price by a few cents a barrel to cover the cost, but the purchasing agent informed Herb that his competitors were paying the kickback and so should he.

As Herb shuffled his papers trying to decide what to do about Kim's demand, he came across a memo that had just arrived from Marv. Apparently, the internal auditors were raising a fuss about Herb's high entertainment and miscellaneous expenses. Marv wanted to set up an off-the-books cash fund that Herb could use to pay off government clerks and officials, and Marv wanted to know what Herb thought about the idea.

Questions

1. How does Herb's environment differ from what he might find in the United States?
2. What should Herb do about Kim's request?
3. What problems could Herb run into with Marv's suggestion of an off-the-books cash fund? What benefits would there be?
4. How do Herb's different situations relate to the Foreign Corrupt Practices Act?
5. Given Herb's situation, how do you feel about the effort of U.S. regulatory agencies to impose their rules on U.S. companies operating abroad under local laws?

14

The Future

As Peter Drucker has eloquently observed, we are living in an age of discontinuity. In these times, most analyses of historical problems and their solutions are not likely to be particularly useful. Moreover, the discontinuities of the modern age make forecasting extremely hazardous, particularly forecasting the future of accounting in either domestic or international contexts. Nevertheless, problems in prognostication do not dissuade us from crystal balling.

There appear to be several significant trends which will call for innovative and creative accounting solutions. Many of these trends point toward unilateral national efforts, occurring in different countries at different times, or along different lines at the same time. An example is accounting for inflation. Other trends suggest multilateral efforts by several countries working in concert. This variety will be more difficult to achieve because multilateral efforts require harmonization of disparate national accounting goals and systems, as described in Chapter 3. Regardless of the approaches taken, accountants in all countries must begin now to prepare for the future. This chapter highlights what we feel will be the most important problems related to accounting. Not all these problems are international per se in the sense that they concern accounting problems unique to international business operations. Many of them—inflation accounting, social responsibility accounting, the role of accounting in economic development—have a more national focus. However, they are all international in the sense that many countries and companies will be confronted with them and there could be considerable benefits to be gained if everyone were to learn what each country is doing to solve them and with what degree of success.

INFLATION

As was described in Chapter 8, double-digit and even triple-digit inflation rates have become disconcertingly commonplace and persistent.
While this phenomenon has generated a number of national approaches
to accounting for inflation, they share one objective in common: to find a
better way to measure the impact of inflation on a firm's financial
position.

As additional countries encounter the disruptive and distorting impact of inflation on their economies and societies, there will be increased
efforts to develop and refine new approaches to inflation accounting. As
we gain experience, and as managers, accountants, and accounting
information users of all kinds become more sophisticated, most of the
age-old resistance to inflation accounting should be overcome. Of
course, a great deal of creative work and sheer diligence will have to be
invested. But it appears that the trend is toward abandoning the stable
monetary unit premise and the almost religious adherence to the historical cost basis of value measurement: every accountant should prepare
for this fundamental shift in accounting.

We will not speculate as to the method of inflation accounting that
will ultimately become dominant. In the final analysis each country will
have to decide which method is best for its particular environment.
However, in order to make the best and most appropriate decision, a
country should carefully and exhaustively study all the approaches being
taken and the results experienced by other countries. The economic and
societal disruptions resulting from distorted accounting information that
is *not* adjusted for inflation are too great to be ignored or inappropriately
handled. The elimination of inflation is largely the domain of national
governments, but the elimination of the inflation-distorted accounting
information on which business, government, and societal groups base
their decisions is the domain of *accountants*.

MACROACCOUNTING

The growing intrusion of governments into national economic activity
constitutes a worldwide trend. At minimum, government involvement
has increased in the area of economic activity *guidance*, such as wage
and price guidelines, tax incentives, and national economic plans. At
maximum, government involvement has encompassed outright ownership of economic enterprises, comprehensive wage and price controls,
and regulation of all business activities. In between have been various
degrees of regulation, control, and ownership, often restricted to certain
sectors of the economy or certain types of enterprise or types of activity.

Increased government involvement in the economic sector points toward more uniform and standard accounting procedures, more of a macro approach to accounting, and hence less tolerance of accounting flexibility at the enterprise level. More standard charts of accounts and a more legalistic approach to accounting are likely to result. Whether these predicted changes in accounting are desirable will once again depend on the country. And as is the case with inflation accounting, accountants should play a major role in deciding whether the changes are desirable or even feasible and, if they are, in developing the appropriate accounting systems and procedures. To do this properly, accountants must thoroughly understand all the issues and approaches.

Superimposed on increased government involvement in economic activity is the growing government and societal concern about the effects of industrialization on issues such as income distribution. While often assumed to be part and parcel of the growing socialist political movement in the world, this phenomenon is also taking place in countries such as Germany and the United States. Accounting will undoubtedly be called on to measure the impact of business and other organizations' operations on income distribution within the society, as well as other societal impacts. Broadly speaking, this phenomenon is called social accounting.

SOCIAL RESPONSIBILITY AND
SOCIAL ACCOUNTING[1]

As pointed out in Chapter 9 social accounting is inexorably intertwined with social responsibility. It is clear that a new social consciousness is emerging globally, although to different degrees in individual countries. Intelligent and prudent managers should realize that their organization's success rests not just on a profit performance but also on social performance. That is, a firm survives not just on profits but also on its broader contribution to society. Because there is a symbiotic relationship between a firm and the society in which it operates, a firm must contribute to the *net* benefit of society if it is to survive. Thus a firm which creates wealth and power for a few individuals by making worse the lives of thousands of others is *not* contributing to the net welfare of the society. And while such firms have existed for decades, it is unlikely that society, with its new social consciousness, will allow them to continue in the future.

[1]We are particularly indebted to Professor Edmund Marques of CESA (France) for much of the material in this section.

Two Viewpoints

There are two ways to look at the social responsibility of firms. The first is to regard social responsibility issues as undesirable, although perhaps unavoidable, constraints against the firm's only true objective—the maximization of profit. From this viewpoint, social and profit objectives are incompatible. The second approach is to view social and economic objectives as compatible but nonetheless requiring careful balance in all decisions made by the firm. The trick is to find the golden mean, the proper balance of social and economic objectives.

There are also two distinctly different implications for governments in these approaches to social responsibility. In the first approach, the implication is that social responsibility is the province of government. That is, it is up to the government to define what social responsibility is and to pass appropriate legislation to make firms act accordingly. This approach also suggests that business is socially irresponsive and there-fore must be regulated and monitored. The alternate approach suggests that business itself *can* be socially responsible and is capable of self-regulation. If management considers the wider social effects of its business decisions and acts prudently and appropriately, there will be no need for extensive government regulation or involvement in firms' decision making.

National Differences

The nature of the interactions among firms and their constituencies, and the value system of their countries, ultimately determine what constitutes social responsibility and social responsiveness. As was shown in Chapter 2, these patterns of interaction vary considerably from one country to another. In Yugoslavia, for example, workers' councils in each company are responsible for making management decisions, a pattern consistent with Yugoslavia's heavy socialist orientation in both government and society. In some Scandinavian countries the socialist orientation is also extensive and has resulted in considerable action with regard to social responsibility. It has also resulted in a significant amount of social accounting and reporting by firms in various forms, particularly in Sweden.

At the other extreme are countries with little socialist orientation or objectives. In one subset of this group, which includes a large number of less-developed countries, the business sector is tightly controlled by a few dominant families, resulting in a high concentration of wealth and power among a few, and widespread poverty everywhere else. As might be expected, there is comparatively less social responsibility or respon-siveness in these countries.

The other major subset of this nonsocialist group encompasses most of the highly industrialized countries. In the United States, there has historically been great emphasis on individualism, the work ethic, freedom of choice, and a form of economic Darwinism at both the individual and company level. Based on the notion of capitalism developed by Adam Smith, even with individuals pursuing their own selfish self-interest, society as a whole benefits from the mysterious working of an invisible hand. It has become clear, however, that even in the United States there remain economic and social inequities in need of redress. This perception—found to an even greater extent in Europe, along with a growing degree of social orientation—is most evident in France, Italy, and the United Kingdom. It has also been accompanied by growing participation of workers in management decision making. This process, which in Europe is called *co-determination*, has taken various forms, including significant representation from the rank and file workers on the company boards of directors. Already a law in Germany, codetermination is likely to become law throughout Europe in this decade.[2]

Thus to varying degrees in the major countries throughout the world, social responsibility and responsiveness are increasingly important.

Accounting Implications

Regardless of the environment in which a company operates, some interaction must take place between the company and its constituencies. To a traditionalist, a company's major constituents are its shareholders; hence the need and practice of communicating financial information by way of the classic annual report. However, a firm has a much wider array of constituents, including employees, creditors, suppliers, customers, governmental authorities, and even the general public.

Social responsibility's broadest accounting implication is twofold. First, the firm has an obligation to report on its activities to all its constituencies. Second, all these constituencies have a right to obtain information from the company. In a narrower sense, a distinction can be drawn between a *legal* right and a *social* right. At the present time, most firms accept the legal obligation to report to those constituencies that have a legal right to obtain information—although the acceptance is often grudging and reluctant. For example, firms supply financial information to shareholders and tax authorities, environmental information

---

[2]For more information on codetermination, see K. H. Biedenkopf, *Mitbestimmung Im Unternehmen Deutscher Bundestag,* 6, Wahlperiode, VI/334, 1970; Robert Kuhne, *Co-determination in Business: Workers' Representatives in the Boardroom* (New York: Praeger, 1980); and Alfred L. Thimm, "Decision Making at Volkswagen: 1972–1977," *Columbia Journal of World Business,* Vol. 11, Spring 1976, pp. 94–103.

to environmental agencies, and employment information to government employment agencies.

There is far less acceptance of the obligation to supply information to constituents who do not have a legal right to obtain it, unless the firms believe it to be in their own best interest to do so. For example, firms supply financial information to potential creditors or customers, or they supply information on company policies to academicians. Thus while the legal right to know does not pertain exclusively to ownership or government power, it remains for most firms a fundamental criteria or precondition. However, in defense of companies' reluctance to provide all information requested by all constituencies, certain important and pragmatic considerations must be taken into account. These include the identifiability of the constituency itself, the kinds and amount of information requested, the legitimacy of the need for the information requested, the cost and benefit of generating and furnishing the information, and the sensitivity of the information.

Identifying Constituencies

Identifying the constituency itself is not always an easy task, particularly as one moves away from groups that interact closely and frequently with the firm to those that do not. In the former group are government authorities, shareholders, employees, and the firm's principal creditors, suppliers, and customers. In a second group are *potential* investors, creditors, suppliers, customers, and so on. In a third group are members of the general public not realistically included in any of the other groups.

The major accounting implications of the identifiability of the group are the firm's ability to know and understand (1) the information needs of the requesting group, (2) the likelihood of the same or similar information being requested by members of other groups, and (3) the ease of communicating information to the group.

For example, it is relatively easy for a firm to furnish information to tax authorities because it is a readily identifiable group. The firm knows specifically what information the group wants and in what format, and the dissemination of the information is fairly straightforward and direct: the company files a tax report with the appropriate agency. A similar situation exists between the firm and its shareholders in terms of the identifiability of the group, its information desires, and the ease of communication—this time by means of the annual report to, and an annual meeting with, the shareholders.

However, no similar situation exists in the case of the general public. Various groups of the general public that need or want information are more difficult to identify, even assuming that a firm wants to identify them. In addition, the information each subgroup wants may be different, and ultimately there remains the problem of how to get the information to those who request it. At the extreme, one could visualize thousands upon thousands of persons individually being sent whatever information each requested. For all these reasons, the identifiability of information-seeking groups is an important consideration with definite accounting implications.

What Information to Supply

The *specificity* of information requested also has considerable accounting implications. A specific, concise request is easier to satisfy than a broad, vague request. For example, details of a company's profits for the past ten years are easier to furnish than an assessment of the firm's "impact" on a community for the same period. An added complication is that the requester's definition of impact may not be the same as the firm's. Of related importance is the accessibility of the information. Even though the request may be very specific, the information itself may not be available, or be available only at considerable expense. In terms of the impact example above, some of the information may be generated with considerable effort, but many of the *indirect* impacts may not be ascertainable with any validity no matter how much time and effort is expended.

The requester's *need* for information is another important consideration. In this sense, a request based on a passing curiosity should be treated differently from a genuine interest with an attendant legitimate need. Admittedly, this leaves open the question of who is to determine the legitimacy of the need, but more often than not, this is not a problem. A related issue pertains to the *urgency* of the request. Certain information is more important in terms of its timeliness than others. For example, the timeliness of response in a legal suit is critical whereas a request for information for a more general purpose is less urgent.

How Much Will It Cost?

Another consideration is *cost*. Firms are not in business to supply information but to make and sell products or services at a profit, and to provide employment. Supplying information to everyone who asks for it can in itself create jobs if more accountants are hired to generate the information and answer the requests. However, excessive deployment of a company's scarce resources for this purpose could have negative and conceivably ruinous effects on the company, causing far greater negative employment effects in terms of firings or lay-offs.

For example, the extensive reporting requirements imposed on all firms by the U.S. government may cost a small firm as much as $30,000 per year.[3] One might well argue that the social benefit derived from the information is low compared to its cost. But could the cost be a contributing factor to the lower level of profitability of small businesses and to their higher level of bankruptcy? What would happen if these firms had to generate and supply even more information to their constituencies? However it could also be argued that firms are not divulging information which could be furnished with relatively little additional cost or effort for the benefit of their constituencies. Company sales and profit forecasts are a classic example of the latter, as are financial reports presented in a more segmented fashion than customarily shown in annual reports.

How to Handle Sensitive Information

The final problem of providing information concerns the sensitivity of the information requested, particularly from the standpoint of competition. In a society based on individual ownership and competition, secrecy has distinct advantages and is often considered both an individual right and necessary condition. An example is the legal protection of ideas and products by patents. Competitors are eager to obtain all kinds of information about a firm's current activities and future plans. Most countries recognize the right and need of a company to withhold certain competitively sensitive information. Such rights, however, do not exist for information critical to national defense, security, or (in some countries) economic planning. Nor should they exist when firms withhold information about activities that cause injury to someone. Once again, the problematic question is, *who* is to determine the degree of sensitivity of the information.

Measurement Problems

Even if this Gordian knot of problems could be untied, accountants would face yet another battery of problems having to do with social accounting. Not the least is how can—and should—one measure and evaluate a whole series of events and impacts which historically have not been accounted for at all.

Economic and social events are so interrelated and complex that it is extremely difficult to precisely relate one to the other, particularly given the limits of accounting as a tool when applied to social issues and events. Currently, social accounting probably raises more questions than it answers—and perhaps creates more problems than it solves. But growing worldwide concern clearly suggests that the interrelationship of business and social activity will continue to be scrutinized and that some

---

[3]Commission on Federal Paperwork, *Final Report* (Washington: Government Printing Office, 3 October 1977), p. 66.

new system of measurement and analysis will be needed. This implies a movement away from the traditional "wealth" accounting to "welfare" accounting,[4] and the need for accountants to prepare for and assist in this transaction.

SEGMENTED REPORTING

As was described in Chapter 9 segmented reporting is currently—and will continue to be for the future—a topic of interest in international accounting. With the continued expansion and complexity of international business, the clamor for greater segmentation will undoubtedly increase. The reasons are evident: Perhaps the most significant is that multinational firms operate in many countries but do not disclose the extent of these operations or their impact on a *particular* country. They either make little mention of international results or they provide only worldwide, consolidated information. Yet employees, customers, creditors, and host governments are increasingly interested in the multinationals' activities in their country vis-à-vis those in other countries. Their concerns encompass comparative sales, prices, employment, wages, benefits, research and development activities, profits, and taxes. As was pointed out in Chapter 9, such information is not currently being made available by most multinational firms.

However, several major efforts are underway to require considerably more segmented reports. From an accountant's perspective, compliance with this trend will not be inordinately difficult, since most of the information is already contained within existing information systems. However, it would clearly increase the size of corporate reports. More importantly, it would probably pose some problems for a firm's relationships with similar constituents in different countries. For example, the company's employees in Brazil might demand the same benefits as their counterparts in Germany.

Problems in Drawing Segments

Another concern is the way in which the geographic segments themselves are drawn. A financial analyst cannot readily determine the financial risks to which a company's operations are exposed because most geographic segments contain countries with considerably different degrees of political and economic stability. Thus, even in segmented reports, the financial risks are not readily discernible. For example, a

[4]For more details see Edmond Marques "The Firm: Its Impact on Society; Introducing Societal Accounting," a paper presented at the Georgia World Congress Institute's conference on "Exploring the Brave New Worlds of Accounting," Atlanta, Georgia, 8 September 1978.

firm may disclose the financial results from its operations in Germany, Italy, Iran, and Saudi Arabia in a segment entitled Europe and the Middle East. The economic and political stability in Germany is different from that in Italy, and vastly different from that in Iran. While it is unlikely that firms will have to disclose all financial information on a country-by-country basis, risk analysis would be vastly improved by segmented reporting based on areas with similar degrees of economic and political stability.

Many problems would still remain. Who would determine the degree of risk in each country? Would all companies reach similar risk assessments? What happens when a country moves from a low-risk to high-risk category in terms of segment comparability to previous years? In sum, there is still a lot of work to be done by accountants in this area.

PUBLISHING CORPORATE FORECASTS

No accounting textbook would be complete without a discussion of the issue of publishing corporate forecasts. The basic arguments against publishing company forecasts continue to center on problems associated with accuracy and accountability, auditing difficulties, and possible competitive effects.[5]

Can a Forecast Be Accurate?

The accuracy issue is a valid one: forecasting the future is an extremely difficult and imprecise art. Obviously, however, this does not dissuade companies from making internal forecasts. With proper sensitivity analysis and adequate cautionary provisions, there is little reason to believe that intelligent users of corporate forecasts would interpret or use them any differently than intelligent managers. In addition, it can be argued that a forecast prepared by the company itself should be more accurate than those made by someone else.

Who Is Accountable for the Forecast?

The accountability argument appears to be less valid than the accuracy argument. The question here is will employees, creditors, stockholders,

[5]See for example, R. Barefield and E. Comiskey, "The Accuracy of Forecasts of Earnings Per Share," *Journal of Business Research*, July 1975, pp. 241–251; B. Basi, K. Carey, and R. Twark, "A Comparison of the Accuracy of Corporate and Securities Analysts' Forecasts of Earnings," *The Accounting Review*, April 1976, pp. 244–254; R. Copeland and R. Marioni, "Executives Forecasts of EPS Versus Forecasts of Naive Models," *Journal of Business*, October 1972, pp. 497–512; Financial Executives Institute, "How Accurate Are Forecasts?" *Financial Executive*, March 1973; B. L. Jaggi, "Further Evidence of the Accuracy of Management Forecasts vis-à-vis Analyst's Forecasts," *The Accounting Review*, January 1980, pp. 96–101.

and others with vested interest in the firm hold management account-able for meeting the forecast. On one hand, one might argue that management *should* be held accountable. However, assuming the forecast properly recognizes various contingencies, management should not be held accountable if the plans are not achieved because unfavorable events forecasted actually do occur.

How Is a Forecast Audited?

The above arguments apply also to accountability from the external auditor's perspective. The difficulty in auditing forecasts remains a valid but not an insurmountable problem.

A company's external auditors are typically well-versed and knowledgeable about the company and its industry, and this knowledge places them in a reasonable position to assess the company's forecast and its underlying assumptions. Admittedly, there may need to be a separate auditor's opinion to stress the cautionary nature of the forecast and perhaps to assess its reasonableness and comprehensiveness. This second kind of opinion would not be that difficult to initiate or that complicated to understand. Already auditors in many countries, *including* the United States, are coping with price-level-adjusted statements, which are inherently imprecise, and with some corporate reports that include management forecasts.

Do Forecasts Reveal Competitive Information?

The competition issue revolves around the likelihood of competitors gleaning important information about the company's future activities. First, while this might be true if information were divulged about which competitors were not already aware, given the amount of existing industrial espionage and cross-hiring of executives, particularly in the United States, it is not too likely. Second, a forecast would have to be very specific and very detailed to be of real use to a competitor, which is seldom the case. And third, it could be argued that if *all* companies had to publish their forecasts, the basic competitive position would not change—that is, they would all have each other's forecasts.

Forecasting Problems for Multinationals

If preparing a company forecast for a domestic company is fraught with difficulties and dangers, it is much worse for a multinational firm, which has to forecast changing conditions in many different countries for many different product lines. In addition, the firm must forecast changes in exchange rates and the ways in which changes in one of its markets affect its operations in other markets. Thus preparing a forecast is a lot more difficult and hazardous for a multinational than for a domestic company.

Once again, however, the inherent risks and difficulties do not dissuade companies from preparing such forecasts for internal management purposes. Possibly, requiring publication of forecasts would improve the forecasting process and result in better management!

Desirability of Forecast Publication

Certainly from an investor's or creditor's standpoint, access to company forecasts is desirable. By and large, a company's major creditors are already able to get such information directly from the company. So why should not this information be available to investors, particularly those in the United States, which is supposedly investor oriented? In addition, governments could use such forecasts for economic planning. Finally, in a world in which the right to know is increasingly being demanded, it would appear that the publishing of company forecasts is a legitimate issue. Accountants can already provide most of the information that would be required. What remains is the development of the best procedures for reporting it.

However, a prudent conclusion would be that the future of forecasting is more cloudy than clear. Although more groups are warming to the idea, the majority still appears cold to the prospect. And, as is the case for most changes in accounting practice, until sufficient pressure is brought to bear on the issue, the likelihood of change is rather small. However, as forecasting becomes less of an art and more of a science, and as pressures for external financing become greater, one can predict more disclosure of corporate forecasts. It is clearly an area where accounting has considerable room and opportunity to grow.

BALANCE OF PAYMENTS ACCOUNTING

As international trade and investment flows continue to increase, national governments will become more concerned with balance of payments accounting and impacts. In simplest terms, a country's balance of payments records the net flow of funds into and out of a country. In one sense, a country's balance of payments is similar to a company's income statement in that a *deficit* in the balance of payments indicates more funds flowing out than in and, in general, a deteriorating competitive position. Similarly, one can draw parallels between exports and sales (revenues) and imports and purchases (expenses). There are of course many interesting differences between balance of payments accounting and traditional corporate financial accounting. In U.S. balance of payments accounting, for example, debits are on the right and credits are on the left, virtually all accounts are estimated, and technically the balance of payments *always* balances, making it more like a company's balance sheet than its income statement.

The increasing concern of governments about their balance of payments does not pertain to differences from an accounting standpoint, but there are accounting implications of this increased government concern. Many governments are now requesting or requiring balance of payments reports and projections for company operations. For example, what were or will be the net balance of payments effects of a company's yearly operations? In countries such as the Philippines, this kind of information is used as part of an assessment procedure in deciding to accept or reject a company's request to invest in the country. For example, proposed investments that will generate a balance of payments surplus are given priority over those that will generate a deficit. Related information has also been used to enact legislation or otherwise control firms' activities which worsen a country's balance of payments position, such as sending dividends out of the country or paying out funds for intracorporate R&D expense allocations. Examples of some possible balance of payments effects of a company's activities are listed in Table 14–1. In the future it appears that more accountants—and certainly those working for multinational enterprises—will have to be familiar

TABLE 14–1. Some Balance of Payments Effects of Multinational Firms' Activities

DONOR COUNTRY*		HOST COUNTRY†	
ACTIVITY	BALANCE OF PAYMENTS EFFECT	ACTIVITY	BALANCE OF PAYMENTS EFFECT
Capital investment outflow	Negative	Capital investment inflow	Positive
Export of equipment or material to affiliated or unaffiliated buyers	Positive	Import of equipment and material from affiliates or nonaffiliates	Negative
Sale of technology, patents, or trademarks via license or fee	Positive	Purchase of technology, patents, or trademarks via license or fee	Negative
Sale of management services or allocation of other headquarters overhead	Positive	Purchase of management services or being billed for headquarters overhead	Negative
Imports of material, parts, or finished products	Negative	Export of material, parts, or finished goods	Positive
Receipt of dividends from subsidiaries	Positive	Payment of dividends to parent or affiliates	Negative

*Donor country refers to the country in which the firm making the investment is headquartered.
†Host country refers to the country that *receives* the investment.

with balance of payments accounting and the impact of their company's operations on the country's balance of payments.

NATIONALIZATION AND EXPROPRIATION

One of the greatest risks a multinational faces is a government takeover of its operations and assets, either by nationalization of the industry or by expropriation of the specific company or subsidiary. Either act harms the multinational, directly and indirectly. Indirectly, the takeover disrupts the firm's operations and causes *opportunity* losses—the loss of future profits and opportunities because the multinational is no longer in business there. Such takeovers also result in direct financial losses if the government does not pay adequate compensation for the assets taken over.

The Accountant's Role

While accountants can do little to prevent such takeovers, they can and do play an important role in determining the amount of compensation that *should* be claimed by the multinational. By international law, governments are supposed to pay fair compensation to companies whose assets have been taken over. In reality, however, most governments have not paid fair compensation, and even where compensation has been paid, most companies have received considerably less than book value. This then raises the question of what role accountants can play? The answer lies in investment insurance claims. U.S.-based multinationals can insure their investments against losses due to expropriation and nationalization. The major insurer is the Overseas Private Investment Corporation (OPIC), an agency of the U.S. government. The basic reimbursement is the value of the investment minus whatever the foreign government pays to the firm in the way of compensation. Because most foreign governments pay little if any compensation, the account's role is to estimate the value of the foreign investment for OPIC coverage and reimbursement purposes.

Determining Value

Historically, OPIC has considered the value of the foreign investment to be essentially book value. In recent years, however, several companies have successfully argued that the real and appropriate value of the investment loss should be a going concern value. This procedure involves determining and estimating the opportunity losses mentioned above, in addition to the book value losses. Estimations are necessary because in most cases there is no true stock market share price available to act as a proxy for the going concern value of the operation. Thus, it is up to the accountants to arrive at an estimate of the going concern value. This process takes most accountants into largely uncharted waters. It is an area where some innovative and creative accounting work can be done. With rising nationalism and general distrust of multinationals around the world, government takeovers are likely to continue, further underscoring the need for accountants to prepare for this kind of work.

ACCOUNTING'S ROLE IN ECONOMIC DEVELOPMENT

In the vast span of human history, only recently has accounting been recognized as important to economic development. Accounting plays several roles in this process, ranging from systematization to analysis. Among its many attributes, accounting requires and forces the clarification, measurement, categorization, and storage of information related to economic activity. It has been argued that this systematization is both a precondition and a continuing condition for economic development at both micro and macro levels. Accounting's analytical aspects, and to perhaps a lesser extent its reporting aspects, are also essential to the decisions mandated by economic development. An example would be the accounting role in providing information to governments for economic planning and monitoring. Thus, accounting has an integral relationship with economic development that the twentieth century world has really just begun to understand and appreciate.

Recent Examples

Many developing countries have explicitly recognized its importance and have sought to develop an accounting system which facilitates economic development yet remains consistent with their particular environments, as was described with regard to Egypt in Chapter 2. Egypt's dual accounting system reflects its dual objectives. Most of the industrial sector and economic growth are the direct responsibility of large government-owned companies. For planning and directing economic growth, the government developed and installed a complex, comprehensive, uniform accounting system for these firms. The management and accounting sophistication required by this complex system in terms of personnel was also available in these firms. At the same time, the government recognized that the rest of the economic sector consisted of thousands of very small enterprises—few of which had the capability to adopt the complex accounting system. Therefore, the government decided to exempt these firms from the new system and, in essence, to let them continue with the old system.

A similar approach was instituted by Peru in the 1970s.[6] Following the military takeover in 1968, the Revolutionary Government of the Armed Forces began to effect broad social and economic changes, including the nationalization of key industries. While the economy of Peru today is a mixture of state-owned, privately owned, and collectively owned enterprises, the state's role has continued to grow. Two principal factors led to significant government influence in the accounting sector: (1) the increased need for uniform accounting data by government users and regulators, and (2) a relatively weak and unsophisticated accounting profession. In 1973 a government agency called Comision Nacional Supervisora de Empresas y Valores (CNSEV) released a resolution setting forth accounting requirements for large-scale enterprises in five areas:

1. The general requirements for presentation and auditing of statements.
2. The disclosure requirements in the financial statements.
3. The notes to the financial statements.
4. Supplementary information and the contents of the auditors reports.
5. The auditing requirements.

The preamble to the resolution highlighted the importance of the new guidelines:

> Financial statements prepared in accordance with uniform rules and appropriately examined constitute a basic element for the analysis of the financial situation and the results of operations of an enterprise and an indispensable source for the global study of important sections of the national economy. At the same time such statements contribute fundamentally to aid in judgment on decisions by banks, financial institutions, and others as to the operations they may enter into, as well as to provide adequate information to investors. . . .[7]

Concurrent with CNSEV proposals and under the direction of the Ministry of Economy and Finance, a general accounting plan called "Plan Contable General" was developed. This is a uniform system of accounting for enterprises and was designed with three things in mind: managerial needs, macroeconomic needs, and the customs that apply to

---

[6]See Lee Radebaugh, "Environmental Factors Influencing the Development of Accounting Objectives, Standards, and Practices in Peru," *International Journal of Accounting,* Fall 1975, pp. 39–56.
[7]See Arthur Andersen & Co. (Peru), "Regulations for Reporting on Financial Statements in Peru," February 1973, p. 1.

accounting in Peru. It was intended that the plan would form a base of reliable information on which the national accounts (macro statistics) could be prepared, as well as provide useful information for managers, shareholders, workers, creditors, and others. Adherence to the plan is required for all firms with gross revenues in excess of $1.25 million, approximately 2 percent of the 60,000 to 70,000 firms in Peru. All other firms continue to operate under the minimum accounting rules established in the Company Law in 1966. Once again, the uniqueness and duality of an economy dictated the uniqueness and duality of the accounting system.

There is also a recognition by international accountants that accounting can be transferred or adapted from one country to another in order to speed up the recipient country's accounting and economic development. It is clearly a growing responsibility for accountants to design and devise ways to make better use of accounting as both a technology and a tool for economic development.

CLOSING THE BOOKS

We hope that you have enjoyed learning something about the international accounting, and that what you have learned will be of some use to you, directly or indirectly, tangibly or intangibly, sooner or later. Like the path to harmonization, the path to becoming an international accountant or even an internationalized accountant is not quick or easy. No international accounting textbook or course is sufficient; firsthand experiences are also required before a true understanding can be achieved. It is clear that more and more accountants worldwide will have such opportunities to confront in the future, and we hope that our book will provide a good foundation for the building of international accounting understanding and personal/professional development.

STUDY QUESTIONS

14-1.   Discuss the possible implications of the worldwide trend toward more macro-oriented accounting systems on the accounting systems of countries with an independent orientation such as the United States or the United Kingdom.

14-2.   Discuss the major accounting implications and problems posed by social responsibility accounting.

14-3.   Most multinational enterprises which provide segmented reports draw their segments on a broad geographic basis. Discuss why this method may not be particularly useful for investors or creditors interested in the financial risk of the company involved. How might the segments be redrawn to provide more useful information? What new accounting problems might result from your suggestions?

14–4. What are the major costs and benefits, from a multinational firm's perspective, of providing the kinds of segmented information described in question 3?

14–5. Discuss the major reasons for and against firms' publishing their corporate forecasts.

14–6. Discuss the importance of accounting in terms of its role in facilitating or impeding economic development.

14–7. If accounting can be considered a kind of technology, what would be some of the problems of attempting to transfer this technology from one country to another?

14–8. If you were given the responsibility for designing an accounting system for a newly independent developing country, what major factors would you consider in deciding which country's accounting system to model yours after?

14–9. Of all the topics mentioned in this chapter as likely to be important in the future, which do you believe are the ones needing the most attention quickly? Why?

14–10. Now that you have read this book and increased your knowledge about international accounting, what other steps could you take to further enhance your understanding?

Bibliography

Chapter 2

Abu-Jbarah, Hani Mahmoud. "A Subentity Basis for Financial Reporting by Multinational Firms: A Cluster Analysis Approach." Unpublished Ph.D. Dissertation, University of Wisconsin, 1972.

Alhashim, Dhia D., and S. Paul Garner. "Postulates for Localized Uniformity in Accounting." *Abacus*, June 1973, pp. 62–72.

American Accounting Association. "Report of the American Accounting Association Committee on International Accounting, 1974–75." *Accounting Review*, Supplement 1976, pp. 70–196.

American Institute of Certified Public Accountants. *Professional Accounting in 30 Countries*. New York: AICPA, 1975.

Bedford, Norton M., and Jacques P. Gautier. "An International Analytical Comparison of the Structure and Content of Annual Reports in the European Economic Community, Switzerland and the United States." *International Journal of Accounting*, Spring 1974, pp. 1–44.

Beeny, J. H. *European Financial Reporting—France*. London: Institute of Chartered Accountants in England and Wales, 1976.

―――. *European Financial Reporting—West Germany*. London: Institute of Chartered Accountants in England and Wales, 1976.

Benston, George J. "Public (U.S.) Compared to Private (U.K.) Regulation of Corporate Financial Disclosure," *Accounting Review*, July 1976, pp. 483–498.

Bevis, Herman W. *Corporate Financial Reporting in a Competitive Economy*. New York: Macmillan, 1965.

Burgert, A. "Common Features and Difference Between Commercial and Tax Balance Sheets in the Netherlands." *Journal UEC*, v. 8.

Business Europe. "European Mergers: Playing Binationality for All That It's Worth," 2 July 1976, pp. 211–212; "Italian Firms Turn to Independent Auditing," 10 October 1976, p. 327.

Campbell, Robert W. *Accounting in Soviet Planning and Management.* Cambridge, Mass.: Harvard University Press, 1963.

Chastney, John G. "On to International Accounting." *Accountancy*, July 1976, pp. 76–80.

Choi, Frederick D. S., and Gerhard G. Mueller. *An Introduction to Multinational Accounting.* Englewood Cliffs, N.J.: Prentice-Hall, 1978, chapter 2.

Clapp, Charles L. "National Variations in Accounting Principles and Practices." *International Journal of Accounting*, Fall 1967, pp. 29–42.

Crum, William F. "The European Public Accountant." *Management Accountant* (NAA), March 1975, pp. 41–44.

Davidson, David. "Fiscal Influences on Financial Reporting." *The Accountant*, 2 August 1973, p. 150.

Davidson, Sidney, and John M. Kohlmeier. "A Measure of the Impact of Some Foreign Accounting Principles." *International Journal of Accounting*, Fall 1967, pp. 183–212.

DeVoe, Raymond F. Jr. "Under the Southern Cross: The Role of Monetary Adjustment in Brazil's Economic Miracle." *Financial Analysts Journal*, September/October 1974, pp. 32–41.

Dietrich, Wilhelm. "The European Parliament Discusses the EEC Commission's Directive Relating to the Right of Professional Accountants to Establish a Practice and Render Services Freely." *Journal UEC*, January 1972, pp. 14–17.

The Economist (London), Intelligence Unit. "In Depth: Financial Disclosure in Europe—Differences in Accountancy Plague Harmonization Efforts." *Multinational Business*, May 1972, pp. 35–43.

Enthoven, Adolf J. H. *Accountancy and Economic Development Policy.* North Holland, 1973.

European Federation of Financial Analysts Societies (EFFAS). *Corporate Reporting in Europe*, Paris 1970.

Gail, Wilfred. "Common Features of and Difference Between Commercial Balance Sheets for Taxation Purposes in the Federal Republic of Germany." *Journal UEC*, v. 8.

Gimpel, Bruno. "The Accounting Profession in Italy." *Arthur Andersen Chronicle*, April 1956, p. 124.

Gorelik, George. "Notes on the Development and Problems of Soviet Uniform Accounting." *The International Journal of Accounting*, Fall 1973, pp. 135–148.

———. "Soviet Accounting, Planning and Control." *Abacus*, June 1974, pp. 13–25.

Gray, S. J. *EEC Accounting and Reporting: A Comparative Guide to Legal Requirements.* International Centre for Research in Accounting, 1976.

Hatfield, H. R. "Some Variations in Accounting Practice in England, France, Germany and the United States." *Journal of Accounting Research*, Autumn 1966, pp. 169–182.

Hendriksen, Eldon S. *Accounting Theory*, rev. ed. Homewood, Ill.: Richard D. Irwin, 1970, 643 pp. See especially Chapter 1, The Methodology of Accounting Theory.

Hole, R.C., and M.A. Alkier. "German Financial Statements." *Management Accounting*, July 1974, pp. 28–34.

Institute of Chartered Accountants in England and Wales (ICAEW). *Accounting Principles and Practices in European Countries*. 1972.

Jaggi, B. L. "The Impact of the Cultural Environment on Financial Disclosures." *International Journal of Accounting*, Spring 1975.

Jaruga, Alicja A. "Recent Developments in Polish Accounting: An International Transaction Emphasis." *The International Journal of Accounting Education and Research*, Fall 1974, p. 1.

Kafer, Karl. "European National Uniform Charts of Accounts." *International Journal of Accounting*, Fall 1965, pp. 67–83.

———. *Theory of Accounts in Double Entry Bookkeeping*. Monograph 2, Center for International Education and Research in Accounting, University of Illinois, 1966.

Kaminski, Horst. "Recommendations of the EEC Commission for the Fourth Directive on the Harmonization of Accounting Regulations." *Journal UEC*, April 1972, pp. 122–130.

Kramer, Richard L. "Status Report on Auditing in the European Community." Auditing Symposium III, University of Kansas, 13–14 May 1976 (mimeographed).

Lafferty, Michael. *Accounting in Europe*. Cambridge, England: Woodhead, Faulkner, 1975. Published in association with National Westminster Bank.

Louwers, Pieter C. "The European Public Accountant: A Different View." *Management Accounting* (U.S.), September 1975, pp. 43–46. (Response to an article on the same subject in the same journal by William S. Crum, March 1975, pp. 41–44, 54.)

Marrian, Ian, and Hugh Christie. "Italian Accounting Renaissance." *Accountant's Magazine*, October 1972, pp. 479–483.

McDougal, E. H. V. "Professional Qualifications and the EEC." *Accountant's Magazine*, October 1972, pp. 479–483.

McLean, Alasdair D. *Business and Accounting in Europe*. Westmead, England: Saxon House, 1973.

———. "Group Accounts in the EEC: A Look at Some of the Proposals of the Draft Seventh Directive," *Accountant's Magazine*, June 1976, pp. 211–212.

———. "Societas Europea—A Consideration of the Proposals for the European Company." *Accountant's Magazine*, December 1971, pp. 631–640.

Mills, Robert H., and Abbott L. Brown. "Soviet Economic Developments and Accounting." *Journal of Accountancy*, June 1966, pp. 40–46.

Morris, Richard. *Corporate Standards and the Fourth Directive* (Research Committee Occasional Paper No. 2). London: Institute of Chartered Accountants in England and Wales, 1974, 107 pp.

Mueller, Gerhard G. "Academic Research in International Accounting." *International Journal of Accounting*, Fall 1970, pp. 67–81.

———. "Accounting Principles Generally Accepted in the United States versus Those Generally Accepted Elsewhere." *International Journal of Accounting*, Spring 1968, pp. 91 ff.

———. "International Experience with Uniform Accounting." *Law and Contemporary Problems*, Autumn 1965, pp. 850–873.

Murphy, Mary E. "Comparative Professional Accountancy—South America." *Accounting Review*, July 1960, pp. 471–475.

———. "The International Practice of Public Accounting." *Accountancy*, June 1962, pp. 487–491.

Oldham, K. M. *Accounting Systems and Practice in Europe*. Farnsborough, Hampshire, England: Gower, 1975.

Parker, R. H. "Concepts of Consolidation in the EEC." *Accountancy*, February 1977, pp. 72–75.

Perridon, Louis. "Accounting Principles, An Academic Opinion." *Journal UEC*, October 1974, pp. 213–224.

Price Waterhouse & Co. *Doing Business In . . .* (Denmark, France, Germany, Italy, Republic of Ireland, Grand Duchy of Luxembourg, Netherlands, United Kingdom). New York: Price Waterhouse, most recent edition, various paginations.

———. *EEC Bulletin No. 23*. Brussels: Price Waterhouse, May 1976, pp. 1–4.

———. (U.S.A.). *Guide for the Reader of Foreign Financial Statements*, rev. ed. New York: Price Waterhouse, 1975.

———. International. *A Survey in 46 Countries: Accounting Principles and Reporting Practices* (text in English, French, German, Spanish). London: Price Waterhouse, 1975, 264 pp. plus index.

Radebaugh, Lee H. "Environmental Factors Influencing the Development of Accounting Objectives, Standards, and Practices in Peru." *International Journal of Accounting*, Fall 1975, pp. 39–56.

Seidler, L. J. "A Comparison of the Social and Economic Status of the Accountancy Profession in the United States and the United Kingdom." *The Accountants' Magazine* (Scotland), September 1969.

Swoboda, Peter. "Comparison of Consolidated Financial Statements in the United States and West Germany." *International Journal of Accounting*, Spring 1966, pp. 9–24.

Sy Ap, Washington. "Professional Practice in Developing Economies." *Journal of Accountancy*, January 1967, pp. 41–45.

Tyra, Anita I. "Financial Disclosure Patterns in Four European Countries." *International Journal of Accounting*, Spring 1970, pp. 89–99.

Venu, S. "Public Enterprise Profits in Socialist Economies—A Survey of Concepts and Their Application." *Chartered Accountant* India, May 1975, p. 523.

Volpi, Edoardo. "Accounting and Financial Reporting Aspects of the EEC Company Law Harmonization Program and the Proposed European Company Structure." *Proceedings,* Accounting and Finance in Europe Conference, London: The City University, Graduate Business Center, 1976, pp. 3–23.

Watts, Tom. "Company Accounts in Europe: Revising the Fourth Directive." *Accountant,* 9 May 1974, pp. 590–594.

Wilkinson, Theodore. "United States Accounting as Viewed by Accountants of Other Countries." *International Journal of Accounting,* Fall 1965, pp. 3–14.

Yang, J. M. "Accounting in a Free Economy." *Accounting Review,* July 1959, pp. 442–451.

Zeff, Steven A. *Foreign Accounting Principles in Five Countries: A History and an Analysis of Trends.* Champaign, Ill.: Stipes Publishing, 1971.

Chapter 3

Accountants International Study Group (AISG). *Reporting by Diversified Companies,* 1972.

———. *Consolidated Financial Statements.* 1973.

———. *International Financial Reporting,* 1975.

Choi, Frederick D. S. "Global Finance and Accounting Uniformity in the EEC." *Michigan Business Review,* September 1976, pp. 24–27.

Choi, Frederick D. S., and Gerhard G. Mueller. *An Introduction to Multinational Accounting.* Englewood Cliffs, N.J.: Prentice-Hall, 1978, chapter 6.

Commission of the European Communities. *Amended Proposal for a Council Regulation on the Statute for European Companies.* Luxembourg, 1975.

———. *Amended Proposal for a Fourth Council Directive for Coordination of National Legislation Regarding the Annual Accounts of Limited Liability Companies.* Brussels, 1974.

———. *Proposal for a Seventh Directive Concerning Group Accounts.* Brussels, 1976.

Cummings, J. P. "Forging International Accounting Standards." *Tax Executive,* July 1975, pp. 352–359.

European Federation of Financial Analysts Societies (EFFAS), Permanent Commission on Standardization. *Report on Standardization Project,* 1967

Hauworth, William P. "Problems in the Development of Worldwide Accounting Standards." *The International Journal of Accounting,* Fall 1973, pp. 23–34.

International Accounting Standards Committee (IASC). International Accounting Standard No. 3, *Consolidated Financial Statements.* 1976.

————. International Accounting Standard No. 6, *Accounting Responses to Changing Prices.* 1977.

McMonnies, P. N. "EEC, UEC, ASC, IASC, IASG, AISG, ICCAP-IFAC, Old Uncle Tom Cobbleigh and All." *Accounting and Business Research*, Summer 1977, pp. 162–167.

Miller, J. Irvin. "Multinational Corporations: The U.N. Report." *Arthur Andersen Chronicle*, October 1975, pp. 4–12.

Stamp, Edward. "The EEC and European Accounting Standards: A Straitjacket or a Spur?" *Accountancy*, May 1973, pp. 9–16.

————. "Uniformity in International Accounting Standards: A Myth or a Possibility?" *Canadian Chartered Accountant*, December 1971, pp. 450–482.

Stein, Eric. *Harmonization of European Company Laws.* Indianapolis: Bobbs-Merrill, 1971.

Chapter 4

Brittain, Bruce. "Tests of Theories of Exchange Rate Determination." *Journal of Finance*, May 1977, pp. 519–529.

Edwards, David. "Trading Room." *MBA*, June/July 1978, pp. 12–25.

Evans, Thomas G. *The Currency Carousel.* Princeton, N.J.: Dow Jones, 1977.

Field, Peter. "IMF Now: DeLarosiere's Troubled Institution." *Euromoney*, October 1978, pp. 14–29.

Frenkel, Jacob A., and Harry G. Johnson, ed. *The Economics of Exchange Rates.* Reading, Mass.: Addison-Wesley, 1978.

Goodman, Stephen H. "No Better Than the Toss of a Coin." *Euromoney*, December 1978, pp. 75–85.

Kubarych, Roger M. *Foreign Exchange Markets in the United States.* New York: Federal Reserve Bank of New York, August 1978.

Lederer, Walther. "How the U.S. Balance of Payments Affects the Dollar." *Euromoney*, March 1978, pp. 85–93.

Meadows, Edward. "How the Euromarket Fends Off Global Financial Disaster." *Fortune*, 24 September 1979, pp. 122–135.

Pinsky, Neil J., and Joseph G. Kvasnicka. "The European Monetary System." *Economic Perspectives*, November/December 1979, pp. 3–10.

"Playing the Rate Spread Between Continents." *Business Week*, 30 January 1978, p. 75.

Trueger, Arthur I., Charles Ramond, Bainsley Best, and Bruce Smith. "The Forecasters Reply." *Euromoney*, March 1979, pp. 96–101.

Wallich, Henry C. "What Makes Exchange Rates Move?" *Challenge*, July/August 1977, pp. 39–40.

Chapters 5 and 6

Accounting Standards Committee. Proposed Statement of Accounting Practice—ED21. *Foreign Currency Transactions*. London: ASC, 6 October 1977.

Cooper, Kerry, Donald R. Fraser, and R. Malcom Richards. "The Impact of SFAS #8 on Financial Management Practices." *Financial Executive*, June 1978, pp. 26–31.

Choi, Frederick D. S., and Gerhard G. Mueller. *An Introduction to Multinational Accounting*. Englewood Cliffs, N.J.: Prentice-Hall, 1978, chapter 3.

Dukes, Roland E. *An Empirical Investigation of the Effects of Statement of Financial Accounting Standards No. 8 On Security Return Behavior*. Stamford, Connecticut: Financial Accounting Standards Board, 1978.

Evans, Thomas G., William R. Folks Jr., and Michael Jilling. *The Impact of Statement of Accounting Standards No. 8 on the Foreign Exchange Risk Management Practices of American Multinationals: An Economic Impact Study*. Stamford. Connecticut: Financial Accounting Standards Board, 1978.

Financial Accounting Standards Board. Statement of Financial Accounting Standards No. 8. *Accounting for the Translation of Foreign Currency Transactions and Foreign Currency Financial Statements*. Stamford, Connecticut: FASB, October, 1975.

George, Abraham M. "Cash Flow versus Accounting Exposures to Currency Risk." *California Management Review*, Summer 1978, pp. 50–55.

Hepworth, Samuel R. *Reporting Foreign Operations*. Ann Arbor, Michigan: University of Michigan, 1956.

International Accounting Standards Committee. International Exposure Draft 11. *Accounting for Foreign Transactions and Translations of Foreign Financial Statements*. London: IASC, 1978.

Lorensen, Leonard. *Accounting Research Study No. 12*. "Reporting Foreign Operations of U.S. Companies in U.S. Dollars." New York: AICPA, 1972.

Parkinson, R. MacDonald. *Translation of Foreign Currencies: A Research Study*. Toronto, Canada: Canadian Institute of Certified Public Accountants, 1972.

Radebaugh, Lee H. "Accounting for Price-Level and Exchange-Rate Changes for U.S. International Firms: An Empirical Study." *Journal of International Business Studies*, Fall 1974, pp. 41–56.

Rodriguez, Rita. "FASB No. 8: What Has It Done For Us?" *Financial Analysts Journal*. March/April 1977, pp. 40–47.

Shank, John K. "FASB Statement 8 Resolved Foreign Currency Accounting—Or Did It?" *Financial Analysts Journal*, July/August 1976, pp. 55–61.

Shank, John K. and Shamis, Gary S. "Reporting Foreign Currency Adjustment: A Disclosure Perspective." *The Journal of Accountancy*, April 1979, pp. 56–65.

Walker, David. "Currency Translation: A Pragmatic Approach." *Accountant*, 9 March 1978, pp. 311–313.

Watt, George C., Richard M. Hammer and Marianne Burge. *Accounting for the Multinational Corporation.* New York: Financial Executives Research Foundation, 1977, chapter 6.

Chapter 7

Ankrom, Robert K. "Top Level Approach to the Foreign Exchange Problem." *Harvard Business Review*, July/August 1974, pp. 79–90.

Aubey, R. T., and R. H. Cramer. "Use of International Currency Cocktails in the Reduction of Exchange Rate Risk." *Journal of Economics and Business*, Winter 1977, pp. 128–134.

Battersby, Mark E. "Avoiding Risks by 'Parallel Lending.' " *Finance Magazine*, September/October 1975, pp. 56–57.

———. "Swapping Risk for Reward." *Financial Executive*, May 1975, pp. 22–25.

Bell, Geoffrey. "The New World of Floating Exchange Rates." *The Journal of Portfolio Management*, Spring 1977, pp. 25–28.

Choi, Frederick D. S., and Gerhard G. Mueller, *An Introduction to Multinational Accounting.* Englewood Cliffs, N.J.: Prentice-Hall 1978, chapters 5 and 7.

Cooper, John. "How Foreign Exchange Operations Can Go Wrong." *Euromoney*, May 1974, pp. 4–7.

Duerr, Michael G. *Protecting Corporate Assets Under Floating Currencies.* New York: Conference Board, 1975.

Dufey, Gunter. "Corporate Finance and Exchange Rate Variations." *Financial Management*, Summer 1972, pp. 51–57.

Eiteman and Stonehill. *Multinational Business Finance.* Reading, Mass.: Addison Wesley, rev. ed., 1979, Chapters 3 and 4.

Fieleke, Norman S. "The 1971 Flotation of the Mark and the Hedging of Commercial Transactions Between the United States and Germany." *Journal of International Business Studies*, Spring 1973, pp. 43–59.

Folks, William R. Jr. "Decision Analysis for Exchange Risk Management." *Financial Management*, Winter 1972, pp. 101–112.

———. "The Optimal Level of Forward Exchange Transactions." *Journal of Financial and Quantitative Analysis*, January 1973, pp. 105–110.

Fountain, John. "Premium Dollars." *Financial Analysts Journal*, March/April 1975, pp. 70–76.

Giddy, Ian H. "Why It Doesn't Pay to Make a Habit of Forward Hedging." *Euromoney*, December 1976, pp. 96–100.

Gull, Don S. "Composite Foreign Exchange Risk." *The Columbia Journal of World Business*, Fall 1975, pp. 51–69.

Hagemann, Helmut. "Anticipate Your Long-Term Foreign Exchange Risks." *Harvard Business Review*, March/April 1977, pp. 81–88.

Imai, Yutaka. "Exchange Rate Risk Protection in International Business." *Journal of Financial and Quantitative Analysis*, September 1975, pp. 447–456.

Jacque, Laurent. *Management of Foreign Exchange Risk*. Lexington, Mass.: Lexington Books, 1978.

Kohlhagen, Steven W. "Evidence on the Cost of Forward Cover in a Floating System." *Euromoney*, September 1975, pp. 138–141.

———. "Optimal Hedging Strategies for the Multinational Corporation Without Exchange Rate Projections." Paper presented at the 29 December 1975 meetings of the Academy of International Business, Dallas, Texas.

Leff, Nathaniel. "International Sourcing Strategy." *Columbia Journal of World Business*, Fall 1974, pp. 71–79.

Litaer, Bernard A. "Managing Risks in Foreign Exchange." *Harvard Business Review*, March/April 1970, pp. 127–138.

———. *Financial Management of Foreign Exchange*. Cambridge, Mass.: MIT Press, 1971.

Makin, John H. "The Portfolio Method of Managing Foreign Exchange Risk." *Euromoney*, August 1976, pp. 58–64.

Mattlin, Everett. "Playing the Currency Game." *Institutional Investor*, May 1976, pp. 83–96, 124.

Neukomm, Hans U. "Risk and Error Minimization in Foreign Exchange Trading." *Columbia Journal of World Business*, Winter 1975, pp. 77–85.

Prindl, Andreas. R. *Foreign Exchange Risk*. New York: Wiley, 1976.

———. "Guidelines for MNC Money Managers." *Harvard Business Review*, January/February 1976, pp. 73–80.

Ricks, David. "A Model for the Prediction of a Country's International Monetary Reserves: Theory and Application." Ph.D. Thesis. Bloomington: Indiana University, 1970.

Serfass, William D. Jr. "You Can't Outguess the Foreign Exchange Market." *Harvard Business Review*, March/April 1976, pp. 134–137.

Shapiro, Alan C., and David P. Rutenberg. "Managing Exchange Risks in a Floating World." *Financial Management*, Summer 1976, pp. 48–58.

Chapter 8

Accounting Standards Committee. "Statement of Standard Accounting Practice No. 16: Current Cost Accounting." *Accountancy*, April 1980, pp. 99–110.

———. "Guidance Notes on SSAP No. 16: Current Cost Accounting." *Accountancy*, May 1980, pp. 129–144.

Beresford, Dennis R., and John R. Klein. "International Accounting in the U.S. and U.K.—A Comparison." *Journal of Accountancy*, August 1979, pp. 75–78.

Brennan, W. John. "Accounting for Changing Prices: An International Perspective." *Accountant*, 28 April 1977, pp. 467–470.

Choi, Frederick D. S. "Foreign Inflation and Management Decisions." *Management Accounting*, June 1977, pp. 21–27.

————. "Price Level Adjustments and Foreign Currency Translation: Are They Compatible?" *International Journal of Accounting Education and Research*, Fall 1975, pp. 121–143.

Choi, Frederick, D. S., and Gerhard G. Mueller. *An Introduction to Multinational Accounting*. Englewood Cliffs, N.J.: Prentice-Hall, 1978, chapter 3.

Committee on International Accounting. "The 1973 Annual Report of N. V. Philips—The Netherlands." *Accounting Review*, Supplement 1976, pp. 107–133.

Financial Accounting Standards Board. Statement of Financial Accounting Standards No. 33; *Financial Reporting and Changing Prices*. Stamford, Conn.: FASB, 1979.

Hale, David. "Inflation Accounting and Public Policy Around the World." *Financial Analysts Journal*, September/October 1978, pp. 59–60.

International Accounting Standards Committee. "Treatment of Changing Prices in Financial Statements: A Summary of Proposals." *Accountancy*, May 1977, pp. 74–79.

Woo, John C. H. "Accounting for Inflation: Some International Models." *Management Accounting*, February 1978, pp. 37–43.

Chapter 9

Arpan, Jeffrey. "International Differences in Disclosure Practices." *Business Horizons*, October 1971, pp. 67–70.

Baker, H. Kent, Robert H. Chenhall, John A. Haslem, and Roger H. Juchau. "Disclosure of Material Information: A Cross-National Comparison." *International Journal of Accounting Education and Research*, Fall 1977, pp. 1–18.

Barrett, M. Edgar. "The Extent of Disclosure in Annual Reports of Large Companies in Seven Countries." *International Journal of Accounting Education and Research*, Spring 1977, pp. 1–25.

Benston, George J. "Public (U.S.) Compared to Private (U.K.) Regulation of Corporate Financial Disclosure." *Accounting Review*, July 1976, pp. 483–498.

Beresford, Dennis R., and Stewart A. Feldman. "Companies Increase Social Responsibility Disclosure." *Management Accounting*, March 1976, pp. 51–55.

Choi, Frederick D. S. "European Disclosure: The Competitive Disclosure Hypothesis." *Journal of International Business Studies*, Fall 1974, pp. 15–23.

Choi, Frederick, D. S., and Gerhard G. Mueller. *An Introduction to Multinational Accounting*. Englewood Cliffs, N.J.: Prentice-Hall, 1978, chapter 4.

Emmanuel, C. R., and S. J. Gray. "Segmental Disclosures by Multibusiness

Multinational Companies: A Proposal." *Accounting and Business Research,* Summer 1978, pp. 169–177.

Financial Accounting Standards Board, Statement of Financial Accounting Standards 14. *Financial Reporting for Segments of a Business Enterprise.* Stamford, Conn.: FASB, 1976.

Gray, S. J. "Segment Reporting and the EEC Multinationals." *Journal of Accounting Research,* Autumn 1978, pp. 242–253.

Hussey, Roger. *Who Reads Employee Reports?* St. Edmund Hall, England: Touche Ross, October 1979.

International Accounting Standards Committee. International Accounting Standard 1, *Disclosure of Accounting Policies.* London: IASC, 1975.

————. International Accounting Standard 5, *Information to Be Disclosed in Financial Statements.* London: IASC, 1977.

Linowes, David F. "The Accounting Profession and Social Progress." *Journal of Accountancy,* July 1973, pp. 32–40.

Parker, R. H. "Explaining National Differences in Consolidated Accounts." *Accounting and Business Research,* Summer 1977, pp. 203–207.

Shoenfeld, Hanns-Martin. *The Status of Social Reporting in Selected Countries.* Urbana, Ill.: Center for International Education and Research in Accounting, 1978.

Task Force on Corporate Social Performance. *Corporate Social Reporting in the United States and Western Europe.* Washington, D.C.: Department of Commerce, July 1979.

Chapter 10

Arpan, Jeffrey S. *International Intracorporate Pricing: Non-American Systems and Views.* New York: Praeger, 1972.

————. "Multinational Firm Pricing in International Markets." *Sloane Management Review,* Winter 1972–1973.

Barrett, M. Edgar. "Case of the Tangled Transfer Price." *Harvard Business Review,* May/June 1977, pp. 20–28, 32, 36, 176, 178.

Bawley, Dan. "The Multinational in Search of a Tax Haven." LKHH *Accountant,* 52, 4 (1972), pp. 32–42.

Brantner, Paul F. "Taxation and the Multinational Firm." *Management Accounting* (U.S.), October 1973, pp. 11–16, 26.

Briner, Ernst K. "International Tax Management." *Management Accounting* (U.S.), February 1973, pp. 47–50.

Carley, William M. "International Concerns Use Variety of Means to Cut U.S. Tax Bills." *Wall Street Journal,* 16 October 1972, p. 1.

Choi, Frederick D. S., and Gerhard G. Mueller. *An Introduction to Multinational Accounting.* Englewood Cliffs, N.J.: Prentice-Hall, 1978, chapter 9.

Chown, John. *Taxation and Multinational Enterprises.* London: Longman, 1974.

Conference Board. *Interdivisional Transfer Pricing.* New York: Conference Board, 1967.

Ernst & Ernst. *Foreign and U.S. Corporate Income and Withholding Tax Rates.* New York: E&E, January 1976 (updated periodically).

"Flexible Pricing." *Business Week,* 12 December 1977, pp. 78–81, 84, 88.

Greene, James. "Intercompany Pricing Across National Frontiers." *Conference Board Record,* October 1969.

Greene, James, and Michael G. Duerr. *Intercompany Transactions in the Multinational Firm.* New York: Conference Board, 1970.

Holdstock, Peter. "Some Thoughts on International Tax Planning." *Price Waterhouse International Tax News,* December 1975, pp. 1–4.

Horngren, Charles T. *Cost Accounting: A Managerial Emphasis,* 4th ed. Englewood Cliffs, N.J.: Prentice-Hall, 1977, p. 675.

Howard, Frederick. "Overview of International Taxation." *Columbia Journal of World Business,* Summer 1975, pp. 8–9.

Kalish, Richard H., and John P. Casey. "The Dilemma of the International Tax Executive." *Columbia Journal of World Business,* Summer 1975, pp. 52–57.

Keegan, W. J. "Multinational Pricing: How Far Is Arm's-Length?" *Columbia Journal of World Business,* May/June 1969, pp. 57–66.

Milburn, Alex J. "International Transfer Transactions: What Price?" *CA Magazine* (Canada), December 1976, pp. 22–27.

Moore, Russell M., and George M. Scott, eds. *Introduction to Financial Control and Reporting in Multinational Enterprises.* Austin: Bureau of Business Research, University of Texas, 1973, pp. 52–57.

National Association of Accountants, *Management Accounting for Multinational Corporations,* Vols. I and II. New York: NAA, 1974. A collection of selected readings, several of which address the subject of Chapter 10.

Obersteiner, Erich. "The Management of Liquid Fund Flow Across National Boundaries." *International Journal of Accounting,* Spring 1976, pp. 91–101.

Price Waterhouse & Co., *Corporate Taxes in 80 Countries.* New York: Price Waterhouse, July 1976 (updated periodically).

———. *Information Guide for U.S. Corporations Doing Business Abroad.* New York: Price Waterhouse, March 1976 (updated periodically).

Prindi, A. R. *Foreign Exchange Risk.* New York: Wiley, 1976.

Rutenberg, D. "Maneuvering Liquid Assets in a Multinational Company: Formulation and Deterministic Solution Procedures." *Management Science,* June 1970, pp. 671–685.

Sharav, Itzhak. "Transfer Pricing—Diversity of Goals and Practices." *Journal of Accountancy,* April 1974, pp. 56–62.

Shulman, J. S. "Transfer Pricing in the Multinational Firm." *European Business,* January 1969, pp. 46–54.

Solving International Pricing Problems. New York: Business International, 1965.

Stobaugh, Robert B. et al. *U.S. Taxation of United States Manufacturing Abroad: Likely Effects of Taxing Unremitted Profits.* New York: Financial Executive Research Foundation, 1976.

"Tax Reform—Foreign Income." *Journal of Accountancy.* November 1975, pp. 34–48.

Thomas, Arthur L. "Transfer Prices of the Multinational Firm: When Will They Be Arbitrary?" *Abacus*, June 1971, pp. 40–53.

Chapter 11

Adams, Mathew T., and Robert J. E. Henry. "Tax Consequences of Foreign Currency Fluctuations." *Tax Executive*, July 1978, pp. 301–335.

Akhtar, M. A. "Taxation of Corporate Income: Some European Approaches." *Federal Reserve Bank of New York Quarterly Review*, Summer 1977, pp. 27–32.

Bruce, Charles M. "New Rules Taxing Americans Working Abroad." *Taxes*, February 1979, pp. 79–84.

Burge, Marianne, and Joe O'Broin. "Tax Planning for Irish Operations (Part I)." *Tax Adviser*, April 1978, pp. 233–242.

Burns, Jane O. "Exports and the Tax Reform Act of 1976." *International Tax Journal*, February 1978, pp. 810–823.

Casanegra de Jantscher, Milka. "Tax Havens Explained." *Finance and Development*, March 1976, pp. 31–34.

Choi, Frederick D. S., and Gerhard G. Mueller. *An Introduction to Multinational Accounting.* Englewood Cliffs, N.J.: Prentice-Hall, 1978, chapter 8.

Cliff, Walter C. "Pairing: A Technique for Avoiding CFC Status and Other Burdens of U.S. Taxation." *Taxes*, August 1979, pp. 530–537.

Kalish, Richard H. "Intercompany Pricing: How to Handle an International Tax Examination." *Tax Adviser*, April 1978, pp. 196–218.

Lundy, Daniel F. "Tax and Accounting Effects of Foreign Currency Fluctuations." *Tax Executive*, January 1976, pp. 135–143.

Patrick, Robert J. Jr. "A Comparison of the U.S. and OECD Model Income Tax Conventions." *Law and Policy in International Business* 2, 1978, pp. 613–718.

Plaia, Michael C. "Use of Holding Companies Can Cut Impact of Allocation Requirements." *Journal of Taxation*, February 1978, pp. 122–124.

Polk, Raemon M. "Financial and Tax Aspects of Planning for Foreign Currency Exchange Rate Fluctuations." *Taxes*, March 1978, pp. 131–142.

Sanden, B. Kenneth. "VAT: What, How, Where." *Tax Adviser*, March 1973, pp. 150–157.

Welch, William H. "Planning Techniques for Maximizing Foreign Credit Benefits." *Taxes*, August 1978, pp. 462–469.

Chapter 12

Anthony, Robert N. *Planning and Control Systems: A Framework for Analysis.* Boston: Harvard Business School Division of Research, 1965.

Bursk, Edward C., et al. *Financial Control of Multinational Corporations.* New York: Financial Executives Research Foundation, 1971.

"Cash Management: The Art of Wringing More Profit from Corporate Funds." *Business Week,* 13 March 1976, p. 63.

Chandler, Alfred D. Jr. *Strategy and Structure.* Cambridge, Mass.: MIT Press, 1962.

Choi, Frederick D. S. "Multinational Challenges for Managerial Accountants." *Journal of Contemporary Business,* Autumn 1975, pp. 51–68.

Choi, Frederick D. S., and Gerhard G. Mueller. *An Introduction to Multinational Accounting.* Englewood Cliffs, N.J.: Prentice-Hall, 1978, chapter 8.

Churchman, C. West. *The Systems Approach.* New York: Dell Publishing, 1968.

"A Corporate Viewpoint." Interview with Walter Wriston, Chairman of Citicorp, by Randolph L. Denosowicz. In *Columbia Journal of World Business,* Fall 1977, pp. 125–128.

Davis, Gordon B. *Management Information Systems: Conceptual Foundations, Structure, and Development.* New York: McGraw-Hill, 1974, pp. 403–409.

Dearden, John, and Bruce D. Henderson. "New System for Divisional Control." *Harvard Business Review,* September/October 1966, p. 144.

Dickie, Paul M., and Niranjan S. Arya. "MIS and International Business." *Journal of Systems Management,* June 1970, pp. 8–12.

Duerr, Michael G., and John M. Roach. *Organization and Control of International Operations.* New York: Conference Board, 1973.

Fantl, Irvin L. "Control and the Internal Audit in the Multinational Firm." *International Journal of Accounting,* Fall 1975, pp. 57–65.

Farag, Shawki M. "The Problem of Performance Evaluation in International Accounting." *International Journal of Accounting,* Fall 1974, pp. 45–54.

Garrison, Ray H. *Managerial Accounting: Concepts for Planning, Control, Decision Making.* Dallas: Business Publications, 1976, pp. 216–228.

Goetz, Billy E. "Transfer Prices: An Exercise in Relevancy and Goal Congruence." *Accounting Review,* July 1967, p. 437.

Gorab, Robert S. "Effective Management Controls and Reporting Policies for the Multinational Company." *Selected Papers 1970,* Haskins & Sells, pp. 399–400.

Hawkins, David F. "Controlling Foreign Operations." *Financial Executive,* February 1965, pp. 25–56.

"International Auditing Goes International." *Business International,* 13 January 1967, pp. 15–16.

Knortz, Herbert C. "Controllership in International Corporations." *Financial Executive,* June 1969, pp. 54–60.

Koontz, Harold. "The Management Theory Jungle." *Journal of the Academy of Management*, December 1961, pp. 174–188.

Loftus, Joseph X. "Putting the Brakes on Your Foreign Audit Fees." *Price Waterhouse Review*, 3 (1976), pp. 16–19.

Mauriel, John J. "Evaluation and Control of Overseas Operations." *Management Accounting* (U.S.), May 1969, pp. 35–38.

McInnes, J. M. "Financial Control Systems for Multinational Operations: An Empirical Investigation." *Journal of International Business Studies*, Fall 1971, pp. 11–28.

Meister, Irene W. *Managing the International Financial Function*. New York: Conference Board, SBP #133, 1970.

Moore, William P. "Satellites May Revolutionize American Business Methods." *St. Louis Post-Dispatch*, 10 January 1978, p. 40.

Morsicato, Helen. *Currency Translation and Performance Evaluation in Multinationals*. Ann Arbor, Mich.: UMI Research Press, 1980.

Murray, J. Alex. "Intelligence Systems of the MNC's." *Columbia Journal of World Business*, September/October 1972, pp. 63–71.

"Report of the Committee on International Accounting." *Accounting Review*, Supplements to Volumes 48 and 49, 1973 and 1974, pp. 120–167 and 250–269.

Robbins, Sidney M., and Robert B. Stobaugh. "The Bent Measuring Stick of Foreign Subsidiaries." *Harvard Business Review*, September/October 1973.

Rueschhoff, Norlin G. *International Accounting and Financial Reporting*. New York: Praeger, 1976.

Scott, George M. "Financial Control in Multinational Enterprise—The New Challenge to Accountants." *International Journal of Accounting*, Spring 1972, pp. 55–68.

————. "Information Systems and Coordination in Multinational Enterprises." *International Journal of Accounting Education and Research*, February 1974, p. 87.

Vancil, Richard F. "What Kind of Management Control Do You Need?" *Harvard Business Review*, March/April 1973, pp. 76–82.

Watt, George C., Richard M. Hammer, and Marianne Burge. *Accountng for the Multinational Corporation*. New York: Financial Executives Research Foundation, 1977.

White, John D. "Multinationals in Latin America: An Accent on Control." *Management Accounting* (U.S.), February 1977, pp. 49–51.

Woo, John C. H. "Management Control Systems for International Operations." *Tempo* (Touche Ross), Summer/Fall 1970, p. 39.

Zenoff, David B. "Profitable, Fast Growing, but Still the Stepchild." *Columbia Journal of World Business*, July/August 1967, pp. 51–56.

Zenoff, David B., and Jack Zwick. *International Financial Management*. Englewood Cliffs, N. J.: Prentice-Hall, 1969, chapter 12.

Chapter 13

AICPA International Practice Executive Committee. *Professional Accounting in 30 Countries*. New York: AICPA, 1975.

Baruch, Hurd. "The Foreign Corrupt Practices Act." *Harvard Business Review*, January/February 1979, pp. 32–34, 38, 44–50.

Bradt, John D. "The Foreign Corrupt Practices Act and the Internal Auditor." *Internal Auditor*, August 1979, pp. 15–20.

Choi, Frederick D. S., and Gerhard G. Mueller. *An Introduction to Multinational Accounting*. Englewood Cliffs, N.J.: Prentice-Hall, 1978, chapter 4.

Ernst & Whinney. *Worldwide Statutory Audit and Reporting Requirements*. New York: E&WI, 1979.

Financial Executive, July 1979. Several articles about the U.S. Foreign Corrupt Practices Act.

Lee, Marikay. "The International Auditor." *Internal Auditor*, December 1978, pp. 43–47.

Light, Walter F. "The Internal Auditor's Job as Seen by a Multinational Company President." *Internal Auditor*, June 1976, pp. 29–34.

Loftus, Joseph X. "Putting the Brakes on Foreign Audit Fees." *Price Waterhouse Review*, 21, 3 (1976), pp. 16–19.

Mann, Richard W., and Derek H. Redmayne. "Internal Auditing in an International Environment." *Internal Auditor*, October 1979, pp. 49–54.

McKee, Thomas E. "Auditing Under the Foreign Corrupt Practices Act." *CPA Journal*, August 1979, pp. 31–35.

Pomeranz, Felix. "International Auditing Standards." *International Journal of Accounting*, Fall 1975, pp. 1–13.

Schwartz, Ivo. "Harmonisation of Accounting and Auditing in the European Community." *Accountant's Magazine* (Scotland), December 1977, pp. 508–510.

Stamp, Edward, and Maurice Moonitz. *International Audit Standards*. London: Prentice-Hall International, 1978.

Tooman, Lee D. "Starting the Internal Audit of Foreign Operations." *Internal Auditor*, November/December 1975, pp. 56–62.

Weinstein, Arnold K., Louis Corsini, and Ronald Pawliczek. "The Big Eight in Europe." *International Journal of Accounting*, Spring 1978, pp. 57–71.

Wu, Frederick, and Donald W. Hackett. "The Internationalization of U.S. Public Accounting Firms." *International Journal of Accounting*, Spring 1977, pp. 81–91.

Chapter 14

Accountants International Study Group (AISG). *Consolidated Financial Statements* (1973).

———. *International Financial Reporting* (1975).

American Accounting Association. "Report of the Committee on Non-Financial

Measures of Effectiveness." *Accounting Review* Supplement, 1971, pp. 165–211.

―――. "Report of the Committee on Accounting in Developing Countries, 1973–1975." *Accounting Review* Supplement, 1976, pp. 199–212.

―――. *Accounting Education and the Third World,* 1978.

Arthur Andersen & Co. (Peru). *Regulations for Reporting on Financial Statements in Peru,* February 1973.

Barefield and Comiskey. "The Accuracy of Forecasts of Earnings Per Share." *Journal of Business Research,* July 1965, pp. 241–251.

Basi, B., K. Carey, and R. Twark. "A Comparison of the Accuracy of Corporate and Securities Analysts' Forecasts of Earnings." *The Accounting Review,* April 1976, pp. 244–254.

Belfi, John R. "Transferring Technology in a Multinational Service Industry." *Arthur Andersen Chronicle,* January 1975, pp. 16–21.

Belkaoui, Ahmed. Review of "Accounting and Developing Nations," by George M. Scott. *CA Magazine,* November 1974, pp. 16–18.

Beresford, Dennis R., and Stewart A. Feldman. "Companies Increase Social Responsibility Disclosure." *Management Accounting* (U.S.), March 1976, pp. 51–55.

Biedenkopf, K. H. *Mitbestimmung Im Unternehmen Deutscher Bundestag.* 6, Wahlperiode, VI/334, 1970.

Choi, Frederick D. S., and Gerhard G. Mueller. *An Introduction to Multinational Accounting.* Englewood Cliffs, N.J.: Prentice-Hall, 1978, chapter 10.

Commission of the European Communites. *Proposal for a Seventh Directive Concerning Group Accounts* (Brussels, 1976).

Conference Board. *Understanding the Balance of Payments.* New York: Conference Board, 1970.

Copeland, R. M., and R. J. Marioni. "Executives Forecasts of EPS Versus Forecasts of Naive Models." *Journal of Business,* October 1972, pp. 497–512.

Cummings, J. P. "Forging International Accounting Standard." *Tax Executive,* July 1975, pp. 352–359.

De La Mahotiere, Stewart. "The Multinational's Role in a Changing World." *Accountancy,* March 1976, pp. 28–30.

Emmanuel, C. R., and S. J. Gray. "Corporate Diversification and Segmented Disclosure Requirements in the USA." *Journal of Business Finance and Accounting,* Autumn/Winter 1977.

Enthoven, A. J. H. "Standardized Accountancy and Economic Development." *Management Accounting* (U.S.), February 1976, pp. 19–23. (Reprinted from *Finance and Development,* March 1973.)

―――. "Social and Political Impact of Multinationals on Third World Countries (and Its Accounting Implications)." Plenary Session Paper, 60th Annual Meeting. American Accounting Association, Richardson, Texas: University of Texas at Dallas, 1976 (monograph).

Ernst & Whinney. *Social Responsibility Disclosure: 1977 Survey of Fortune 500 Annual Report.* Cleveland. 1977.

Gray, S. J. "Segment Reporting and the EEC Multinationals." *Journal of Accounting Research*, Autumn 1978, pp. 242–253.

Hauworth, William P. "Problems in the Development of Worldwide Accounting Standards." *International Journal of Accounting*, Fall 1973, pp. 23–34.

International Accounting Standards Committee (IASC). International Accounting Standard No. 3, *Consolidated Financial Statements* (1976).

———. International Accounting Standard No. 6, *Accounting Responses to Changing Prices* (1977).

Financial Executives Institue. "How Accurate Are Forecasts?" *Financial Executive*, March 1973.

Jaggi, B. L. "Further Evidence of the Accuracy of Management Forecasts vis-à-vis Analyst's Forecast." *The Accounting Review*, January 1980, pp. 96–101.

Kuhne, Robert. *Co-determination in Business: Workers' Representatives in the Boardroom.* New York: Praeger, 1980.

Linowes, David F., "The Accounting Profession and Social Progress." *Journal of Accountancy*, July 1973, pp. 32–40.

Marques, Edmond. "The Firm: Its Impact on Society; Introducing Societal Accounting." Paper presented at Georgia World Congress Institute Conference on Exploring the Brave New Worlds of Accounting, Atlanta, Georgia, 8 September 1978.

National Foreign Trade Council, Inc. "The Balance of Payments." *Memorandum* 9845, April 22, 1971.

Robinson, Richard. "The Future of International Management." *Journal of International Business Studies*, Spring 1971, pp. 60–70.

Scott, George, with Pontus Troberg. *Eighty-eight International Accounting Problems in Rank Order of Importance.* American Accounting Association, 1980.

Thimm, Alfred L. "Decision Making at Volkswagen: 1972–1977," *Columbia Journal of World Business*, Vol. 11, Spring 1976, pp. 94–103.

Index